Rock Climbing
NEW MEXICO
&
TEXAS

by
Dennis R. Jackson

FALCON

Guilford, Connecticut
An imprint of The Globe Pequot Press

A **FALCON** GUIDE®

Cover photos by Stewart Green

Library of Congress Cataloging-in-Publication Data

Jackson, Dennis, 1941–
    Rock climbing New Mexico & Texas / by Dennis R. Jackson.
        p.   cm.
    "A Falcon guide"—T.p. verso.
    Includes bibliographical references and index.
    ISBN 1-56044-483-5
    1. Rock climbing—New Mexico—Guidebooks. 2. Rock climbing—Texas—Guidebooks.
3. New Mexico—Guidebooks. 4. Texas—Guidebooks. I. Title.

GV199.42.N6J33 1996   96-38829
796.5'223'09789—dc20   CIP

♻ Text pages printed on recycled paper.
Manufactured in the United States of America
First edition/Second printing

CAUTION
Outdoor recreational activities are by their very nature potentially hazardous. All partici-
pants in such activities must assume the responsibility for their own actions and safety.
The information contained in this guidebook cannot replace sound judgment and good
decision-making skills, which help reduce risk exposure, nor does the scope of this book
allow for disclosure of all the potential hazards and risks involved in such activities.
    Learn as much as possible about the outdoor recreational activities in which you par-
ticipate, prepare for the unexpected, and be cautious. The reward will be a safer and more
enjoyable experience.

CONTENTS

Acknowledgments v

New Mexico Rock Climbing Areas vi

Texas Rock Climbing Areas vii

map legend viii

key to topo drawings ix

Introduction 1

What's not covered 3

Geology 3

Granitic rocks 4

Sedimentary rocks 4

Volcanic rocks 6

Equipment 7

Climbing dangers and safety 7

Objective dangers 9

Access and environmental
considerations 11

Ethics 14

Using this Guide 15

Rating system 17

NORTHERN NEW MEXICO

Taos Area Crags

Questa Dome 24

Heart of Stone Rock 31

John's Wall 38

Dead Cholla Wall 43

Tres Piedras Rocks 51

South Rock 58

Lookout Shelf 58

Mosaic Rock—West End 59

Mosaic Rock 61

Middle Rock 64

West Rock 1 68

Sundeck Wall 68

North Rock 69

Raton Area Crags

Sugarite Canyon State Park 71

White Rock–Los Alamos Area Crags

White Rock Crags 77

The Overlook 83

The Old New Place 88

Below The Old New Place 89

The Playground 93

The Y 96

North Wall 98

South Wall 101

Jemez Mountains Area

Cochiti Mesa Crags 103

Eagle Canyon 110

Cochiti Mesa 118

Vista Point 132

The Dihedrals 132

Cacti Cliff 134

Disease Wall 139

Las Conchas 141

Roadside Attraction 145

Cattle Call Wall 145

Gateway Rock 146

Chilly Willy Wall 148

Love Shack Area 148

Gallery Wall 150

Dream Tower 150

The Sponge 151

The Leaning Tower 153

CENTRAL NEW MEXICO

Albuquerque Area

Sandia Mountain 157

The Shield 164

The Needle 167

Muralla Grande 169

Torreon 171

Mexican Breakfast 172

Palomas Peak 174

Entrance Area 179

The Slab 179

The Franks 179

Showdown Wall 181

Transition Zone 181

The Dihedral Area 182

Randy's Wall 182

The Far Side 182

Red Light District 183

Socorro Area

Enchanted Tower 185

The Frog Prince Area 191

Rapunzel's Wall 192

The Enchanted Tower 194

Humpty Dumpty Wall 197

Sleeping Beauty Wall 197

Captain Hook Area 198

Midnight Pumpkin Wall 199

Pogue's Cave Area 201

Socorro Box 202

Waterfall Wall 205

Fillet a Papillon Wall 206

Red Wall 207

Corner Block 208

North Wall 210

SOUTHERN NEW MEXICO

Las Cruces Area

Organ Mountains 214

The Citadel 219

Southern Comfort Wall 221

The Tooth 222

The Wedge 225

Sugarloaf 225

Doña Ana Mountains 229

Bear Boulders 233

Checkerboard Wall 233

The Columns 235

Other Doña Ana Areas 236

Deming Area

City of Rocks State Park 237

Carlsbad Area

Sitting Bull Falls 243

The Rose Bud Wall
(a.k.a. "The Warm-up Wall") 246

The Big Horn Wall 248

TEXAS

West Texas Area

Hueco Tanks State Historical Park 251

North Mountain 261

Cakewalk Wall 262

The Central Wall 264

Indecent Exposure Buttress 267

Fox Tower 271

End Loop Wall 271

End Loop Boulder 272

West Mountain 272

Natural Buttress 272

Three Lobe Buttress 273

The Eagle 274

East Mountain: Pigs in Space Buttress .. 275

The Great Wall 275

Point of Rocks 277

Pecos River Gorge 284

The Gecko Wall 291

The Random Wall 293

The Lawless Wall and Lawless Cove 295

Slain Buffalo Wall 297

Whiskey Wall 297

Shaman Wall 301

Metalogic Wall and Dock Wall 301

The Dock Wall 303

Big Bend National Park 303

Austin Area

Enchanted Rocks State Natural Area 309

The Backside Area 316

Buzzard's Roost 322

Other Park Crags 325

Dallas Area

Lake Mineral Wells State Park 326

Appendix A: Futher Reading 330

Appendix B: Rating System Comparison 331

Appendix C: Shops, Guide Services, Gyms 332

Appendix D: Services 334

Appendix E: Emergency Services 336

Appendix F: Glossary 337

Index 341

About the Author 358

ACKNOWLEDGMENTS

Many people helped make this guide possible. I wish to thank Doug Couleur, Jean DeLatallaide, Paul Drakos, Jim Graham, Ed Jaramillo, Dave Pegg, Peter Prandoni, Lee Sheftel, Ken Sims, and Mark Thomas for their input on the New Mexico crags and Ian Spencer-Green for bouldering info at Hueco Tanks. Billy Blackstock provided valuable information about the Big Bend region. John Gogas contributed to Point of Rocks, Pecos River Gorge, and Sitting Bull Falls. Ken Sims, Ph.D., wrote and contributed the geology information. My sincere thanks to all of you.

My editor Stewart Green and graphic artist Martha Morris were involved in this project from start to completion. Stewart also added his considerable photographic expertise. I could not have done it without these two. My heartfelt thanks to both of you.

Thanks also to Tyler Bowser and especially Paul Drakos for sharing the many road trips and routes. Let's do it all again soon. I'll leave my notebook at home next time.

Finally, I want to thank my wife Carol for her constant support and encouragement during this two and one-half year project. When I got overwhelmed, Carol was always there for me. Carol also helped with many of the topos for the crags. I promise to leave my rack and rope home on our next vacation, darling.

Every effort has been made to ensure the accuracy of the route descriptions and other information in this book. The real world, however, is constantly undergoing revision. If you find any discrepancy between a piece of New Mexican or Texan rock and how it is described in the following pages, let us know. Please send all corrections, additions, and comments to Zoidian@aol.com.

NEW MEXICO CLIMBING AREAS

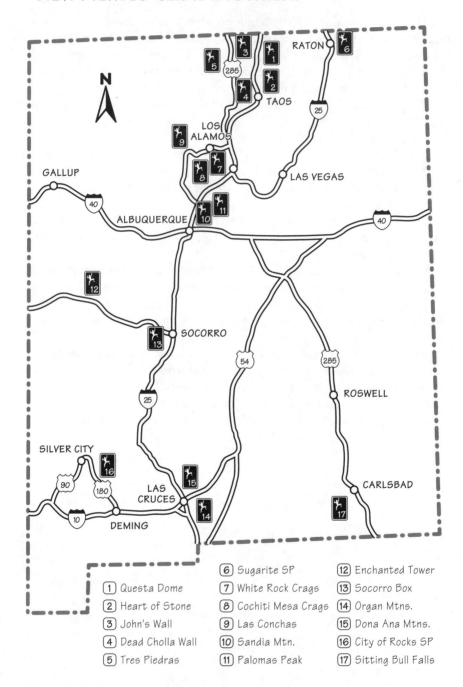

1. Questa Dome
2. Heart of Stone
3. John's Wall
4. Dead Cholla Wall
5. Tres Piedras
6. Sugarite SP
7. White Rock Crags
8. Cochiti Mesa Crags
9. Las Conchas
10. Sandia Mtn.
11. Palomas Peak
12. Enchanted Tower
13. Socorro Box
14. Organ Mtns.
15. Dona Ana Mtns.
16. City of Rocks SP
17. Sitting Bull Falls

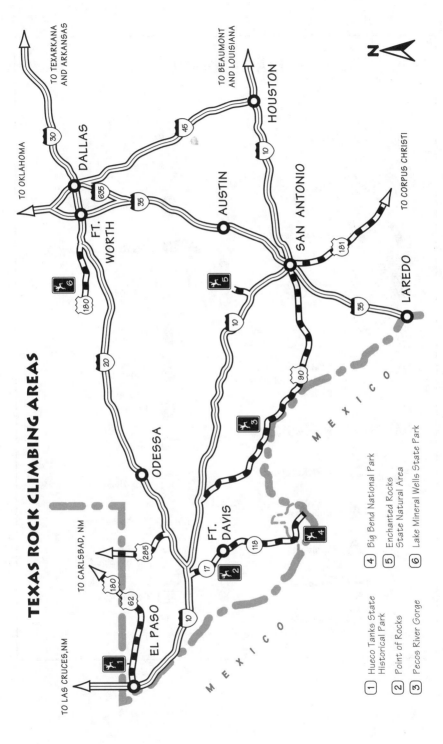

TEXAS ROCK CLIMBING AREAS

1 Hueco Tanks State Historical Park

2 Point of Rocks

3 Pecos River Gorge

4 Big Bend National Park

5 Enchanted Rocks State Natural Area

6 Lake Mineral Wells State Park

MAP LEGEND

 Trail

 Interstate

 Paved Road

 Gravel Road

 Unimproved Road

 State Line, Forest, Park, or Wilderness Boundary

 Waterway

 Lake/Reservoir

 Building

 Camping

 Gate

 Mile Marker

 Town

 City

 Climbing Area

 Crag/Boulder

 Cliff Edge

 Mountain Peak

 Trailhead

 Parking

 Interstate

 U.S. Highway

 State Highway

 County Road

 Forest Road

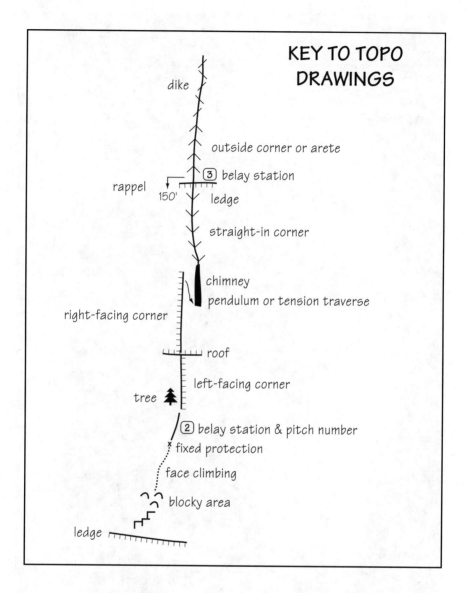

KEY TO TOPO DRAWINGS

dike

outside corner or arete

③ belay station

rappel

150'   ledge

straight-in corner

chimney

pendulum or tension traverse

right-facing corner

roof

left-facing corner

tree

② belay station & pitch number

✗ fixed protection

face climbing

blocky area

ledge

lb.	lieback	thin	thin crack(to 1 ½")
chim.	chimney	3rd	class 3
ow	off-width	4th	class 4
HB, RP	very small chocks	KB	knife blade
TCU	small camming devices	LA	lost arrow

Ian Spencer-Green swings up the classic *Wailing Banshee* (5.11c/d), Below the Old New Place, New Mexico. *Photo by Stewart M. Green.*

INTRODUCTION

Welcome to the sunny southwestern states of New Mexico and Texas. The vast area covered in this guidebook, more than 388,400 square miles, is home to many excellent rock climbing crags. Climbers from all over the world are discovering what New Mexico climbers have always known. The state's stunning beauty, quality and quantity of rock, lack of crowds, and friendly scene all make for a rich climbing experience. The great expanse of Texas, the second largest state in the Union, offers less rock, but none of it less than excellent. New climbing areas are being developed, particularly in the limestone regions and Davis Mountains of west Texas, to complement the existing world-class Hueco Tanks State Historical Park and the not-so-famous but exquisite Enchanted Rocks State Natural Area.

Those unfamiliar with New Mexico usually envision a desert landscape complete with cactus and shimmering heat. Although the state has a dry, warm climate, this image is, of course, too narrow. Visitors are treated to pristine scenery whether in mountains up to 13,161 feet in elevation in the northern part of the state or in the more desert-like basin and ranges in the southern part. In New Mexico the average July temperature is 74 degrees Fahrenheit and the average January temperature is 34 degrees F. The southern areas of the state are generally much warmer in both summer and winter. Several mountain ranges tower over the high Chihuahua Desert that makes up much of southern New Mexico and west Texas, offering relief from the desert heat. Being aware of climatic variations at different elevations and latitudes allows climbers to pursue their sport year-round in New Mexico and Texas.

The majority of climbing in New Mexico is on granite, basalt, limestone, and rhyolite, a softer volcanic rock formed by intense heat and pressure of volcanic ashes. The basalt is found along the great Rio Grande Rift zone in central and northern New Mexico. This massive geologic structure starts near Leadville, Colorado, and extends well into Texas. The dramatic landscape west of Taos is a good place to view the rift. Other volcanic areas are the result of localized volcanic action both east and west of the rift. Good examples of volcanism can be found in the Jemez Mountains west of the rift, which include the White Rock crags and Cochiti Mesa area, and the high plains east of the Sangre de Cristo range around Raton. The granite climbing is found on the western side of the Sangre de Cristo Mountains, Sandia Mountain, Doña Ana, and Organ Mountains. The granite domes of Tres Piedras in the Tusas Mountains, the westernmost southern extension of the Rocky Mountains, are the only granite on the western side of the rift. Limestone climbing is getting jump-started with the development of Palomas Peak and Sitting Bull Falls. New Mexico and Texas both have an excess of limestone, insuring unlimited rock for future development.

Sport climbers and traditional climbers alike will enjoy New Mexico and Texas crags. New Mexico has enjoyed a long history of traditional climbing both on the shorter basalt crags and on the longer mountain rock liberally located throughout the state. Sport climbing enthusiasts have discovered great climbing on faces between the cracks at traditional areas and on softer rock thought unclimbable ten years ago. The development of Cochiti Mesa and other cliffs in the immediate area demonstrates that much more of New Mexico rock is climbable. Excellent sport climbing crags continue to be developed.

Texas climbing is conducted mainly in state parks administered by the Texas Parks and Wildlife Department. Compared to other public lands, visitor use—particularly climbing—is more formally managed in these parks. Be on your best behavior. The Texas Parks and Wildlife Department has a long history of working with climbers through local clubs and the Texas Climber's Coalition. The cooperation between these agencies is exemplary and could be viewed as a model for climbers everywhere. Do your part when visiting to favorably represent climbing.

The climbing gems of the Texas Park system are Hueco Tanks State Historical Park and Enchanted Rock State Natural Area. If you can't have a good time climbing in either of these areas, consider other recreational activities. Lake Mineral Wells State Park is not as well known but is the most visited climbing area in Texas. Toproping only is allowed here on more than 80 routes up a metamorphosed sandstone cliff. The newly developed limestone crags at the Pecos River Gorge and the seldom visited Point of Rocks both require long road trips but are worth the effort. A visit to Big Bend National Park in the same area reveals abundant adventure possibilities in a sea of limestone. The beauty of this area alone makes a visit worthwhile. In Texas, most of the climbable rock found outside public lands is on private property. The slogan "Texas friendly spoken here" does not apply if you're caught climbing where you are not supposed to be. Don't even try. Pecos River Gorge is an example of where climbers and private land owners are cooperating. With any luck, this will start a trend.

WHAT'S NOT COVERED

This guide essentially covers every developed crag in New Mexico not on tribal lands or private land where climbing is prohibited. Climbers wishing to climb on tribal lands should consult with local tribal officials. Several recent ascents of Shiprock on the Navajo Reservation in northwest New Mexico demonstrate that permission is not necessarily out of reach. This can be a time-consuming process at times more challenging than the climb itself, so plan accordingly. The Brazos Cliffs, surely one of New Mexico's most beautiful and intriguing cliffs, is privately owned and presently closed to climbing. The Los Alamos Mountaineers are the only group authorized to climb here. The access situation at the Brazos changes periodically, so climbers interested in the area should contact the Mountaineers to stay abreast of the situation.

The small limestone sport crags and bouldering areas around Austin and San Antonio, Texas, are not covered in this guide. First-time visitors may wish to check out the local favorite, Reimer's Fishing Ranch, in the Austin area. Many 5.10 to 5.11 climbs in a beautiful setting are found here. These areas are covered in *Central Texas Limestone* and *Texas Limestone II* by Jeff Jackson and Kevin Gallagher. If in the area you can ask a friendly local for beta and advice.

GEOLOGY

The rocks in New Mexico and Texas are diverse and offer a range of climbing from multi-pitch traditional routes on granite domes and sandstone spires to single-pitch sport climbs up pocketed faces and cracks on volcanic lava flows. The rocks we see and climb on today are a product of both the regional tectonic forces and the local geologic processes that have been operating in this area since the Precambrian era, about 2 billion years ago.

In New Mexico and Texas most of the climbing is represented by three different categories of rock type: granitic, sedimentary rocks (predominantly limestones and sandstones), and volcanic rocks (basalts, andesites and rhyolites). The granitic rocks, particularly those in the Sangre de Cristo Range and Sandia Mountain, represent the oldest rocks. These crystallized deep in the crust during the Earth's early history and during previous episodes of mountain building. The sedimentary rocks, such as the limestones at the Pecos River Gorge or the sandstones in western New Mexico, represent a time in the Earth's middle history when inland seas and sandy deserts moved back and forth across this area. The volcanic rocks, such as the welded tuffs on Cochiti Mesa or the basalts at Sugarite and White Rock, are a result of recent extensional forces that thinned the crust and fragmented this region of the North American continent as well as forming large-scale topographic features such as the

Rio Grande Rift and the Basin and Range region.

Although a variety of tectonic forces and geologic processes have played a role in forming the different rock types in this region, the Rio Grande rift is the geological feature most responsible for exposing much of its climbable rock. This rift runs roughly north-south from southern Colorado to western Texas, and is a result of recent crustal thinning and extension. This extension resulted in large-scale normal faulting that exposed a number of older plutonic and sedimentary rocks along the margins of the rift and created extensive magmatism within and just outside the rift.

GRANITIC ROCKS

Although the term "granite" refers to a very specific composition, for most climbers the classification is much broader, referring instead to almost all varieties of silicic intrusive rocks. This classification, which is both adequate and accurate, is based on the rock's climbing texture—a coarse, granular texture often studded with large knobs or crystals of feldspar, and its color and appearance—generally a pinkish to grayish-colored rock containing quartz, feldspars, mica, and other less abundant minerals.

In the New Mexico and west Texas regions, the majority of the granitic rocks occur along the mountain ranges on the eastern margin of the Rio Grande Rift. Exceptions to this are the Precambrian granites and quartz monzonites of Tres Piedras found along the western margin of the rift at the foot of the Tusas Mountains. The granitic rocks of the Sangre de Cristo Range and Sandia Mountain exposed along the rifts northern section are Precambrian in age, whereas the quartz monzonites and syenites at Hueco Tanks along the southern section of the rift were intruded much later during the Tertiary Period. The granites found in Enchanted Rocks State Natural Area are not in the rift system but are part of the Llano Uplift, a giant batholithic structure that was intruded and crystallized 1.2 billion years ago and was subsequently uplifted and eroded.

SEDIMENTARY ROCKS

Sedimentary rocks are a record of ancient landscapes and times. When complete, this memory can record in explicit detail events such as the transgression and regression of inland seas which inundated this area during the Pennsylvanian and Permian and left behind large limestone reefs; the large sandy deserts which swept across in the Mesozoic Era leaving behind sandstones which later eroded into sheer cliffs, desert towers, and petrified sand dunes; or the inter-layered sand and shale deposits of ancient tidal mud flats and shallow lakes that recorded the footprints of dinosaurs.

New Mexico and Texas offer a sedimentary sequence that ranges from the Cambrian Period (about 560 million years ago) up through the present

Ian Spencer-Green on *Pumping Huecos* (5.11a), The Sponge, Las Conchas, New Mexico. *Photo by Stewart M. Green.*

Quaternary. Of the many sedimentary rocks exposed only a few are climbable. Most of the climbing is on the Pennsylvanian age limestones of the Madera Formation which caps Sandia Mountain and the Permian age limestones at the Pecos River Gorge. This is part of the El Capitan reef system and includes the Guadalupe Mountains and the caves of Carlsbad Caverns. Western New Mexico's numerous sandstones, including the Zuni and Entrada sandstones, are exposed as cliffs and towers within and along the margin of the Colorado Plateau. Most of these cliffs, however, are on tribal lands and therefore not readily accessible to climbers.

VOLCANIC ROCKS

Volcanic rocks represent magmas from inside the deep Earth. Typically, ancient volcanic flows cooled relatively quickly at the surface and formed a climbing texture different from that of granitic rocks. The smaller crystal size gives the rock a finer-grained, less granular texture, often replete with pockets. As the rock cooled, it contracted, particularly at the top and bottom of the flow. This caused fracturing in polygonal patterns. When exposed in cross-section these fractures give the cliff faces of lava flows their characteristic columnar appearance and, of course, make for lots of good crack climbing.

Finally, differences in the processes by which volcanic rocks are extruded and then deposited impart a big difference in the feel of the rock and the character of the climbing. In general, volcanic eruptions occur as either lava flows or as explosively erupted deposits. Lava flows, which are typical of the basalts in New Mexico, are generally massive, compact rocks with stretched pockets and abundant cracks. In explosively erupted deposits such as the welded flow deposits in the Bandelier Tuff on Cochiti Mesa, large volumes avalanched down the side of the volcano. With ash flow tuffs, the degree of welding is critical in determining the climbability of the rock. In general, it is the center part of the rock unit, which cooled slowly and is the most welded, that we climb on. In contrast, the less welded, softer parts of the Bandelier Tuff are the areas where the Anasazi chose to carve out homes at nearby Bandelier National Monument.

While most of the basalt climbing in the Jemez Volcanic Field and throughout New Mexico is consistently good, climbing on the Bandelier Tuff is restricted to the areas which are most densely welded. In many places the climbing character of the Bandelier Tuff has been improved by a "desert varnish" surface. While this surface can significantly improve the climbing quality of the rock, it also is deceptive as it makes the quality of the rock appear better than it actually is.

EQUIPMENT

Many of the classic traditional routes were put up in the "pre-Friends" era, so almost any manufactured piece of protection will do on your rack. Camming units, referred to in the text as SLCDs, TCUs, Friends, and camming units are generally carried these days for most routes. A double set of units up to 4", a set of stoppers, RPs or similar small wires, runners, quickdraws, shoes, and a 165' rope is sufficient for most routes. Refer to route descriptions for more specific route information. When in doubt, carry extra gear. Many routes require installing a belay with gear, and each climber's comfort level between protection points varies so be thoughtful when you rack out. A windshirt, rain gear, wool cap, and descent shoes are optional but desirable on many mountain routes. Wearing a helmet is always recommended especially on mountain routes and even when standing below the shorter crags at all areas. New Mexico cliffs are particularly vulnerable to rock fall from other climbers setting up topropes, etc. Water-bottles may be tough to deal with on a climb but are recommended equipment on all but the shortest routes. Camel up (drink a lot) before you leave the ground, carry some, and have some waiting when you return to your pack and car.

Sport routes generally require only quickdraws to clip bolts for protection. Some routes in both New Mexico and Texas were equipped with bolts taking into consideration the availability of gear placement possibilities. This is especially true at Hueco Tanks and Cochiti Mesa crags. A sport rack will often include TCUs, wires, and a range of Friend sizes from 0.5 to 3.5. One 165' rope is sufficient for most sport routes. A 150' rope is sufficient for some crags, and a 200' rope is often useful but never mandatory.

CLIMBING DANGERS AND SAFETY

Have you lost a friend in a climbing accident? Many of us have or know of a person killed while climbing. This is dangerous stuff. Don't think of it as anything different. Once you leave the ground all sorts of errors can occur. Newer climbers, nurtured in the friendly confines of a climbing gym, are particularly vulnerable. Experience gained in a gym falls short of equipping climbers for the real world of rock. Experiential learning outdoors under the tutelage of experienced climbers is the best teacher. Newcomers to the sport should avail themselves of all the instruction and mentoring possible. Experienced and inexperienced climbers can always make each outing a learning experience. Always climb within your abilities, be bold but not foolish, and watch out for yourself and your partner. Following are some ideas and suggestions to make your climbing more fun and safe.

8

Paul Drakos on the roof on *Question of Balance* (5.11) on Questa Dome, Taos Area Crags, New Mexico. *Photo by Marc Sheppard.*

Make a rule (Rule #1) for yourself to never to hit the deck (fall to the ground). This is especially important near the start of a climb. Ask yourself, is the first protection placed so I will not hit the ground when I climb above it?

Assess your own abilities in regard to the climbing difficulties.

Before you weight the rope on any rappel or lowering situation, look back through the entire system. This relates back to Rule #1, never fall to the ground. Are the anchors good? Is the rope through the anchors? Am I tied in? Is my harness doubled back? Is my belayer ready?

Before you leave the ground, check through your system and your partner's system. Are both harnesses doubled back? Are you both tied in? Does the belayer need an anchor? Do you have what you need to lead and belay? Do you have descent information? Can you get down before reaching the top if you have to?

Avoid climbing beneath other parties. If someone chooses to climb below you, be extra cautious not to drop anything on them. Place lots of protection, particularly near the bottom of routes and in soft rock areas. This relates back to Rule #1.

When rappeling, tie a knot in each strand of rope if you are unsure that they reach the ground or when in multiple rappel situations.

On lowering situations, tie a knot in the bottom end of the rope, or better yet insist that the belayer be tied in. This will keep the rope from passing through the belay device if the rope is not long enough.

OBJECTIVE DANGERS

Objective dangers are the ones that are going to happen no matter what you do. Your only recourse is to recognize and be prepared to deal with the many situations found in an outdoor environment. Be thoughtful and vigilant regarding your safety on the way to the climb, on the climb, and on the descent. Consider yourself on task and vulnerable to injury until you return to your car.

Use all fixed protection with caution. Do not be cavalier in your attitude about bolts and other fixed gear found on many routes. Older bolts are particularly suspect. Weathering, holding repeated falls, and poor placements all contribute to their danger. Back these up whenever possible and do your best not to fall on them. Never rappel, lower, or toprope from a single piece of gear. Build redundancy into any life support system so that failure of one part is not catastrophic to the whole system.

Rocks falling from above represent one of the biggest dangers to climbers. These rocks can be dislodged by weather conditions, yourself, other climbers, or animals. Stay out of the fall-line at the bottom of cliffs, seek overhangs or

Josh Morris on the classic boulder problem *45 Degree Wall* at Hueco Tanks, Texas.
Photo by Stewart M. Green.

other safe areas. When at the top, be particularly careful not to dislodge rocks even if you think no one is down there. This is just good practice and besides, someone unknown to you may be there. When climbing, test suspect-looking holds and warn your belayer whenever climbing through a loose section. Set belays off to the side of the line of ascent whenever possible.

Learn to identify and avoid poison oak and poison ivy. These are common in many crags in this book. Wasps, bees, ticks, and rattlesnakes are common to many areas also. Look for the presence of any wasp or bees nest on routes and then select another route. Avoid agitating these critters. Ticks are generally active in late spring and early summer. Check your clothing and body for these blood suckers and remove them immediately. Rattlesnakes are common in New Mexico and Texas. Be thoughtful about where you walk and sit. Do not kill any snakes. Simply leave the area and leave the snake alone. Rarely is a person bitten by a snake and if so, envenomation occurs only a small percentage of the bites. If bitten, treat the bitten area as a break by splinting and immobilizing, evacuate quickly and seek medical attention.

A complex terrain and large area produces a varied climate for New Mexico. The state ranges in elevation from 13,161 feet on Wheeler Peak in the Sangre de Cristo Mountains to 2,817 feet where the Pecos River flows into Texas. Expect high summer temperatures throughout the state with cooler temperatures in the mountains. Climbing slows down in the New Mexico winter except for the Dona Ana and Organ mountains. It is possible to climb any crag in this guide with the exceptions of Questa, Heart of Stone, and Sandia Mountain, on warmer winter days. Thundershowers and attendant lightning dangers are a serious consideration during the months of June through August. New Mexico is second only to Florida in lightning strikes. Be aware, equipped, and able to deal with this killer (over 300 deaths a year in the United States) when climbing, camping, or hiking.

Texas areas are generally warmer in the winter and hotter in the summer. The immense area encompassed by Texas, 266,807 square miles, also produces a diverse climate. The state ranges in elevation from 8,000 feet (near the Point of Rocks) to sea level. Heat, wind, and flash floods are common objective dangers encountered in Texas climbing situations. It only rains 10 inches a year in the Big Bend country, which "isn't bad," as the locals say, "if you're not here the day it does it." Avoid flashfloods in watercourses when hiking, climbing, or camping in the desert areas if rain showers are possible in the surrounding area.

In both states, drink lots of water to stay hydrated. This will help avoid heat exhaustion and the killer, heatstroke. It is impossible to drink too much water and most of us do not drink nearly enough. A minimum of two quarts is barely adequate in these arid climates; try for a gallon and your fun and safety on the rock will be improved. Seek out shade whenever the opportunity arises in desert environments. Wear a hat, cover your skin, and limit your activity to cooler mornings, evenings, and shaded crags.

ACCESS AND ENVIRONMENTAL CONSIDERATIONS

The most compelling factor in agreeing to write this guidebook was the opportunity to pass on to visitors information on how to preserve and protect the climbing crags in my home state of New Mexico and neighboring Texas. All of these areas exist in a fragile equilibrium of environmental and access concerns. What each of us does or does not do will dictate the very future of climbing in these areas.

Climbing is undergoing a paradigm shift in the 1990s. No longer can we support the "maverick" mentality that has long been part of the lore and legend of climbing. All climbers must recognize how their individual actions affect all of us. What came through clearly, time after time, in talking with land managers is that climbing will be treated like any other use on public lands. Climbers will have to jump through the same bureaucratic hoops and comply with the same regulations as any other interested potential user. The

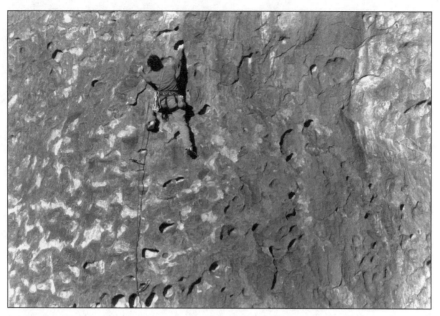

A climber on *Alice in Bananaland* on The Front Side at Hueco Tanks, Texas. *Photo by Stewart M. Green.*

message I got over and over was that land managers were willing to work with climbers. What was disturbing most to them was the cavalier attitude of individuals who unilaterally took it upon themselves to develop areas (i.e. drill holes, place bolts, and create "social trails") without prior consultation or regard for existing plans or regulations. Most areas were unprepared to deal with this sudden increase in climbing activities. The discovery of bolts and trails where once there were none forced closures until required regulations could be met and management plans developed. As climbing becomes more and more popular, we should not see regulation as an impediment or a disability but rather use it as an opportunity for validation and increased use. We will do more to ensure the integrity of climbing on public lands everywhere by cooperating with land managers than by being antagonistic toward them.

In researching this book, I spent more than two years traveling to every area, climbing, talking with climbers and land managers, and doing other attendant tasks that it takes to put a book of this scope together. One aspect that became crystal clear is that many climbers appear to be no different than the general population when it comes to taking care of the natural environment. Perhaps I overreacted because my expectations are higher, but I did observe an astonishing disregard for the very medium that we ply our craft on. The most obvious incursions on the environment were an inordinate amount of trash, cigarette butts, used tape, copious chalk use, unnecessary trails, and chipped, filled, drilled, or otherwise enhanced holds. Why, I asked myself, do climbers not know how to comport themselves outdoors or do they not care? The answer eludes me, but what is clear is that we must become better stewards of our crags. The appropriation of skills and knowledge of acceptable outdoor behavior is possible for all, but the application and use must come from realizing our connection to the larger world outside our individual insular egos. Make it a practice to tread lightly wherever you go. Respect the area, the people who will visit after you, and yourself. If you can leave each area as good as or better than you found it, you will have done no harm. Following are some general suggestions on how you can help.

Carry out everything you carry in. Pick up other trash as you find it and carry it out also.

Use existing approach and descent trails. Avoid shortcutting and causing extra erosion. Soil erosion destroys plants and ground cover, leading to degradation of the area. Try to belay off a boulder instead of that lush grass ledge at the crag base. Do not chop down trees or tear off limbs that might interfere with the first few feet of a route. Use a longer approach or descent route if necessary to protect sensitive ecological areas. Be prepared to deal with crapping in the outdoors. Shit happens but yours doesn't have to happen for everybody else. Carry toilet paper, matches, and a small trowel. If you do not have a trowel, use a stick. Select an area away from where other humans are likely to visit, dig a "cat-hole" into the humus layer of soil, do your business, carefully burn paper (just bury it if there is danger of starting a fire), and cover with a heavy rock.

Practice low-impact camping techniques. Use sites that show signs of previous use. If you must have a fire, use existing fire rings. Don't tear down local trees for firewood; anticipate your needs and bring your own. Let the fire burn down to white ashes and cover with a thin layer of dirt before leaving. If there are more fire rings than needed, dismantle the unnecessary ones. Cook with a stove. Crumbs and other food particles attract ants; take care in preparation, when eating, and clean up. Construct a small sump hole and screen out particles of food when washing dishes. Be considerate of other campers in the area in terms of noise and other distractions. Respect wildlife and all other special closures.

Join and contribute your energies and financial support to organizations such as the American Mountain Foundation and the Access Fund. Become involved in any way you can to protect and preserve the natural environment.

ETHICS

Put more than one rock climber together for any length of time and a debate of ethics is certain to happen. This usually boils down to a debate on "style," how the route is put up and in what fashion is it climbed. So-called "traditional" climbers were able to contain this debate within a relatively small community until only recently when European methods and styles were introduced to the general climbing scene. Two seemingly opposite styles of climbing have emerged, setting "sport climbers" and "traditional climbers" into defensive and offensive stances. Now debates often become ugly and highly charged with strong feelings expressed. Bolt wars, character assassination, and blows have resulted. What's wrong with this picture? We must agree to disagree with more civility, but the rock should never become the innocent victim. Bolt wars in the long run are harmful to individuals and to the rock. Nor should the very existence of climbing be threatened by actions of thoughtless individuals in either camp. It is best in the long run for the future of climbing to leave petty grievances behind and unite in an effort to make sure climbing is still around in the 21st century.

The style in which a climb is accomplished is a personal choice. There is purity and beauty in the ground-up tradition, of accepting only what the rock offers for protection and technique. The talent, power, and training required to pump out difficult gymnastic moves on a sport climb is an equally valid facet of climbing. One is not better than the other, they are just different expressions of the same game. Can they co-exist? Of course. Climbing is only enriched by diversity. What we must do is find the middle path so that one does not destroy the other. At the heart of this matter are the issues of bolting, rock alternation, and environmental impact to the crags.

Bolting should only be carried out if it is a legal practice for the area and in accord with local traditions. Those who place bolts should seriously consider each and every placement. Bolting should be done only after consulting with land managers and not be at variance with local traditions. This will avoid closures and acrimony. Choose a natural line that ends at a natural stance, then toprope the line first to assess its worth and to locate where the bolts should be placed. Placing bolts next to a protectable crack is never acceptable. The important considerations are the worthiness of the route and the reliability (safety) of the fixed pro. Don't let the rappel-down style lead to over-bolting a line or to adding bolts to existing lines. Consider each route a gift for everyone.

If climbers can't agree on everything, we must agree on one thing: altering the rock to make it climbable or more comfortable is simply not acceptable. Placing a bolt is already considered alternation by many land managers and has been cited as reason to close areas. When the time comes that the crags come under closer scrutiny and the glue, chipped handholds, and other count-less alternations to the rock are discovered, lots of areas are going to get shut down. It is a punishable crime to alter any rock on public land. That this must be legislated is lamentable. Climb with what the rock gives you to climb on or don't climb it. This might mean you have to get better or the route simply can't be climbed—yet. Don't destroy future hard climbs. This guide omits any route that is obviously altered. Some may have made it in but these mistakes are in no way a validation of the viability of the route.

It would be tragic if misbehavior from new visitors forces any closures of our crags. This could happen if new visitors fail to honor each area's specific rules and regulations around the many delicate access issues. The most vulner-able area in this guide is Tres Piedras. Be ultra careful here to not offend the owner of the private land on which some of the rocks lie. A stop at the ranger station to pick up maps is highly recommended. Please read and adhere to information found in "Restrictions and access issues" for all the crags. A guide-book is a tacit invitation to visit an area. Come on down but please bring your manners, leave your chisels, and, while here, respect our crags.

Using this Guide

Rock Climbing New Mexico and Texas is a complete guide to New Mexico crags and the popular areas of Texas. More than 750 routes are described here with words, photographs, and topos. A locator map at the front of the book shows the general locations of the main climbing areas.

Each area write-up includes: an **Overview**, which may include a brief sum-mary of the climbing history and local ethics; **Trip planning information**, which includes condensed summaries of specific information on each area; **Direc-tions** and **Maps** to find the areas; and specific climbing **Route descriptions**, which in many cases are accompanied by photos with overlays and maps iden-tifying routes and showing the locations.

The Overview describes the setting, the type of rock, and climbing. Also included are recommendations for climbing equipment as well as some dis-cussions of local climbing history and ethics.

Trip planning information offers a brief synopsis of the following categories:

Area description: A brief summary of the area.
Location: Reference to largest nearby towns, major roads, or natural land-marks.

Camping: Information on nearby developed campgrounds and suggestions for camping in undeveloped sites. When available, addresses or phone numbers are given in Appendix D.

Climbing season: What time of year is best for visiting an area.

Restrictions and access issues: Important issues to be aware of, such as private land, parking, safety, and land use.

Guidebooks: Published sources of information for the area.

Nearby mountain shops, guide services, and gyms: The name of the nearest town with these services is given here. For a full listing of addresses and phone numbers, by town, see Appendix C.

Area write-ups include:

Finding the crag: Description and how-to-get-there map with directions starting at nearest major road and town.

The crag name: Detailed discussion of location, special information pertaining to equipment, approaches, and descents.

Route descriptions: Routes are listed numerically, with the name and rating followed by a brief discussion of the location and nature of the climb, special equipment recommendations, length, and descent information. An overview map of each climbing area and photos—showing cliffs and route locations—accompanies the descriptions. The road map legend and key to topo map symbols are located at the front of the book on pages viii and ix.

Appendices offer further reading (Appendix A); rating comparison charts (Appendix B); a list of climbing equipment shops and clubs (Appendix C); a list of campgrounds, restaurants, and other services (Appendix D), and phone numbers and addresses for emergency services such as Search and Rescue and hospitals (Appendix E).

An **index** in the back of the book lists all proper names (names of areas, people, and climbs) alphabetically.

A book of this magnitude requires a wide selection of routes of all difficulties and lengths. Errors will creep into route descriptions due simply to the sheer diversity and number of routes detailed here. The area and crag descriptions have been carefully checked and double-checked by a wide range of active New Mexico and Texas climbers to maximize the book's accuracy. Be forewarned, however, that things on paper aren't always as they are in reality. Take every route description with a grain of salt. This book is not intended to carry you up any rock route. It will get you to the base of the cliff and point you in the right direction, but the rest is up to you and your sound decisions. This book is not a substitute for your own experience and judgment.

Almost all of the routes included in this guide are worth climbing. Routes not worth climbing have usually been omitted or described as "not recommended." If a route is especially good, words like "quality" and "excellent" may be included in the route description. Star ratings have been deliberately omitted in an effort to avoid queues and a diminished experience for everyone. These are generally subjective opinions that may or may not be true for every climber. Every climber has his or her own unique experience on every route. There are many fine routes in this guide to choose from. You are invited to decide for yourself what looks right and feels best on any given day.

RATING SYSTEM

This book uses the Yosemite Decimal System, the usual American grading scale, to identify the technical difficulty of the routes. Remember that ratings are totally subjective and vary from area to area. This book has tried to bring a consensus to the grades, but previously listed grades for routes have been relied on in most cases. Small rating variances are found in each area. Taos and Organ Mountain climbs seem to be more conservative (read harder) than other areas. Easier sport climbs (5.8 to 5.11) seem to be harder to translate to the YDS system, although the standard of difficulty on the higher end of the scale is comparable to European grading. Older traditional routes conform to early Colorado and California ratings established at the same time. The present sticky rubber and better pro might make them slightly easier, but climbers will still find them solidly rated.

Texas ratings are fairly consistent but vary from area to area also. Many of the older bolted climbs have been retro-bolted, which on some level makes them seem slightly easier. 5.9 can start feeling like 5.10 when you're 40 feet out as opposed to 10 feet out! Experienced crack climbers may also find the few crack routes to be slightly over-rated in malnourished Texas crack country. Use all ratings as a starting point in any area and expect a one to two letter grade, or even a full grade variation, from what you are accustomed to at your home area.

Many routes listed also have protection or danger ratings. These routes generally have little or no protection and a climber who falls could sustain serious injuries or death. R-rated climbs have serious injury potential. X-rated climbs have groundfall and death potential. Remember, however, that every route is a possible R- or X-rated climb.

Mountain travel is typically classified as follows:

Class 1—Trail hiking.

Class 2—Hiking over rough ground such as scree and talus; may include the use of hands for stability.

Class 3—Scrambling that requires the use of hands and careful foot placement.

Class 4—Scrambling over steep and exposed terrain; climbing difficulty is relatively easy, but a long fall could result in injury because of exposure. The lead climber trails a rope, uses natural formations for protection if available, and is on belay.

Class 5—Climbing on steep and exposed terrain where a fall would definitely result in injury or death. Hands and feet only are used for upward progress, no direct or artificial aid is employed. Ropes, belays, running belays (protection), and related techniques are used.

The Yosemite Decimal System (YDS) used to rate Class 5 climbing fails to follow mathematical logic. It is now an open-ended scale where the 5 denotes the Class and the difficulty rating is tacked on behind the decimal point, with 5.0 being the easiest and 5.15 (read five-fifteen) being the hardest (to date). When it was originally developed, 5.9 was the theoretic upper end of the scale. When routes were climbed that were obviously harder than 5.9, new "numbers" were invented to denote the difficulty. When a route has had too few ascents for a consensus or the estimated difficulty rating is unclear, a plus (+) or minus (-) subgrade may be employed (5.9+ or 5.12- for example). Where there is a consensus of opinion, additional subgrades of a, b, c, and d are used on climbs rated 5.10 and above. Occasionally two letters may be used such as 5.12b/c. This is because the grade still requires consensus or is height dependent, or subject to some other qualifier.

As originally intended, routes are rated according to the most difficult move. Some climbs may be continuously difficult, seeming more difficult than other routes rated the same but with only one or two hard moves. In some instances, routes will be described as "sustained" or "pumpy" to give an indication of the continuous nature of the climbing. Also, differences in strength and reach as well as distance between protection points may be factors contributing to rating variations. Where these factors seem significant, they may be pointed out in the written descriptions.

Aid climbing—using artificial means to progress up the rock—has a different set of ratings.

Class 6—Aid climbing; climbing equipment is used for progress, balance, or rest; denoted with a capital letter A followed by numbers progressing from 0.

A0—Equipment may have been placed to rest on or to pull on for upward progress.

A1—Solid gear placements and aid slings (etriers) are used for progress because the climbing is too difficult to be free climbed.

A2—Gear placements are more difficult to install and support less weight than an A1 placement.

A3—Progressively weaker placements, more difficult to install; may not hold a short fall.

A4—Placements can support body weight only; long falls can occur.

A5—Enough A4 placements that result in falls of 50 feet or longer.

A pitch or rope-length of technical climbing may have a combination Class 5 and Class 6 rating such as 5.9A4, meaning the free climbing difficulties are up to 5.9 with an aid section of A4 difficulty. On the route "topo" drawings or marked photos in this guide, the crux (most difficult section) often is marked with the difficulty rating.

An additional grade denoted by Roman numerals I through VI is given to some longer routes. This generally refers to the commitment in terms of length and time requirements of the climb. Climbers should also consider other factors such as technical difficulties, weather, logistics, and the approach and descent. Typically a Grade I takes a few hours to complete, Grade II up to half a day, Grade III most of the day, Grade IV all day, Grade V usually requires a bivouac, and Grade VI takes two or more days.

Ian Spencer-Green on *Entertaining Mike Tyson* (5.13b), Palomas Peak, New Mexico. *Photo by Stewart M. Green.*

An additional "danger" rating may be tacked on to some climbs. Where the protection may not hold and a fall could result in injury or death, an R or X may be added. A route rated 5.9R may mean that the protection is sparse or "runout" or that some placements may not hold a fall. X-rated routes have a fall potential that can be fatal, unless one has the confidence and ability to solo a route safely with absolutely no protection and without falling.

See Appendix B for a table comparing the American system (Yosemite Decimal System) to the British, French, and Australian systems.

Injuries sustained from falls are always possible, even on routes that can be well protected. This guide does not give a protection rating nor does it provide detailed information on how, when, or where to place protective hardware. Suggested "standard" gear racks are described in the overview for each area, and some recommendations are made on types and sizes of protection that may be useful on some climbs. But safety and the level of risk assumed are the responsibility of the climber.

Sport climbers should also eye their prospective route and count the number of bolts. Bolt counts are given for many routes, but things change on the real rock. Some bolts may be hidden, added, subtracted, or miscounted. Always carry extra in case the count is wrong or you drop a quickdraw. Remember to consider what you need for the anchors and for lowering. Again, it's always really up to you to provide your own safety. Climb safe, climb smart, and have fun!

Northern New Mexico

REGION

Taos Area Crags

Overview

The Taos climbing area includes Questa Dome, Heart of Stone Rock, John's Wall, Dead Cholla Wall, and Tres Piedras Rocks. Excellent climbing is found on the cliffs at all these areas. Multi-pitch routes on some of New Mexico's best granite is found here, along with quality sport and traditional routes on basalt cliffs. Climbers can scale Questa Dome in a pristine mountain setting in the Latir Wilderness Area or on lofty crags overlooking the Rio Grande from its cliffed rim.

Development of the area started in the early 1970s on John's Wall, a small basalt cliff with both trad and sport routes near the put-in for boaters embarking on the very exciting Taos Box in Rio Grande Gorge. John's Wall offers great crack climbing on a vertical basalt cliff above the Rio Hondo, a pleasant creek that tumbles over worn boulders. Enjoyment of this area is diminished by the recent vandalism to the rock cliff. Oil splatters at the start of some routes must be negotiated to reach the good climbing on the upper wall.

The Taos Box river run, a challenging Class IV section of whitewater, ends at Taos Junction Bridge 15 miles to the south. Above the river take-out sits Dead Cholla Wall, the area's newest developed crag. The wall is primarily a sport climbing cliff with excellent 5.10 and 5.11 routes protected by modern bolts. The crag yields great views of the Rio Grande Gorge and the snowcapped Sangre de Cristo Range from its rimrock vantage point.

Questa Dome, looming above a narrow canyon sliced into the western flank of the Sangre de Cristos, offers the area's longest routes with several superb 4- to 5-pitch lines scaling its grey granite wall. One of the most highly regarded New Mexico routes, *Question of Balance*, is located here. Heart of Stone Rock, a smaller version of Questa Dome, yields several 3- and 4-pitch routes. These two areas require placing gear, although fixed anchors and fixed protection are found on some routes.

TAOS AREA CRAGS

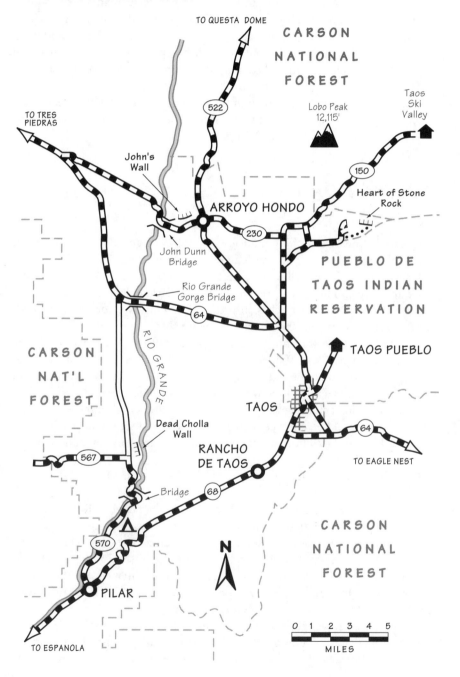

TO QUESTA DOME

CARSON
NATIONAL
FOREST

Taos
Ski
Valley

Lobo Peak
12,115'

522

TO TRES
PIEDRAS

John's
Wall

150

Heart of Stone
Rock

ARROYO HONDO

230

John Dunn
Bridge

PUEBLO DE
TAOS INDIAN
RESERVATION

Rio Grande
Gorge Bridge

64

RIO GRANDE

TAOS PUEBLO

CARSON
NAT'L
FOREST

TAOS

64

Dead Cholla
Wall

TO EAGLE NEST

567

RANCHO
DE TAOS

Bridge

68

CARSON
NATIONAL
FOREST

570

N

PILAR

TO ESPANOLA

0 1 2 3 4 5
MILES

Tres Piedras, situated on the southern end of the Tusas Mountains, is a pleasing mountain area of granite ridges and small domes. West of Taos and the Gorge, this area is a favorite of locals and features many 1- to 2-pitch routes from 5.6 to 5.12. These are mostly bolt-protected with additional gear placements often necessary. Climbers will encounter many 1/4" bolts and fixed pins at the Taos area crags on routes established prior to the late 1980s. Use these with extreme caution and back up the fixed gear whenever possible.

The Taos area is reached from the north via New Mexico Highway 522 (it's Colorado Highway 159 north of the border). From the south, exit Interstate 25 at Santa Fe onto Saint Francis Drive and follow road signs north to Taos on U.S. Highway 285 and NM 68.

QUESTA DOME

OVERVIEW

Questa Dome, overlooking the Rio Grande's deep gorge and broad valley, lies on the western flank of the Sangre de Cristo Range in the Latir Peak Wilderness north of the village of Questa. The 500' granite dome offers good crack and face climbing in a pristine mountain setting. The routes on Questa Dome vary from 2 to 5 pitches in length. Currently six routes along with several variations ascend the southwest-facing cliff.

Questa Dome is a traditional climbing area. Bolting and power drills are banned in the Latir Peak Wilderness. Visiting climbers should be aware that long runouts are encountered on many routes, some with serious fall and injury potential. Help is a long way off from this remote crag. Use your best judgment and don't climb beyond your abilities. Climbers attempting any lines on the dome should be competent at placing gear and setting belays. Also be prepared for thin face climbing, long runouts on hard climbing, and devious route-finding.

Climbing history: Bold routes were established on the Questa Dome's excellent rock in the 1970s and 1980s. Paul Horak was the first to test Questa's steep complicated faces. Ken Trout, Peter Prandoni, and Mike Roybal all lent their considerable talents to connect the discontinuous crack systems and intricate face moves necessary to summit this fine crag. The crag's classic route is *Question of Balance*. This 4-pitch line, established in 1970 by Paul Horak, Mark Dalen, Glen Banks, and Dave Balz, is a bold statement up the dome's obvious line. Only *Tooth or Consequences* in the Organ Mountains rivals *Question of Balance* for quality, experience, and position.

Questa Dome has experienced a resurgence in popularity in the 1990s with some new route activity and the replacement of the original 1/4" bolts on some enduring classic lines. Dan Parks, Doug Coleur, and others are leading

QUESTA DOME

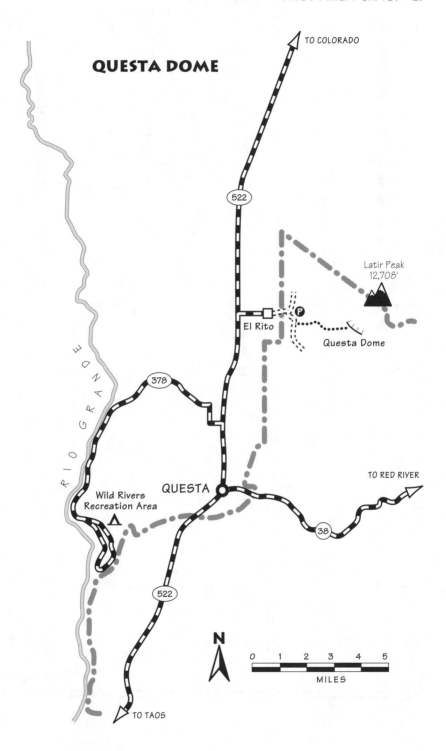

TO COLORADO

522

Latir Peak
12,708'

El Rito

Questa Dome

378

RIO GRANDE

TO RED RIVER

QUESTA

Wild Rivers
Recreation Area

38

522

TO TAOS

N

0 1 2 3 4 5
MILES

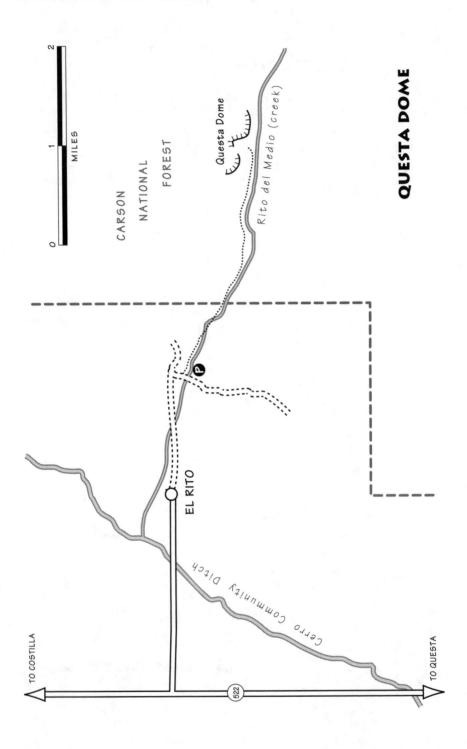

0 1 2

MILES

CARSON

NATIONAL

FOREST

Questa Dome

Rito del Medio (creek)

EL RITO

Cerro Community Ditch

522

TO COSTILLA

TO QUESTA

QUESTA DOME

this new development. Many of the routes, however, still rely on old bolts. Use with caution. Back up all bolts, particularly at belay stations, with gear whenever possible.

Good cragging is also found on most of the Dome's other routes making Questa Dome worthy of many visits. It's rarely crowded, with only occasional parties encountered on weekends. Climbers can expect quiet weekday visits. If the weather turns bad or the dome is too crowded for your tastes, consider the Nutcracker Rocks directly west of the dome. These granite crags, reaching heights of 200', receive little attention from most climbers. The rocks offer fine 1- and 2-pitch crack lines. Climbing here is a satisfying experience of solitude and discovery.

Rack: Bring a full rack of Friends, wired stoppers, RPs, a dozen quickdraws, runners, and a 165' rope. An extra rope can be helpful if retreat is necessary.

Descent: Descent from the summit is to the east or right side of the dome. Walk east from the summit, pass over the top of a gully, and follow a faint trail trending down and right through trees. Eventually you will emerge at the base of the Dome's east flank near the rock's base. Allow 30 minutes for the descent.

Trip Planning Information

Area description: Questa Dome, a 500' granite dome, offers some excellent multi-pitch traditional routes in a spectacular mountain setting.

Location: Northern New Mexico. In the Latir Wilderness north of Taos.

Camping: No established campgrounds in the area. Good camping is available about 13 miles away at the BLM Wild Rivers Recreation Area on the rim of the Rio Grande Gorge. Head north from the town of Questa a few miles to New Mexico Highway 378. Turn west on NM 378 and follow signs to the recreation area. The area offers 21 campsites in 5 campgrounds on the rim.

Climbing season: Late May to late October, depending on snow conditions. July through September are best months. Expect afternoon thunderstorms during the summer months.

Restrictions and access issues: Questa Dome lies in Carson National Forest. Access was an issue in the past but was mitigated by the inclusion of the dome in the Latir Wilderness Area. It is necessary to pass private property to reach the trailhead. Please exercise good judgment when passing through. No motorized equipment, including power drills, is allowed in the wilderness area. Limited parking at the trailhead. Lock your car. Four-wheel-drive recommended to drive all the way to the parking area.

Guidebook: A description of *Question of Balance* is in *Taos Rock*, a self-published guide by Cayce Weber and Ed Jaramillo. It's available at Mudd N-Flood Review and Taos Mountain Outfitters. An account of the first ascent appeared in *Climbing Magazine* issue 44.

Nearby mountain shops, guide services, and gyms: Taos. There are no climbing gyms in the area.

Services: The small village of Questa offers limited services including a convenience store, several restaurants, and a gas station. Full services are found in Taos, 20 miles south on NM 522, and in Red River, 15 miles east of Questa on NM 38.

Emergency services: Call 911.

Nearby climbing areas: Heart of Stone Rock, John's Wall, Dead Cholla Wall, Tres Piedras.

Nearby attractions: Rio Grande Wild and Scenic River, Red River, Red River Fish Hatchery. Taos attractions include Taos Plaza and Kit Carson Park, Taos Pueblo, Enchanted Circle Scenic Byway, Rio Grande Gorge Bridge, Wheeler Peak Wilderness Area. Good boating, fishing, backpacking, and hiking is found in the BLM's Wild Rivers Recreation Area. Reach it via the Wild Rivers Back Country Byway north of Questa via NM 378 and NM 522.

Finding the crag: Questa Dome is accessed from the north and south via NM 522 between Taos and the Colorado border. The turnoff is about 7 miles north of the village of Questa and about 13 miles south of the Colorado-New Mexico border. Turn east at a sign announcing El Rito (right from the south, left from the north) toward the mountains on a narrow paved road. Make sure to turn at El Rito and not Tres Ritos Ranch. Questa Dome is the prominent, large granite buttress in view as you drive in. The trailhead is 2.1 miles from the highway and requires four-wheel drive for the last mile. The pavement turns to gravel at 0.9 mile, where it is joined by a road coming in from the left. Continue straight here. After passing a large house on the left, the road gets much rougher. When the road comes to a T junction, go right for 0.2 mile to a small parking area on the left. The trail starts here and climbs steadily up the El Rito Creek to Questa Dome. When you are close to the dome, the trail travels close to the creek. To reach Nutcracker Rocks, look for a faint trail forking off left in this area. For Questa Dome, continue following the creek until it is possible to easily hike left to the base of the dome. Allow 35 to 40 minutes for the approach hike.

1. **Que Wasted (a.k.a. Sequestered)** (III 5.12-) From the toe of the southwest prow of the rock, walk uphill 50' to where a prominent dihedral reaches the ground. At this point the dihedral is a groove. **Pitch 1:** Climb easy slabs and the groove up and right to where it is possible to do a balance traverse around a bulge to the right. This puts you on the slabs to the right of the prominent left-facing corner. Climb up to belay below a flake roof. 150'. **Pitch 2:** Climb over the flake roof (5.10-) then up slab and crack climbing to a belay from gear in a shallow pod. 150'. **Pitch 3:** Difficult face climbing (5.12-) is protected by small nuts to easier terrain above. Belay on a large sloping ledge. 100'. **Pitch 4:** Climb up left to a hand crack

behind short pillars. Climb this to a ledge on top. The crux slab is next. Move up then right to difficult mantle protected by bolts. Belay 50' farther from gear at the base of a water groove/crack. **Pitches 5 and 6:** Follow cracks and grooves up and right for 2 pitches to the top, 5.8-5.9, slightly runout. **Descent:** From summit walk off east(right).

2. **Question Of Balance** (III 5.11) This excellent route, one of New Mexico's very best, offers 5 long pitches on excellent granite. The route, wandering up connecting crack systems on the main face, is high quality, sustained, and very enjoyable. **Rack:** Bring a standard rack with sets of Friends up to a #4, TCUs, and wired stoppers, some runners, and two 165' ropes if retreat is necessary. Begin the route a little left of the rock's center directly below a 2-bolt chained belay stance 150' above. **Pitch 1:** Start up and aim for a short right-curving flake. Jam a 2" crack up the flake. At the top of the flake, continue up and left across a slab (5.9) under a roof. Climb back right to a fixed piton under the roof. (The original way traversed left here to a mantle (5.10+) then back right on easy climbing.) Pull over the roof (5.11 crux) and continue up and right in a thin crack to some difficult face moves (5.10). End at the 2-bolt belay. 150'. **Pitch 2:** Climb up a right-angling finger crack past a fixed pin. Go left where the crack pinches down and then up right, passing an overlap to another right-trending, fingers to small hands crack to a 1 bolt, 1-pin belay stance. Gear placements are also available. 150'. **Pitch 3:** Drop down several feet and traverse right across a dike 12', then head up right via thin cracks and face climbing (5.9 and 5.10) to where it is possible to traverse left under a large obvious roof. End at a hanging belay (2 bolts) almost directly above the second belay stance and below a notch in the roof. 140'. **Pitch 4:** Step left from the belay and face climb up to the roof. Jam over the roof (5.10) to easier climbing above. Run the rope out by climbing and traversing up right (sparse protection) and belay below a small groove of trees. **Pitch 5:** A short fourth class pitch to the small grove of trees that are about 150' below the summit. Third class up easy rock to the right. **Descent:** Climb easy rock to the large trees near the east or right side of the summit. Angling up and right from the end of Pitch 4 will speed things up a bit. When on easy ground, walk east or right above the top of a gully and turn down a slope through the trees by following a faint trail down and contouring right or west. The trail ends at the base of the east flank of Questa Dome and near the rock base. Allow 20 to 30 minutes for the descent.

3. **Aero Questa** (5.12-) **Pitch 1:** Climb the 1st pitch of *Question of Balance*. **Pitch 2:** Move left past 2 bolts to a belay at bottom of obvious water streak. **Pitch 3:** Climb water streak to horizontal dike and move left on dike past natural pockets. Then climb over a bulge onto another dike and belay. **Pitch 4:** Follow bolts up the face to a pin and bolt belay. **Descent:**

Multiple rappels from end of Pitch 4, or traverse right and go to the summit via *Question of Balance*.

3a. **Project** (5.12) On 3rd pitch of *Aero Questa*, continue straight up water streak following a bolt line. The climbing above the horizontal dike is harder than the climbing below the dike. **Descent:** Either rappel the route or traverse into *Question of Balance*.

4. **Another Pretty Face** (5.11) 2 pitches of thin face climbing up to the 2nd belay on *Question of Balance*. Rope up at same place as *Tostados*

QUESTA DOME

Comquesta. **Pitch 1:** Climb slabs to left of dihedral. Difficult climbing leads to better pro in cracks. Climb corners to top of two large flakes. Belay on ledge at top of second flake. **Pitch 2:** Difficult face climbing protected by 1/4" bolts leads up and left to join *Question of Balance*. 120'.

5. **Tostados Comquesta** (5.10) This climb follows the major right-facing dihedral on the right side of the rock. **Pitch 1:** easy climbing on the face right of the dihedral up to a sling belay below a roof. **Pitch 2:** Either stay with the crack or move right (5.9 either way) for enjoyable climbing over the roof, into a crack, then up a face to a 2-bolt belay. These 2 pitches can be done as one but require a 165' rope and some simul-climbing. **Pitch 3:** Climb straight up past 2 bolts then into the main crack system to a belay. Crux pitch. **Pitch 4:** Straight up via moderate then easy climbing to the top.

5a. **Project** (5.12?) This route proposes to turn the right side of the major roof system. Tentative grade is 5.12.

HEART OF STONE ROCK

OVERVIEW

Heart of Stone Rock, tucked into a narrow canyon, rises 300' above twisting Arroyo Seco Creek in the mountains north of Taos. This granite crag, a smaller version of nearby Questa Dome, yields some excellent climbing on surprisingly solid granite. First-time visitors may be intimidated by the lack of protection and the initial impression of poor rock quality. Early Taos climbers, however, were undeterred and established several multi-pitch routes in bold traditional style. Most of this activity occurred in the late 1970s and early 1980s. Development has since slowed, except for Ken Sims' fine 1-pitch variation to *Laid Back Limey*. This variation is named for Edwin Terrell, a talented climber from Santa Fe that was tragically killed climbing in the Himalayas. Both of the crag's routes are somewhat inobvious affairs that ascend a variety of edges, pockets, flakes, and cracks. Climbers should be adept at route finding and willing to run it out on the sparsely protected sections.

Other efforts are being made farther upstream by Taos area climbers. The abundant rock in the area will almost certainly yield additional climbing gems, although explorers will have to endure long hikes and be equipped for creative protection.

Don't confuse Heart of Stone Rock with the nearby El Salto climbed by early Taos climbers. They referred to some of the large granite formations north and west of the crag. Climbing possibilities exist there for those willing

Paul Drakos climbing *Laid Back Limey* (5.9+) on Heart of Stone Rock, north of Taos, New Mexico. *Photo by Dennis Jackson.*

to undertake difficult approaches and use creative route-finding skills. Several 5.7 routes were established on the original El Salto which look like exciting affairs. Check with locals for information about these and other possibilities in this area. Remember that all these rocks are on private land. A low-key, user-friendly approach by visitors is necessary to ensure the future of climbing here. Read and adhere to information in the "Restrictions and access issues" section below.

Rack: A standard rack with a selection of wired stoppers, TCUs, slings, a double set of Friends or other camming devices, and a 165' rope are required for Heart of Stone routes.

Descent: Descent is somewhat devious and involves rappels and downclimbing on the northwest side of the rock. At the summit, walk to the left, then downclimb to a tree equipped with rappel slings. From here either rappel 120' or continue downclimbing (somewhat loose and steep) to the descent gully. The 2-rope rappel eliminates the downclimbing and ends on easier terrain near the low-angle gully on the north side of the crag. The bolts to the right of Heart of Stone route protect an ice climb that forms up periodically on the black water streak. The suspect-looking rappel anchors passed on the 2nd pitch of *Laid Back Limey* is also part of the ice climb. Ignore the bolts and anchors during any rock climbing descent.

Trip Planning Information

Area description: Heart of Stone offers a small selection of 3-pitch routes on a 350' granite crag.

Location: North-central New Mexico.

Camping: Camping near the crag is not allowed, recommended, or advised. The best public campsites are in Carson National Forest east of Taos and at Orilla Verde Recreation Area (BLM) next to the Rio Grande between Taos and Espanola. This pleasant area offers four developed campgrounds and one primitive campground. This fee area is operated on a first-come basis. Reach Orilla Verde by driving north on New Mexico Highway 570 from NM 68 at Pilar about 15 miles southwest of Taos.

Climbing season: Heart of Stone lies in a mountain environment. Climbing is possible after the spring snow melt and before the arrival of winter snow. April through November are generally the best months. Early spring runoff may make the creek crossings difficult. The area is best during the hot summer months of July to September. Expect regular afternoon summer thunderstorms.

Restrictions and access issues: A $3 fee per person is required to enter this privately owned area. Pay at the Quintana residence on the approach road. Failure to pay will result in possible fines and ill-will toward climbers. There are no present restrictions on climbing, partially because there is very little climbing activity and climbing is poorly understood by the area's owners. If visitation increases, this will surely change. Please treat this sensitive area with caution and respect.

Guidebook: None.

Nearby mountain shops, guide services, and gyms: Taos. There are no gyms in the area.

Services: Casa Fresen, in the small village of Arroyo Seco, can provide pre-climb espresso, coffee, and pastries. Nearby Taos offers a full range of tourist services, including gas, lodging, and food, with a choice of more than 80 restaurants.

Emergency services: Call 911. Ambulance service and hospital in Taos.

Nearby climbing areas: John's Wall, Dead Cholla Wall, Questa Dome, Tres Piedras Rocks.

Nearby attractions: Taos history and culture (Martinez Hacienda, Kit Carson Home and Museum, and Governor Bent House Museum and Gallery). Also Taos Pueblo, Wheeler Peak and Latir Peak wilderness areas, whitewater boating on the Rio Grande, and, in winter, skiing at Taos Ski Valley, Red River, Ski Rio, Angel Fire, and Sipapu.

Finding the crag: From Taos go north through town to the blinking light at the junction of U.S. Highway 64 West, NM 522, and NM 150. Turn east onto NM 150. Signs point toward Taos Ski Valley and Arroyo Seco. In the village of Arroyo Seco the road makes a sharp curve to the left where signs direct traffic to the Taos Ski Valley. Do not make this turn. Instead, continue straight ahead (starts as gravel, turns to pavement) for about 1 mile to the Quintana residence where you pay your fees ($3 per person as of 1994) and receive your permit. You will be glad you did this when you return to find your car in the same place and condition you left it. This green house is on the left-hand or north side of the road and has a sign in the trees announcing that permission and fees are required. The road turns to gravel just past the sign. Most visitors are interested in seeing El Salto ("the falls"), a popular waterfall and picnic site which is located farther up the road. Leave your permit visible on the dash to avoid confusion. You may want to mention that you plan on hiking up the *cañoncito* although this is not mandatory (See "Restrictions and access issues" section). Continue on the dirt road for about 0.7 mile and park by a creek just before several large houses. Parking is limited and some creativity and more walking may be required. Do not park at the private residences. The trail starts on the south side of the creek and goes east or upstream. Count on 45 minutes of hiking up a good trail that eventually places you at the base of the 350' crag at creek level. Cross the creek to access all routes.

The crag faces west. Routes are described left to right.

1. **Heart of Stone and The Edwin Terrell Memorial Route** (5.11) This line ascends Heart of Stone and the excellent but difficult *Edwin Terrell Memorial Route* variation. Start near the left end of the formation. Locate a

HEART
OF
STONE

variation

.10d

original route

.11

XX

fixed
piton

.10+

1

series of of small trees up the cliff face. **Pitch 1:** Start just to the right of the bottom tree in a large crack system that ascends to a large right-slanting roof system. Climb up 30' and exit left into a shallow right-slanting crack. Climb the crack (5.10+) past a fixed pin. Move right and face climb up to a left-facing corner. Stay with the corner until it is possible to exit right and up to a 2-bolt belay stance. 165'. **Pitch 2:** Clip a bolt protecting a hard move (5.11) up to a belay stance by trees at the base of an attractive slab with two cracks, or continue on either of the following variations. The original ascent line face-climbs left, turns the roof on the left, then goes up to the summit (5.9). The *Edwin Terrell Memorial* (5.10d) takes the left-hand thin crack up to the middle of the roof, over it to the right-angling system. 2 fixed pins plus gear protect this difficult (5.10d section). Continue through a slot and belay. **Pitch 3 or 4:** Take the most obvious line (moderate climbing) to the top.

2. **Laid Back Limey** (5.9+) **Pitch 1:** Begin from a flat, sloping boulder in the creek upstream from *Heart of Stone* and climb straight up to a hole in the rock 25' up. Gear placements protect this section. From the hole continue straight up past a bolt and angle up right to a water streak. Continue up the streak to a good stance in a dished-out area just above a poorly placed bolt at about 150'. **Pitch 2:** Climb either the left- or right-hand crack systems above the belay. The right system is unprotectable, moderate rock, while the left system (preferable alternative) offers some protection but involves a traverse back to the right-hand system. Continue up right to the streak and establish a belay convenient to your exit crack of choice. **Pitch 3:** At least 3 choices exist here. The easiest way off is to establish the belay as far left as possible under and right of the large fins. From here, traverse right to an easy crack-chimney system to the top. The other two options are the thin finger crack splitting the face (5.10) and the hand crack on the right side (5.9+).

2 pitches to top

HEART OF STONE ROCK
"LAID BACK LIMEY"

2

JOHN'S WALL

OVERVIEW

John's Wall, a.k.a. Hondo Cliffs, is a roadside 70' basalt cliff and the original and oldest Taos climbing area. The south-facing crag tucks into a narrow side-canyon just east of the John Dunn Bridge at the bottom of the 650' deep Rio Grande Gorge in northern New Mexico. A selection of fine crack and face routes ascends the cliff offering good, easily accessible climbing. Vandalism to the cliff and area, however, detracts from the pleasant surroundings and climbing experience. Several new routes are on another cliff farther left and around the corner just opposite the put-in for the Taos Box section of the river in the gorge itself. These climbs are in the 5.10 and 5.11 range.

Climbing history: Convenient access and a pleasant setting deep in the scenic Rio Grande Gorge attracted area climbers to John's Wall in the early 1970s. Skills developed here allowed climbers to turn their attention to other area challenges including the granite faces of Heart of Stone and Questa Dome and the less intimidating but bold climbs at Tres Piedras. John's Wall, named for the nearby John Dunn Bridge, has suffered vandalism dating back to 1910. The most recent incident was the splattering of a petroleum-based substance on the bottom third of the wall. This, plus the usual graffiti, detracts from enjoying the crag's excellent face and crack routes.

Many of the older routes are protected by old 1/4" bolts which should be used cautiously. Back up all bolts whenever possible with gear.

Rack: A standard rack here should include quickdraws, wired stoppers, and camming units or nuts up to #4 Friend.

Descent: Descend by walking off the west end (towards the river) or east end of the cliff. Some bolted routes have fixed lowering stations with chains. Setting up topropes is problematic due to rock fall danger, difficulty in getting to established anchors below the cliff-top, and lack of anchor placements above the cliff. Use caution whenever walking along the cliff-top to avoid knocking loose blocks and boulders onto belayers, climbers, and on-lookers below.

Trip Planning Information

Area description: John's Wall offers face and crack climbs on a 70' basalt cliff in the bottom of the Rio Grande Gorge.

Location: North-central New Mexico, northwest of Taos.

Camping: Camping opportunities are limited in the immediate area. The road that veers left at the bridge over the Rio Hondo goes downstream on the east side of the river. This is a heavily used fishing area and generally occupied. Camping is not permitted at the BLM boat launch site. Primitive and established camping sites are plentiful in Carson National Forest. Go east

Dennis Jackson leads *Amazon* (5.9), at John's Wall, New Mexico.
Photo by Stewart M. Green.

from Taos on U.S. Highway 64 toward Eagle Nest. Developed campgrounds are found in this area.

Climbing season: Year-round. Occasional cold temperatures in the winter limit the number of climbable days. The south-facing wall can be uncomfortably hot during the summer. Spring and fall offer the best weather.

Restrictions and access issues: The crag is administered by the Bureau of Land Management. There are no current restrictions on climbing.

Guidebook: The area is partially covered in the non-bound, self-published guide, *Taos Rock III* by Cayce Weber and Ed Jaramillo. The guide is available at Taos Mountain Outfitters and Mudd N-Flood Review.

Nearby mountain shops, guide services, and gyms: Taos. There are no gyms in the area.

Services: Nearby Taos offers a full range of tourist services, including gas, food, and lodging. Visitors can choose from over 80 restaurants.

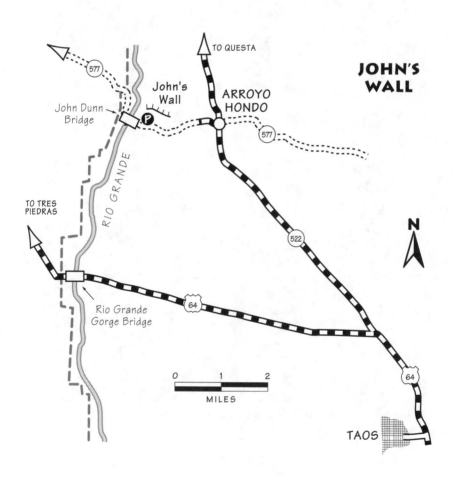

Emergency services: Call 911. The nearest phone is at Herb's Lounge on New Mexico Highway 522 at Arroyo Hondo. Ambulance service and Holy Cross Hospital are in Taos.

Nearby climbing areas: Heart of Stone Rock, Dead Cholla Wall, Tres Piedras, Questa Dome.

Nearby attractions: A heavily used, natural hot spring is located downstream on the west bank of the Rio Grande. Drive across the John Dunn Bridge, continue west a short distance to the first switchback, and locate a trail heading down to the river. At peak runoff, the spring is under water. Another hot spring, Mamby Hot Spring, is located downriver on the east bank. Access via a trail by walking or driving down the road that veers left at the Rio Hondo bridge crossing. The hot spring is about 3 miles downstream. Other attractions include Taos Plaza, Kit Carson Park, Taos Pueblo, Enchanted Circle Scenic Byway, San Francisco de Assisi Church in Ranchos de Taos, Rio Grande Gorge Bridge, Picuris Pueblo, Carson National Forest, Wheeler Peak Wilderness Area. Good boating, fishing, and swimming are found in the Rio Grande Gorge area. Mountain biking on dirt roads and hiking trails can also be found. Wild Rivers Back Country Byway is west of Questa.

Finding the crag: From the south, go north from the blinking light on the north end of Taos on NM 522 about 7 miles to Arroyo Hondo. From the north, drive south on NM 522 to the village of Arroyo Hondo. At Arroyo Hondo turn west on paved NM 577 just over the bridge on the Rio Hondo. The road begins as pavement, then turns to dirt. John's Wall is a little more than 2 miles from Arroyo Hondo on the right or north side of the road where it crosses a small bridge over the Rio Hondo. The John Dunn Bridge crosses the Rio Grande a short distance past the climbing area.

Routes are described left to right. Descend either from lowering anchors or walk off the west end (preferable) or east end.

1. **Awkward Chimney** (5.8) Climb up through broken rock to ledge, then up chimney.

2. **Rope-a-Dope** (5.7) Start at blocks on left end of ledge; climb the face between *Awkward Chimney* and *Deception*.

3. **Deception** (5.8) Start on right side of broken rocks with bushes and a cholla cactus, then climb up the dihedral to the top.

4. **The Trapeze** (5.10) Start from large ledge 10' off the deck just below a dark gouged-out section with a steep, attractive crack going to the top. Classic.

5. **Heaven Above** (5.10) Start on the right side of the upper part of the ledge. Up an overhang to a flake and crack to the top. 3 cold shuts to lower from. Classic.

6. **Unnamed** (5.12) Start at ground level, then up an attractive face to *Heaven Above* anchors. Difficult and sustained. Usually top-roped. 3 bolts.

7. **The Bulges** (5.9) Start up oil-splattered rock to a curving crack system, over bulges and up a steep, thin crack to summit. Good pockets but strenuous near top. Classic.

8. **The Nose** (5.10a) Moderately difficult climbing (5.9 and 1 bolt) to a ledge atop the bulbous nose formation (Central Block). Face climb up the quality blunt arete above to chained anchors. One of the most popular lines on the crag. Classic. 3 bolts.

9. **Memory Lane** (5.8) The large dihedral to the right of *The Nose*. Named in memory of Lane McMurry. Bring medium pro.

10. **The Face** (5.9+) Same start as *The Nose*, only work up right from bolt 1 onto steep face right of arete to 2-bolt anchor with chains. 5 bolts.

11. **Route 66** (5.7) Start right of *The Face*. Up the obvious left-facing dihedral. Shares anchors with *The Face*.

12. **Unnamed** (5.8) Start same as *Amazon*. Step left at 1st bolt onto slabby face between aretes. Waltz upwards on great holds and pockets to a 2-bolt lowering anchor. 5 bolts.

13. **Amazon** (5.9) Begin on far right side of cliff. Pick easiest way through choss rock section to a bolt, pull up into a classic right-facing corner. Jam and stem corner (5.8) to blocky roof. Turn crux roof (5.9) on the left. Belay with gear and slings on the cliff rim.

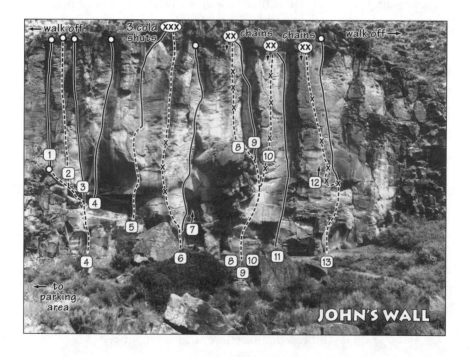

DEAD CHOLLA WALL

OVERVIEW

Dead Cholla Wall, offering marvelous views to complement great climbing, sits along the cliffed rim of the 600' deep Rio Grande Gorge. The Rio Grande rushes silently through the steep, rocky canyon below with the Taos Valley and the Sangre de Cristo Mountains looming to the east. The 60' cliff, composed of vertical and overhanging red and black basalt, is just one of many crags in the immediate area that invite further exploration. Future routes will necessitate longer walks than the short 5-minute approach to Dead Cholla Wall, but climbers will be rewarded with ample opportunities to climb and explore this beautiful area.

More than 20 sport routes are currently established at Dead Cholla Wall. All are equipped with new 3/8" bolts. Several good crack climbs that readily accept gear also scale the escarpment. Most of the routes offer steep face climbing on small, positive, in-cut holds. Toproping is possible, although many of the lowering anchors are located well below the top of the cliff. The ledges atop most of New Mexico's basalt cliffs are stacked with loose, precarious rocks and boulders. Take extra care to protect yourself and those below from falling rocks when approaching the crag and when setting up an anchor on the rim. Also watch for rattlesnakes in boulderfields during summer and fall.

Climbing history: Ed Jaramillo and Cayce Boyce, long-time Taos climbers, found Dead Cholla Wall while searching out sport climbing possibilities closer to Taos in 1989. The crag was named after a large dead cholla cactus found on the approach to the climb. Today, the crag is also known as Pilar. Cayce and Ed were amazed at the quality of the rock, the views, and the climbing possibilities. Since this initial foray, the number of routes has doubled. Almost all of the lines are in the 5.10 to 5.11 range, making this crag popular for sport climbers moving up the numbers. Panorama Wall (not covered in this guide), a prominent southeast-facing cliff on the rim almost a mile north of Dead Cholla Wall, offers a few natural lines and a partially bolted face route.

Rack: A rack for the sport climbing routes is up to ten quickdraws. Small gear placements (TCUs, RPs, and wired stoppers) are occasionally found and recommended for extra security. The cracks are all easily protected with a standard rack of camming units and wired stoppers. A 150' rope suffices for all routes.

Descent: Lower from anchors or walk off.

Martha Morris leads *Fun* (5.7), Dead Cholla Wall, New Mexico.
Photo by Stewart M. Green.

Trip Planning Information

Area description: Dead Cholla Wall, a 60' basalt cliff, offers many sport routes on the west rim of the Rio Grande Gorge.

Location: North-central New Mexico, about 10 miles southwest of Taos.

Camping: Primitive camping is possible near the parking area on the canyon rim. Practice low-impact camping and be low-key if you choose to camp here. A good alternative is a short distance away in developed fee sites in the Orilla Verde Recreation Area along the Rio Grande. This area, operated on a first-come, first-served basis, can be crowded during spring and summer. Advance reservations are not possible so plan accordingly. Additional camping can be found in nearby Carson National Forest.

Climbing season: Early spring to late fall are best. The east-facing cliff provides early morning sun and afternoon shade.

Restrictions and access issues: Dead Cholla Wall is located on Bureau of Land Management (BLM) land. No restrictions are currently in place. All public land management agencies are reviewing their management of climbing activities. Climbers may wish to inquire about new BLM regulations before visiting. The residents of Pilar will appreciate you driving slowly through their village.

Guidebook: Some of the early routes are covered in the self-published guide *Taos Rock*, by Cayce Weber and Ed Jaramillo.

Nearby mountain shops, guide services, and gyms: Taos. There are no gyms in the area.

Services: All services are found in Taos, including gas, groceries, dining, and lodging. The village of Pilar has a restaurant, The Yacht Club, and a bed and breakfast. Historic Embudo Station, 10 miles south on New Mexico 68, is pleasantly located next to the river and serves excellent food and local brews.

Emergency services: Call 911. The nearest telephones are in the Orilla Verde Recreation Area at the visitor center and in the Taos Junction and Orilla Verde campsites. Holy Cross Hospital, on the south end of Taos, is the nearest hospital.

Nearby climbing areas: John's Wall, Heart of Stone Rock, Questa Dome, Tres Piedras.

Nearby attractions: Taos Plaza, Kit Carson Park, Taos Pueblo, Enchanted Circle Scenic Byway, San Francisco de Assisi Church in Ranchos de Taos, Rio Grande Gorge Bridge, Picuris Pueblo, Carson National Forest, Wheeler Peak Wilderness Area. Good boating, fishing, and swimming is found in the Rio Grande Gorge area. Mountain biking on backroads and hiking trails can also be found.

Finding the crag: Access to the area from NM 68 is currently possible only via NM 570 at Pilar, 15 miles southwest of Taos. The northern access road just west of the Rio Grande Gorge Bridge that leads south to NM 570 is

DEAD CHOLLA WALL

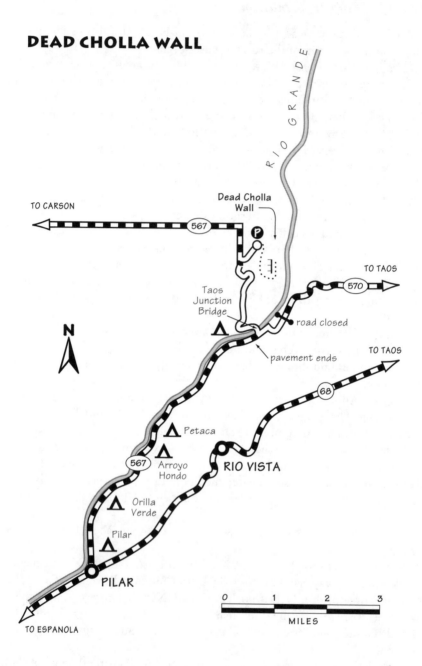

TO CARSON

RIO GRANDE

Dead Cholla
Wall

567

Ⓟ

Taos
Junction
Bridge

TO TAOS

570

road closed

pavement ends

TO TAOS

68

N

Petaca

567

Arroyo
Hondo

RIO VISTA

Orilla
Verde

Pilar

PILAR

TO ESPANOLA

0   1   2   3

MILES

currently blocked by a massive land slide with no immediate plans for reconstruction. Check with the New Mexico Highway Department at (800) 432-4269 for the status of this road section.

To reach the crag, turn north from NM 68 at Pilar onto paved NM 68. Drive along the Rio Grande through Orilla Verde Recreation Area for about 6 miles to the Taos Junction Bridge. Cross the bridge (the road becomes NM 567) and continue about 1.6 miles up the winding dirt road until the road becomes paved again. Go 0.2 mile on the pavement and take the first dirt track on the right. The parking area lies 0.3 mile on this level road above the gorge's western rim. At this point you are north (up-river) of the crag, which is only a 5-minute walk away. The crag trail is visible on the clifftop just below and to the south (down-river) as you look east toward the gorge. The trail leads across the cliff's top, then drops down and around the crag's southern end.

1. **Jam Time** (5.10b) One of the few crack climbs on the crag. Classic finger crack requiring placement of gear.

2. **Blind Faith** (5.11) Place gear before the 1st bolt, then follow excellent stemming to the top up white left-facing dihedral. 3 bolts and 2 anchors.

3. **Queso's Delight** (5.11+) Thin finger crack on left-facing wall. Runout and difficult on gear placements.

4. **Lava Flows** (5.11) One of crag's best climbs. Up arete and face. 5 bolts to anchors. Small cam in horizontal crack down low protects first 20'.

DEAD CHOLLA WALL

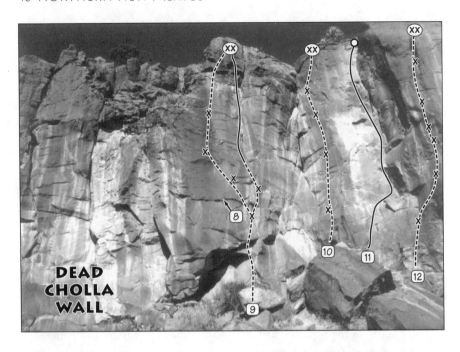

DEAD
CHOLLA
WALL

DEAD CHOLLA WALL

5. **Open Season** (5.10) Start in the finger crack and continue up the corner on right side of prow. 2 bolts and 2 anchors.

6. **Cholla Backstep** (5.11) Climbs obvious corner system. 1 bolt protects the crux.

7. **Hageemoto** (5.11+) After bolt 5, layback a steep section, then traverse left to 2 anchors. 5 bolts.

8. **Merge Left** (5.10+) Clip first bolt of *Gorge Yourself*, traverse left and follow 3 more bolts up red face to *Gorge Yourself's* anchors.

9. **Gorge Yourself** (5.10+) Ascends thin corner system to double anchors. Wires and TCUs necessary after 2 bolts.

10. **Just Arose** (5.11) Climbs red streak just right of broken dihedral. 4 bolts protect difficult balance moves. 2 lowering anchors.

11. **After the Pillar Came Down** (5.10) A thin crack requiring TCUs and stoppers. Belay on clifftop.

12. **Toxic Socks** (5.11+) Delicate steep face climbing up beautiful red wall. 6 bolts to 2 anchors.

13. **Special Ed** (5.11) Thin crack/corner route. Crux is pulling the roof near top. 5 bolts to double anchors.

14. **Fun** (5.7) The easiest line on the crag. Face climb right wall of large obvious corner past 2 bolts, then up the crack above. Bring small and medium Friends for pro. 2 bolts to 2 anchors.

DEAD CHOLLA WALL

15. **Games** (5.10+) Begin at *Fun's* start and work up right around arete onto steep wall. Small holds lead to smears near the top. 5 bolts and double anchors.

16. **Corrido Del Norte** (5.11) Every climb has its own tale. Work up a beautiful pale face past 4 bolts to 2-bolt anchor.

17. **No Lines** (5.11) Climb flakes to face to crack. Bring small to medium pro. Shares anchors with *No Waiting*. 3 bolts.

18. **No Waiting** (5.11) Thin face climbing up white-streaked face. 4 bolts to a 2-bolt anchor.

19. **Twisted Feet** (5.11) Begin right of large right-facing dihedral. Long reaches and stemming up the white face past 5 bolts to 2-bolt anchor.

20. **Doc's Dangle** (5.10) Clip the first 2 bolts of *Somebody Loaned Me a Bosch*, then left and up past 2 more bolts.

21. **Somebody Loaned Me a Bosch** (5.10) Same start as *Doc's Dangle*, but move up right after 2nd bolt. 2 more bolts lead to 2-bolt anchor.

22. **Either Or** (5.11) Quality moves up face right of thin crack. 4 bolts to 2-bolt anchor.

23. **Esmerelda** (5.11) An exciting start makes this climb one of the best here. Face climb up steep wall right of blunt arete and left-leaning corner on far right side of cliff. 5 bolts to 2-bolt anchor.

DEAD CHOLLA WALL

TRES PIEDRAS ROCKS

OVERVIEW

The Tres Piedras crags (Spanish for "three rocks") rise up surprisingly above the high mesa that overlooks the Rio Grande Gorge to the east. This is the only granite climbing area on the west side of the Rio Grande rift zone in New Mexico. The area's excellent rock, pristine mountain setting, and pine-scented forest offer a welcome summer alternative to the hot environments at adjacent basalt climbing areas along the Rio Grande to the east. The granite here differs from Questa Dome and Heart of Stone in the mountains north of Taos in both color and texture but is of equal quality. Most routes are 1-pitch face lines up slabs and vertical to overhanging walls. Several fine crack climbs are found as well.

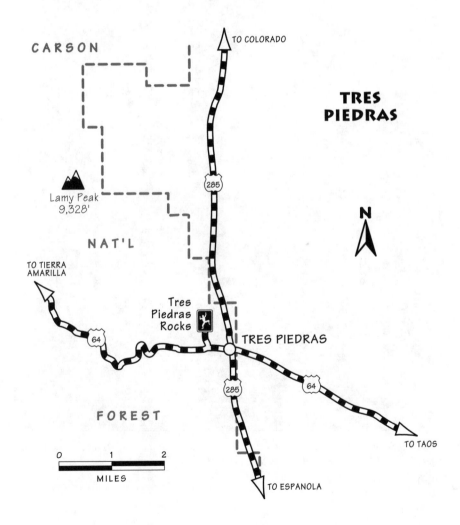

Dennis Jackson belays Martha Morris up *Dirty Black Nightmare* (5.10) on Mosaic Rock, Tres Piedras, New Mexico. *Photo by Stewart M. Green.*

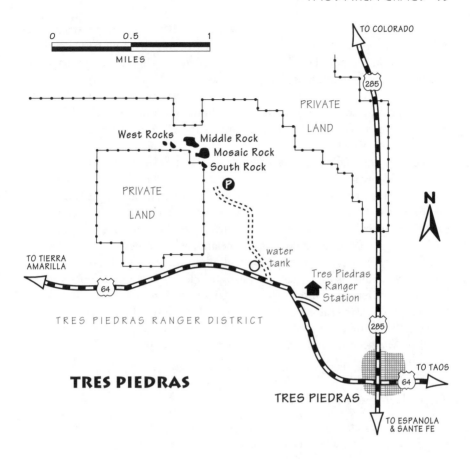

This old-time area possesses a strong traditional background and ethic, although sport routes have made a recent appearance. Many of the new climbs were installed from the ground up. Newer routes are identified by their more plentiful 3/8" bolts, some with chained anchors at the top. Most of the older routes are protected by old 1/4" bolts. Be alert for occasional gear placements to back up these bolts. Some of them are over 20 years old and should be used with caution. Expect long runouts between bolts on the older routes. Taos area climbers have recently retro-bolted most of the 1/4" bolts on Mosaic Rock. On all routes, the absence of established anchors necessitates that the belay be installed with gear and a walk-off descent is required.

Climbing history: A talented group of Taos climbers began exploring Tres Piedras in the early 1970s. Ed Jaramillo, Cayce Weber, and Bruce Holthouse led a strong group of climbers in establishing the area classics. Most of these older climbs are nerve-wracking affairs requiring laser-like focus between widely spaced and often dubious protection. Sample the 5.10 grade on classics like

Seaman Girl and *Better Red than Dead,* or ratchet it up on the strung-out 5.10+ *Holthouse to Hell.* Amp it up more by trying anything between these two routes on the popular Mosaic Wall. This steep face offers the area's best and largest concentration of difficult routes.

Climbers of all abilities will enjoy Tres Piedras. Most lines lie in the 5.9 to 5.11 range with lots of lower fifth class climbing on lower angle slabs. The hardest climb at TP is 5.12. Climbing during the week can be a solitary experience with crowds seldom an issue.

Access is the key issue at Tres Piedras. The USDA Forest Service and a private land owner share management of the area. The former seems moderately receptive to climbing activities but the latter much less so. Visiting climbers should hold themselves to a strict code of conduct while at the area. Doing anything less will surely cancel out our current climbing privileges at this wonderful cragging area. Locals would not be amused if this jewel was lost due to climber misbehavior. Remember that climbing here as well as at all other areas in this guide is a privilege, not a right. Please read and comply with all information presented in the "Restrictions and access issues" section below.

Rack: A standard rack for most routes includes a set of wired stoppers and camming units up to 3", as well as quickdraws, runners, and a 165' rope. A 200' rope is often helpful. Many climbs have chickenheads and knobs large enough to be tied off.

Trip Planning Information

Area description: Tres Piedras offers 1- to 2-pitch traditional and sport climbs on quality granite slabs and steep faces.

Location: North-central New Mexico.

Camping: Because of delicate access issues for these crags, climbers should consider alternative camping sites away from the crags. Impact and access problems are best served if camping is not done near the area. Consult with the rangers at the Ranger Station on the west side of the town of Tres Piedras for other camping areas. Be vigilant about leaving a clean site and do not camp on private land. Water and sanitation facilities are not available. Fires are not recommended. Additional primitive camping can be found on national forest about 2 miles south on U.S. Highway 285 along Forest Road 22. Developed campsites can be found at Hopewell Lake, about 15 miles west on US 64.

Climbing season: Late April to early November is the prime time to climb Tres Piedras. Expect cooler conditions in the early spring and late fall. Regular afternoon thundershowers are almost guaranteed during the warm summer months. Snow covers the area from late November to early March, with US 64 often closed due to drifting snow.

Martha Morris edges up *Zorro* (5.10a) in Aspen Alley at Tres Piedras, New Mexico.
Photo by Stewart M. Green.

Restrictions and access issues: As with many climbing areas in New Mexico, access to Tres Piedras Rocks is a volatile, dynamic issue. At least some of the rocks are on private property with the remainder being on national forest land. Although the precise boundaries of public and private land are questionable, local consensus holds that South Rock and access from the south to all other rocks, is on private land. The Ranger Station, located 0.5 mile west of the Village of Tres Piedras en route to the rocks, provides climbers with a map detailing the public areas. All visitors should avail themselves of this information. The facility is closed on weekends. Write to Tres Piedras Ranger District, P.O. Box 728, Tres Piedras, NM 87577, for the map if anticipating a weekend visit. The private land owner, Mr. Gus Foster, has been moderately receptive to requests to climb on his land and should be consulted to have total rock access. Although it is doubtful he will appreciate an increase in requests, his phone number is posted at the climbing site. Increased visitation to this area will undoubtedly affect the future of climbing in this special area. Please conduct yourself in a responsible manner. Additional new route activity is limited and is further discouraged by a ban on bolting.

Guidebook: A classic unbound, self-published guidebook by Cayce Weber and Ed Jaramillo has been circulating since 1981. Cayce and Ed are Taos locals responsible for many of the climbs at Tres Piedras. The guide is available at Taos Mountain Outfitters and Mudd N-Flood Review.

Nearby mountain shops, guide services, and gyms: Taos. There are no climbing gyms in the area.

Services: Cozart's Hunting and Fishing Supplies in the village of Tres Piedras is a well-stocked general store and gas station. The Diner next door offers moderately priced meals. Taos, 30 miles away, offers all tourist services.

Emergency services: Contact the Ranger Station for emergencies on national forest land. If closed, the nearest public phone is at Cozart's Hunting and Fishing Supplies in the village of Tres Piedras. Taos has the nearest hospital.

Nearby climbing areas: John's Wall, Dead Cholla Wall, Heart of Stone Rock, Questa Dome.

Nearby attractions: Ojo Caliente Mineral Springs (30 miles south on US 285).

Finding the crags: The small village of Tres Piedras is located at the junction of US 285 and New Mexico Highway 64, about 25 miles south of the New Mexico-Colorado border, 30 miles west of Taos, and 80 miles north of Santa Fe. From Taos, access NM 64 just north of town and drive about 30 miles west on NM 64 to the junction of US 285. When approaching from the Santa Fe area, drive north on US 84/285 and be alert for signs near the south end of Espanola that direct you around the town to US 84/285. At the first stop light in Espanola just past Dandy's Burgers, turn left (west) across the Rio Grande.

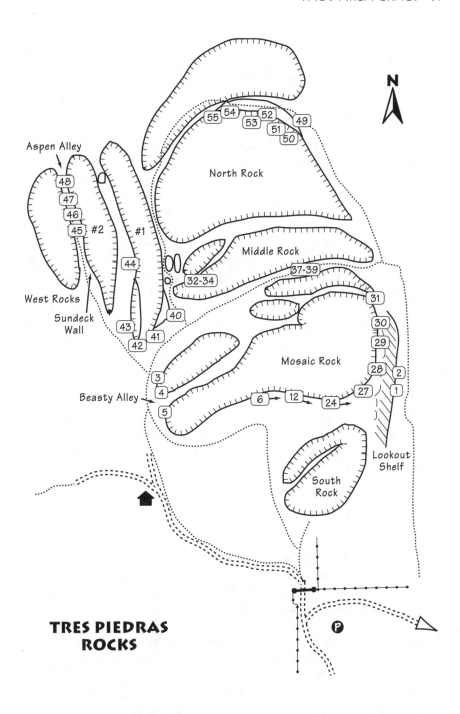

TRES PIEDRAS ROCKS

At the next light turn right following signs to Abiquiu, Tierra Amarilla, and Chama, and then bend left at the next light. Continue about 7 miles to where US 84 and US 285 divide and make a right turn on US 285. Stay on this road, passing through Ojo Caliente, all the way to the village of Tres Piedras.

From the junction of US 285 and US 64 in Tres Piedras at the blinking light, travel west on route US 64. It is about 0.5 mile to the ranger station (open M-F, 8 a.m. to 4:30 p.m.), where you can get local information and a map of the climbing area. Continue 0.2 mile west past the ranger station and look for an unmarked dirt road on the right. Turn here, go right past a graffiti-covered water tower, and continue 0.4 mile to a T junction, where you turn left and go a short distance to the parking area next to a fence and gate. The rock immediately north is South Rock, which is on private land.

The Tres Piedras crags are made up of five distinct rocks from 70' to 150' in height. From the parking area, South Rock is in view about 100 yards to the north. By walking around its left (west) end and turning north you come to the Mosaic Rock, the area's most popular rock. Continue left around the west end of the Mosaic Wall and turn northeast to reach Middle Rock. Directly north of Middle is North Rock. Access it by going around the right end (east) of Middle rock. Access West Rocks by going left (west) from Middle Rock.

SOUTH ROCK

Remember this rock is on private land. You must have permission to climb here. At least 6 routes are found on the west flank and south face. Most are thinly protected face climbs or routes requiring gear placements. Routes are not covered in this guide.

LOOKOUT SHELF

Approach Lookout Shelf from the parking area by crossing the fence to the right of the gate onto national forest land. Walk north and slightly east toward the east end of South Rock. Keep walking below South Rock then turn north to get to base of Lookout Shelf. This east-facing cliff is topped by a wide granite ledge and offers good views to the east.

1. **Unnamed** (5.10c/d) Start under a large triangular roof near south end of cliff. Difficult climbing up and right leads to a traverse to gain a finger and hand crack that jams to the top.
2. **Unnamed** (5.11c) Bolt-protected thin face climbing on positive holds leads up and left to the summit of the rounded block.

MOSAIC ROCK—WEST END

Just after passing the far west end of Mosaic Rock, Beastie Alley, a deep, foreboding chasm, is encountered. This narrow canyon divides Mosaic Rock from another rock to the north. *Pony Express* is the first route to the right of Beastie Alley and *Danger Mouse* and *Thunder Toad* are about 45' farther left. Beastie Alley has several established routes, although the rock is of lesser quality.

3. **Danger Mouse** (5.11a) Difficult face climbing and underclings past 4 bolts to a fixed anchor. Lower from here.

4. **Thunder Toad** (5.10a/b) Climb the face up through a series of horizontal cracks. TCU placements possible. Shares anchors with *Danger Mouse*.

5. **Pony Express** (5.9) Not pictured. The first climb right of Beastie Alley. 4 bolts up a fine slab with several bulges to a 2-bolt anchor. A 200' rope required for lowering or rappelling back to start. With shorter ropes, rappel north into Beastie Alley.

TRES PIEDRAS
WEST END OF
MOSAIC ROCK

MOSAIC ROCK

The greatest concentration of climbs at Tres Piedras is found on Mosaic Rock's long south-facing wall. When belaying on the ground for these routes you are on private land. The area left of *Dirty Diagonal* is called the Mosaic Wall. To descend routes not equipped with lowering anchors, gain the rock summit and descend the east end of the rock via moderately tricky downclimbing. Routes are listed left to right.

6. **Seaman Girl** (5.10b/c) Farthest left climb on Mosaic Wall just to right of a thin right-facing crack. Third class up a low-angle ramp system to get to start. Clip a suspect bolt, then climb straight up using crack for TCU placements, past the 2-bolt anchor for *Mama Jugs*. Then left and up to the right-trending crack system just below the summit. Belay at end of crack. Creative gear placements necessary on entire route. Descend to the east.

7. **Mama Jugs** (5.8) About 25' right of *Seaman Girl*. Runout, no bolts, creative gear placements necessary. 2-bolt anchor. Rappel from here or continue to top on upper portion of *Seaman Girl* for good 2-pitch climb.

8. **T.B.O.L** (5.11+) Up to a large flake then straight up. TCUs and wires helpful. 4 bolts.

9. **Techtonic** (5.11+) Start by a small 3' tree, then straight up via 4 bolts. 1st bolt is high. Sustained and classic.

10. **Techweenie** (5.11+) Start about 5' right of the small tree, then straight up via 5 bolts to a 2-bolt anchor. Lower from here. Crux is going through the bulge.

11. **Tech-no-star** (5.12) Straight up the black streak to a tree growing on the cliff. 3 bolts. Sustained and classic. Rappell from tree.

12. **Dirty Diagonal** (5.7) Climb the crack and adjacent chickenhead-studded face. 2 bolts on left have been added for anchors to toprope this climb from the ledge. If leading, continue past bolts and belay on large ledge above.

13. **Five Years After** (5.9+) Originally started on the large ledge then to the upper large grassy belay ledge via 3 bolts. Most parties now start at ground level (#14) and climb up to the lower large ledge via 1 bolt, then continue to the upper belay ledge (5.9+) or lower from the the 2-bolt anchor (5.7).

14. **Chickenheads** (5.7) Start at ground level or on the right end of the ramp/buttress to the right of *Dirty Diagonal*, then straight up following chickenheads. Creative pro.

15. **Fried Chickens** (5.8) Sparsely protected climbing in a shallow crack/corner. Merges with *Chickenheads* on upper portion.

TRES PIEDRAS
WEST END OF MOSAIC WALL

16. **Better Red than Dead** (5.10b/c) Face climb up to a slanting crack, then right and up to the first bolt. Continue straight up past the second bolt past a thin crack to a small ledge. The easier finish is to climb up and left via chicken heads to the west end of the large grassy ledge. (200' rope required or install an intermediate station.) A more difficult alternative from the small ledge is to climb the upper section of *Holthouse to Hell*. Rack of wires, TCUs, and camming units up to 2.5". Classic Tres Piedras face climbing.

17. **Holthouse to Hell** (5.10c) Another area classic. Start on low-angle crack about 15' left of *Serpentine Crack*. Rack wires, TCUs, camming units to 2.5" to supplement 5 bolts. Good belay ledge at end of green streak.

18. **Serpentine Crack** (5.8) Starts as a chimney then goes up to large belay ledge.

19.

(5.11) Start just right of *Serpentine Crack*, undercling a flake and clip a bolt. The original way went straight up slinging chickenheads and using natural pro (small TCUs), or you can merge with *Serpentine Face*.

20. **Serpentine Face** (5.11-) Start in *Serpentine Crack* and then traverse right on unprotected seam (5.9) to clip 1st bolt on face.

20a. **Direct Start** (5.11) Starts at ground level. Merges with *Serpentine Face* low.

21. **Bolts to Nowhere** (5.12b) Starts on *Direct Start*, then traverses right to steep blank face. Steep and thin up a blank face. Unfinished project. Lower from last bolt.

22. **Holthouse's Haulsack** (5.11+) A steep line following fixed pins and bolts. A small Friend is helpful at beginning.

23. **Cryin' in the Rain** (5.9) Start in a crack and turn the roof above on its left.

24. **Dirty Black Nightmare** (5.11+) Start is same as *Cryin' in the Rain,* then follow bolts right that merge with bolts on prominent black streak. An alternate start to *Black Streak*.

25. **Black Streak** (5.10) Same start as *Clean Green Dream,* then straight up past bolts in the black streak.

26. **Clean Green Dream** (5.9) Start from the top of a large block. A bolt protects overhangs. Exit to the right near the top of the crack and climb a bolted face to just below the summit.

27. **Walking Dread** (5.10+) Easier start is by traversing from right to left to the 1st bolt. Harder start is to go straight for 1st bolt over overhangs.

28. **Bienvenidos** (5.10a/b) 2 bolts. Gear placements protect the prominent crack behind a large pine tree.

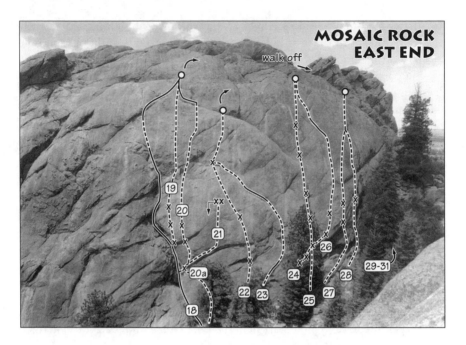

29. **Baby Cakes** (5.8) Not pictured. Climb through 2 large overhangs.

30. **Raise the Titanic** (5.12) Not pictured. Just downhill and left of the descent route. Fixed pins and bolts augment gear up an overhanging crack.

31. **Summer Dreams** (5.7) Not pictured. Right and around the corner of the descent route. Start in a crack behind a small pine tree growing on the cliff's northeast side. Above the crack, face climb on large "boiler plates" to a 2-bolt anchor 100' up. Seldom climbed; some suspect rock.

MIDDLE ROCK

Descend the west or east end of the rock. Routes listed from left to right.

32. **Cowboy Bob's Chicken Head Delight** (5.9+) Scramble up the rounded west ridge of Middle Rock to a depression under a hole through the entire rock. Start right and angle up the finger crack on the right side of a small face replete with chickenheads. Traverse right to a row of chickenheads slanting up and right below a horizontal finger crack. Use knobs for footholds to the end of the crack, then up right via large chickenheads to *Fingerfest*. Continue up left of the final large chickenhead. Easy climbing leads up right to a belay stance from gear. Keeping the rope to the left of the final large chickenhead helps protect the second. Wires, TCUs, and

slung chickenheads for protection. Committing, seldom climbed, and classic.

33. **Fingerfest** (5.10d/11a) Start same as *Cowboy Bob's* but continue up the finger crack and gain the long slanting finger crack on the right. Continue to end of the crack, then up to top. Wires, extra TCUs and small Friends. Gear required for the belay. Sustained, committing, and seldom climbed.

34. **Cowgirl Pump** (5.11-) From the west base of the rock, choose to third, fourth, or fifth class up the low angle slab to the large angling crack system below *Cowboy Bob's* and *Fingerfest*. Belay here and start climbing up and right to join *Cowboy Bob's* on the foothold chickenheads. Finish on *Cowboy Bob's*.

35. **Bats in the Belfry** (5.8) From the base, fourth class up the low-angle slabs and install a belay at the base of the hand crack. Climb the hand crack to the summit.

36. **Unknown** (5.9) Not pictured. Start about 70' right of *Bats in the Belfry*. Quality climbing up 4 bolts to a 2-bolt belay.

37. **Dragon's Lair** (5.11c) RPs protect the lower section, then 3 bolts up a green lichen streak. Gear required for the belay. Walk off to the right or east.

38. **Grandma's Cancer** (5.11d/12a) 5 bolts lead up a vertical face. Gear needed for the belay. Walk off to the right or east.

39. **Raging Chicken** (5.11d) 3 bolts up a face with chickenheads. Gear required for belay. Walk off to the right or east.

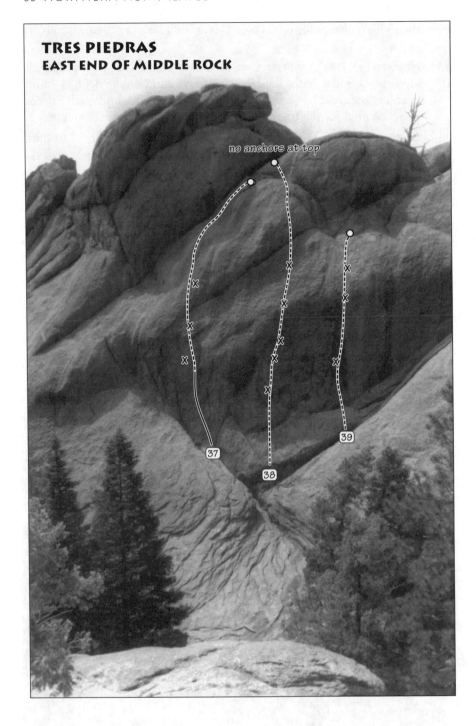

TRES PIEDRAS
EAST END OF MIDDLE ROCK

no anchors at top

37

38

39

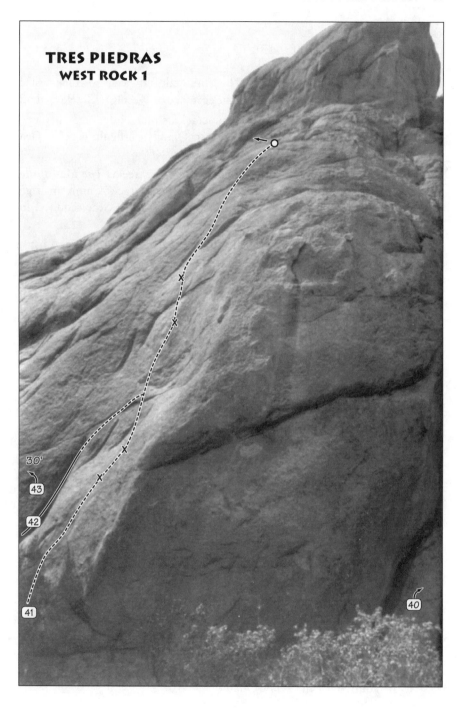

TRES PIEDRAS
WEST ROCK 1

WEST ROCK 1

Routes listed from right to left.

40. **The Alien** (5.9+) Not pictured. This climb takes the central crack system on the detached pillar making up the east face of West Rock 1. Rappel off.

41. **The Mad Bolter** (5.11) Start in a thin crack behind a large tree, then up 2 bolts to join *How Ed's Mind Was Lost*. Quality, difficult; 4 bolts. Gear required for the belay. Walk off to left or west.

42. **How Ed's Mind Was Lost** (5.9) Behind the same tree as *The Mad Bolter* and to the left of the thin crack is another larger crack. Climb this right and up to a good belay ledge (2 bolts on headwall). Gear required for anchors. Walk off to the left or west.

43. **New Rage** (5.9+) Start about 30' left of *How Ed's Mind Was Lost*. 2 bolts, with a hard start up to a belay stance left of *The Mad Bolter* and *How Ed's Mind was Lost*. Walk off to left or west.

44. **Geez Louise** (5.8RX) Not pictured. Located up the gully between 2 dead trees laying on the face. One 1/4" bolt about two-thirds of the way up protects the route. Seldom climbed. Be ready to run this one out.

SUNDECK WALL

Continue walking west from West Rock 1 to Aspen Alley, an attractive aspen-filled gully that opens up to the right or north. This area is sometimes referred to as West Rock #2. Routes, described right to left, are located near the north end of the gully. Descend either to the south (easier, longer), or downclimb a low-angle chimney to the north (more exposed but shorter).

45. **Zorro** (5.10a) Start directly below 1st bolt. TCUs protect the crack above the second bolt. Gear required for top anchors. 2 bolts. Quality.

46. **Unnamed** (5.8+) Face climb up to the right-angling finger crack. Face climb above this to a small tree. Belay off gear. Quality.

47. **Gila Monster** (5.9+/10) Start between the black water streaks. TCUs work in the horizontal crack between bolts 3 and 4. A 5.9 variation clips the 1st 2 bolts, then traverses left to a water groove. Gear up to 2" required for the belay. Quality. 4 bolts.

48. **Digital Dilemma** (5.11a) Start on a small flake behind a large ponderosa pine. Climb up for about 10', then move left, then up widely spaced bolts. Gear required for the belay. Quality.

NORTH ROCK

All routes, described left to right, are on the north side of North Rock. Recent activity here has produced a 5.12a, 5-bolt sport climb up a beautiful green and yellow lichen streak. The remaining routes are 1970s vintage, sparsely protected face and crack climbs. Most of these seldom climbed routes feature ground fall potential. Descend all routes by walking off to the right or west end.

49. **Unnamed** (5.12) 5 bolts up a green and yellow lichen streak to 2 cold shuts.

50. **King Crack** (5.9R) The first crack to the right of Number 49. Climb the crack, then face climb up to cold shut anchors. Protection is difficult and marginal.

51. **Queen Crack** (5.10X) 100'. Face climb up to a fist-size groove offering amorphous jams and marginal protection. Traverse right onto face near the top. No pro after the traverse. Gear required for belay. Both cracks can be toproped by using long extensions at the top or with a 200' rope.

52. **Unnamed** (5.9+X) Face climb up right side of black streak. Bottom section protectable with TCUs, wires, and small Friends. Top part protected by a single 1/4" bolt. Gear required for belay anchors.

53. **Unnamed** (5.9+X) Face climb on right side of a thin fin-like feature. Two 1/4" bolts on upper section. Gear required for belay anchors.

54. **Back of Jack** (5.10-X) 2 old 1/4" bolts is all you get. Ground fall potential. Gear required for belay anchors.

55. **Eyes That Lie** (5.10) Difficult slab climbing up and right past three 1/4" bolts. This is the best protected of all the slab routes on this side. Gear required for belay anchors.

RATON AREA CRAGS

SUGARITE CANYON STATE PARK

OVERVIEW

Sugarite Canyon State Park, located just south of the Colorado border and north of Raton, is remote and off-the-beaten track but well worth a visit. The park features excellent 70' basalt cliffs atop the east rim of Little Horse Mesa. Fine climbing is found on the area's many cracks and pocketed vertical faces. The cliffs were deposited as basaltic lava flows from the numerous volcanoes

The main cliff at Sugarite Canyon State Park, New Mexico. *Photo by Dennis Jackson.*

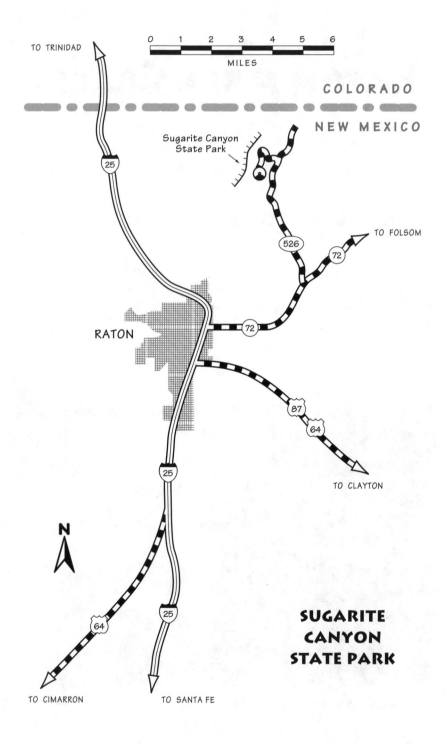

SUGARITE
CANYON
STATE PARK

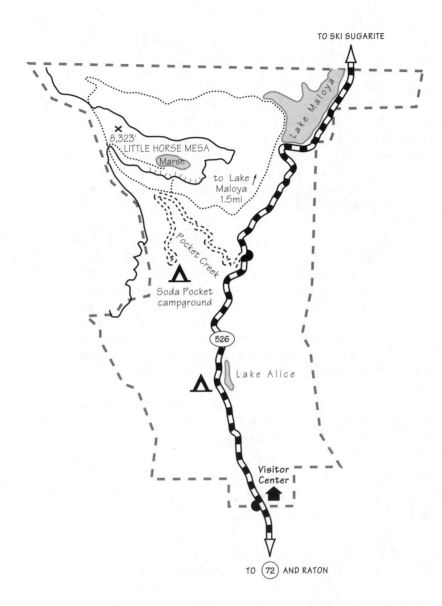

TO SKI SUGARITE

Lake Maloya

✕
8,323'
LITTLE HORSE MESA

Marsh

to Lake
Maloya
1.5mi

Pocket Creek

Soda Pocket
campground

526

Lake Alice

Visitor
Center

TO 72 AND RATON

SUGARITE CANYON
STATE PARK

that dot northeastern New Mexico. More than 100 extinct volcanoes rise above the shortgrass prairie here. The best known is 8,215' Capulin Mountain, an almost perfectly shaped cinder cone 30 miles east of Raton.

Climbing history: Sugarite escaped the attention of the larger climbing community until the early 1990s. Most of the climbing until then was done by a small contingent from northern New Mexico. Visiting Colorado climbers accounted for the intensive route development in the early 1990s. The indiscriminate use of power drills and the resulting bolt-studded routes up the cliffs resulted in the park closing all cliffs to climbing while surprised officials evaluated the situation. The park staff has since authorized rock climbing with a moratorium on bolting until a final climbing management plan is developed. All of the previously placed bolts were removed or mangled by an unknown party.

The quality of climbing here is similar to the popular Los Alamos basalt crags. A big difference is the absence of crowds, providing many opportunities for solitude. There are numerous premium steep crack routes in the 5.7 to 5.11 range with steep face climbing on positive holds and pockets between the cracks. Many of the face routes can be toproped. This generally requires extra long runners or a short rope. The installation of top anchors would be the first logical step in developing the cliffs. Pioneering new routes requiring bolts is no longer allowed, although this situation could change in the future. Stop in at the visitor center to pay entrance fees before climbing and ask for current information.

Rack: Bring long runners or extra rope to secure top-rope anchors on the mesa rim above. A standard rack of cams through fist-size will protect most cracks. Stoppers and TCUs are also useful. A 150' rope gets you up and down most routes.

Descent: Rappel.

Trip Planning Information

Area description: Sugarite State Park features 70' basalt cliffs with many crack and face routes that are led or toproped.

Location: Northeastern New Mexico. North of Raton near Colorado border.

Camping: Convenient camping is found in Sugarite State Park. Fees and limits apply. Area information, brochures, and maps are available.

Climbing season: Early spring to late fall.

Restrictions and access issues: Bolting is not allowed in the park. All issues involving climbing activities are under study by park officials. Ask at the visitor center for any climbing restrictions.

Guidebook: None.

Nearby mountain shops, guide services, and gyms: None.

Services: All facilities and services are found in Raton.

Emergency services: Contact the visitor center for any assistance required in the park. The nearest public phone is at the visitor center. Call 911 in the Raton area for emergency assistance.

Nearby climbing areas: Cimarron Canyon, about 50 miles west on New Mexico Highway 64, is a developing area worth a visit as much for its beauty as for the quality and quantity of its climbing.

Nearby attractions: Sugarite Park (visitor center, fishing, hiking, and natural beauty), Capulin Volcano National Monument, Folsom Museum, Santa Fe National Historic Trail, Maxwell National Wildlife Refuge, Raton Museum, and Cimarron Canyon State Park.

Finding the crag: Sugarite State Park is 3 miles south of the Colorado-New Mexico border. From the north end of Raton on Interstate 25, take exit 452. Look for signs to Sugarite State Park, Ski Sugarite, and Folsom. Drive about 3 miles east on NM 72 and turn north on NM 526, where signs point to Sugarite State Canyon Park. Drive less than 2 miles to the visitor center on the right. Continue 2.2 miles north on NM 526, turn left, and drive 1.2 miles to Soda Pocket Campground and the climbing area. This road is generally open from April to late November. Park in a pullout on the left before the campground.

To reach the top of the cliff, hike north on the trail marked by signs for Little Horse Mesa and Lake Maloya (4.5 miles). Turn right once atop the mesa and walk along the rim several hundred yards to a small marshy lake. Turn south and rappel down the cliffs. First-time visitors find this is the easiest route to the crags.

A shorter but somewhat more difficult route is to head east from the parking pullout toward Lake Maloya on another trail marked "Lake Maloya 1.5 miles." About 100 yards from the sign turn north (left) on a faint trail that eventually ascends a low-angle brushy break in the cliffs to reach the mesa. Turn right at the top and go to the marshy lake to set up the rappel. An unimproved trail is farther along the east Lake Maloya trail. This reaches the bottom of the cliffs after bushwhacking and scrambling. Future access solutions will likely include improving this access trail.

Bob D'Antonio at The Overlook, White Rock Crags, New Mexico.
Photo courtesy of Bob D'Antonio.

WHITE ROCK–
LOS ALAMOS AREA
CRAGS

WHITE ROCK CRAGS

OVERVIEW

These easily accessible cliffs are beautifully situated on the rim of White Rock Canyon with the Rio Grande coursing its way far below to Cochiti Lake 20 miles to the south. The most popular White Rock crags are The Overlook, Below the Old New Place, The Old New Place, The Playground, and The Y. All but The Y are clustered within a mile of each other on the east side of the village of White Rock. All offer fine views, quality climbing, and easy access. The Y is less than 5 miles north of White Rock below New Mexico Highway 502.

Although White Rock is historically a traditional area, sport climbing enthusiasts have found fertile ground on the steep blank faces between the cracks. Quality, well-protected sport routes are now found on most of the area's crags. A typical day sees climbers of both persuasions peacefully playing on the same crag.

Crack climbers can expect steep, strenuous finger to hand cracks on excellent rock with ample opportunities for gear placements. Crack routes range in difficulty from 5.7 to 5.11+ and are sure to both test and improve anyone's jamming skills. A rack of camming units, wired stoppers, and a 150' rope are sufficient for most routes. All crack routes are 1 pitch and generally require placing belay anchors at the top.

Sport climbers find strenuous, technical routes on vertical to overhanging rock. Most routes are equipped with 3/8" bolts and lowering anchors. Be alert for occasional gear placement opportunities such as small Friends or tri-cams in pockets on some routes for additional pro. A dozen quickdraws and a 150' rope complete the sport climbing rack.

Climbing history: White Rock climbing dates back to the early 1950s; the

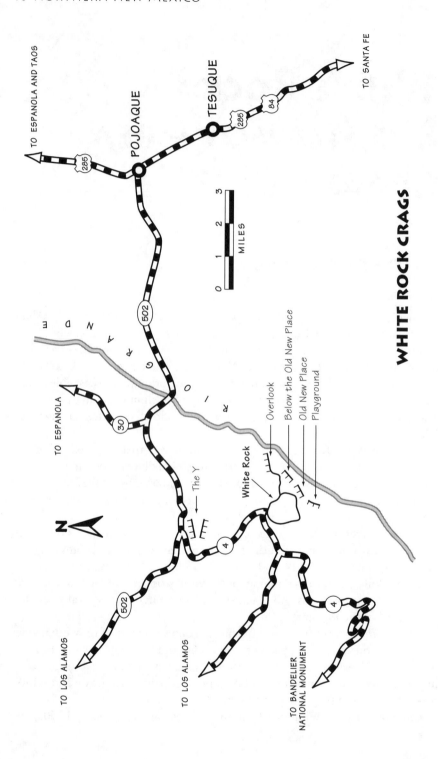

WHITE ROCK CRAGS

earliest explorations were led by members of the Los Alamos scientific community. George Bell, a member of the 1953 K2 Expedition, teamed with a strong and adventuresome group to test the area's steep unrelenting cracks beginning in 1952. The venerable Los Alamos Mountaineers, founded in 1952 by Don Monk and Kermith Ross, were active on the smaller cliffs as well as surrounding areas. The Mountaineers continue to be active and have brought some much needed leadership in resolving climbing and access issues. Layton Kor, the prolific Colorado climber, visited White Rock in 1968, solidifying the 5.9 grade and giving impetus to new exploration. Mike Roybal, a talented young New Mexico climber, honed his skills here as well. The "discovery" of The Y in 1970 by Len Margolin and Jim Porter pushed area standards into the then rarefied 5.10 and 5.11 grades. *The Nose,* New Mexico's first 5.12 and perhaps one of the first routes with this rating in the country, was established at The Y by Mike Roybal in 1974. Chances are, no matter where you climb in northern New Mexico, Mike Roybal was there first and ticked the best routes. Other pioneers include Bob Taylor, Don Liska, Mike Williams, Carl and Lou

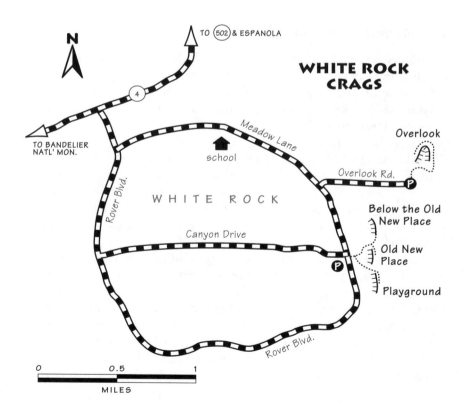

Horak, Bill Hendry, Jim Porter, Len Margolin, Larry Campbell, Norbert Ennslin, and Carl Keller.

White Rock's early test pieces were splitter cracks and dihedrals ascended in traditional style. The local practice of toproping the harder, difficult-to-protect faces gave way to rap-bolting in the summer of 1989. *Wailing Banshees* (5.11b) established on Below the Old New Place owns the distinction of being the first rap-bolted route in the White Rock area. The following eight months saw the establishment of 17 more bolted routes on Below the Old New Place plus rap-bolting at the popular Overlook area. This development was led by Tom MacFarlane, Brian Riepe, Peter Gram, Rick Smith, Mike Schillaci, Chris Vandiver, Lee Sheftel, and Bob D'Antonio. This departure from the long-established tradition of putting routes up from the bottom sent shock waves throughout the climbing community. Long-time local activists Norbert Ennslin and Rick Smith organized a series of meetings to openly discuss the bolting question and future new route opportunities. The outcome was that several crags were identified as off-limits to bolting. They were and still are The Playground, The Y, The Old New Place, and The New New Place. Bolting is allowed in all other areas. Visiting climbers, however, should leave their drills at home as new route possibilities are very limited.

Trip Planning Information

Area description: Excellent 50' to 70' basalt cliffs offer a wide selection of bolted sport routes and traditional crack climbs.

Location: Central New Mexico. Northwest of Santa Fe near Los Alamos.

Camping: No camping in the immediate area. Overnight camping is not allowed in Overlook Park nor anywhere in White Rock or at The Y. The best nearby public campground is 12 miles west of White Rock on NM 4 at Bandelier National Monument. Juniper Campground, on the rim of Frijoles Canyon, offers pleasant, wooded sites with water and restrooms. The fee area is on a first-come, first-served basis and quickly fills up in summer. Primitive off-road camping is available in many parts of Santa Fe National Forest. Check with locals for other ideas. Avoid camping on private land and nearby Pueblo Indian land.

Climbing season: Year-round. Early spring to late fall offers the best weather. The east and southeast-facing cliffs provide morning sun and afternoon shade. Summer days can be hot; early morning and late afternoon are the best times. Spring days are often windy; many of the cliffs, however, are sheltered from the wind. Climbing is possible on the White Rock crags on all but the coldest winter days. The cliffs' southern exposure combined with the black rock allows enjoyable winter climbing; mornings are best.

Restrictions and access issues: The cliffs are on Los Alamos County land.

Ian Spencer-Green on *Face Off* (5.12a) at the Overlook, White Rock Crags, New Mexico. *Photo by Stewart M. Green.*

The Y is a detached segment of the Bandelier National Monument. A climbing management plan is not developed for this area, although this could change. Be careful not to climb near the petroglyphs here. The county has not imposed any restrictions on the other crags largely due to the pro-active efforts of the local climbing community led by the Los Alamos Mountaineers Club (LAMC). Bolting is permitted at The Overlook, Below The Old New Place, The Doughnut Shop, The Underlook, The Sununu Place, The Lounge, and Pajarito. Bolting is not allowed at The Playground, The Old New Place, The New New Place, and The Y. Visiting climbers, however, should leave their drills at home as new route possibilities are limited. Stay on existing trails along the rim and en route to the crags to minimize human impact on the area. An effort is being made to limit the number of trails found on the mesa overlooking the cliffs. Please stay on the main trail. Cautions include: loose rock on the cliff tops, rattlesnakes, cacti, and primitive access trails.

Guidebook: *Sport Climbing in New Mexico* by Randal Jett and Matt Samet, 1991. Also *Rock and Ice Magazine* issues 36 and 40.

Nearby mountain shops, guide services, and gyms: Los Alamos, Santa Fe.

Services: Food, fuel, and lodging can be found in the village of White Rock. Nearby Los Alamos, the "Atomic City," offers more variety and entertainment possibilities. Santa Fe offers complete visitor services.

Emergency services: Call 911. The nearest public phone is in White Rock at the corner of NM 4 and Rover Drive. The Los Alamos Medical Center at the corner of Diamond and Trinity Drives in Los Alamos offers 24-hour emergency care.

Nearby climbing areas: Cochiti Mesa cliffs, Las Conchas.

Nearby attractions: Bandelier National Monument (34,000 acres of designated wilderness, great hiking, visitor center, and self-guided tour of the pueblo ruin Tyuonyi in Frijoles Canyon). A self-guided hike to the Tsankawi Unit of the monument is a short distance north of White Rock. Park at a designated lot on NM 4. Also: Bradbury Science Museum at the Los Alamos National Laboratory; Rio Grande and Rio Chama rafting, canoeing, and kayaking; fishing; backpacking; mountain biking; and Indian pueblos along the Rio Grande.

Finding the crags: The village of White Rock is 30 miles northwest of Santa Fe and 10 miles southeast of Los Alamos. Approach the area via U.S. Highway 285 between Santa Fe and Espanola. Turn west from US 285 onto NM 502 just north of the roadside village of Pojoaque. Signs point west toward Los Alamos and Bandelier National Monument. After 7 miles, the highway crosses the Rio Grande. Continue west past the junction with NM 30 and head uphill on a four-lane highway. The highway divides about 4 miles later, with NM 502 going to Los Alamos. Stay on NM 4 toward White Rock. Go 4.1 miles to a left turn on Rover Blvd. into the village of White Rock. Drive one block, turn left on Meadow Lane, and go about 0.8 mile. Turn left again on Overlook Road to reach The Overlook, or continue another 0.5 mile on Meadow Lane to the public access trail located on the east side of Meadow Lane between house addresses 719 and 721 to reach the other crags. Refer to specific directions for each crag for trail access.

THE OVERLOOK

The Overlook, a V-shaped cliff with east and northwest faces, sits directly below a ridge and a popular observation point that overlooks the Rio Grande in White Rock Canyon and the distant Sangre de Cristo Range. The views from the point and the cliff are spectacular and make any visit worthwhile. The 60' Overlook crag, one of New Mexico's premier basalt areas, offers excellent climbing on more than 40 routes that include both bolted sport lines and great cracks.

Climbers of all abilities will enjoy this area. Many of the sport routes are in the moderate 5.10 to 5.11+ range. The east face features many steep hand and finger cracks from 5.8 to 5.11. Popular routes include *Bosker Boozeroo, Boy What Assholes (You Guys Turned Out To Be), Paul's Boutique, No Exit, Holy Wall, Sale at Mervyn's,* and *Thorazine Dream. Overture* (5.12b/c) and *On Beyond Zebra* (5.12c/d X) are local test pieces. The *Cholla Wall* is a popular toprope problem that the bold leader can ascend using small gear placements in shallow pockets. Local consensus keeps this superb route off-limits to bolting.

Rack: Bring a rack of 12 quickdraws and a 150' rope for the sport routes. Most have lowering anchors. A rack of Friends or other cams to 3.5" along with a set of wired stoppers and a few TCUs are needed to jam any of the cracks. Tri-cams are also useful in some of the small pockets. Bring some slings to set belay or toprope anchors atop the cliff. Use extreme caution not to knock any loose rock down on climbers below.

Descent: Walk around the cliff to the south on the access trail or lower from bolt anchors.

Finding the cliff: Reach The Overlook from NM 4 in White Rock by turning left on Rover Blvd. Signs direct you to Overlook Park. Go 1 block and turn left on Meadow Lane. Go 0.8 mile through a residential area and make another left turn on Overlook Road. Pass sports playing fields and reach a dead end parking area for the Overlook viewing area. Walk north past the railings at the observation deck onto a narrow rocky ridge. At the end of the rocky ridge, locate a rough trail that drops right or southeast toward the Rio Grande. Follow the trail down and around to the south end of The Overlook crag. The trail leads north along the base of the east face (main climbing area) to the point of the ridge prow. Here it turns sharply west to reach the north-

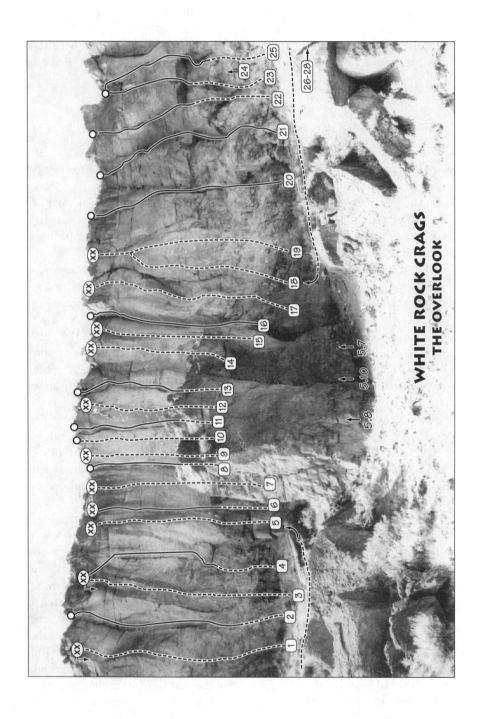

WHITE ROCK CRAGS
THE OVERLOOK

west face. Routes are listed left to right from the southern end of the main southeast-facing cliff.

1. **Bosker Boozeroo** (5.11a) 7 bolts plus anchors. First climb on the cliff. Up a steep arete.
2. **Squeeze Chimney** (5.10+) No bolts. After the short chimney, a finger and hand crack leads to a dihedral. Belay at the top.
3. **Boy, What Assholes (You Guys Turned Out To Be)** (5.10b) 5 bolts plus anchors. Excellent face and arete climbing.
4. **5.8 Crack** (5.8) No bolts. Steep and difficult to protect at the top.
5. **Paul's Boutique** (5.11b) 5 bolts plus anchors. Steep arete and face climbing.
6. **Headwall Crack Left** (5.8) No bolts. Quality jams to the top.
7. **No Exit** (5.12a) 5 bolts plus anchors. Difficult at top. Quality.
8. **Headwall Crack Right** (5.9) No bolts. Quality jams up to a difficult finish. Step right to top of *Double Vision/Ream Dream* and belay off gear or continue to the top.
9. **Double Vision/Ream Dream** (5.10d or 5.11c) 5 bolts plus anchors. 5.10d if arete is used.
10. **Cholla Wall** (5.10) No bolts. An area classic. Generally toproped. Gear placements marginal. No bolts by local consensus. Classic.
11. **Cholla Crack** (5.9) No bolts. Classic finger and hand jams to the top. 3.5" SLCD useful at top.
12. **Holy Wall** (5.10a) A fun pocket route. 5 bolts to 2-bolt chains. One of the most popular routes on the crag. Pocket and face climbing.
13. **Holy Crack** (5.9+) No bolts. Quality lead.
14. **Sale at Mervyn's** (a.k.a. **Dave's Face**) (5.10c) 5 bolts plus anchors. Excellent face and pocket climbing. An area favorite.
15. **Way Beyond Zebra** (5.11b) 5 bolts plus anchors. Excellent face and pocket climbing. An area favorite.
16. **Polly's Crack** (5.8) No bolts. Fingers and hands to the top.
17. **Thief in Time** (5.12d) 5 bolts plus anchors. Start in a right-facing crack on the right or in *Polly's Crack*. Small pockets up an overhanging face. Go right at upper arete.
18. **Narcissistic Dream** (5.11+) A former toprope problem with bolts added for leading. Thin and difficult.
19. **Face Off** (5.12a) 6 bolts plus anchors. Considered the best of its grade on the crag.

20. **M.C. Epic** (5.8) No bolts. Start in an overhanging hand and fist crack to easier climbing above. Belay at top.

21. **Captain Smarmbag** (5.10) No bolts. A difficult finger crack around a roof to easier climbing above. Belay at top.

22. **Box Overhang Left** (5.8+) No bolts. Fingers and hand jams on the left side of the large roof. Classic.

23. **Len's Roof** (5.11a) No bolts. Climb up choss rock to the right of the center crack. Strenuous hand jams lead to easier climbing above.

24. **Overture** (5.12b/c) Missing hangers. Seldom done.

25. **Box Overhang Right** (5.8) No bolts. Hand and fist jams lead to easier climbing above. Belay at top.

26. **On Beyond Zebra** (5.12b R) Not pictured. Just to the right of *Box Overhang Right*. 4 bolts plus anchors. Ground fall potential getting to 2nd bolt.

27. **5.9 Crack** (5.9) Not pictured.

28. **Thorazine Dream** (5.11d) Not pictured. Difficult moves over a small roof to a slab with 2 bolts, then past a horizontal crack (TCU placement possible). Up 3 more bolts to a 2-bolt anchor. Quality.

The following routes are located around the corner from *Thorazine Dream* on the cliff's northwest face.

29. **View With a Room** (5.11b) Scramble up to a short steep face, then up 3 bolts to a 2-bolt anchor.

30. **Overlord** (5.11a) 4 bolts up a face/arete to chains.

31. **Overlard** (5.10c) On the right side of the roof. Joins *Overlord* and shares anchors.

32. **Overripe Fresh-squeezed California Females** (5.11b) 4 bolts and 2 tied-off holes to a 2-bolt anchor. Suspect old webbing.

33. **The D'Antonio Approach** (5.12a) 4 bolts up the face left of a wide crack. Shares anchors with *Overripe Fresh Squeezed....*

34. **Huecos Rancheros** (5.10c) Located about 60' right of *The D'Antonio Approach*. The most popular route on this side. 3 bolts up large pockets to a 2-bolt anchor.

35. **Unknown** (5.11+) 3 bolts up a steep face with chimney on left and a finger crack on the right.

36. **Just Say No To Jugs** (5.11a) Large pockets up an overhanging face. 4 bolts plus anchors.

37. **Overlichen** (5.11a) Climb up to the arete then right around to a face.

38. **Chocolate Thunder** (5.11d) 4 bolts up a black arete to anchors.

39. **Hammertime** (5.12a) Start on top of a blocky shelf, then up 4 bolts on the arete to a 1-bolt lowering station.

40. **Citizen Of Time** (5.11d/.12a) 4 bolts up a black face.

41. **Crisis In Utopia** (5.11a/b) A finger crack in a left-facing corner. No bolts, gear required.

42. **Primal Scream** (5.12a) Climb up past 2 bolts, then left and up a steep face/arete to anchors.

43. **Overkill** (5.11a) Move right at 2nd bolt of *Primal Scream*, then up a black pocketed face to anchors.

The following 3 routes are right of *Overkill*.

44. **Lubme** (5.12a/b) Start up choss rock to 2 bolts, then left up more choss to a steep face. 1-bolt lowering station. Poor quality.

45. **Unknown** (?) Clip first 2 bolts of *Lubme*, then up the arete/prow. Contrived.

46. **Putterman Gully Jump** (5.9+) Go right at bolt 1 of *Lubme*, then 6' right and up 4 bolts on a black face. A contrived route.

THE OLD NEW PLACE

The Old New Place, a 60' east-facing basalt crag, is a long-time local toprope area. Most of the climbs can be and often are led. At least eight high-quality hand and finger cracks ranging from 5.8 to 5.11+ ascend the cliff. A rack of camming units up to 3" plus a good assortment of wired nuts and stoppers is sufficient to lead most routes. Toprope and belay anchor placements are plentiful on top. Long runners are often necessary. The Old New Place by local agreement is a no-bolt area. Please respect local traditions. Watch, as always, for loose rocks on the cliff top when setting anchors.

None of the routes have names following a long time area tradition that allows each visitor to ascribe a name and rating of their own. Be forewarned that the cracks are as difficult as any other in the area.

To reach the crag follow the directions provided in the Overview section of the White Rock Crags. Drive through White Rock's residential area east of NM 4 and reach the public access trail on the east side of Meadow Lane between house addresses 719 and 721. Follow the trail through the swinging gate, walk toward the rim, and turn left or north on the trail closest to the rim. Follow the trail northeast along the rim for about 150 yards to the top of a small knoll on the rim. This is the top of The Old New Place. Walk a short distance left (north) and descend the north side of a gully down through rock bands on the north flank of The Old New Place. Turn right or south to the cliff base.

Rack: A standard rack complete with wires, TCUs, and camming units is necessary for the crack routes. Doubles in most sizes is often helpful. Long extension runners for setting topropes are often necessary.

Descent: Walk back down the approach trail.

BELOW THE OLD NEW PLACE

Below the Old New Place, an excellent 65' basalt crag, is a superb sport climbing crag with 19 bolted lines. It also offers quality crack routes. Below the Old New Place is just north and, not surprisingly, below the Old New Place. Recommended routes include *Monsterpiece Theater, Flesh Eating Gnats, Ralph's Dilemma, Manic Crack, Adam Ant, Wailing Banshees, P.M.S., Fat Boy's Don't Cry, Sardonic Smile,* and *Color of My Potion.*

Rack: All the cracks are led with a rack of camming units up to 3" and wired stoppers. Cracks range in difficulty from 5.9 to 5.11. A rack of 10 quickdraws suffices for all the sport routes. Most have lowering anchors. Some crack climbs will require setting a belay atop the crag. Watch for loose rock on the cliff edge.

Finding the cliff: To reach the crag follow the directions to The Old New Place. From the north end of The Old New Place, continue switchbacking downhill a short distance, then left for about 50 yards to the base of Below

The Old New Place. Routes are listed left to right.

1. **Putterman Cracks** (5.9) Converging finger cracks to a slightly loose section. Use one, the other, or both cracks for different problems. Belay at top off gear or from a 2-bolt anchor 10' right.

2. **Scandinavian Airlines** (5.10c) The arete to the right of *Putterman Cracks*. 3 bolts to a 2 bolt anchor. Difficult clips. Quality.

3. **Inflight Movie** (5.12a) Difficult moves up the face and arete to *Scandinavian Airlines* anchors.

4. **Monsterpiece Theater** (5.12a) Long steep face with 6 bolts to a 2-bolt anchor. Quality.

5. **Little Shop of Horrors** (5.12a) Start in the crack, then left out on the face after about 25'. 3 bolts, shared anchors.

6. **Polyester Terror** (5.10a) Climb the right-slanting finger crack up to the triangular roof, then left to the top.

7. **Ralph's Leisure Suit** (5.11c or 5.12a) Steep climbing via 5 bolts to a 2-bolt anchor under the triangular roof. 5.12a if crack on the left is ignored.

8. **Ralph's Dilemma** (5.10) A thin crack and stemming problem to the apex of the triangular roof, then right and up to a 2-bolt anchor shared with *Flesh Eating Gnats*.

9. **Flesh Eating Gnats** (5.11c) Start from ground level and just to the right of *Ralph's Dilemma*. Climb straight up the arete via 5 bolts to a 2-bolt anchor. Quality.

10. **Ralph's Revenge** (5.9) Climb up to a ledge 10' off the ground, then up a finger crack. Belay at the top or from *Adam Ant* anchors. Difficult near the top. Quality.

11. **Adam Ant** (5.12a) Start on the same ledge as *Ralph's Revenge,* then up the face to the right of the crack via 4 bolts to a 2-bolt anchor. Quality.

12. **Wailing Banshees** (5.11b/c) Avoid a ground fall by traversing in from the left, then up a steep arete to shared anchors with *Adam Ant*. Quality.

13. **Manic Crack** (5.11) Quality climbing up a difficult steep finger crack.

14. **Manic Nirvana** (5.12b/c) On the face between *Manic Crack* and *Lost Nerve*. 4 bolts.

15. **Lost Nerve** (5.10c) A steep and strenuous finger crack.

16. **L Dopa** (5.9+) A finger crack curving up and right to a large ledge with a 2-bolt anchor.

17. **P.M.S.** (5.11c) 3 bolts up the steep face bracketed on the right by a steep arete. Using arete makes the climb 5.10a. Shared anchors with *L Dopa*.

WHITE ROCK CRAGS
BELOW THE OLD NEW PLACE

18. **I Dogged Your Wife and She is a Doofus** (5.11a/b) Start on a large ledge, then up 3 bolts to a 1-bolt lowering station.

19. **Instant Dogma** (5.10c/d) Start on face between 2 ledges, then up 3 bolts left of a sharp arete. No anchors.

20. **Fat Boys Don't Fly** (5.12b/c) 4 bolts up a white face, over a bulge to a 1-bolt lowering station. The climb is .12b going right after the 3rd bolt and .12c going straight up from the bolt.

21. **Unknown** (?) Up the arete left of a roof. Shares anchors with #22.

22. **Unknown** (?) 5 bolts up a less than vertical face between 2 cracks, to a 2-bolt anchor.

23. **Sardonic Smile** (5.11d) Thin pocket and face climbing up a steep white face to a 2-bolt anchor.

24. **Color of My Potion** (5.12a) An arete and face climb to *Sardonic Smile* anchors.

25. **Strong Urge to Fly** (5.12b) Start just left of the ledge shaded by a tree. 2 clips to a bulge, then 2 more to widely spaced anchors.

26. **Unnamed** (5.12b) Start from the ledge, then up a black face/arete to a 2-bolt anchor.

27. **Got a Nightstick, Got a Gun, Got Time on My Hands** (5/11c) The farthest right climb on the cliff. Start from upper shelf, then up a black arete to a 2-bolt anchor.

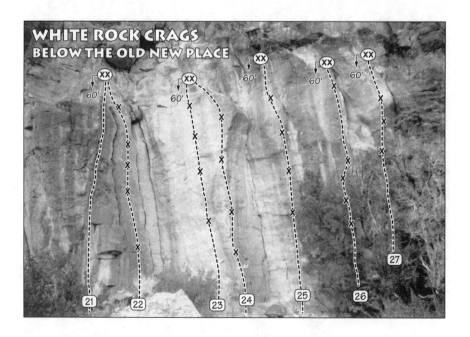

WHITE ROCK CRAGS BELOW THE OLD NEW PLACE

THE PLAYGROUND

The Playground, a 70' basalt cliff, offers some of the best and most concentrated crack climbs in the White Rock/Los Alamos area. Only The Overlook just up-canyon boasts as much diversity and challenge for crack masters. The 30 routes at The Playground range in difficulty from 5.9 to 5.12. Expect steep, strenuous climbing on solid basalt with generally good gear placements. Great views of the Rio Grande in White Rock Canyon, a short approach, the quality climbing, and a friendly local scene makes The Playground a superb alternative to the nearby busy sport crags.

No bolts are found on this traditional cliff. Climbers must place gear to protect the many finger and hand cracks. Routes can also be toproped. The most popular routes are the strenuous *Unrelenting Nines, First Strike* (a 5.12c with ground fall potential that's usually toproped), *Original Horak Route, The Flying A* up a quality 5.10+ corner, popular *Beginner's Crack*, and *The Blowhole* up a sustained, overhanging 5.10b dihedral. Many routes here are unnamed. This is a local tradition with different names applied as new climbers "discover" the area. All the routes and variations, however, are worth jamming.

Rack: Bring a rack of Friends or other cams through 3" or hand-size, along with a set of wired stoppers. A few hexes, TCUs, RPs, and tri-cams might prove useful on some lines. Set up belays on the broken ledge above the cliff to bring up your second. Toprope anchors, using gear and long slings, are also easily constructed on this ledge. Be careful not to trundle any boulders or loose rock from the ledge onto unsuspecting innocents below. Good bouldering is found along the cliff base.

Descent: Descend by rappel or walk down either end of the cliff.

Finding the cliff: To reach The Playground from NM 4 in White Rock, turn left onto Rover Blvd. Go 1 block and turn left onto Meadow Lane. Continue past the turnoff to Overlook Park about 0.5 mile and park near a public access trailhead between houses numbered 719 and 721 on the left or east side of Meadow Lane. A sign here says "Motor Vehicles Prohibited." Walk east down the cement trail through a swinging gate to the main rim trail. Turn right (south) on this trail. It follows the area between the cliff top and a fence on the right. Locate an easy downclimb in a gully on the north end of the crag about 300 yards from the gate. Finding the downclimb is important for easy access. It may be difficult to find the first time. Sometimes there is a wooden playhouse with a colorful roof behind the fence on the right. A broad flat area below the wall's base is visible just before starting down. Scramble down the rough trail between the north edge of the cliff and a detached basalt pillar. Routes are listed from right to left.

1. **The Blowhole** (5.10b) The first climb encountered after the downclimb. Thin jams led up to the "blowhole" about 20' up. Continue up and right to top.

2. **Unnamed** (5.9+) 5 paces to the left of *The Blowhole*. A thin flake leads up to a finger crack in a dihedral. Turn triangular roof on left.

3. **Battle of the Bulge** (5.11b/c) Tips and stemming past a bulge in a finger crack under the rightmost of a set of 3 roofs.

4. **Barlow's Buttress** (5.9) Edges and crack climbing lead up to middle roof (as in *Battle of the Bulge*). Go right around roof.

5. **Fingertip Layback** (5.10d/11a) Tips to a left-curving hand crack, then up a good crack to the left-most roof. Turn roof on right.

6. **Upper Left Roof** (5.9) Low angle face climbing leads to a right-facing dihedral going up to the left-most roof. Turn on right.

7. **Advanced Start** (5.10c/d) Good hand jams for 10', then hand traverse left to main crack.

8. **Beginners Hand Jam** (5.9) Perfect hand jams to thin hands to fingers.

9. **Cactus Climb** (5.10a/b) Face and crack climb to the right of 2 cracks.

10. **Unnamed** (5.10d/.11a) Finger crack to flakes to a shallow dihedral.

11. **Black Wall** (5.9) Face climb up to flakes to gain a good size ledge. Continue up and left via a thin crack.

12. **Mr. Foster's Lead** (5.9) 2 parallel cracks lead to a crack system to the right

WHITE ROCK CRAGS
EAST END OF PLAYGROUND

of a tree at the top.

13. **Vulture Roof** (5.11b/c) Face and crack climb up 10' to a large orange roof. Difficult moves over the roof lead to a crack system going up and right.

14. **Unnamed** (5.11b/c) 4 paces to the left of *Vulture Roof*. Climb straight up for 20', then right and up thin cracks.

15. **The Cheeks** (5.11a/b) Difficult climbing up to a bulbous roof, then right and up an inside dihedral.

16. **Unnamed** (5.9+/10-) Climb up to the left side of the bulbous roof, then up and right via cracks to a short left-facing corner.

17. **Unnamed** (5.11) 2 paces left of #16. Straight up to a crack system.

18. **Unnamed** (5.10a) Thin cracks lead up 25' to a triangular roof. Continue up crack system on left of roof.

19. **The Flying A** (5.10d/11-) Start in a 5' rectangle, move up and over two blocks to a left-facing dihedral. The face to the left is a 5.12a toprope problem.

20. **Texas** (5.8) Easy climbing leads up to a flake. Layback around to the right.

21. **Zander Zig Zag** (5.10d) Same start as *Texas*. Go left at bottom of flake.

22. **Original Horak Route** (5.9) The right trending crack system 6 paces left of *Texas*.

WHITE ROCK CRAGS
WEST END OF PLAYGROUND

23. **First Strike** (5.12c X) 3 paces left of *Original Horak Route*. A quality toprope problem.

24. **Unnamed** (5.10b) Climb right side of flake that has a large hole near its top. Continue up a thin right-trending crack.

25. **Unrelenting Nines** (5.11b/c) 5 paces left of #24. A thin, steep crack bottom to top.

26. **Unnamed** (5.11a) Start in a 10' black streak, then up and right via a thin crack.

27. **Unnamed** (5.11d) Start uphill of #26, then up and left.

THE Y

The Y, sitting in an abrupt canyon below the Y roadwork east of Los Alamos, is a popular basalt crag divided into two sectors—the North Wall and the South Wall. The 60' cliffs offer more than 30 toprope and lead routes. The area's superb crack climbing, easy access, and friendly scene contribute to its popularity. The Y's steep finger and hand cracks, sharp overhangs, and occasional dicey face moves on pockets and edges give first-time New Mexico visitors a sampling of what awaits them at the other fine basalt crags surrounding White Rock. The Y also serves as the Los Alamos area's usual climbing introduction for beginners. This roadside crag has a quiet, pleasant ambiance, with a trickling creek that flows year-round except during the hot summer months. Avoid drinking or splashing in the water because of its suspect upstream origins in the Los Alamos area.

The Y is near the eastern edge of the Pajarito Plateau, a large sloping mesa composed of river gravels, lava flows, and volcanic ash deposits and deeply dissected by tumbling creeks that rush eastward to the Rio Grande's canyon from snow fields on the Jemez Mountains. The Y's cliffs formed when basaltic lava erupted from vents and fissures of the ancient Jemez Volcano. The lava blanketed underlying river gravels with an 80' layer that quickly cooled into basalt, forming hexagonal columns. Later erosion from snow melt and flash floods excavated this abrupt little canyon, leaving today's steep canyon walls for climbers to pursue their vertical craft.

Climbing history: The Y was "discovered" by local climbers Len Margolin and Jim Porter in 1970. That first day they ascended three of today's classics—*Boy Scout, The Ramp,* and *Ratshit Cave.* Other lines were quickly ascended that year, including *Wisconsin,* a route up the North Wall's center that uses both sides of a Wisconsin-shaped flake. *Spiral Staircase,* the area's first 5.11, fell to Margolin in 1973. A less talented and non-thinking climber later chiseled out the initial holds and eased the grade. (This route—plus *Six Pack Crack* immediately to the left, and *Ringjam* and *Ratshit Cave* immediately to the right—are off-limits to climbing because of their proximity to petroglyphs.) The following year Mike Roybal established *The Nose,* a thin face problem rated 5.12a X. Most folks toprope this audacious lead, New Mexico's first 5.12 route.

Toproping with lots of hanging is the normal course of climbing action here, although most routes can be easily led. Weekends are often crowded with topropes occupying the more popular routes. The scene is friendly, however, with most willing to share ropes and beta information. School and rescue groups also use the area. If it is too crowded, visit one of the other fine nearby climbing areas at White Rock.

It is possible to climb here all year long, although colder winter days can limit opportunities. The best weather is in spring and fall. By alternating routes on the north and south walls, sun can be found or avoided throughout the year. Summer days can be hot.

The Y is located within Bandelier National Monument, and is subject to National Park Service climbing restrictions. No bolting or power drills are allowed by an agreement between park officials and local climbing groups. Please avoid climbing on or near the petroglyphs located at the base of the cliff. Any climbing activity can damage these important and precious parts of American prehistory. Other archeological sites are found in the immediate area. Please do not disturb or pot-hunt. It's against the law. Also watch for rattlesnakes in the warmer months and use caution on the cliff top when setting topropes. Lots of loose rock is found on the rim and is easily trundled onto others below.

All of the routes at The Y are worth climbing. The North Wall (south-facing) offers the greatest concentration of climbs. The more popular routes include *Triple Overhang* (5.10), *Open Book* (5.8), *Wisconsin* (5.10-), *The Nose* (5.12a), *Beastie Crack* (5.10b), *The Three Mother Cracks* (5.10c, 5.10a, and 5.11b), and *The Porter Route* (5.7). The shady South Wall has fewer climbs but more opportunities for moderate routes. *Cavemantle* (5.10a), *Twin Cracks* (5.7), and *Little Roof* (5.7) are the most popular.

Both walls are easy to access to set toprope anchors. Easy scrambling just upstream from *Little Roof* reaches the top of the South Wall. Extra long runners are useful to tie off trees and boulders for anchors above both walls. Exercise caution on the cliff tops to safeguard yourself and others below. There are no bolts at The Y. This is a traditional area. Lead on gear or toprope only please. Placing gear for protection is necessary.

Rack: Bring a rack that includes sets of wires, TCUs, and Friends. An occasional large cam might be required.

Descent: Descend from the north cliff top by following a trail west, then left and down into the canyon. Resist the temptation to turn left to early too avoid getting cliffed out.

Finding the crag: The Y is located on a detached unit of Bandelier National Monument that protects the Anazazi ruin of Tsankawi. The crag lies south of NM 502, 7 miles east of Los Alamos and 25 miles northwest of Santa Fe. Most climbers will approach from the north (Espanola) or south (Santa Fe) on US 285. Turn west onto NM 502 just north of the roadside village of Pojoaque. Follow signs toward Los Alamos and Bandelier National Monument. After about 7 miles the road crosses the Rio Grande and an exit to Espanola. Proceed up a long hill on a divided highway until the road divides with NM 502 going to Los Alamos and NM 4 to White Rock. Drive toward White Rock on NM 4 for about 0.7 mile until it is possible to pull off in a large parking area on the right. Use this area to turn around and head back east toward Santa Fe on NM 502. This is necessary because it is impossible to cross over the divided highway when approaching from the east. Go 0.9 mile back and park as soon as possible alongside a fence when the guard rail on the right ends. The cliffs are less than 100' away through the fence to the south. Walk south to the top of the crag's North Wall. A trail goes west (turn right on the cliff top) and drops down into the canyon. Go left or downstream about 50' to access the first routes.

To reach The Y from Los Alamos drive east on NM 502 to its junction with NM 4. Continue east and park about 0.9 mile after the exit to Santa Fe.

NORTH WALL

1. **Six Pack Crack** (5.11b/c) Thin crack and face climbing through the roof. Closed to climbing.

2. **Spiral Staircase** (5.11b) A crack just to the right of *Six Pack Crack*. Closed to climbing.

3. **Ringjam** (5.10d/11a) Up to the right side of the roof, then slightly left and up. Closed to climbing.

4. **Ratshit Cave** (5.10b/c) Left around the roof. Closed to climbing.

5. **Batshit Roof** (5.10+) Go either left or right at the roof system.

6. **Triple Overhang** (5.10) The hard start can be avoided by entering from the right to make a 5.8 climb.

7. **Open Book** (5.8+) One of the most popular climbs at the Y. Thin jams at the start defeat many attempts.

8. **Broadway** (5.8) Start to the right of *Inside Dihedral* and traverse left at the ledge.

8a. **Hard Start** (to *Broadway*) (5.11+) An arete problem. No protection; best to toprope.

THE Y
NORTH WALL

8b. **Less Hard Start** (to *Broadway*) (5.9) The thin vertical crack to the right of the arete.

8c. **Inside Dihedral** (5.8) Join *Broadway* after moving right, then back left or join *The Notch*.

9. **The Notch** (5.10c/d). Difficult moves straight up from the right side of the ledge.

10. **El Queso Grande** (5.12d/13a) Difficult moves to the left of the roof close to the ground to the left of *Wisconsin*.

11. **Wisconsin** (5.10-) An area classic. Difficult to protect, generally toproped.

12. **The Nose** (5.12a) Difficult to protect, missing hangers on face above the roof, usually toproped. The direct start is harder.

13. **Beastie Crack** (5.9+) A thin crack up to a small roof with ground fall potential. Protect the lower part with TCUs, but best not to fall. Go left or right after the roof.

14. **Herb's Roof** (5.9) Up and over the roof to the face above. Excellent route.

15. **Original Open Book** (5.8) Go right under the roof.

16a. **Left Mother** (5.10c/d) The first of the *Three Mothers*. Excellent steep jamming.

16b. **Middle Mother** (5.10a/b) The easiest of the *Mothers*. Fun.

THE Y
EAST END OF THE NORTH WALL

16c. Right Mother (5.11b/c) The hardest *Mother*. Thin jams. Good practice.

17. IDBI Wall (5.11b/c X) Best to toprope.

18. The Ramp (5.9) Go straight up through the overhang for a harder finish.

19. Porter Route (5.7) Easy jams on the right side of the roof.

20. Monster (5.10) Seldom led. Good jams to the top.

21. Hessing Route (5.7) Easy to toprope, easy to lead. An area favorite.

22. Lizard Man (5.8 X) Best to toprope.

SOUTH WALL

23. Cavemantle (a.k.a. **Heel Hook** and **Apeshit**) (5.10a/b) Heel hook the roof, then jam the crack above. Hard to protect first moves; easy to install anchors at top for toprope. The climb just to the left is a 5.12+ toprope problem.

24. Black Mantel (5.10 X) Good toprope problem.

25. Twin Cracks (5.7+) Wires and small gear protect 2 finger cracks. A popular toprope problem.

26. Little Roof (5.7) Hard for its grade below roof.

Ian Spencer-Green pulls the roof on *The Prow* (5.11b/c), Cochiti Mesa's mega classic line, New Mexico. *Photo by Stewart M. Green.*

JEMEZ MOUNTAINS AREA

COCHITI MESA CRAGS

OVERVIEW

A pleasant mountain setting, stunning views, easy approaches, and a multitude of excellent bolted sport routes make the Cochiti Mesa Crags one of New Mexico's most popular sport climbing venues. The most popular crags are Eagle Canyon,Cochiti Mesa, Cacti Cliff, and Disease Wall. Several other crags are also under development in the area. Ask locals for the latest information on these. A smattering of fine cracks are also found here on the four main crags. The best concentration of crack routes are found on The Dihedrals at Cochiti Mesa.

Pocket climbing on steep vertical faces and aretes is characteristic of the area. Routes from 5.9 to 5.13 ascend cliffs up to 80' high on good quality rhyolite or welded tuff rock. These cliffs are made of the more densely welded parts of the Bandelier Tuff formation which were deposited during the caldera-forming eruptions of the Jemez Volcano. The volcano, about the same size as Mount St. Helens before its 1980 eruption, spewed out roughly 100 times more material than St. Helens. This volcanic activity is relatively recent in geologic time, occurring some one million years ago. The beautiful Jemez Caldera is all that remains of this once massive stratovolcano.

Climbing history: Development of the crags started in 1987 in response to the closure of the popular Cochiti Canyon climbing area along the Rio Grande by the Tribal Council of Cochiti Pueblo. Locals had long enjoyed the vast amount of solid basalt cliffs found there, and with its closure were forced to look elsewhere. The softer rhyolite rock found in what was to be called the "Cochiti Mesa" area had been visited in the 1970s when many of the cracks in The Dihedrals were first climbed, including the classic *Apprentice* by Mark Hesse, Peter Prandoni, and Mike Roybal. Ken Sims and others were active in the area through the 1980s. *Bookworm,* a sustained and quality crack, was completed by Ken Sims in 1989. The route is unrepeated as of 1996.

The steep, unprotected faces that came to be known as Cochiti Mesa were ignored until rap-bolting and other sport climbing techniques were introduced to the area. Early pioneers included Todd Skinner, John Duran, Ed Romback, Tom Wezwick, Lee Sheftel, Doug Couleur, Adam Read, Jean DeLataillade, Doug Pandorf, and Tom Kalakay. *Touch Monkey* ushered in the 5.13 grade to the area in 1989.

The bolts at all the Cochiti Mesa Crags come in a variety of sizes and types. Some are obviously better than others. Many of the original bolts have been replaced for safer climbing, although visitors should always use caution when trusting single bolts and in route selection. Welded tuff is a very soft rock with a thin, hard surface coating that actually makes climbing feasible. Effective bolts need to be the largest and longest available sizes and placed in well-drilled holes. Unwelded cold shuts are used as lowering anchors for many climbs. Use these for lowering only. On many routes it is possible to back up these anchors. This is especially important for toproping.

Rack: A rack of ten quickdraws, sometimes augmented by wired stoppers and TCUs is sufficient for most routes. A rack should include camming units up to 3.5". Place these units as deep as possible and take the time to put in lots of gear for extra protection in this soft rock area. Most crack routes require gear for the belay and a rappel or walk-off descent.

The real Cochiti Mesa is identified on USGS maps as farther west from the climbing area. Don't let this confuse you when using these maps. The early developers of the area didn't pinpoint the present crag's location and the name given to the cliff is unlikely to change.

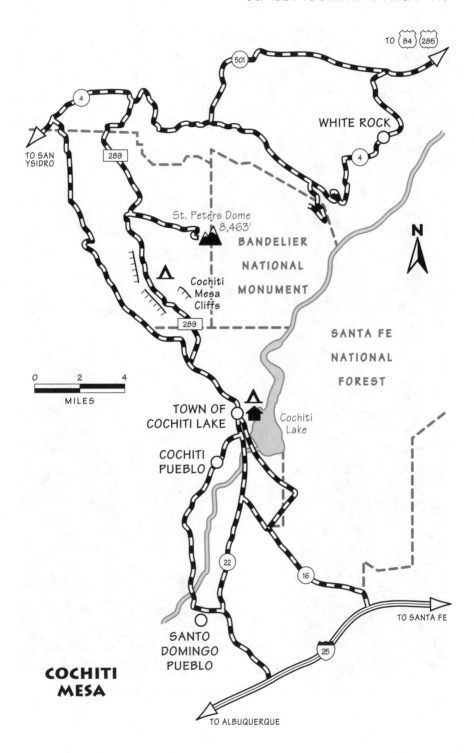

TO 84 285

501

WHITE ROCK

4

4

TO SAN
YSIDRO

289

St. Peters Dome
8,463'

BANDELIER

NATIONAL

MONUMENT

Cochiti
Mesa
Cliffs

289

SANTA FE

NATIONAL

FOREST

0   2   4
MILES

TOWN OF
COCHITI LAKE

Cochiti
Lake

COCHITI
PUEBLO

22

16

TO SANTA FE

SANTO
DOMINGO
PUEBLO

25

COCHITI
MESA

TO ALBUQUERQUE

N

Jay Coglin on *Banana Rama* (5.10c), Eagle Canyon, Cochiti Mesa, New Mexico. *Photo by Dennis Jackson.*

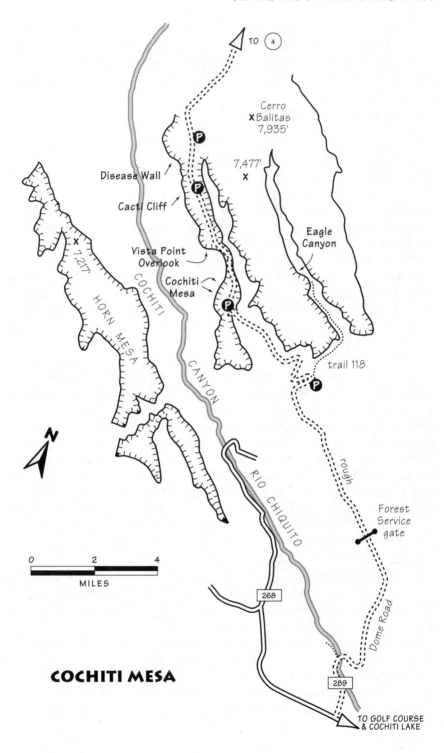

TO (4)

Cerro
X Balitas
7,935'

7,477'
X

Disease Wall

Cacti Cliff

Eagle
Canyon

X 7,217'

HORN MESA

COCHITI

Vista Point
Overlook

Cochiti
Mesa

CANYON

trail 118

N

rough

RIO CHIQUITO

Forest
Service
gate

0   2   4
MILES

268

Dome Road

289

COCHITI MESA

TO GOLF COURSE
& COCHITI LAKE

Chipping and other hold enhancement techniques were used at many of the crags on Cochiti Mesa. This guide attempts to omit any route where such activity has obviously occurred. Erosion problems at Eagle Canyon and Cochiti Mesa are a current issue. Please tread lightly in all areas and use existing trails.

Trip Planning Information

Area description: Cochiti Mesa crags offer excellent sport climbing routes from 5.8 to 5.13c on 30' to 80' welded tuff cliffs.

Location: North-central New Mexico in the Jemez Mountains.

Camping: Undeveloped campsites can be found near the climbing areas on Forest Road 289. Water and facilities are not available. Avoid camping on Cochiti Pueblo land south of the Santa Fe National Forest boundary. Developed sites in Bandelier National Monument are about 20 miles east and at nearby Cochiti Dam.

Climbing season: The Cochiti Mesa Crags are at 7,000'. Climbing is best from spring to late fall. Climbing is possible on warmer winter days, though the road may be impassable. The south-facing cliffs provide warm afternoons and cool mornings. Eagle Canyon's north-facing cliffs are a good choice on hot summer days.

Restrictions and access issues: All crags lie within Santa Fe National Forest. Eagle Canyon is included in the Dome Wilderness Area, which prohibits motors of any kind. No other restrictions on climbing are presently in place. Limited parking can be problematic on busy days at Cochiti Mesa and Eagle Canyon. Heavy use of the popular North Cliffs at Cochiti Mesa has seriously impacted the area. Please leave as little evidence of your visit as possible. In 1996, the Forest Service is scheduled to release new management plans concerning climbing on all forest land. Climbers are encouraged to stay abreast of current regulations in this changing situation. FR 289 is closed by gates near the northern entrance off New Mexico Highway 4 and at the forest boundary on the southern end during and after wet conditions. When open, the road is always rough but generally passable by high-clearance vehicles. Check on road conditions with the Jemez Ranger District, (505) 829-3535.

Guidebook: Crags in the Cochiti Mesa area are covered in *Sport Climbing in New Mexico* by Randal Jett and Matt Samet, 1991. A guide to Cochiti Mesa appeared in *Climbing Magazine* issue 133. Cacti Cliff is covered in *Rock and Ice* issue 40 and *Climbing Magazine* issue 124.

Nearby mountain shops, guide services, and gyms: The nearest mountain shops are in Los Alamos, Santa Fe, or Albuquerque.

Services: An Alsups convenience store with snacks, groceries, liquor, and auto fuel is in the town of Cochiti Lake. A laundromat and Ritz's Pizza and Deli is next door. All services are available in Santa Fe and Albuquerque.

Jean DeLataillade on *Handsome Parish Ladies* (5.13a), at Eagle Canyon, Cochiti Mesa, New Mexico. *Photo by Matt Gray.*

Emergency services: The nearest phone is located at the convenience store in Cochiti Lake. Call 911 for emergency assistance. Nearest hospital is in Santa Fe.

Nearby climbing areas: White Rock crags, Sandia Mountain, Palomas Peak, and Las Conchas.

Nearby attractions: Tent Rocks, Cochiti Pueblo, Santo Domingo Pueblo, San Felipe Pueblo, Bandelier National Monument, Jemez State Monument, Jemez Pueblo, Rio Grande, Cochiti Lake, Spence Hot Springs, and good dining and commercial bath houses in Jemez Springs. Santa Fe includes St. Francis Cathedral, San Miguel Mission, Santa Fe Opera, Santa Fe Plaza, El Rancho de las Golondrinas (preserved Spanish colonial village 15 miles south of Santa Fe), Northern New Mexico cuisine, shopping, and museums. Albuquerque attractions include Coronado State Monument, Petroglyphs National Monument, and Sandia Crest and Peak Tram.

Finding the crags: All of the crags are reached from the Albuquerque and Santa Fe areas from Interstate 25 or from the north (Los Alamos/White Rock area) via NM 4 and FR 289. Cochiti Mesa crags all lie within Santa Fe National Forest 20 miles west of Los Alamos and 60 miles north of Albuquerque.

From the south take I-25 north toward Santa Fe and turn north at Exit 259 onto NM 22 to Santo Domingo Pueblo. Continue about 13 miles to the town of Cochiti Lake. From the north, take I-25 south toward Albuquerque and turn right at Exit 264 onto NM 16 to Cochiti Pueblo. After about 6 miles, turn right at signs to Spillway and "Welcome to Town of Cochiti Lake." (Alternately, continue on NM 16 to NM 22 and turn right to the town of Cochiti Lake.) Drive through Cochiti Lake a short distance to the golf course, then continue 0.9 mile past the golf course to a right on a dirt road, FR 289. Look for a brown wooden building on the left just past the turn off. This poorly marked road is sometimes signed "Dome Road to State Road 4." Depending on weather conditions, the road can be rough to impassable, although cars with high clearance usually have no problem.

The parking area for Eagle Canyon is about 3.4 miles from this turn and 1 mile before the Cochiti Mesa parking area. It is 7.1 miles from the town of Cochiti Lake to the Cochiti Mesa parking area. Cacti Cliff is a short distance north of Cochiti Mesa parking. Continue a short distance to the Vista Point Overlook; not signed, but obvious. A Forest Service gate here is usually locked until mid-April depending on road conditions. Continue 0.5 mile from here to a small parking area on the left or south side of the road by a relatively tall pine tree. Disease Wall parking is 0.3 mile farther north from the Cacti Cliff parking area. Park here as best you can on either side of the road. Additional parking, camping, and alternate access to Disease Wall is a short distance farther north. Refer to each crag's description for trail directions from the parking areas.

EAGLE CANYON

Eagle Canyon, a smaller version of nearby Cochiti Mesa, offers 28 routes equipped with 3/8" bolts and lowering anchors. The routes, up to 80' long, ascend huecos and pockets up vertical welded tuff faces. Many consider the rock quality here superior to the more popular Cochiti Mesa cliffs. Climbs range in difficulty from 5.9 to 5.13, with many in the 5.10 and 5.11 range. Only limited crack climbing opportunities exist. Most of the lines were established by John Duran, Ed Rombach, and Tom Wezwick in the early 1990s.

Eagle Canyon is Cochiti Mesa's premier summer crag. When all the other area crags are baking under the noon sun, Eagle Canyon's cliffs are cool and shady. The north-facing wall offers welcome relief from the heat-absorbing black basalt at White Rock and the sun-drenched walls farther up the mesa. Expect summer daytime high temperatures in the 70s and 80s with cool nights. Autumn also offers great climbing weather at Eagle Canyon. Winters, however, can be cold and snowy in the shadows. Sunnier south-facing walls on the other crags are better choices on cold days.

Rack: A rack of quickdraws and a 165' rope is sufficient for most routes.

Descent: Most routes are equipped with lowering anchors. It is possible to scramble down the right or west end on the cliff.

Finding the cliff: Follow above directions to FR 289 accessed 0.9 mile northwest of the Cochiti Golf Course. Drive approximately 3.4 miles on this rough dirt road (high clearance required) to the parking area. FR 289 can also be accessed from the north via NM 4 about 9 miles west of Los Alamos. The parking area is about 9 miles south this way, although on a generally better road. From the parking area, which is the trailhead for the Dome Wilderness, walk northwest or left of Trail 118 to an abandoned flat road overgrown with chamisa plants. This is the original Trail 118 that was rerouted because of erosion problems. After about 0.3 mile, turn left up the canyon just before a washed-out area of the trail. An easy-to-follow trail leads up through an impressive stand of ponderosa pine to the northeast-facing cliff. The routes are on the left or south side of the canyon. Look for the climber access trail to the base of the routes after about a 3-minute hike up the main canyon. Most of the erosion problems in the climbing area are associated with these short trails, so use extra care to minimize your impact.

Routes described left (down canyon) to right (up canyon) when viewed from the bottom of the cliff.

1. **Kona** (5.12a) The farthest left climb on the cliff. Scramble to end of ledge system about mid-height on cliff. Small pockets up 5 bolts to anchors.

2. **Pepto-Dismal** (5.11c /d) Excellent pocket climbing up a slightly laid back face. 6 bolts and anchors.

3. **Maalox Moment** (5.11a) An area favorite. Small pockets past a large depression. 7 bolts and anchors.

4. **Wannabee** (5.11c/d) Small pockets and thin face climbing over a small roof. 4 bolts and anchors.

5. **Killer Bee** (5.9+) The easiest climb in Eagle Canyon. 7 bolts and anchors.

6. **Indecent Insertion** (5.12b) Start to left of chimney and climb a prow up to an arete. Shares anchors with *Killer Bee*. 8 bolts.

7. **New Wave** (5.11c) Start to right of chimney in a scoop, then through several bulges and a steep face. 6 bolts and anchors.

8. **Old Wave** (5.9) The best of the 2 crack climbs on the cliff. Perfect hands to the *Tutti Frutti* anchors on the right. Hand-size camming units protect the crack. Use anchors for *Tutti Frutti*.

9. **Tutti Frutti** (5.11a) Clip a low bolt and boulder to an hourglass-shaped scoop. 5 bolts and anchors.

10. **Jug Abuse** (5.12a) Start about 35' right of *Tutti Frutti* to the right of a chimney and left of a large flake. 8 bolts, shares last bolt and anchors with *Turkey Baster*.

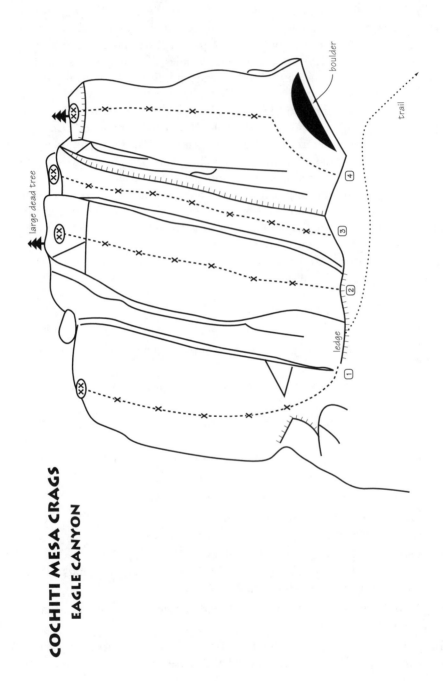

COCHITI MESA CRAGS
EAGLE CANYON

boulder

trail

large dead tree

ledge

1 2 3 4

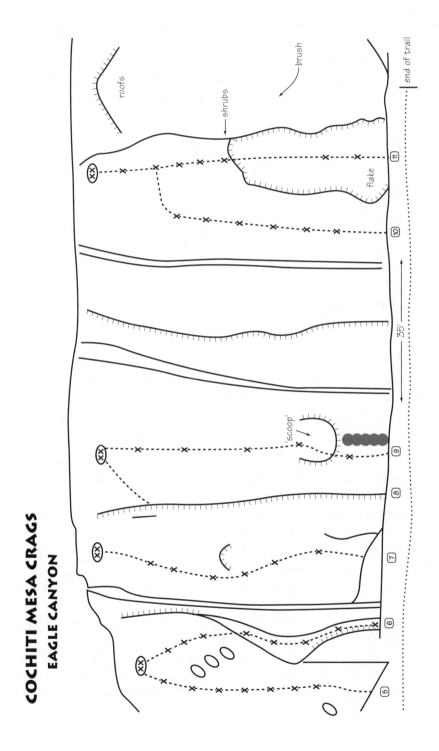

COCHITI MESA CRAGS
EAGLE CANYON

11. **Turkey Baster** (5.10c) Start in middle of large flake, climb past a bush to a 2-bolt anchor. 7 bolts.

12. **Manhattan** (5.10c) If climbing at previous route area, descend to the access trail going up from the canyon bottom and take the right fork. Scramble up to a sloping ledge and climb a long pitch up 8 bolts to a 2-bolt anchor. A 165' rope required to lower from here. An area favorite.

13. **Unnamed** (5.11b) Quality climbing up 13 bolts to a 2-bolt anchor.

14. **Unnamed** (5.11c) 12 bolts plus anchors. Start at bottom of cliff, then up to a roof and left to anchors for #13.

15. **The Blade** (5.12a/b) Start on low-angle face to left of a tree with a dead tree attached to it. 5 bolts and anchors.

16. **Unnamed** (5.11a) Start on left wall of amphitheater. Steep and thin climbing up to right of arete. 5 bolts and anchors.

17. **Handsome Parish Lady** (5.13a) Start high near upper right side of amphitheater. 6 bolts and anchors. 3 bolts protect an upper variation, also 5.13a.

18. **E Pluribis Cruxi Unum Puripus** (5.11b) 5 bolts and anchors. One of the crag's newest routes. Excellent.

19. **Racist Fantasy** (5.12a) The black streak protected with 8 bolts plus anchors. Very popular.

20. **Accrojovia** (5.12b) 8 bolts plus anchors. Recommended.

21. **Omdulation Fever** (5.12c) 7 bolts plus anchors. Recommended.

22. **Are You Lichen It** (5.11c) Six bolts plus anchors. Recommended.

23. **Earth Monster** (5.11d) Sustained thin face climbing over a bulge then up to a 2-bolt anchor. 7 bolts. Difficult clips. Very popular.

24. **Psycho Thriller** (5.11c/d) Difficult between 1st and 3rd bolt. Sustained, but easier above. 7 bolts plus anchors. An area favorite.

25. **Banana Rama** (5.10c) First bolt is suspect; #1 Friend in crack adds security. Serpentine around the arete to a 2-bolt anchor shared with *Psycho Thriller*. 9 bolts. An area favorite.

26. **The Wrong Mr. Wong** (5.8) No topo. Located about 40' right (west) of *Banana Rama*. A moderately aesthetic hand crack offering mediocre climbing. Belay off gear placements.

27. **Ego Maniac** (5.11c) No topo. Located about 30' right of *The Wrong Mr. Wong*. 6 bolts up a steep face. Gear required for the belay.

28. **Mr. Wong's Zipper** (5.10b) No topo. Located about 30' to the right of *Ego Maniac*. A splitter finger crack up to a seam. No bolts on this route. Gear required for the belay. Grade needs confirmation on this seldom climbed route.

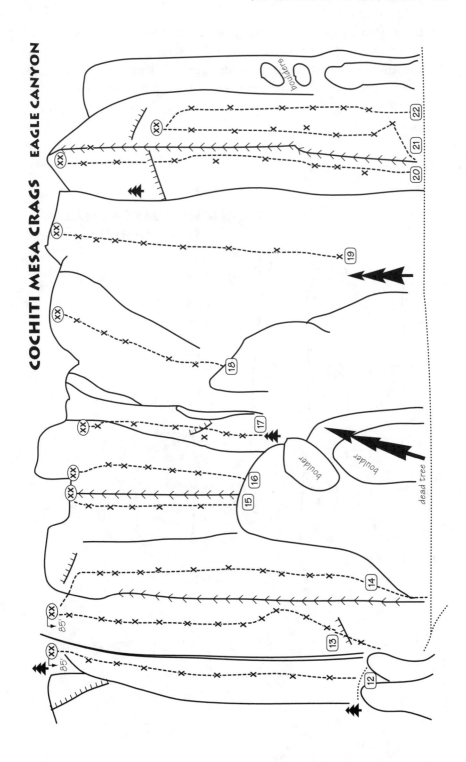

29. Bunga Bunga (5.12a) Starts low on west end of the rock. A quality route up 10 bolts that angle right and up to 2 cold shuts.

30. Didgemaster (5.13c) The area's hardest climb. Done by Jean DeLataillade in the fall of 1991. A short radically overhanging face up to 2 cold shuts. Unrepeated as of fall 1995.

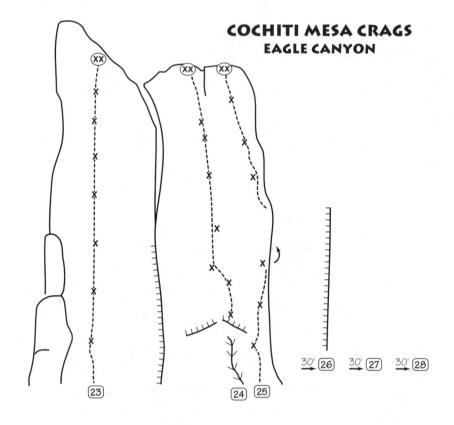

COCHITI MESA CRAGS
EAGLE CANYON

COCHITI MESA CRAGS
EAGLE CANYON

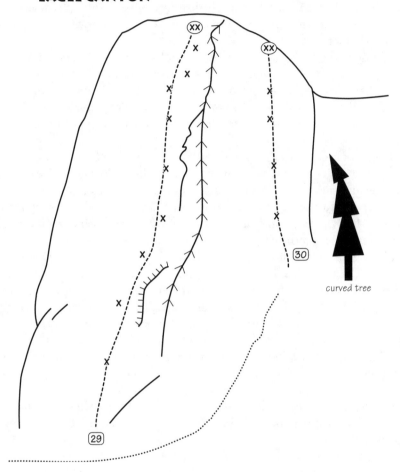

curved tree

COCHITI MESA

Cochiti Mesa is the largest, most developed, and most popular of the Cochiti Mesa crags. More than 50 established routes range in difficulty from 5.8 to 5.13. Pocket climbing and thin face climbing on steep vertical faces up to 80' high is characteristic of the area.

Although the sport routes are the principle attraction at Cochiti Mesa, an excellent assortment of finger and hand cracks are found in The Dihedrals, about 250 yards north or left of the main cliff band. Climbing possibilities were sought here in the late 1970s when many of the classic lines were ascended. Routes range from 5.8 to 5.11+. Most of the routes require doubles in all sizes of gear.

Rack: A rack of quickdraws and 150' rope is sufficient for most sport routes. TCUs and larger SLCDs are sometimes necessary. A longer rope can be advantageous on the longer South Cliff routes and The Dihedrals.

Descent: Most sport routes are equipped with unwelded cold shut anchors for lowering. Descent from traditional routes without fixed anchors is by rappel from small trees on the cliff.

Finding the cliff: Follow directions in the Cochiti Mesa Crags Overview to FR 289 accessed 0.9 mile northwest of the Cochiti Golf Course. Drive 4.4 miles on this rough dirt road (high clearance recommended) to the parking area on both sides of the road. The parking area is just past a canyon that has been filled with dirt to allow crossing and just before a sharp right-hand turn. FR 289 can also be accessed from the north via NM 4 about 9 miles west of Los Alamos. The parking area is 8 miles south from the highway on a generally good dirt road. The trail to the cliffs starts on the west side of the road and goes gently uphill to the northwest. A short walk ends atop the cliffs. Locate an easy one-move downclimb by a large dead tree where the cliff band narrows. This downclimb divides the South and North cliffs. After the downclimb, turn left or south to access routes 1 through 34 or turn right or north to reach routes 35 through 62 and The Dihedrals area. Routes 1 through 34 are described left to right. Routes 35 through 62 are described right to left when viewed from the base of the cliffs.

SOUTH CLIFF

Routes described left to right when viewed from the base of the cliff.

1. **Leslie's Little Fingers** (5.12b) 4 bolts, no anchor. Visible to the left from the top of the downclimb. Short, steep, and seldom climbed.
2. **Mononucleosis** (5.12c) 6 bolts and anchors. Mono-doigt and thin face climbing.
3. **Unknown** (5.10b/c) 5 bolts plus anchor. A recent addition. The thin arete left of *Crackerjack*.

4. **Just Say No To Crack** (5.10a/b) 5 bolts and anchors. Face climb up a low-angle face. An area favorite.

5. **Crackerjack** (5.9+) Quality hand crack climbing up to tree anchors back from cliff top.

6. **Dinabolic** (5.12a) 6 bolts and anchors. Steep face climbing.

7. **The Prow** (5.11b/c) 4 bolts and anchors. Climb up a low-angle arete to a juggy overhanging prow above. One of the area's top classics.

8. **Double Jeopardy** (5.12b/c) Variation. 2 bolts plus anchors.

9. **End of the French Revolution** (5.11b) 3 bolts and anchors with gear placements possible at roof. Runout 5.8 face climbing leads to a small roof split by a fist crack.

10. **Another Lichen Nightmare** (5.11a) 5 bolts and anchors. Small pockets up a low-angle face lead to a left-angling ramp.

11. **Dreamscape** (5.12a) No bolts, gear required. An attractive left-leaning finger and tips crack on a northwest-facing wall. Trees for anchors. An area classic.

12. **Shadowdancer** (5.12c or 5.12d) Start up *Dreamscape*, then right to overhanging dark face. The higher traverse onto the face is .12d. Excellent technical route.

13. **Terminal Ferocity** (5.11d) Start in *Dreamscape* crack up to first bolt of *Shadowdancer*, then right to a sloping ledge. 3 more bolts lead to a 2-bolt anchor.

14. **Velocity Unto Ferocity** (5.12a/b)10 bolts and anchors. Start in a right-facing corner at the base of the cliff right of *Dreamscape* and pass a small roof then up steep face climbing.

15. **Crack A Smile** (5.10b/c) Start in a left-facing corner capped by a triangular roof. The off-size crack above roof ends at a small ledge.

Routes 16-20 are accessed via rappel from the cliff-top via anchors for *Confusion Say*. Anchors are about 45' south of the top of *Dreamscape* area.

16. **Desert Storm** (5.11c) 4 bolts plus anchors. Clip first 2 bolts of *Desert Shield*, then work up left to 2 more bolts.

17. **Desert Shield** (5.11a) 4 bolts and anchors. Go right at second bolt of *Desert Storm*.

18. **Confusion Say** (5.11a) 4 bolts and anchors.

19. **Unknown** (5.7) Crack.

20. **Unknown** (5.8+) Crack.

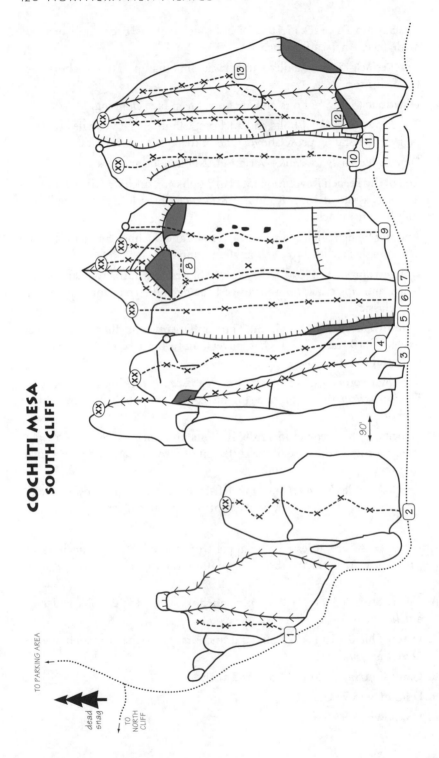

COCHITI MESA
SOUTH CLIFF

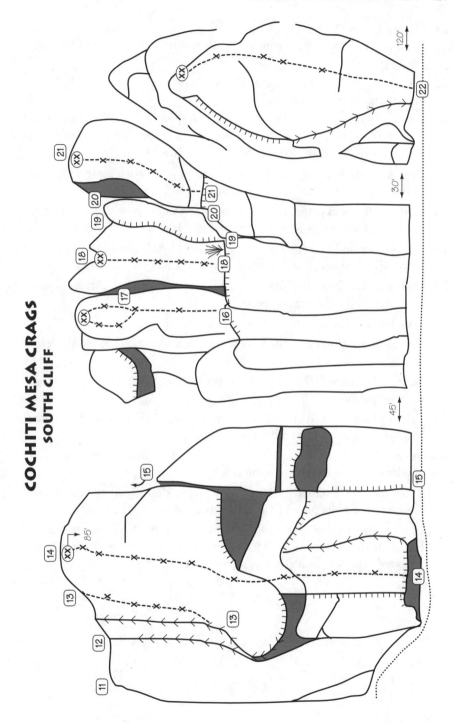

COCHITI MESA CRAGS
SOUTH CLIFF

21. **Lumpy Gravy** (5.10d/11a) 4 bolts and anchors on a steep featured face. Walk down gully to left (from cliff top) to start route. The extra anchors are a mystery.

22. **Acid Rain** (5.10c) 4 bolts and anchors. A low-angle slab with 4 bolts. Go left at top of slab to anchors.

23. **Cardinal Sin** (5.13a) 8 bolts and anchors. Rappel from cliff top to chained belay station. This is 45' up from the cliff base. Face climb to a steep arete with a triangular roof. Cochiti Mesa's newest 5.13. Quality.

24. **Rocket In My Pocket** (5.11d/.12a) 6 bolts plus anchors. Start on face left of low angle arete. Go left at 4th bolt.

25. **Finger in the Socket** (5.11b/c) 6 bolts, shares anchors with *Rocket In My Pocket.* Start same as *Rocket,* then right at 4th bolt.

26. **Kids in Toyland** (5.12c) 5 bolts and anchors. Start just to left of off-size crack. Climb steep arete, then face climb to anchors.

27. **Olympian Crack** (5.13a) Toprope. Use trees for anchors on cliff top. Routes to the left and right are chipped.

28. **Sanadine Dream** (5.11b) 8 bolts. 2-bolt anchor.

29. **Crystal Suppository** (5.11d) 5 bolts and anchors. Face climb to the left of an arete.

30. **Strange Attractor** (5.11c) 6 bolts, lower from last bolt. Difficult climbing up a steep arete.

31. **Fainting Imam** (5.12b/c) No bolts, gear required. A thin crack/edge layback to a 2-bolt anchor. Originally rated 5.13a.

32. **Immaculate Deception** (5.12c/d) 6 bolts and anchors. Face and pocket climbing by a thin right-slanting crack.

33. **Tolerated and Excused** (5.10c) A low-angle slab 5' left of *Immaculate Deception.* 2 bolts plus TCUs in the horizontal crack near top.

34. **Illusion Dissolution** (5.11c) 8 bolts plus anchors. A long aesthetic face line with small pockets at start. Start about 50' right of *Tolerated and Excused.* The last climb on this section of the cliff.

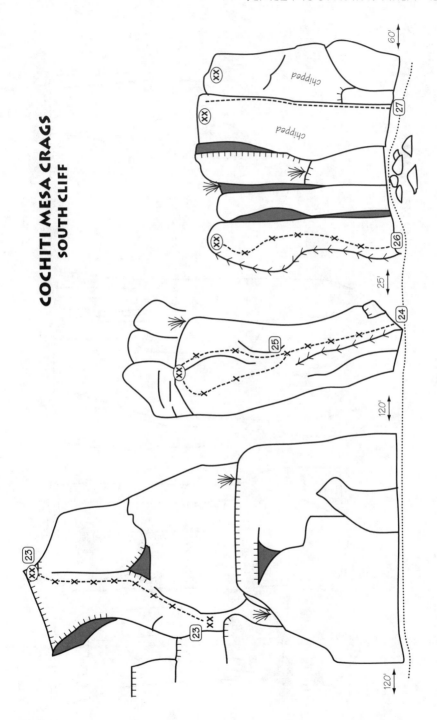

COCHITI MESA CRAGS
SOUTH CLIFF

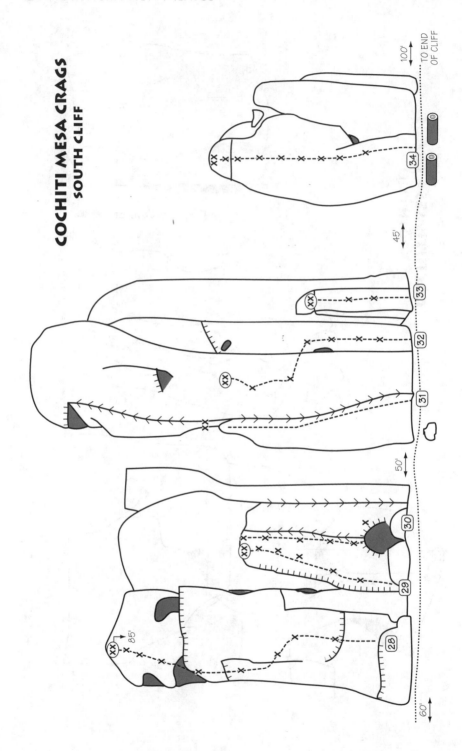

COCHITI MESA CRAGS
SOUTH CLIFF

NORTH CLIFF

The following routes on the North Cliff, are located to the right, north, after the one-move downclimb. Described right to left looking at the cliff.

35. **Napoleon Blown-Apart** (5.11b) 2 bolts and anchors.

36. **Grunge up the Munge** (5.9+) A seldom climbed off-width crack left of *Napoleon Blown Apart.*

37. **Proctologist's Fantasy** (5.12b) 2 bolts and anchors. Camming units protect the lower section. Difficult at the bulge.

38. **Praise the Lunge** (5.11b/c) 4 bolts and a fixed pin plus anchors. Up a blunt arete. An area favorite.

39. **Unknown** (5.11a/b) Crack. No bolts. The thin parallel cracks between 2 off-size cracks.

40. **Gunning for The Buddha** (5.12a) 5 bolts and anchors. Small pockets to a small ledge/crack, then more small pockets to anchors. Good route.

41. **Lainbo** (5.12b) 6 bolts and anchors. Start on top of boulders. Climb a short arete then left to a steep face.

42. **Holy Wars** (5.11a) 3 bolts and shared anchors. Finish on *Back to Montana.*

42a. **Montana Deviate** (5.9+) A 2-bolt variation to *Holy Wars* or climb a wide crack to a left-slanting crack, then past 2 bolts to anchors for *Back to Montana.*

43. **Back to Montana** (5.11c/d) 4 bolts and anchors. Small pockets lead to big pockets and a ledge, then up right.

44. **Mr. Toad's Wild Ride** (5.10c/d) 1 bolt plus gear placements. Jam and layback a hollow left-facing flake with a bolt at its top. A steep finger crack leads to anchors.

45. **Touch Monkey** (5.13a) 6 bolts and shared anchors. Small pockets up a steep southwest-facing wall. An area classic.

46. **Digital Pleasures** (5.12b) 4 bolts and anchors. Follow steep arete just left of *Touch Monkey,* then up right in a thin crack.

47. **Empty and Meaningless** (5.12b) 6 bolts and anchors. Steep face and pocket climbing. Start just left of a left-facing dihedral.

48. **Unknown** Chipped route.

49. **Monkey Lust** (5.9+/10a) 4 bolts and anchors. Start by gaining the top of a large boulder via an easy chimney next to the cliff. One of the area's best moderates.

50. **Unknown** (5.9) 4 bolts and anchors. On the west face of the large boulder in front of the cliff. A quality moderate route.

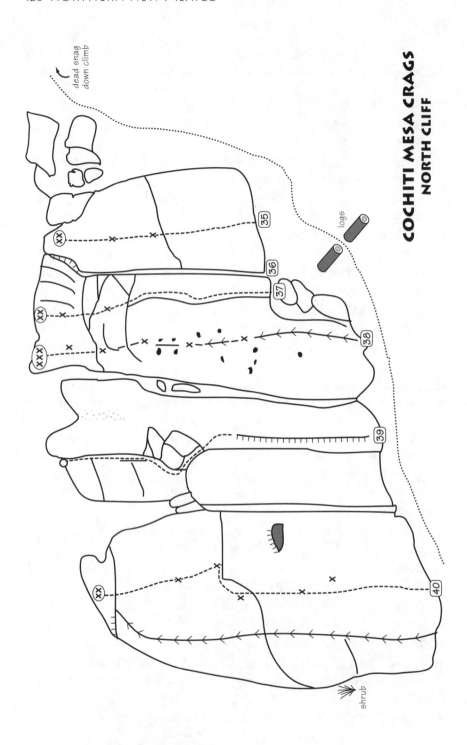

COCHITI MESA CRAGS
NORTH CLIFF

dead snag
down climb

logs

shrub

35
36
37
38
39
40

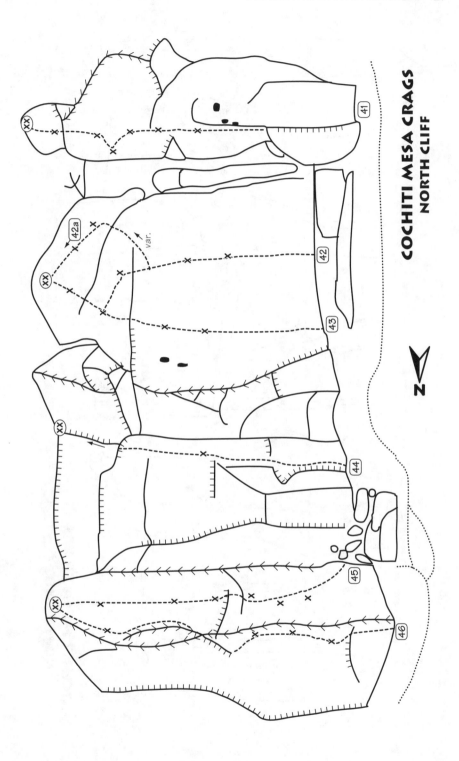

COCHITI MESA CRAGS
NORTH CLIFF

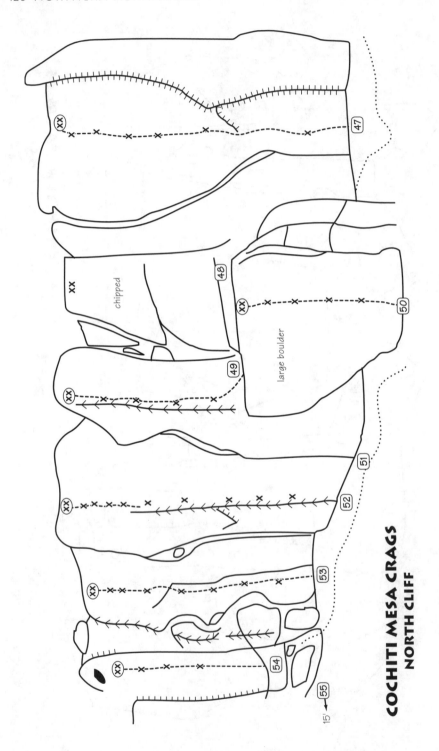

chipped

large boulder

COCHITI MESA CRAGS
NORTH CLIFF

COCHITI MESA CRAGS
NORTH CLIFF

51. Cochiti Classic (5.10) No bolts. Start in an attractive hand crack. Climb up through a wide loose section to a left-leaning vertical fist crack. Camming units to 4".

52. La Espina (5.12a) 9 bolts and anchors. Face and arete climbing. Quality route.

53. Thief in Time (5.12a) 7 bolts and anchors. One of the area's newest lines. Recommendable.

54. To Catch A Thief (5.11b/c) 3 bolts and anchors. A moderately angled face to small pockets. Good new route.

55. Unknown (5.8 or 5.10a) Located about 15' left of *To Catch A Thief* on a short rock behind trees. 25' of moderate face climbing. Using left edge makes climb 5.8.

56. Pickpocket (5.11b) 5 bolts and anchors. On a separate cliff down and left from the main cliff. Quality.

57. Open Mouth Syndrome (5.11b) 7 bolts and anchors. To the left of *Pickpocket*. Excellent.

58. Project On the left side of the cliff.

Routes 59-60 are located on the cliff band up and left of the main area. Access this area by hiking uphill and slightly left from *Open Mouth Syndrome* on a good trail for about 250' to a dark face left of a dihedral.

59. The Boya From La Jolla Who Stepped On A Cholla (5.11a) Start left of a dihedral. Ascend a dark brown face. 6 bolts and anchors. A popular recommended route.

60. New Age Nightmare (5.11c) Start in a loose slanting off-width crack up a ramp to a 7-bolt face and anchors. Recommended.

The following 2 routes (no topos) are worth climbing and best approached from the cliff top. From the top of the downclimb that divides the cliff, walk right or north along the cliff top, then right and up to the next level. A faint trail eventually reaches anchors for *The Boya From La Jolla*... about 200 yards from the top of the downclimb. Past here are 2 dead snags sticking out over the rim. Locating these from below before you start will help. The top of *Shunning Theocracy* is 25' past (north) of the first snag, and the top of *Path of the Doughnut Man* is about 65' north of the second one. Rappel to base of both routes.

61. Shunning Theocracy (5.11d) 6 drilled pins. No anchors. Soft rock.

62. Path of the Doughnut Man (5.12a/b) Rap down a 60' face with 6 bolts and a 1-bolt belay anchor on a ledge with a cactus on it. Preclip the 1st bolt above the belay on the way down. A large Friend can back up the belay. Recommended. No anchors.

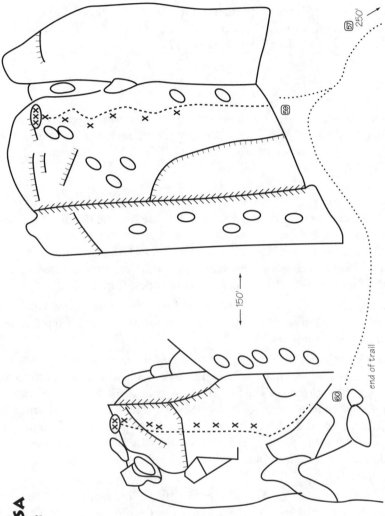

COCHITI MESA
UPPER CLIFF

VISTA POINT

Several established routes lie below the Vista Point overlook. Some of these routes are worth searching out. The approach is by rappel or by a loose and somewhat dangerous downclimb. At least one serious accident has occurred here. Be cautious, careful, and thoughtful. Ask locals about *Coming of Age* (a 5.6 bolted face), *Adolescent Fantasy* (5.10), *Stridex* (5.11d), *Wasted Youth* (5.11c), and *Fortuitous Circumstance* (5.12a).

THE DIHEDRALS

In addition to several quality sport routes, this area offers the best crack climbing in the Cochiti Mesa area. Approach via a faint trail heading left or north below the main cliff band from the *Touch Monkey* area. Routes described right to left.

63. **Inchworm** (5.11a) On the left side of an alcove on the right side of the crag. Scramble up the slope a short distance to a hand and off-size crack leading to a ledge with a small oak tree. Belay on this ledge or continue up the attractive thin-finger crack (crux). Extra TCUs are helpful here. Belay at a good stance from some funky anchors. Descend from here or climb the corner above (.10b/c) and rappel (2 ropes) from a tree.

64. **Art Gecko** (5.12a) Climb first part of *Inchworm* to the ledge with a small oak tree. Climb past 6 bolts up a face with small pockets. Rappel (2 ropes) from trees at top of cliff.

65. **Bookworm** (5.11d) The longest (2 pitches) and most sustained crack climb at Cochiti Mesa. **Pitch 1:** Face and crack climb past 2 fixed pins to a fist crack through a roof. The first 20' is the crux. A 5.8/5.9 hand crack above the roof ends at the ledge below the difficult *Inchworm* fingertip crack. **Pitch 2:** Climb the thin finger crack of *Inchworm,* then the thin corner (5.10b/c) above to the top. **Rack:** Small TCUs and wires protect this seldom climbed section. **Descent:** Via a 2-rope rappel from a tree. Unrepeated as of 1996.

66. **The Apprentice** (5.11b/c) About 15' left of *Bookworm.* Start in a steep chimney capped by a narrow chockstone. Continue up the hand and finger crack above. Classic. **Rack:** Take at least a double rack of Friends and TCUs and runners for the rappel. **Descent:** Descend via a 2-rope rappel from trees at top of cliff.

67. **Autobahn** (5.8+) Start 12' left of *The Apprentice.* Moderate crack climbing up a dark corner to a triangular roof, then left up a finger crack. **Rack:** Carry a hand and fist rack plus runners for the rappel. **Descent:** Via a 2-rope rappel from trees.

68. **Eternal Spring** (5.10) About 75' left of *Autobahn*. Climb a short moderate section up to a spacious ledge with several small oak trees. Belay from here or continue up an awkward left-facing corner that becomes a perfect hand crack. Belay on a good ledge from your own gear. **Rack:** Carry at least a double set of Friends to 3.5". **Descent:** Scramble left to rap anchors on a tree. 145', 2-rope rappel. Excellent, reminiscent of Canyonlands cracks.

69. **Indiscipline** (5.11a) Left of *Eternal Spring* past a prominent arete. Start in a corner. Climb onto a wavy face to an arete. Runout on 5.11 climbing near top. Gear placements protect bottom section. **Descent:** 145' rappel from trees (same as *Eternal Spring*).

70. **Discipline** (5.11d R) About 50' left of *Eternal Spring*. Start up a finger crack to a roof. Climb the arete to the right past 4 bolts to a tree with slings. **Descent:** 120', 2-rope rappel.

71. **Wyoming Saw** (5.10b/c) 7' left of *Discipline*. Climb a hand crack past a shrub to a chimney capped by a small roof. Difficult climbing above roof in a thin crack to trees for an anchor. **Descent:** 2-rope rappel from here.

72. **Cactus War** (5.10a/b) Same start as *Wyoming Saw*. Climb chimney to the small roof and traverse left into a crack system with shrubs and cactus. The initial moves of the traverse are difficult to protect; be extra careful not to fall here. Recommendable. **Descent:** Rappel from *Wyoming Saw*.

73. **Marlboro Country** (5.11a) Left of *Wyoming Saw*, left of the obvious arete. Thin crack climbing using RPs and TCUs. **Descent:** Rappel from *Wyoming Saw*.

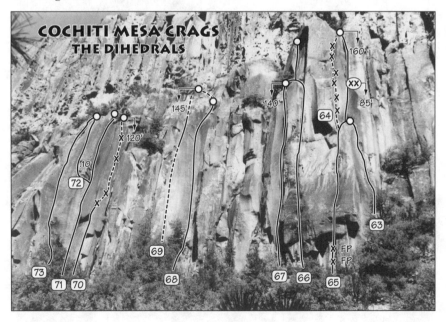

CACTI CLIFF

Cacti Cliff, with an excellent selection of sport routes plus a few cracks, offers a good alternative to the more popular and often crowded Cochiti Mesa. The southwest-facing crag yields quality sport routes and cracks up vertical 50' to 75' welded rhyolite tuff walls. The rock, considered equal or better than Cochiti Mesa, features small huecos and pockets. The pale salmon-colored rock was deposited from violent ash eruptions of the nearby Jemez Volcano.

Difficult, strenuous, and well-protected sport routes ascend this beautifully situated cliff. Cacti Cliff is noted for its excellent arete routes. Almost 25 routes grace the crag, including thirteen 5.12s and two 5.13s. Some sculpted and manufactured holds, however, detract from the fine climbing. Four superb crack routes, including the difficult *Crank Addiction* (5.12b/c), are also found here.

Rack: A rack for Cacti Cliff should include lots of quickdraws, TCUs, and camming devices to 4". Tape may be useful to avoid tweaking finger tendons on mono-doigt pockets.

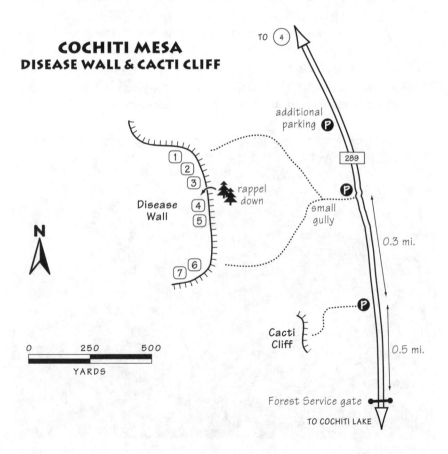

COCHITI MESA
DISEASE WALL & CACTI CLIFF

Descent: It is possible to lower from 2-bolt anchors on all routes except *Gravity's Angel* and the crack routes. For these, either rappel from nearby trees or walk to the top of the right or south end of the cliff and scramble down.

Finding the cliff: Follow directions in the Cochiti Mesa Crags Overview to FR 289 accessed 0.9 mile northwest of the Cochiti Golf Course. Drive about 4.4 miles on this rough dirt road (high clearance recommended) to the parking area for Cochiti Mesa. FR 289 can also be accessed from the north via NM 4 about 9 miles west of Los Alamos. Continue past the parking area a short distance to Vista Point (not signed, but obvious) and a Forest Service gate. Drive 0.5 mile north of the gate to a parking area on the left (west) side of the road by a relatively large pine tree. Cacti Cliff is about 150 yards below the parking area. From the parking area, walk down and slightly right to a faint trail that traverses left across the upper cliff's rim. Look for a steep narrow gully on the right going down close to the cliff's edge. This is direct but fairly steep. Alternately, descend the broader slope a little farther ahead and turn right when the cliff comes into view on your right. The approach is short, less than 5 minutes, and only nominally difficult to locate the first time.

Routes are described right to left from the cliff base.

1. **Cross-eyed and Painless** (5.12a) The first arete on the right end of the cliff. Technical moves. 5 bolts and anchors.

2. **Reach Or Bleach** (5.12b) To the left of *Cross-eyed and Painless* on the same face. TCUs protect the horizontal crack. Reachy and hard at the bottom, easier above. 4 bolts, shares anchors with *Cross-eyed*.

3. **Technobiscuit** (5.12b) Steep slab climbing with 5 bolts and anchors. Good rest opportunities.

4. **Hump Me Dump Me** (5.12c) A classic arete climb with exciting moves. 5 bolts, 2-bolt anchor.

5. **Premature Infatuation** (5.11c) Start in the smaller, short crack system left of a long off-size crack. Gear placements possible up to a steep face on the right with 4 bolts and anchors.

6. **Pendejo Park** (5.10b) Start at ground level and boulder up to a short curving hand crack. Face climb past 2 bolts near top. Gear placements necessary. Lower from welded cold shuts.

7. **Unknown** Chipped route.

8. **Cheese Grater** (5.10c).Climb up to large ledge to start. Fingers and hand-size crack. Install belay at top.

9. **Slums of Bora Bora** (5.12c) Start from same ledge as *Cheese Grater*. Hard cranks up a face with 5 bolts to anchors.

COCHITI MESA
CACTI CLIFF

COCHITI MESA
CACTI CLIFF

10. **Balance of Terror** (5.12a) Start on *Slums of Bora Bora,* then left up the right side of a long, steep arete. 6 bolts, shares anchors with *Slums of Bora Bora.* Classic arete route.

11. **Direct Terror** (5.12c/d) Up the arete from the left end of ledge. *Action Indirect,* a 5.13a variation, leaves *Balance of Terror* at the roof, then joins *Crank Addiction.*

12. **Crank Addiction** (5.12b/c) Start on *Izimbra,* then right to a thin crack. Many TCUs and wire required. Seldom attempted; awaiting first ground-up ascent with no pre-placed gear.

13. **Izimbra** (5.13a/b) Start just to right of a left-slanting thin crack, then up increasingly difficult face climbing to the left of *Crank Addiction.* 8 bolts, anchors, plus gear for the bottom section. Long and sustained. Classic.

14. **Anazazi Momma** (5.10b) Fingers, hands, and fists up a right-facing dihedral. Lowering anchors at top are an option. Friends to 4". A classic multidiscipline crack route.

15. **Funktuation** (5.13b) 8 bolts and anchors. Yet another classic arete. Technical, long, and sustained.

16. **The Sample** (5.12d) Start in a shallow corner, then up a thin finger crack protected by 2 bolts.

17. **Vibrator Dependent** (5.12a) A classic short arete. 4 bolts and lowering anchors.

The following routes are 40' to the left of *Vibrator Dependent.*

18. **Clandestine Desire** (5.11d) Interesting moves up a wavy face to a steep arete (crux). 6 bolts plus lowering station.

19. **Full Cortex Meltdown** (5.12) Start in a finger crack, to a steep face to join with *Clandestine Desire.* Small gear protects the bottom.

20. **Flameout** (5.11a) A strenuous finger crack in a corner. Extra TCUs and wires are useful. 1 bolt and lowering anchors added after first ascent. A classic climb diminished by unnecessary chipped face holds; you can do it without them.

21. **Gravity's Angel** (5.12b/c) Start about 50' left of *Flameout.* Long reaches up a steep face, then over a 3' roof. TCUs helpful after roof. 6 bolts, no anchor.

DISEASE WALL

The Disease Wall, the farthest north crag in the Cochiti Mesa area, offers a small but excellent selection of hard sport routes on its steep southwest-facing cliff. Five quality routes grace the wall's steep huecoed face. The cliff is popular with locals because of its classic hueco and arete routes. Easy access from the nearby road and stunning views of the Rio Grande valley make this small cliff a worthwhile destination. The crag, composed of welded tuff, lies about 300 yards up-canyon or northwest from Cacti Cliff. The easiest approach is from FR 289. All the routes were put up by Jean DeLataillade and Adam Read, along with several other partners. All are bolted sport lines up to 60' high.

Rack: Bring a rack of ten quickdraws and long slings for tying off cliff-top trees for rappel and belay anchors. A selection of thin crack pro is needed for one of the routes. The quality rock here invites future development.

Finding the crag: Follow directions in the Cochiti Mesa Crags Overview to FR 289 accessed 0.9 mile northwest of the Cochiti Golf Course. Drive about 5 miles on this rough dirt road (high clearance recommended) to the Forest Service gate and Vista Point. FR 289 can also be accessed from the north via NM 4 about 9 miles west of Los Alamos. About 0.8 mile north of the Forest Service gate, park as best you can on the left side of the road. Additional parking (and camping) is found 0.2 mile farther on the left. From the obscure small parking area, walk southwest down and slightly right from the left (west) side of the road about 100 yards to a small drainage that drops down to the left or southeast. Follow this gully down (starts small, gets wider and deeper) for about 0.3 mile to the cliff top. This is near the *Endorphin* route. Traverse right across the cliff top about 100 yards to reach the top of *Chicken Pox*. Rappel to the base using trees for anchors to reach all routes. *Endorphin* and *Opiate of the Masses* are about 100 yards right (southeast) of *Bulimia*. Access these by rappel or via a faint brushy trail at the base of the cliff heading southeast.

Routes described left to right when viewed from the base of the cliff.

1. **Common Cold** (5.9) The cliff's only moderate line. Climb a long huecoed face and arete to a 2-cold shut belay. 8 bolts.
2. **Small Pox** (5.12c/d) A hard classic. 5 bolts up a featured face to an overhanging black streak. Belay from a tree.
3. **Chicken Pox** (5.12) Same 5-bolt start as *Small Pox* with a hand traverse right onto a bulging face with 2 bolts. 7 bolts, no lowering anchor.
4. **Anorexia** (5.11a) Climb the off-width crack up to the 1st bolt. Layback the crack and face climb up huecos, bolt-protected, to the top. 5 bolts, no anchors.

5. **Bulimia** (5.11c) Climb an attractive thin corner past 1 bolt to the cliff top. Bring a selection of thin crack pro. Use a tree for belay anchor.

6. **Endorphin** (5.12a) This quality line starts 100 yards right of *Bulimia*. Climb a blunt arete with 7 bolts to a 1-bolt lowering station.

7. **Opiate of the Masses** (5.11c) Start 30' right of *Endorphin* behind a pine tree. Tree climb a large limb to clip the 1st bolt, 5 more bolts lead to an overhanging dihedral. 1-bolt lowering station.

LAS CONCHAS

Overview

Cool summer temperatures, easily accessible rock, great climbing, and wonderful mountain scenery all make Las Conchas a popular climbing area. The area's cliffs, scattered above a pastoral, grassy valley at 8,400', are composed of rhyolite, a volcanic rock spewed millions of years ago during violent eruptions of the Jemez Caldera. The routes here, mostly bolted sport climbs, range from 30' to 60' in height and 5.8 to 5.13c in difficulty. Nine different crags spread out for a mile north of New Mexico Highway 4 along the East Fork of the Jemez River. This is an active climbing area, with new route development continuing. Most of the routes were established by numerous local climbers including Bob D'Antonio, Cam Burns, Mike Schillaci, Chris Vandiver, Mike Baker, and Mike McGill in the early 1990s. Juan Lopez is a more recent activist.

Most of the cliffs are accessed from the parking area for the East Fork Trailhead on the north side of NM 4. The trail heads northwest into the canyon, following the lovely East Fork of the Jemez River. Immediately east of the parking area is Cattle Call Wall, a long cliff with six moderate routes and some suspect toprope anchors. This is a popular instructional and toprope crag. Routes on the left end of the wall can be led (gear placement required), as can a bolted climb near the right end. Roadside Attraction Rock is located just east of Cattle Call Wall. The other crags are encountered by walking northwest or downstream from the parking area and include Gateway Rock, Chilly Willy Wall, Love Shack Area, Gallery Wall, Dream Tower, The Sponge, and The Leaning Tower.

The Mean Leaner, a 5.13a/b problem on The Leaning Tower, saw its first free ascent in April 1996 by Luke Laeser.

The area is popular with fishermen, day hikers, mountain bikers, and campers. Climbers should adopt a low-key approach if developing new routes or when climbing in general. Future Forest Service management of the area will certainly be influenced by all of our actions, so please tread lightly in this fragile area.

Trip Planning Information

Area description: Las Conchas, a small, developing climbing area tucked into the Jemez River's upper canyon, offers many short sport routes in the heart of the Jemez Mountains.

Location: North-central New Mexico. In the Jemez Mountains about 15 miles west of Los Alamos.

Camping: The Las Conchas Campground, on the north side of NM 4 just

Jean DeLataillade on *Mainliner* (5.13c) on the Leaning Tower at Las Conchas, New Mexico. *Photo by Dave Pegg.*

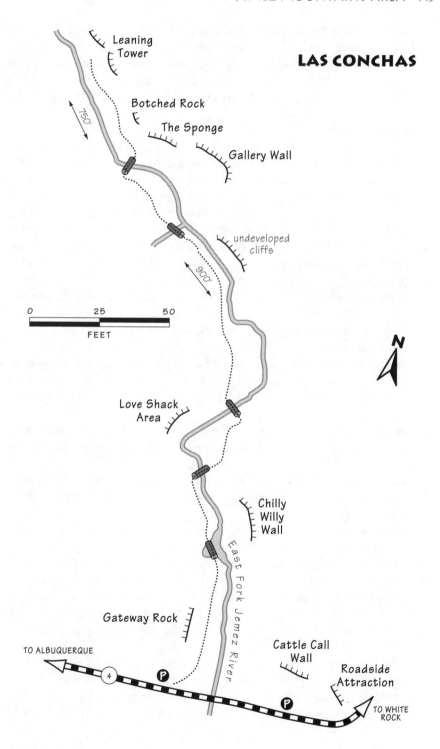

LAS CONCHAS

Leaning Tower

Botched Rock

The Sponge

Gallery Wall

750'

undeveloped cliffs

900'

0   25   50
FEET

N

Love Shack Area

Chilly Willy Wall

East Fork Jemez River

Gateway Rock

TO ALBUQUERQUE

4

P

Cattle Call Wall

Roadside Attraction

P

TO WHITE ROCK

east of the climbing area parking lot, is popular and often crowded. 5 additional campgrounds in the Santa Fe National Forest are found in the immediate area. Free primitive campsites are found south toward Cochiti Mesa along Forest Road 289 from its junction with NM 4 about 7 miles east of Las Conchas. Good camping is also found at Bandelier National Monument farther east toward Los Alamos.

Climbing season: Spring to fall. At 8,400', Las Conchas is primarily a May through October area. Climbing is best during warm summer months. The high elevation limits climbing on all but the warmest winter days. Watch for heavy thunderstorms on summer afternoons.

Restrictions and access issues: Las Conchas lies within land administered by the USDA Forest Service. Presently no restrictions on climbing are in place. As visitation and new routes proliferate, this will surely change. The area is also very popular with anglers, hikers, and campers. Use discretion and good judgment when climbing to favorably represent climbing activities to other user groups.

Guidebook: *Sport Climbing in New Mexico* by Randal Jett and Matt Samet, 1991.

Nearby mountain shops, guide services, and gyms: Los Alamos, Santa Fe, and Albuquerque.

Services: No services in the immediate area. Jemez Springs, 18 miles west, offers fuel, a restaurant, and bed and breakfast options. Good dining and commercial hot spring bath houses are found here. Full services in Los Alamos, 18 miles east.

Emergency services: The nearest phone is in Jemez Springs or Los Alamos, either about 15 miles away. The Los Alamos Medical Center offers 24-hour emergency care.

Nearby climbing areas: The Cochiti Mesa cliffs and the White Rock Area cliffs are about 25 miles southeast. The Sandias and Palomas Peak are about 50 miles south.

Nearby attractions: Excellent hiking, mountain biking, and fishing in the surrounding area. Spence Hot Springs, a local favorite, is west on NM 4, 1.5 miles below the village of La Cueva. Park near a sign advising "No Parking after 10:00 p.m." Walk down and cross the river on a log and up a steep trail ¿ short distance to three excellent pools. Other attractions include Bandelier National Monument, Indian ruins, Jemez State Monument, Jemez Pueblo, Rio Grande, San Ildefonso Pueblo, Los Alamos, Valle Grande, and Santa Fe attractions.

Finding the crags: The Las Conchas climbing area is located along the East Fork of the Jemez River about 20 miles west of Los Alamos and 50 miles northwest of Albuquerque. From Los Alamos take NM 501 to NM 4 and head west toward Jemez Springs. The Las Conchas parking area is about 12 miles west of this road junction. If in the White Rock area, the easiest route is to continue on NM 4 west. Just after passing through the beautiful Valle Grande Caldera, Las Conchas Campground is on the right (north). Continue 0.5 mile to the parking area just past the river. Park in the lot on the north side of the highway and walk northwest or downstream to reach all of the rocks except Roadside Attraction and Cattle Call Wall. These rocks are north of the road and just east of the parking area.

To reach the area from Albuquerque, drive north on Interstate 25 to Bernalillo and turn northwest on NM Highway 44 to San Ysidro. Turn north here onto NM 4 and follow to the parking lot just before the Las Conchas Campground. Las Conchas can also be reached from the Cochiti Mesa Crags by continuing north on FR 289 to its junction with NM 4. Las Conchas is about 7 miles west from here.

ROADSIDE ATTRACTION (NOT PICTURED)

This 60' rock is just north of the road and has 1 route. Park in front of Cattle Call Wall and walk a short distance to the next rock east (right).

1. **Roadside Attraction** (5.12a/b) Bring wires, a 2.5 Friend, and clip the bolt. Poor rock and runout after the roof.

CATTLE CALL WALL

First large rock east of the parking area fronted by a level grassy meadow. Park in front of the rock if this is your destination. This is also a good parking alternative if the main parking lot is full. This is a popular instructional toprope area. One good bolted climb is established near the right end of the rock. The far left end has some leading possibilities plus some bolts for top anchors. Be circumspect in the use of these bolts. Routes are described right to left.

2. **Moon over Belen** (5.6) On the far right end of the rock.
3. **Cowpies for Breakfast** (5.10d) Near the right end of rock. The only bolted lead on this rock leads to a 2-bolt anchor. 6 bolts.
4. **Cow Flop Crack** (5.8) Straight up the crack near the center of the rock. Or start in the right-hand slanting crack.
5. **Pie In Your Eye** (5.6) To the left of the center crack.
6. **Cud for Lulu** (5.8) Usually toproped. Ascends line straight up face on good holds.

7. **Bovine Inspiration** (5.9) Usually toproped.

8. **Ow Now** (5.11a) The face on the far left end of the rock. Multiple possibilities for toproping and leading in this area.

GATEWAY ROCK

The first rock encountered walking north on the trail. Several routes have been established here, although the rock is unattractive. The best choice is a newer bolted climb on the south end. Toprope anchors are in place for the east ridge.

9. **Woof Toof Noof Roof** (5.10+) 4 bolts up to fixed ringed anchors. On the east face is the newest route in the area, 9a, *Drive by Shooting* (5.10-) (no picture). 6 bolts plus a fixed nut to fixed anchors.

CHILLY WILLY WALL (NOT PICTURED)

This wall is on the east side of the river about 200 yards from the parking area just opposite the first log crossing. Access usually involves wading. Nestled away among the pines, this area is often passed by on the way to the climbs in the Sponge area. Several easy-to-locate, good routes and hidden camping spots are found here. Routes are described right to left.

10. **Turkey Sandwich** (5.8) Scramble up to the top of a detached low-angle rock at the extreme southern (right) edge of the rock. Climb up and right to a short chimney, then your choice to the top. Seldom climbed.

11. **Tasty Freeze** (5.9R) Start 25' left of *Turkey Sandwich*. 3 bolts plus wires and camming units to 3.5" protect a steep face and crack.

12, 13, 14. These 3 routes (no harder than 5.9) are on the 30' boulder leaning against the main wall left of the southern end of the rock. All are moderate routes sharing the same anchor.

15. **Wet Willies** (5.11b/c) Start on the main wall behind the 30' boulder's left side. Initial section is mossy and sometimes wet. Camming units through hand-size protect up to a face with 6 bolts.

16. **Donkey Show** (5.10c) About 150' north of *Wet Willies* on the extreme northern edge of the rock. Face climb up to a difficult clip, then past 2 more bolts bracketing a thin crack to a 2-bolt anchor. TCUs and camming units helpful.

LOVE SHACK AREA

Located on the left side of the stream near the second river crossing. These climbs are more difficult to access presently due to the changing river channel along the base of the rock.

17. **Happy Entrails** (5.12d) Start in the left circular depression and climb out and up toward a bush. Move right to clip a 2-bolt shared anchor.

18. **Unknown** Start in the right circular depression and climb out and up to a 2-bolt anchor. Difficult.

GALLERY WALL

On the north side of the river. At the fifth crossing go up-river passing The Sponge and Dream Tower on the way.

19. **Presumed to be Modern** (5.12a/b) 5 bolts lead to a fixed anchor.
20. **Across the View** (5.11d) Climb the black streak to the left of *Presumed to be Modern*. 4 bolts and a fixed anchor.

DREAM TOWER

On the lower left end of the Gallery Wall.

21. **Animal Magnetism** (5.11d) 6 bolts on the right side of the tower. Loose in spots.
22. **Sanctuarium** (5.12b/c) After 4 bolts, move left to join *East Coast Dreams*.
23. **East Coast Dreams** (5.11b/c) 6 bolts and a fixed anchor on the left side of the tower.
24. **Hail Dancer** (5.9) 40' left of *East Coast Dreams*. A low-angle face up to a bolt, then up the arete to a 2-bolt anchor. TCUs and gear up to 3".

LAS CONCHAS
GALLERY WALL &
DREAM TOWER

THE SPONGE

This south-facing cliff with some of the canyon's best rock sits just above the fifth river crossing almost a mile into the canyon.

25. **Hollywood Tim** (5.9+) Begins on the right side of the crag. Start in the crack or face climb up and left to the first bolt. Deceptively difficult pocket climbing and pinches lead past 5 bolts to a 3-bolt lowering station.

26. **Mad Dogs and Englishmen** (5.10b) Clip the first 2 bolts of *Hollywood Tim*, then up and left through a small roof. Continue up past several more bolts to *Hollywood Tim's* anchors. Quality.

27. **Pumpin' Huecos** (5.10d/11a) A superb, pumpy route up a slightly over-hung pocketed wall. Crux above bolt 2. 4 bolts and a 2-bolt anchor. Quality.

28. **Sal's Neuroses** (5.10d/.11) Located on Botched Rock, a small outcrop, 60' left of the Sponge. 30' of climbing (4 bolts) to a 2-bolt anchor. Short with quality moves.

LAS CONCHAS
THE SPONGE

LAS CONCHAS
BOTCHED ROCK

THE LEANING TOWER

Continue about 250 yards downstream from The Sponge to the obvious south-facing outcrop split by a long overhanging crack. The Leaning Tower, the largest rock in the canyon, also offers the hardest routes.

29. **The Mean Leaner** (5.13a/b) The central crack that splits the tower. First ascent by Lucas Laeser. To date, accomplished with pre-placed gear only. No bolts, 3 fixed pins.

30. **Mainliner** (5.13c) A sustained, pumpy, and technical line up the left side of the tower. Completed in the summer of 1995 by Jean DeLataillade. A classic 100' line. Start left of *The Mean Leaner*. 6 bolts lead to a thin crack that slices the upper headwall. Hard face climbing, laybacking, and some thin jams past 6 more bolts plus TCU placements (just below top) lead to a 2-bolt anchor set back from the edge. Rap to base with 2 ropes. The area's most difficult climb to date. Unrepeated as of fall 1995.

31. **Unknown** (5.12b/c) Just left around the corner from *Mainliner*. 5 bolts to a 2-bolt anchor.

32. **Lichen Attack Crack** (5.10b) The obvious, attractive right-facing dihedral 40' left of *Mean Leaner*. 80' of hand jams. Wires and units up to 3.5" plus extras for the belay. Go left to rappel down a loose gully off a tree. Seldom climbed, although quality.

33. **Project** (5.12b/c) On the arete to the left of *Lichen Attack Crack*.

LAS CONCHAS
LEANING TOWER

Central New Mexico

REGION

Darrin Milligan on *Warpy Moople* (5.10+), Muralla Grande, Sandia Mountain, New Mexico. *Photo by Paul Drakos.*

ALBUQUERQUEAREA

SANDIA MOUNTAIN

OVERVIEW

Sandia Mountain, a rugged limestone-capped granite escarpment that towers east of Albuquerque, offers a wealth of adventure climbing on large granite faces. Long approaches, difficult climbing, route-finding decisions, and long descents characterize the area. The routes range in length from 1 to 13 pitches. Sandia's rock quality varies from poor to good, making route selection paramount for a safe and enjoyable experience. The selections in this guide represent some of the best routes on the escarpment. Gaining familiarity with these routes will give first-time visitors a basis to explore this complicated area and the knowledge to seek out other more obscure but quality lines.

Sandia Mountain forms an abrupt and rugged skyline for Albuquerque, New Mexico's largest city. *Sandia* is Spanish for "watermelon." The range's long north-south trending ridge is topped by 10,678-foot Sandia Crest. This lofty point, reached from Albuquerque and Interstate 40 via a 14-mile paved road up Tejano Canyon, overlooks the city's urban sprawl, the broad Rio Grande valley, and distant mountain ranges including the southern tip of the Sangre de Cristo Range above Santa Fe, the Jemez Mountains, and Mount Taylor to the west. The road winds upward from the dry upland desert east of Albuquerque through forests of pine and spruce. A spur highway, New Mexico Highway 165, leaves the crest road after 8 miles and drops down Las Huertas Creek to Placitas and the northern foothills of the Sandia range. This highway accesses the Palomas Peak sport climbing area and passes the famed Sandia Man Cave archeological site. This controversial site, discovered in 1936, dated early man's presence in the New World to 26,000 years ago. Most of the Sandia sierra lies in Cibola National Forest. A spectacular section of the range north of the crest highway is protected within the Sandia Mountain Wilderness.

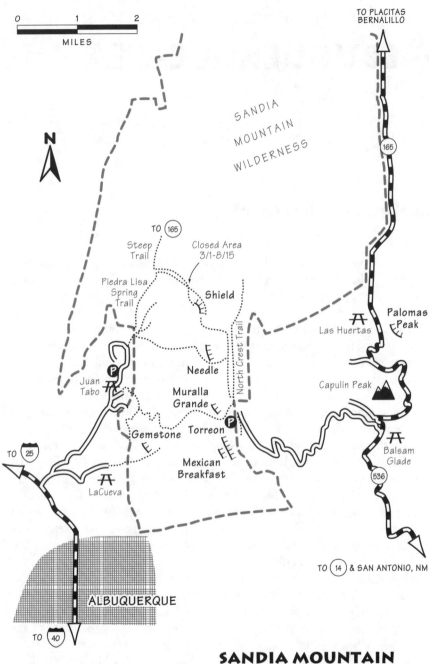

0   1   2
MILES

N

TO PLACITAS
BERNALILLO

SANDIA
MOUNTAIN
WILDERNESS

165

TO 165

Steep
Trail

Closed Area
3/1-8/15

Shield

Piedra Lisa
Spring
Trail

Palomas
Peak

Las Huertas

North Crest Trail

Needle

P

Juan
Tabo

Muralla
Grande

Capulin Peak

Gemstone

Torreon

P

Balsam
Glade

TO 25

Mexican
Breakfast

536

LaCueva

ALBUQUERQUE

TO 40

TO 14 & SAN ANTONIO, NM

**SANDIA MOUNTAIN
& PALOMAS PEAK**

The geology of Sandia Mountain is quite complex. The large cliffs exposed on the west-facing escarpment are composed of an ancient granite that is an aggregate quartz, feldspar, and mica. The granite formed in Precambrian times some one to two billion years ago. During the last five to ten million years, massive blocks of the earth's crust slowly lifted along a fault line on the west edge of today's mountains. Thin layers of limestone and shale dating from the Pennsylvanian Period between 250 and 300 million years ago cap the granite atop the range crest. The limestone bands are prominent along Palomas Peak on the northeast fringe of the Sandias. The Great Unconformity, a 1.1 billion-year erosive gap of missing geologic history, lies between the granite and limestone.

Climbing History: Little is known about early climbing in the Sandias. The Shield seems to have attracted the most attention with ascents as early as the 1930s. An accident claimed the lives of two climbers here in 1938. The East Saddle of the Needle was ascended in 1944. The period between the 1950s and 1960s saw very little recorded activity with the exception of a Dick Ingraham ascent of The Shield in the mid-1960s. The long approach and wild nature of the crag must have reminded Ingraham of his many classic ascents in the Organ Mountains to the south. Bob Kyrlack, Jack and LaDonna Kutz, and Larry Kline were also seeking out harder lines in the late 1960s.

The 1970s were the halcyon years of exploration. Standards rose dramatically during this time with many of the classic lines established on The Shield,

Muralla Grande, and Torreon. Mike Roybal, one of the most talented and prolific climbers that New Mexico has produced, honed his craft here. Mike teamed up with various partners in establishing many of the present classics. Peter Prandoni and Doug Bridgers joined to do many first and second ascents. Both continue to be active in the area climbing scene and pursue high-standard routes. Other activists during the 1970s include Mark Leonard, Gary Hicks, Carlos Buhler, Paul Horak, Rico Meleski, Clark Gray, John Mauldin, Robbie Baker, Charlie Ware, Steve Merrill, Steve Schum, Hans Bede, Ron Beauchamp, Reed Cundiff, David Hammack, Joe Darriau, Thad Meyerriecks, Dennis Udall, Dirk VanWinkle, Wayne Taylor, and Jenny McKernan.

The Sandias continued to be explored in the 1980s with many new routes and areas being discovered. The Techweeny Buttress, featuring upper grade (5.11-5.12) bolt-protected climbs, was developed by Paul Horak, Mark Leonard, Matt Samet, Tom Wezwick, Cayce Weber, Adam Read, Jeff Ash, Dave Dunlap, Bruce Doeren, Wayne Taylor, Steve Verchinski, John Duran, Doug Drumheller, Kathy Kacon, and David Benyak.

Sport climbing enthusiasts will not find many opportunities in the Sandias. A long-standing traditional approach to climbing and a prohibition on motorized drilling limits interest. In keeping with the local ethics, many of the established sport routes were put up in a quasi-traditional style by augmenting bolts with gear placements. *A Date With Death,* the hardest climb in the Sandias, is one example. The first 25' of 5.12c face climbing is protected by #0 RPs; TCUs and wires protect 40' of 5.12a finger crack; and two bolts protect the final 20' of B2 bouldering. Originally rated 5.13c/d by John Duran, the route remains unrepeated and is now thought to be harder.

Presently the Sandias see most climbing activity from locals who repeat the classics and those willing to seek out the sometimes obscure and hard-to-find cliffs that stud the range's west front. Trails to the cliffs are sometimes complicated affairs that require careful hiking and navigating to reach the crag base. On the routes themselves, climbers need to use traditional skills like route finding and placing gear for protection and belays to successfully ascend their chosen line. Climbing in the Sandias requires sound judgment and caution. Objective dangers abound, including loose rock, changeable weather, and lightning. Climbers, especially first-time visitors, should plan on a long day in the mountains when attempting most Sandia routes. The range is not an ideal beginner area. Anyone climbing here should be competent and able to self-rescue should the need arise.

The best routes and rock in the Sandias are found on The Shield, The Needle (sometimes referred to as the Pyramid), Muralla Grande, Torreon, and Mexican Breakfast crag. All of the rock formations on the mountain are approached either from trails starting at the mountain base just east of Albuquerque or by driving to the crest summit and descending trails to the base of the cliffs. The

Shield is approached from both the bottom and the top, although it is usually from the top. The Needle, Muralla Grande, Torreon, Mexican Breakfast are best reached from the top. See individual rock formation route descriptions for more specific directions to the crag bases. A recommended map for first-time visitors is the "Sandia Wilderness Area" map available from the Albuquerque Forest Service office and many local climbing shops.

Other areas (not included in this guide) worth visiting include The Thumb, Lower La Cueva Canyon area, and Upper Echo Canyon . Eight moderate routes ascend the relatively easily approached Thumb, including *Aviary Ort Overhangs* (5.10-), *North Summit Direct* (5.8), and the *Northwest Ridge* (5.6). The Upper Echo Canyon area offers many short crags with difficult climbing on fair to good rock. Six routes ascend Techweeny Buttress. Other routes are on Bush Shark Tower and Yucca Flower Tower. The Lower La Cueva Domes and Gemstone Slabs are easily approached via La Cueva Trail from La Cueva Picnic Area at the range base. On Lower La Cueva Domes try 1-pitch *Mona Feetsa* (5.9) and *Leonardo da Smeari* (5.11a). Farther up La Cueva Canyon lie the Gemstone West Slabs and East Slabs. *The Hiker's and Climber's Guide to the Sandias* gives information on these and other areas in the Sandias.

Rack: A large rack of camming units up to 4", TCUs, RPs, wired stoppers, runners, and quickdraws is sufficient for most Sandia routes. The long crack and face pitches plus belay anchors eat up the pro, making doubles in most sizes mandatory. The few bolts encountered are generally old 1/4" bolts. Back these up whenever possible. Two 165' ropes are useful to facilitate a possible retreat. Water, food, and rain gear are generally necessary on the longer routes. Watch for loose rock, start early, and plan on a long day in the mountains.

Trip Planning Information

Area description: Sandia Mountain, towering east of Albuquerque, offer numerous multi-pitch adventure routes on tall granite crags in remote wilderness settings.

Location: North-central New Mexico, east of Albuquerque.

Camping: There are no developed campgrounds in the Sandia Mountains. All sites on the Sandia Crest are day-use picnic areas only. The nearest developed campsites are about 50 miles south of Albuquerque on the east side of the mountains on the Mountainair Ranger District. Two KOA campgrounds are in the Albuquerque vicinity. Coronado State Park, north of Albuquerque, offers showers and is convenient to NM 165, which travels to the mountain crest.

Climbing season: Late spring to late fall are the best months. Snow depths of 100" are recorded annually in the Sandias. July and August are the rainy months. Be prepared for possible heavy thunderstorms and lightning. As in

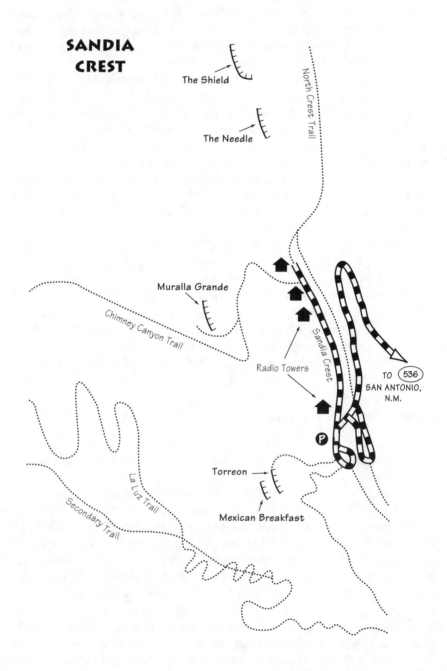

SANDIA CREST

The Shield

The Needle

North Crest Trail

Muralla Grande

Chimney Canyon Trail

Radio Towers

Sandia Crest

TO 536
SAN ANTONIO,
N.M.

P

La Luz Trail

Secondary Trail

Torreon

Mexican Breakfast

any mountain environment, be prepared for changeable weather during any month.

Restrictions and access issues: The climbing areas described here are all located in the Sandia Wilderness Area administered by the Sandia Ranger District of the Cibola National Forest. Motorized drilling is not allowed. A seasonal closure protects peregrine falcon nesting sites from March 1 to August 15. The closure area affects all climbing on The Shield, UNM Spire, Prow, and hiking on the Fletcher and Movie trails. Some routes on the Needle are periodically affected. Call the Sandia Ranger District at (505) 281-3304 for specific closure information. Fines of up to $5,000 and imprisonment up to 6 months can be levied for violating the closed areas.

Guidebook: *Hiker's and Climber's Guide to the Sandias,* third edition, University of New Mexico Press, by Mike Hill, is the complete guide to the area. A guide to the Sandias was also featured in *Rock and Ice* issue 43.

Nearby mountain shops, guide services, and gyms: Albuquerque.

Services: Full services in Albuquerque.

Emergency services: Dial 911 for all emergency services in the Albuquerque area.

Nearby climbing areas: The Cochiti Mesa Crags are 50 miles to the north. White Rock Crags are 90 miles to the north. Palomas Peak sport climbing area is on the northern end of the Sandias.

The Three Guns Springs climbing area with more than 20 bolted 5.8 to 5.12 climbs and abundant bouldering is climbable all year. To get there, drive east on I-40 to Carmel. Head north through the Monticello Estates to the Three Gun Springs Trailhead. Hike about 1 mile north and look for a cluster of large granite boulders on the right.

Good bouldering is found on the designated open space recreational area that runs along the base of the Sandias. Excellent biking and running trails are also located here. Tramway Boulevard accesses all these areas. Exit onto Tramway Blvd. from I-40 East and turn right or east on Copper. Drive less than 1 mile to the end of Copper. Hike about 400 yards on a good trail going north to the popular Copper Street boulders. A short distance north of Copper is Indian School Road. Turn right or east on Indian School to its end and a large parking area. Hike past the large storage tank, then up canyon past a flood control project for more good bouldering and short toprope problems.

Near the northern end of Tramway is the exit to the La Cueva and Juan Tabo Picnic areas. The Luz Trail starts in the Juan Tabo area. Good bouldering is found in the La Cueva Picnic area. Follow signs to both areas.

Nearby attractions: Albuquerque history and culture, Old Town, the Albuquerque Museum, New Mexico Museum of Natural History, Rio Grande Nature Center State Park, Rio Grande Zoological Park, Petroglyph National Monument, and Coronado National Monument. The internationally famous

Balloon Fiesta is held annually in October.

Finding the crags: The trails to all of the described crags begin from the Sandia Crest parking area. To reach the crest from the north or south turn east on NM 165 about 10 miles north of Albuquerque. The road ends 20 miles south at the Sandia Crest parking area. Sandia Crest is also reached from the east via NM 14. Access NM 14 from the south via I-40. From the north or Santa Fe, follow I-25 to the highway junction north of Albuquerque. Turn west on NM 536 at San Antonio, then left at the junction with NM 165. Refer to each crag's description for trail directions from the main parking area atop the Sandia Crest.

THE SHIELD

The Shield offers the area's longest routes (5 to 13 pitches), including *Rainbow Route* (VI 5.9 A4), New Mexico's only Grade VI route. Due to a long approach and an area closure between March and August to protect peregrine falcon nest sites, The Shield sees limited climbing activity. It is a toss-up whether it's best to approach this remote crag from the mountain base or the from the crest. For routes on the east end of The Shield, most seem to prefer coming in from the top. Consult with locals for their advice on this and other logistics when planning to climb here. From the parking area on the crest, walk north through metal gates past the Radio Towers to the North Crest Trail. Stay on the trail for a little more than 1 mile until the trail turns west. A large horseshoe-shaped drainage drops west from here. This is located between the north side of The Needle and the top of The Shield. Downclimb a short limestone cliff band to scree fields to reach the drainage. Continue a long way, an elevation drop of around 1,500', down the canyon to The UNM Spire. Above (north) are slabs at the bottom of the east end of The Shield. Continue down the drainage a little farther until it is possible to scramble up and right to a short gravel filled gully. This provides access to the large ramp below the main face. All the routes described below start from the ramp. If you can find the approach, the routes are easy to find. All of the routes have some loose, easy pitches near the top. Set belays out of the fall line and be extra cautious. Experienced Sandia climbers choose to wear helmets on many Sandia routes.

Descent: Descend by hiking south on the crest ridge back to the Sandia Crest parking area.

Routes are described right to left or east to west.

1. **Rainbow Dancer** (V 5.11a) **Pitch 1:** Start in a groove 100' right of the prominent right-leaning corner below the large arching overhangs (start of the *Rainbow Route*) about mid-height on the cliff. Climb, with poor

SANDIA MOUNTAIN
THE SHIELD

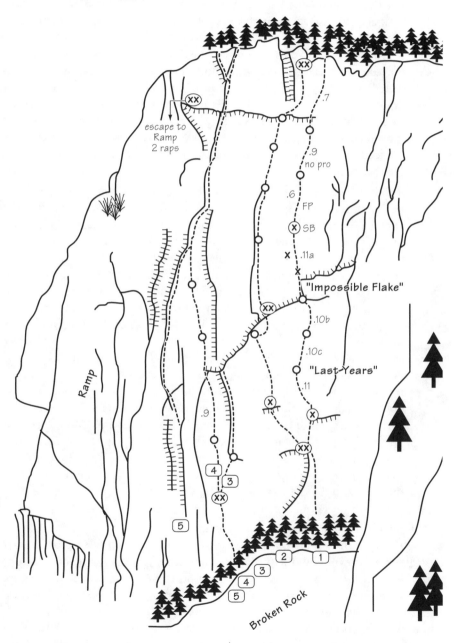

escape to
Ramp
2 raps

.7

.9
no pro

.6

FP

SB

.11a

"Impossible Flake"

.10b

.10c

"Last-Years"

.11

Ramp

.9

4

3

5

2   1

3

4

5

Broken Rock

protection, over a bulge to easier terrain. Belay at established anchors. **Pitch 2:** Follow corners above belay to a large ledge and belay (5.8). **Pitch 3:** Follow a groove off the left end of the ledge for 25', then traverse up left 100' to a hanging belay in a water groove (5.11). **Pitch 4:** Difficult off the belay to easier terrain above. Follow ledges back right to the base of the right end of a large overhang (5.10c). **Pitch 5:** Climb a small corner for 20', then right onto the face above "The Rainbow." Spectacular face climbing goes up then left above the roofs. The pitch (150' can be well-protected and features a 5.10 mantle near the end. Belay in a great position on top of a large flake (5.10b). **Pitch 6:** Crux pitch. Climb up to the left side of "The Impossible Flake," then difficult cracks lead to the 5.11 crux moves. Belay in slings. **Pitches 7, 8, and 9:** Grooves, cracks, and face climbing lead through lesser quality rock to the top. Be extra cautious in this section.

2. **Rainbow Route** (VI 5.9 A4) Modern gear and better techniques may prompt a re-evaluation of the grading for this historic route. Most of the climbing is free with about 100' of aid done with nuts and small pitons on the first ascent. A brief description follows. Complete details should be sought from locals before any attempts. **Pitch 1:** Start at the base of the large overhanging right-trending dihedral. A long pitch up the dihedral ends at a bolted belay stance. **Pitch 2:** Continue up the corner to the left to another bolt. Belay on a ledge. **Pitch 3:** Bolt-protected face climbing leads up and left to the base of the first "Rainbow." **Pitch 4:** Climb up corner above to an aid crack through the roof. Above the roof, climb to belay ledge above. **Pitch 5:** Moderate free climbing leads to fourth class ledges. Follow these to their high point. **Pitch 6:** Near the top of the ledges is an A1 crack that goes over the first roof/bulge to a bent 1/4" bolt. Traverse 40' left on difficult aid (crux) between upper and lower sets of roofs. The corner at the end of the traverse offers better protection. Climb corner to a small belay ledge. **Pitches 7, 8, and 9:** Continue up the corner 2 to 3 pitches to a large blocky ledge below the "Cyclops," a large roof/cave formation near the top of the rock. **Pitches 10 and 11:** 2 more pitches up the corner to the right of the "Cyclops" lead to the top.

The following 3 routes all share a common start.

Procrastination is an easier variation of *Chicken Chop Suey.* **Pitch 1** Start 100' left or downhill of the prominent right-leaning corner that is the start of *Rainbow Route.* A 5.9 move with poor protection accesses an easy ramp. *Procrastination* and *Chicken Chop Suey* follow the corner above for 6 pitches. **Pitch 3 and 4** of *Chicken Chop Suey* go up the left corner and *Procrastination* up the right corner. **Pitches 6 and 7** have loose rock on the ledges. The final pitches go up a large corner to the left of the "Cyclops," a large roof/cave formation near the top of the rock.

Slipping Into Darkness continues left on a ramp after the first pitch of *Chicken Chop Suey* and *Procrastination*. Climb to the base of a ledge/corner about 75' left. Follow the corner for 4 pitches to join with *Chicken Chop Suey* and *Procrastination* on their 7th pitch. Pitch 4 is the crux pitch. Originally aided (A2/3), it can be free climbed (5.10c). **Pitch 5** also originally involved A2 aid in a thin crack.

Rack: A large rack of camming units, including fist-size units, wires, TCUs, runners, and a 165' rope, is needed for all routes. Allow at least 2.5 hours for the approach, a full day of climbing, and 1.5 hours back to the crest parking lot.

3. **Chicken Chop Suey** (IV 5.9) Crux is pitch 4. Quality of rock is fair to good.

4. **Procrastination** (IV 5.8+) Crux is pitch 3. The climbing is mostly 5.7. Usually done in 11 pitches. Quality of rock is fair to good.

5. **Slipping Into Darkness** (IV 5.10c) Extra-small and extra-large gear needed. Quality of rock is good. Some difficult and sustained pitches are found on this route.

THE NEEDLE

The Needle offers the popular 15-pitch *Southwest Ridge* (5.8). A strong party should allow 10 to 12 hours car to car for this route. The route is mostly moderate climbing with a few sections of 5.8. Climbers should be adept at route finding, gear placements, and self-rescue on this remote crag.

The approach is long and arduous. From the crest parking lot, hike right (north) through the metal gates past the radio towers to the North Crest Trail. Continue about 0.5 mile and descend to a limestone band just before a prominent bulge in the crest ridge. Hike down to a saddle to the east of The Needle and bushwack to the base of the Southwest Ridge. Allow a couple hours for the approach. The descent involves descending into a loose gully, then scrambling to easier terrain and up to the crest.

6. **The Southwest Ridge** (IV 5.8) 15 pitches. Start on the west side of the ridge and climb fourth and/or easy fifth class rock about 300' to a large square trough with a prominent cave above. Climb either side of the trough to the right side of the cave and then up to good ledges. Easy climbing above leads to the first notch on the ridge. Retreat is possible from here via a 150' rappel down the east side. From here do many pitches of moderate climbing (some 5.8 moves) to the top. Fifth Avenue, a large tree-

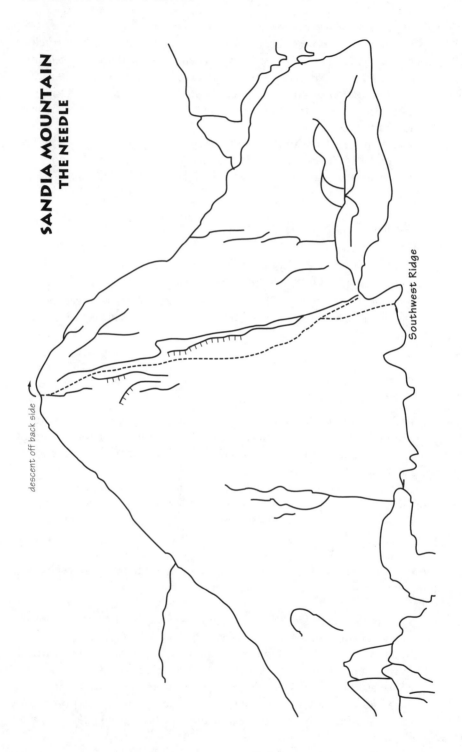

SANDIA MOUNTAIN
THE NEEDLE

descent off back side

Southwest Ridge

covered ledge system, is passed at about pitch 10. Retreat is possible here by walking left or north along the ledges. 4 more pitches (2 of them 5.8) lead to the summit.

MURALLA GRANDE

The towering walls of Muralla Grande offer some fine adventure routes on good quality rock. Climbing here is reminiscent of shorter Black Canyon of the Gunnison routes. The rugged scramble down from the range crest usually commits you to climbing back out because it's a whole lot more pleasant. The recommended route on Muralla Grande is *Warpy Moople* (III 5.9 or 5.10+). The more moderate *Second Coming* (5.9+) is shorter but nearly as good.

To approach Muralla Grande, walk north from the parking lot at Sandia Crest through a large metal gate toward the radio towers. At the hang glider launch point, look down to the north and see most of the approach route to Muralla Grande. Locate an aspen knoll and a large canyon that descends the south side of the crag. Continue walking alongside the buildings on the crest and turn left at building 79B. The trail starts here. Follow it until it eventually reaches the aspen knoll. This is a good place to leave packs to pick up on the way out. Go left at the beginning of the knoll and follow a steep trail down into Chimney Canyon. At the junction of the south side of Muralla Grande and The Chimney, a large rock formation on the south side of the canyon, bear right to the west face of Muralla Grande. The routes on the crag's south face are all moderate 5.8 to 5.9 lines. Continue around the cliff to the west face and the start of *Warpy Moople* directly underneath the large main roof system above. Allow about 1 hour for the approach.

Rack: Carry a large rack of camming units through 3.5", wires, TCUs, quickdraws, and several runners. A 200' rope is handy but not required.

Descent: Hike up the trail to retrieve gear if you left it by the aspen knoll and to get back on the upper section of the Chimney Trail.

7. **Warpy Moople** (III 5.9 or 5.10+) **Pitch 1:** Start below and to the left of a large pine tree, climb a left-facing corner, and then move through a blocky section. Trend right a short distance and establish a belay on a good ledge (130', 5.8). **Pitch 2:** Climb up the corner system, trend up right to establish a belay under a 5' roof directly under the main roof system (5.9). **Pitch 3:** Quality of rock improves on this pitch. Climb up and right to the far right side of the roof, then up right to a good belay ledge (100', 5.8). **Pitch 4:** Climb straight up the corner system on right side of main roof system to a small belay ledge. Friends #0.5, 1.5, and 2 are required to equip belay. **Pitch 5:** Crux pitch. Either climb straight up through the roof

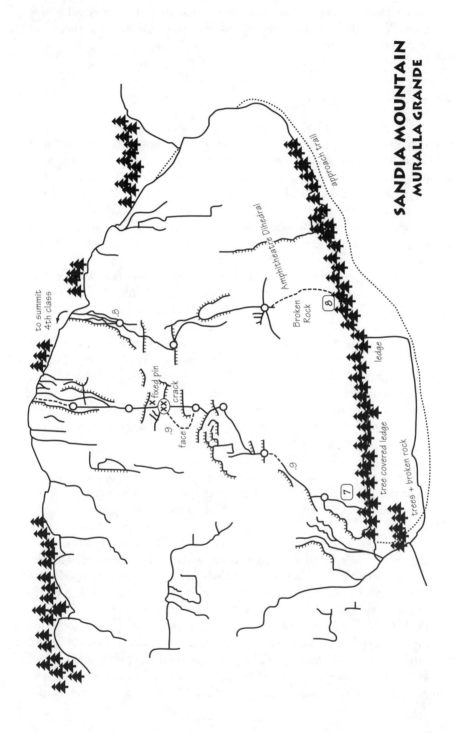

SANDIA MOUNTAIN
MURALLA GRANDE

(5.10+), or traverse left about 15', then up right on 5.9 face climbing to a good ledge with a 2-bolt anchor. **Pitch 6:** Face climb up to a fixed pin, then angle right to a large ledge. Climb the crack above the ledge to a sloping grassy ledge (140'). **Pitch 7:** Climb up the right-facing corner, then up right for a full rope length. (A 200' rope gets to the top). **Pitch 8:** A short easy pitch leads to the top at the westernmost part of the aspen knoll.

8. **The Second Coming** (II 5.8) This 4-pitch climb is easy to locate on the way to *Warpy Moople*. It is located on the south side of Muralla Grande at the end of the descent gully opposite The Chimney, a large rock formation. Look up to the top of the cliff and locate 3 attractive cracks splitting the uppermost section of the wall. The crack on the right is the final of 4 pitches. **Pitch 1:** Start on the left side of the slabs at ground level to gain the top of the large tree-covered ledge system. **Pitch 2:** From the very top tree, take the left crack to near the right end of another vegetated ledge. **Pitch 3:** Climb up to the roof and either continue straight up or face climb around the left side. Belay at the top of large blocks. **Pitch 4:** The rightmost crack is 5.7. Harder cracks are to the left.

TORREON

Torreon features a good selection of routes including the difficult Peter Prandoni and Mike Roybal classic *Voodoo Child* (5.12a) and the 7-pitch *Mountain Momma* (5.10c). This is one of the most popular routes in the Sandia Mountains. Both routes have some fixed gear, although both are traditional lines that require skills at route finding, gear placements, and self-rescue. Some of the best crack and face routes in the Sandia Mountains are found here.

The approach is relatively easy if the correct gully is located. Remember, the top of Torreon is very near the range crest and the approach comes in from the north, then traverses down and south to the cliff base. Locate the trail on the southern end of the parking area by a gate near some stairs. Go right (north) about 150 yards to the second gully. A short downclimb (5.5) on the limestone band next to a dead tree puts you in the gully. Look for an abandoned aspen-log cabin in this area. This is a good place to stash gear for your return. Descend a gully for 400' to 500' to a saddle on the left near the bottom of the gully. Walk left (south) to the base of the West Face of Torreon. Allow 30 to 45 minutes for the approach.

Rack: A standard rack of camming units up to 4" plus extras in 1/2" to 3/4" range.

Descent: Walk to the top of the cliff and rappel off a tree about 100' down to a sloping ledge. This requires some traverse tensioning while on rappel. A short fifth class section leads up and out of the gully to near the "aspen heap" log cabin and continues up to the Sandia Crest.

9. **Voodoo Child** (III 5.12a) Start at the toe of the Southwest Buttress. **Pitch 1:** Start about 80' left of *Mountain Momma*. Climb a left-facing corner to a small ledge at the top of a pillar (60'). **Pitch 2:** Face climb right, then up past 2 bolts. Difficult at beginning, easier above. Belay at the hollow corner below roofs (120 feet). **Pitch 3:** A difficult rounded layback brings you to the roof. Undercling left about 12', then climb over the roof via a strenuous jam crack that leads 100' to a belay station with bolts and chains. This is at *Mountain Momma's* 4th pitch. **Pitch 4:** Climb face and crack up and left to a roof. Turn roof on the right. A short traverse left gets to the base of an overhanging layback/jam crack. Climb the corner to ledge at top of 5th pitch of *Mountain Momma*. Continue on the upper pitches of *Mountain Momma* to the top. **Descent:** Same as *Mountain Momma*.

10. **Mountain Momma** (III 5.10c) Walk along the base of the West Face to the toe of the Southwest Buttress (*Voodoo Child*). *Mountain Momma* follows the large dihedral to the right for 250' before moving left and up corners that lead to the upper face. **Pitch 1:** Start near the south end of the west face in a shallow dihedral system. Face and crack climb up to a 2-bolt belay (5.10a). **Pitch 2:** Ascend difficult face climbing (5.10) on questionable rock to a good hand crack on the right. Follow this to a belay stance. **Pitch 3:** Climb up and left up to top of buttress below a steep short headwall. Belay at ledge with bolts and chains. Rap descent possible from here, straight down *Voodoo Child*. **Pitch 4:** Short but difficult. Climb up to a fixed pin that protects the crux. Crank past the bulge, then climb the crack above to a belay (5.10c). **Pitch 5:** Original way: Face climb around to the left of the blocks and belay on a large ledge (5.9). Recommended variation: Continue up a spectacular crack and over the roofs. When the crack ends, traverse left (look for hidden protection possibilities) to the summit exit cracks. Belay off gear in a corner. **Pitch 6:** Continue up the large crack system and belay in the chimney (5.9). **Pitch 7:** A short easy pitch ends on a shoulder descending from the summit. **Descent:** Rappel or downclimb into the notch and then scramble up and left to the Sandia Crest.

MEXICAN BREAKFAST

Directly below Torreon is a small formation called Mexican Breakfast. Two recommended routes are found here: *Mexican Breakfast Crack* (5.9) and *Tarantula* (5.10). Follow directions to the base of Torreon's west face, then continue down to the base of Mexican Breakfast.

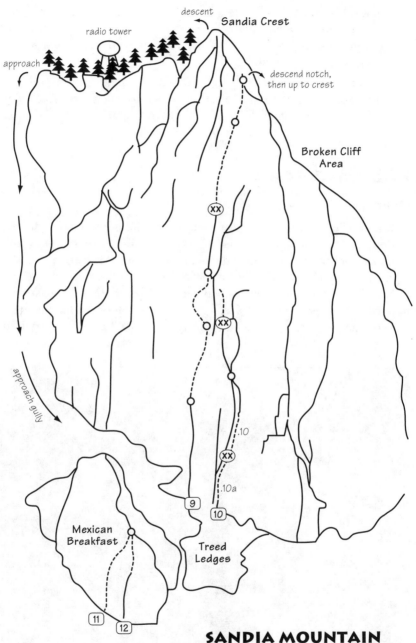

descent

Sandia Crest

radio tower

approach

descend notch,
then up to crest

Broken Cliff
Area

xx

xx

approach gully

.10

xx

.10a

9

10

Mexican
Breakfast

Treed
Ledges

11

12

SANDIA MOUNTAIN
TORREON & MEXICAN BREAKFAST

11. **Mexican Breakfast Crack** (5.9) **Pitch 1:** Climb the off-size crack on the right side of the formation to a large roof. Traverse under the roof to the right and install a hanging belay on the right-hand end. **Pitch 2:** Either continue up the off-size crack above the roof or traverse right for easier and less protected climbing.

12. **Tarantula** (5.10) **Pitch 1:** Climb the thin crack on the face left of *Mexican Breakfast Crack* up to the roof, traverse left to an off-size crack. Jam up and over the roof. **Pitch 2:** Easy climbing straight up to the top of the crag.

PALOMAS PEAK

OVERVIEW

Palomas Peak rises to 8,200' on the northern end of the Sandia Mountains just outside the boundaries of the Sandia Wilderness Area. The peak itself is composed of several layers of madera limestone separated by tree- and shrub-covered slopes. The limestone formed in the vast inland sea that covered much of New Mexico in the Pennsylvanian Period. When the Sandia massif thrust upward, the limestone layers were pushed to the top of the mountains. The cliffs on the peak are separated into many 40' to 70' bands and vary in rock quality.

Brett Spencer-Green on *Funky Junkie* (5.11b), Palomas Peak, New Mexico. *Photo by Stewart M. Green.*

PALOMAS PEAK ACCESS

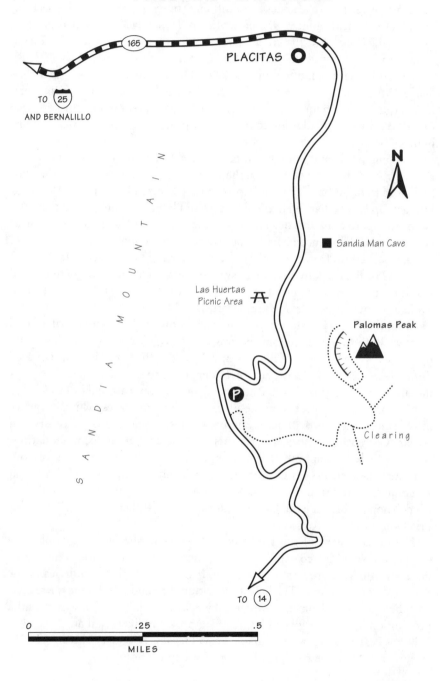

165

PLACITAS ⭘

TO 25
AND BERNALILLO

N

S A N D I A   M O U N T A I N

■ Sandia Man Cave

Las Huertas
Picnic Area ⛱

Palomas Peak
🔺

Ⓟ

Clearing

TO 14

0   .25   .5

MILES

The climbing crag at Palomas Peak averages 50' high and is characterized by vertical to overhanging rock. The alleged "Slab" sector overhangs about 35' in 50' of vertical. The area's most difficult routes are found on this section, including the focal point of the crag, *Turbo Trad* (5.13a), a bolt-protected, overhanging, fingers-to-fist crack. The crack has undergone some enhancing to make it more comfortable. Just left of *Turbo Trad* is *Slab City* (5.13b), completed by Lance Hadfield in late 1995. On the left margin of The Slab is *Snake Dance* (5.13d), presently the crag's most difficult route. Englishman Dave Pegg, from Albuquerque via Sheffield, England, redpointed this testpiece in the fall of 1995. In addition to these burly problems, there are many climbs in the 5.10 to 5.12 grade.

Chipping holds and bolting protectable cracks are an ongoing problem at the crag. A section of The Slab, perhaps the most attractive wall on the cliff, had more than 30 bolts randomly placed to accommodate a photo shoot for Straight Up Holds. Lance Hadfield and Brian Pletta have since filled the holes in an attempt to erase this debasement. Other concerned locals are working at correcting hold enhancements, some chipped subsequent to natural first ascents. Local ethics frown on chipping and other hold enhancements.

Access to the crag involves an easy 30-minute hike on a well-defined trail that leads to the cliff's right-hand end. Be sure to locate and follow this trail to avoid a serious thrash through underbrush.

Climbing history: Interestingly, it was traditional climbers that visited Palomas Peak first, seeking out the crag's few quality crack lines. This development was led by Dave Whitelaw and John Groth. Paul Horak attempted *Turbo Trad* in the mid-1980s before his departure to the East. The subsequent discovery of the area by Lewis Rutherford and Timmy Fairfield in 1993 led to fully equipped sport routes on the blank, overhanging faces. This divergence in styles led to a period of acrimony between the opposing views on style of ascent. Currently a peace of sorts exists at the crag with accommodations tacitly agreed to from both climbing approaches. Sport climbers have concentrated their efforts on unprotectable walls and cracks and left lines that accept gear to the traditionalists. Most of the sport climbs were installed by Mark Thomas, Brian Pletta, Lance Hadfield, Lewis Rutherford, Joey Tefertiller, Eric Gompper, and Lorne Raney.

The development of the Palomas Peak area is ushering in a whole new chapter on New Mexico's sport climbing scene. A wealth of cliffs in the immediate area invite more exploration, with many outside the boundaries of the Sandia Wilderness Area. The limestone within the Sandia Wilderness Area has been held in check from development by a strong traditional presence and a prohibition on motorized drilling. Long approaches likely had an affect also. Palomas Peak's location, just outside the wilderness boundary and an easy 30-minute hike from the road, made it ripe for exploration.

Brett Spencer-Green jams *Crash Test Dummy* (5.11d), Palomas Peak, New Mexico. *Photo by Stewart M. Green.*

Rack: A rack of quickdraws and a 150' rope is sufficient for most routes. The occasional intermittent cracks found throughout the cliff face also accept gear. Expect a minimum of holds on the steep, strenuous, and technical faces.

Descend from lowering anchors.

Trip Planning Information

Area description: Palomas Peak offers many bolted sport routes on a 50' limestone cliff band.

Location: Northeast of Albuquerque in Cibola National Forest.

Camping: None in the immediate area. Undeveloped and less than desirable sites can be found on the road between Placitas and the parking area. There are no developed campgrounds in the Sandia Mountains. All sites on the crest are picnicking, day-use, only. The nearest developed sites are in the Mountainair Ranger District, about 50 miles south of Albuquerque on the east side of the mountains. Two KOA Campgrounds are in the Albuquerque vicinity. Coronado State Park, next to the Rio Grande in Bernalillo just north of Albuquerque, has showers and is convenient to New Mexico Highway 165.

Climbing season: Year-round. Best seasons are spring and fall. Winter access can occasionally be a problem. Summers can be hot.

Restrictions and access issues: There are currently no restrictions on climbing although meetings continue with Forest Service personnel to determine how or if climbing is to be managed. New policies on bolting, trail access, and further route development should be anticipated. Visitors may wish to call the Sandia Ranger District, (505) 281-3304, for updates.

Guidebook: None. Palomas Peak was featured in *Climbing Magazine* issue 155.

Nearby mountain shops, guide services and gyms: Albuquerque.

Services: Nearby Placitas offers a convenience store and gasoline. A supermarket and restaurants are 3 miles farther west. Bernalillo offers more selection. Albuquerque, about 45 minutes away, has full services.

Emergency services: The nearest phone is in Placitas about 7 miles away. Dial 911 for all emergencies. Medical facilities are in Albuquerque.

Nearby climbing areas: Sandia Mountain Wilderness Area, Cochiti Mesa crags, White Rock crags.

Nearby attractions: Sandia Man Cave.

Finding the crag: From Interstate 25, take Exit 242 east on NM 165 to Placitas. From Placitas continue about 7 miles east on NM 165. The road turns to dirt about 2.5 miles farther. Drive almost exactly 5 miles on this dirt road to a parking area on the left identified by 3 large concrete railings. The parking lot is 14 miles from I-25. From the parking area, walk up the road about 25 yards to a good trail just past a large ponderosa pine. This trail contours down into the upper narrows of the valley below (about 10 minutes to the valley). The trail climbs north out of the valley. Head gently uphill directly to the base of the cliff's right end. The trail is easy to follow and generally marked with cairns. Allow 20 to 30 minutes for the approach hike.

Routes are described right to left when viewed from the bottom of the cliff.

ENTRANCE AREA

Located on the right end of the cliff at the end of the approach trail.

1. **Double D** (5.11d) 4 bolts and anchors. Chipped holds are being repaired by locals.
2. **Entrance Exam** (5.10c) 6 bolts and anchors.
3. **Sidewinder** (5.12a) 9 bolts and anchors.
4. **Nature of the Beast** (5.12a) 8 bolts and anchors.
5. **Drop in the Ocean** (5.11c/d) Diagonal left along the flake after the last bolt.
6. **Project** (5.11/5.12?) Crack with a fixed stopper. Lewis Rutherford project.
7. **Fall From Grace** (5.13?) Unfinished project as of January 1995. Bolts and anchors installed. Timmy Fairfield and Dave Pegg project.

THE SLAB

8. **Turbo Trad** (5.13a) 9 bolts and anchors. The obvious bolted overhanging crack.
9. **Slab City** (5.13b/c) 9 bolts and anchors. Bolted overhanging seam.
10. **Snake Dance** (5.13d) Short overhanging right-facing dihedral to an overhanging seam.

THE FRANKS

11. **Project (Sick Man)** Projected grade is 5.14. 4 bolts and anchors. Joe Tefertiller project.
12. **Project (Wooden Jesus)** Projected grade is 5.14. 5 bolts and anchors. Lorne Raney project.

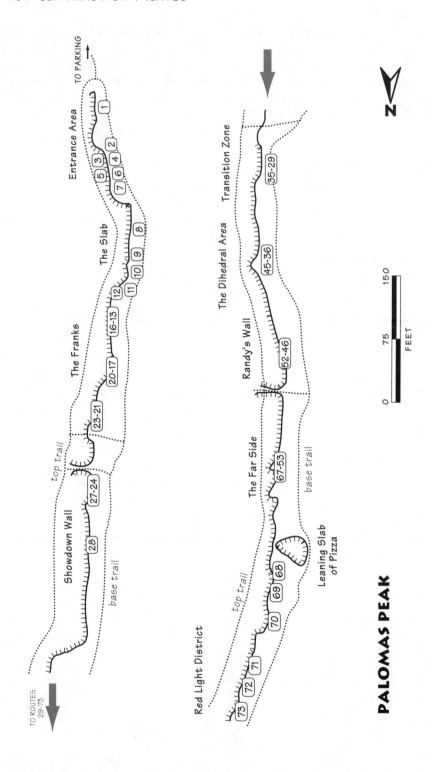

TO PARKING

Entrance Area

TO ROUTES 29-73

The Slab

The Franks

Showdown Wall

top trail

base trail

Transition Zone

The Dihedral Area

Randy's Wall

The Far Side

base trail

top trail

Red Light District

Leaning Slab of Pizza

0   75   150

FEET

N

PALOMAS PEAK

13. **Project (Love Hate Love)** Projected grade is 5.12d/.13a; 4 bolts and anchors. Lorne Raney project.

14. **Junkhead** (5.12a) 3 bolts and anchors.

15. **Dark Dreams** (5.12b) 6 bolts and anchors.

16. **Entertaining Mike Tyson** (5.13b) 5 bolts and anchors.

17. **Crash Test Dummy** (5.11d) 3 bolts and anchors.

18. **Project (Butthead)** Projected grade is 5.12d. 4 bolts and anchors. Shares last 3 bolts and anchors with *Bevis*.

19. **Bevis** (5.13a) 5 bolts and anchors.

20. **Project** Projected grade is 5.13. 4 bolts and anchors. Richard Foust and Eric Robertson project.

21. **Monkey Man** (5.12b) 6 bolts and anchors.

22. **Project** 3 bolts above a 5' roof.

23. **Funky Junkie** (5.11b) 6 bolts and anchors.

SHOWDOWN WALL

24. **Gunslinger** (5.11d) 5 bolts and anchors.

25. **Sidekick** (5.10c) 5 bolts and anchors.

26. **Velcro Booties** (5.11a) 5 bolts and anchors. A 5.10 climb going left at the crux.

27. **Precious** (5.11c) 6 bolts and anchors.

28. **Sweet Jane** (5.12b) 7 bolts and anchors.

TRANSITION ZONE

29. **Wavy Gravy** (5.8) 5 bolts and anchors.

30. **Rode Hard** (5.11c/d) 8 bolts and anchors.

31. **Put Up Wet** (5.11a) TCUs, wires, and 3 bolts. Shares anchors with *Rode Hard*.

32. **Have Slab Will Travel** (5.10c) 4 bolts and anchors.

33. **Support Your Local Bolter** (5.11b) 4 bolts and anchors.

34. **Trigger Happy** (5.9) Crack route. Gear placements necessary. Shares anchors with *Have Slab Will Travel*.

35. **Factory Direct** (5.10c) 4 bolts and anchors.

THE DIHEDRAL AREA

36. **Project (Kick Stand)** Bolts and anchors.

37. **Black Panther** (5.12a) 6 bolts and anchors.

38. **Smoked Salmon** (5.10c) Crack route. Gear placements necessary.

39. **Floating World** (5.11c).

40. **Tina's Rig** (5.12b) 7 bolts and anchors.

41. **Green Eggs and Ham** (5.10c) 6 bolts and anchors.

42. **Quickdraw McGraw** (5.11) 5 bolts and anchors.

43. **Babalouie** (5.10d) 4 bolts. Shares anchors with *Lucky Boy.*

44. **Lucky Boy** (5.11c) 5 bolts and anchors.

45. **Classic Jam Crack** (5.9) Gear placements required to fixed anchors.

RANDY'S WALL

46. **In the Lime-Lite** (5.11c/d) 5 bolts and anchors.

47. **Monkey See** (5.11d) 5 bolts and anchors.

48. **Monkey Do** (5.12a) 5 bolts. Shares same start, first 2 bolts, and anchors with *Monkey See.*

49. **Stemulation** (5.11b) 6 bolts and anchors.

50. **Pretzel Logic** (5.11b) 6 bolts. Shares last 2 bolts and anchors with *Stemulation.*

51. **Kyle's Crack** (5.7) Carry large SLCDs. Fixed anchors.

52. **Unknown** (5.10a R) 2 bolts. Left-diagonaling seam on a ramp to blocks near the top.

THE FAR SIDE

53. **R.I.P.** (5.11d/.12a) 5 bolts and anchors.

54. **Unknown** (5.7/5.8) Off-width crack. Gear placement required.

55. **Midnight Rider** 5.11b/c) 5 bolts and anchors.

56. **Unknown** (5.10c) Zig-zag hand crack. Carry large SLCDs. Shares anchors with *Midnight Rider.*

57. **Curious George** (5.10d) 5 bolts and anchors.

58. **Ramblin' Man** (5.10c) 5 bolts and anchors.

59. **Unknown** (5.9/.10) Face with 1 pin and 1 bolt to a crack.

60. **Unknown** (5.10a/b?) Short face with 2 bolts to a ledge with a small tree.

61. **Chess** (5.10b/c) 7 bolts, fixed stopper, and anchors.

62. **Checkers** (5.10b/c) Shares start, first 2 bolts, fixed stopper, last 2 bolts, and anchor with *Chess*.

63. **Patchwork** (5.10a/b) 9 bolts and anchors.

64. **Lonesome Dove** (5.9) 7 bolts and anchors.

65. **Unnamed** (5.11d/.12a) Toprope problem on the face left of *Lonesome Dove*. Use *Lonesome Dove* anchors.

66. **Tiger By The Tail** (5.10a) 6 bolts and anchors.

67. **Pussy Whipped** (5.8) 5 bolts and anchors. Shares first 4 bolts of *Tiger By The Tail*.

RED LIGHT DISTRICT

68. **Circle K** (5.10d) 4 bolts and anchors.

69. **X-File** (5.10d) 4 bolts and anchors.

70. **The Baltzenator** (5.11a/b) Climb the crack through the roof. Gear placement required up to fixed anchors.

71. **People Mover** (5.7) Bolts and anchor.

72. **Pony Ride** (5.9+) 3 bolts and anchor.

73. **Project (Radio Flyer)** Projected grade is 5.12c. Bolts and anchor.

Ian Spencer-Green climbs *Golden Stairs* (5.11b/c), Enchanted Tower, New Mexico. *Photo by Stewart M. Green.*

SOCORRO AREA

ENCHANTED TOWER

OVERVIEW

South-central New Mexico is a desolate and lonely land. Rough mountains, darkened with forests of pinyon, juniper, pine, and fir, tower above broad, dry valleys coated with sagebrush, short grass, and creosote bush. These remote sierras, including the Magdelena, Bear, San Mateo, Gallinas, and Datil ranges west of Socorro, are, for the most part, unvisited and unpopulated except for the occasional cowboy in search of grazing cattle. Rock outcrops stud the steep mountainsides, their ragged cliffs rising above deep canyons. The Enchanted Tower, one of New Mexico's best sport climbing areas, hides its vertical secrets deep in Thompson Canyon in the heart of the Datil Mountains north of the small village of Datil.

The Enchanted Tower, a 110' semi-detached spire, sits in the middle of a long west-facing band of welded volcanic tuff. Both the tower and the surrounding cliffs offer more than 35 superb sport routes that range in difficulty from 5.8 to 5.13. Almost all of the routes ascend vertical to overhanging rock using pockets, huecos, incut jugs, and face holds. The routes, particularly on the tower, are strenuous and pumpy, but good rests can be found on most lines. The rock quality is generally good, although a few cliffs are somewhat chossy.

Climbing history: The Enchanted Tower climbing area was discovered in 1987 when Bertrand Gramont, a visiting French geology graduate student at New Mexico Tech in Socorro, quickly recognized the canyon's unique possibilities and led a flurry of development. The area was the exclusive domain of Gramont and a small group of New Mexico Tech students until word of the fine climbing reached outsiders. The publication of a guidebook in 1993 further opened up the area. Now climbers from across the United States and Europe visit this remote canyon to enjoy its excellent rock and routes. Pleasant surroundings, free camping, and a friendly scene are extra inducements to visit the Enchanted Tower.

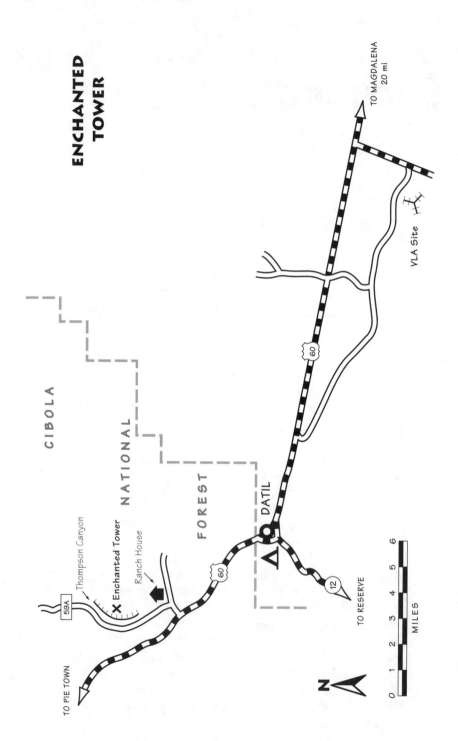

ENCHANTED TOWER

ENCHANTED TOWER
AREA CLIFF OVERVIEW

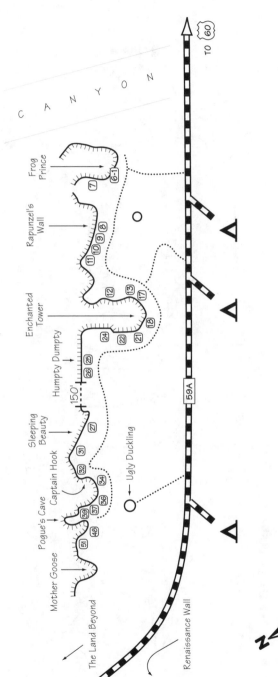

ENCHANTED TOWER
CLIFF OVERVIEW

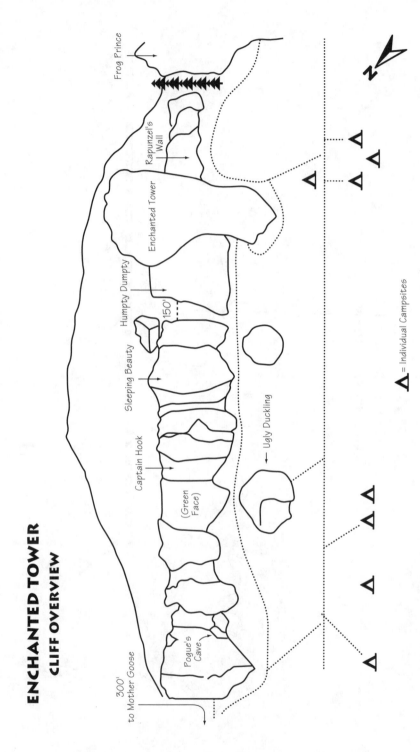

Frog Prince

Rapunzel's Wall

Enchanted Tower

Humpty Dumpty

Sleeping Beauty

150'

Captain Hook

(Green Face)

Ugly Duckling

Pogue's Cave

300'
to Mother Goose

N

△ = Individual Campsites

The canyon lies above 8,000' in the rugged Datil Mountains. April through October offers the best climbing weather. April and May bring mild, warm days with occasional wind. Summer afternoons can be hot on the west-facing cliff, with highs in the 80s and low 90s. Plan on rising early in the morning for your daily route quota. Heavy thunderstorms can occur on summer afternoons. Autumn days are great, with highs in the 70s and cool nights. It's possible to climb here in winter, although snow can block the access road and turn it muddy. Only sunny afternoons are climbable. March is somewhat unpredictable. Plan on cold nights and warm afternoons.

The Enchanted Tower climbing area, reached by a one-lane dirt road off U.S. Highway 60 northwest of Datil, is divided into several sectors. This guide includes the main, easily accessible sectors above the campground. The area's comprehensive guide can direct climbers to other cliffs and routes. All the cliffs are easily and quickly reached via climber's paths from pullouts along the road. The trails below the tower are in dire need of trail design and work before the hillside erodes away.

The Enchanted Tower itself is the centerpiece. It's an abrupt, obvious prow that looms over the camping area and access road. It features long, strenuous routes that range from 5.11 to 5.13. Up and right is Rapunzel's Wall, a short cliff with several bolted moderate lines. About 100 yards farther right or south is The Frog Prince area with the excellent Training Wall. This short, over-hanging wall offers some great 5.12 and 5.13 power climbs. The cliff band north of the Tower yields some popular walls, including The Sleeping Beauty Wall with six routes and Pogue's Cave area. Below the cave and above the road is a 35' boulder, The Ugly Duckling, with a fun 5.9 bolted jug-haul route on its south face. The Mother Goose area near the cliff's north end features good bouldering and routes in the 5.8 to 5.10 range.

The *Child of Light,* currently New Mexico's hardest route at 5.14a, lies north of the main cliffs on the Renaissance Wall on the west side of the canyon. The route works up the overhanging black streak near the wall's center. Glue to reinforce holds and a prosthetic edge constructed to replace a broken hold were employed to establish this Tim Fairfield creation. Easy to find and worth a visit is the Land Beyond, about 1.5 miles farther north of the main cliff band. About twenty short and difficult routes are found here. This crag is on the left or west side of the canyon, 0.3 mile past a windmill.

Trip Planning Information

Area description: The Enchanted Tower and its satellite crags offer some of New Mexico's best sport routes on steep bolted cliffs composed of a coarse welded volcanic tuff.

Location: West-central New Mexico. About 70 miles west of Socorro and Interstate 25.

Camping: Excellent primitive campsites are found throughout Thompson Canyon. The best and most popular sites are among the shady ponderosa pines below the tower. Use established sites whenever possible. Practice low-impact camping. Fires are discouraged to minimize impact. Bring water. Developed sites administered by the BLM are at Datil Wells Campground 5 miles east of the canyon off US 60 just west of Datil. Water is available here.

Climbing season: Enchanted Tower lies at 8,000'. Snow and cold temperatures are common in winter. Late March to early November offer the most climbing days. April, May, September, and October are best.

Restrictions and access issues: The climbing area lies in the Cibola National Forest. No restrictions on climbing are presently in place. The dirt access road is accessible to passenger cars. Wet conditions, however, can make access difficult. The cliffs are an important nesting site for some endangered birds; avoid developing routes or hiking in the various side canyons that serve as the area's last undisturbed nesting sites. Important months for nesting are May through August. Hunting activity is heavy during the fall months. Be mindful of where you hike and wear bright clothing. As with other soft rock sport climbing areas in New Mexico, Enchanted Tower has experienced some hold enhancement. The friable rock and sharp edges make this an attractive and easy practice. Beyond the ethical debate lies the specter that these practices will influence future access and management policies. Please act responsibly when visiting.

Guidebook: *The Enchanted Tower, Sport Climbing Socorro and Datil, New Mexico* by Solomon Maestas and Matthew Jones, 1993.

Nearby mountain shops, guide services, and gyms: None.

Services: Datil offers limited services including a restaurant, gas station, and grocery store. Full services are in Socorro. Being self-sufficient is the best way to visit the Tower.

Emergency services: The nearest phone is in Datil at the Post Office a half block north of US 60. The State Police number is 1-800-922-9221. Call (505)-773-4600 for an ambulance. The nearest hospital is in Socorro 70 miles east.

Nearby climbing areas: The Socorro Box is 8 miles west of Socorro. An undeveloped area with potential for climbing is Water Canyon, about 15 miles west of Socorro on US 60. Turn left (south) on a paved road and drive about 8 miles to the rocks visible from the highway. Good developed camping in Forest Service sites and beautiful scenery complement this area.

Nearby attractions: The Very Large Array, a radio telescope consisting of 27 separate antennas, is about 15 miles east of Datil on US 60 (self-guided tour and visitor center). Also, Mineralogical Museum (on the campus of New Mexico Tech in Socorro) and Bosque Del Apache National Wildlife Refuge (14 miles south of Socorro on I-25). Other attractions include the Quebradas Back Country Byway, Kelly ghost town, Gila National Forest, and El Malpais National Monument.

Finding the cliffs: Enchanted Tower is located in Thompson Canyon in Cibola National Forest about 7 miles northwest of the village of Datil. From the west, take US 60 from Arizona to Datil. From I-25 in Socorro, turn west on US 60 on the south side of Socorro. Drive west 62 miles to Datil. From the blinking traffic light in Datil, continue west on US 60 for 5.2 miles to a right turn (north) onto a dirt road. Drive 0.8 mile to a sharp curve to the left just before a ranch house. This is Forest Road 59A with a sign "Thompson Canyon" a short distance into the canyon. Drive 1.8 miles up the one-lane dirt road to Enchanted Tower.

THE FROG PRINCE WALL

This cliff lies 100 yards right or south of Enchanted Tower. Two trails reach the cliff. A trail leads east from the road. The other contours south from the Tower to the base of the crag. The Training Wall, a short overhanging wall that faces west, is the obvious right wall.

1. **White Queen** (5.13b/c) 6 bolts plus anchors. Follow line of bolts up the right side of The Training Wall to anchors just over the lip. Go left at 2nd bolt to the 2-bolt anchor on *White Knight* for 5.12c/d variation.

2. **White Knight** (5.12c/d) Variation. move left at 3rd bolt of *White Queen*.

3. **Red Queen** (5.13b/c) Variation. Move right at 4th bolt of *Through The Looking Glass*.

4. **Through The Looking Glass** (5.12c) The middle line of bolts. Good pockets and position. Go right at the 3rd bolt and up to anchors on *White Queen* for 5.13b/c variation.

5. **The Frog Prince** (a.k.a. **Babies**) (5.12a) 6 bolts plus anchors. Short, steep, powerful. Excellent route.

6. **Gollum** (5.11b/c) 3 bolts plus anchors. Steep jug haul up left side of wall.

7. **Blind Man's Bluff** (5.11b/c) Located around and up from the left end of the rock near a large ponderosa pine. 4 bolts plus anchor. Somewhat loose.

FROG PRINCE WALL

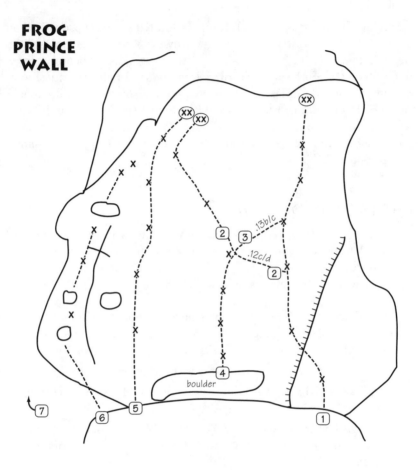

RAPUNZEL'S WALL

A short 40' cliff with moderate routes. Located above and right of the Tower.

8. **Rapunzel's Revenge** (5.8) 4 bolts up the black streak to lowering anchors.

9. **Fee Fi Fo Fum** (5.9) 4 bolts to anchors.

10. **The Thorn Bush** (5.10a) 4 bolts to anchors. Up right side of groove.

11. **The Blind Prince** (5.10a) 4 bolts, finish at anchors of *Blind Man's Bluff*. Fun climbing up steep wall right of groove and above small cave.

ENCHANTED TOWER
RAPUNZEL'S WALL

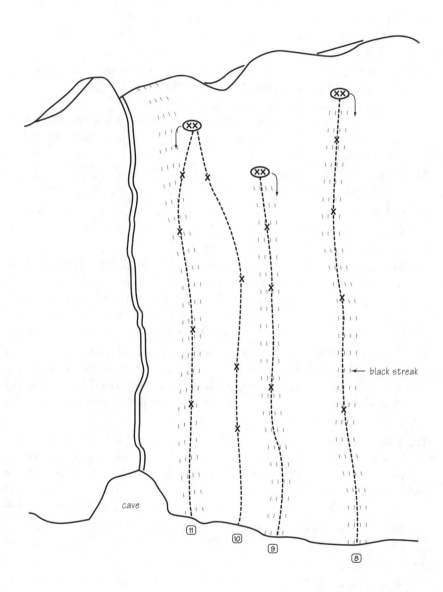

black streak

cave

⑪   ⑩   ⑨   ⑧

THE ENCHANTED TOWER

The area's classic crag. Be prepared for long, strenuous pitches. A 200' rope is useful on many routes. Descent: Walk off from top, lower using the intermediate anchors, or use a 2-rope rappel.

12. **Shipwrecked** (5.12c/d) A great pocket climb up the tower's steep southeast-facing wall. The upper headwall is superb and exposed. 8 bolts to 2-bolt anchor.

13. **Golden Stairs** (5.11b/c) This route climbs the sunny southwest face up a black streak. Begin near left side of face. Difficult face climbing up to 4th bolt then up right on easier climbing past 6 bolts to a 2-bolt anchor. Lower from here or continue to top. Easier left of the black streaks, more difficult between them. **Descent:** Rap with 2 ropes from anchors just below summit.

14. **Medusa** (5.12b) Climb first 6 bolts of *Golden Stairs*, then up left past 4 bolts to 2-bolt belay/lowering station.

15. **Goliath** (5.13a/b) A difficult directissima up the exposed prow. Ascend *Ripped's* 1st pitch. Continue up the wildly exposed prow to 2-bolt anchor. **Descent:** 2-rope rappel from here.

16. **Ripped Van Winkle** (5.12d) A super classic line near the exposed prow edge. **Pitch 1:** start up *Golden Stairs*, after 4 bolts angle up left, then straight up past 5 bolts to 2-bolt belay. **Pitch 2:** go left around arete onto west face. Continue past 5 more bolts to 2-bolt anchor. **Descent:** 2-rope rappel to ground from here. The route can be done in 1 pitch with a 200' rope.

17. **Zee Wicked Witch** (5.12c) This line climbs the northwest face just left of prow. Climb past the first 6 bolts on *Golden Stairs* onto the west face. Work up and over the left end of large roof, then past 4 bolts on upper headwall to 2-bolt anchor. **Pitch 2:** go up and right to join the upper part of *Ripped Van Winkle*.

18. **The Mad Hatter** (5.12d/13a) **Pitch 1:** 5 bolts over the small roofs at the base of Tower's West Face, to a large roof with holes on its left side; up right to join *Zee Wicked Witch*. **Pitch 2:** go up and right of an obvious black streak to a 2-bolt anchor. The climb can be done in 1 long pitch with the midway station useful for back-cleaning. 12 bolts.

19. **Rubber Mission** (5.12d) 6 bolts to a 2-bolt, chained, lowering anchor. 60'.

20. **Jabberwocky** (5.12b) Start on the right end of the shelf on the West Face, up and over the large roof, then past 7 more bolts to 2-bolt lowering station; 85'. Stay to the left of the black streak at the top.

SOUTHEAST FACE OF ENCHANTED TOWER

WEST FACE OF ENCHANTED TOWER

21. **Rumplestiltskin** (5.11d) About 15' left of *Jabberwocky*. 10 bolts up and over the small roof below the narrow black streak, then up and to the right of the black streak. 2-bolt lowering anchors at top.

22. **Once Upon a Time** (5.11c) Not pictured. Begin at common start for *Jabberwocky* and *Rumplestiltskin*. Traverse right above 3rd bolt to the bottom of the black streak. An intermediate belay can be established here. 2-bolt lowering anchor at top. 9 bolts.

23. **Tinkerbell's Nightmare** (5.12b) Not pictured. Located between *Rumplestiltskin* and *Technowitch*. 10 bolts to 2-bolt lowering anchor.

24. **Technowitch** (5.12a/b) Farthest left climb on the Tower. Move up left from the 3rd bolt of *Tinkerbell's Nightmare*. 5 more bolts lead to a 2-bolt lowering anchor.

HUMPTY DUMPTY WALL

Not pictured. The wall to the left of and joined to the Tower. Two routes on the left end of the wall.

25. **Humpty Dumpty** (5.12a/b) Right side of wall. 4 bolts to cold shut lowering anchors.

26. **Bambi** (5.11b) Fun route up steep wall left of *Humpty Dumpty*. 4 bolts. Lower from 1 cold shut and a wired nut.

SLEEPING BEAUTY WALL

Located left of the Tower just past a prominent low-angle break in the cliff.

27. **Cheshire Cat** (5.10b) 4 bolts and 2-bolt lowering anchor just right of a black streak.

28. **Tarred and Feathered** (5.10d) 4 bolts up the black streak to 2-bolt lowering anchor.

29. **Sleeping Beauty** (5.11d) First route left of black streak. 5 bolts, shares anchors with *Glass Coffin*.

30. **Glass Coffin** (5.11a/b R) 3 bolts with ground-fall potential. Can be toproped by leading *Sleeping Beauty* first.

31. **Poison Apple** (5.11b) 5 bolts plus anchors. Use the crack on the right or come in from the left to start.

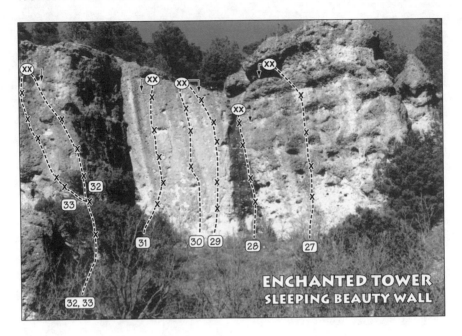

ENCHANTED TOWER
SLEEPING BEAUTY WALL

32. **Sea Hag** (5.11c) 7 bolts plus anchors. Around the corner and left of *Poison Apple*.

33. **Unknown** (5.11+) Clip first 2 bolts of *Sea Hag*, then up and left.

CAPTAIN HOOK AREA

Located above and right of The Ugly Duckling boulder.

34. **Unknown** (5.12a) 4 bolts plus 2-bolt anchor. Up small huecos in the second black streak right of an inset dihedral.

35. **Captain Hook** (5.11a) Overhanging face just left of the inset dihedral. Joins *Peter Pan Flies Again* and shares anchors.

36. **Peter Pan Flies Again** (5.11b) 3 bolts plus anchors. Start on top of choss rock, then straight up to anchors.

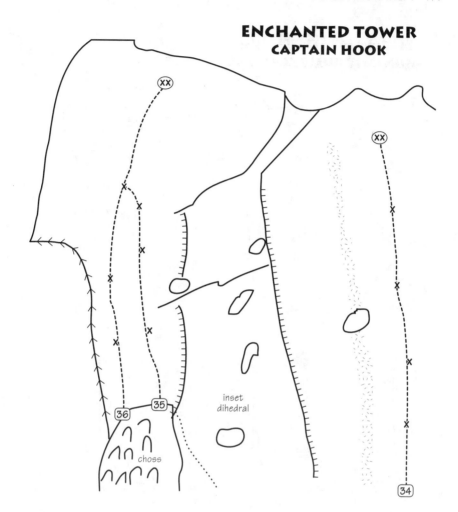

ENCHANTED TOWER
CAPTAIN HOOK

MIDNIGHT PUMPKIN WALL

Located left of *Captain Hook* area and above The Ugly Duckling rock. 3 routes from right to left.

37. Glass Slipper (5.11d) 3 bolts and shared anchors with *Cinderella's Nightmare*. Climb past a bulging ledge, then up the right-hand black streak.

38. Cinderella's Nightmare (5.11c) 4 bolts plus cold shut anchors.

39. Midnight Pumpkin (5.11d) 3 bolts up the left black streak. No anchors.

ENCHANTED TOWER
MIDNIGHT PUMPKIN WALL

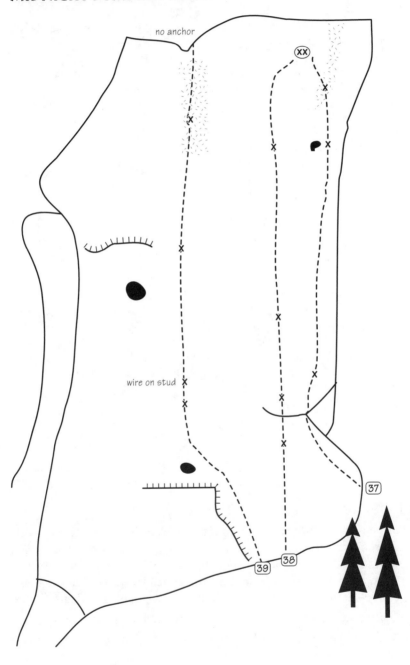

no anchor

wire on stud

POGUE'S CAVE AREA

Located near the left or north end of the main climbing area. The area's second greatest concentration of routes is found here. All routes are worth climbing.

40. **Blessed and Blissed** (5.12a) 5 bolts plus anchors.
41. **Merlin's Mantra** (5.11a) 4 bolts plus anchors.
42. **Ooey Gooey** (5.11a) 5 bolts plus anchors.
43. **Party Pogues** (5.12a) 5 bolts plus anchor.
44. **Pogue's Arete** (5.12a) 3 bolts, shares anchor with *Party Pogues.*
45. **Unknown** (5.10c) 4 bolts plus anchors.
46. **Unknown** (5.11b) 5 bolts plus anchors.
47. **Unknown** (5.11) 7 bolts plus anchors. Watch for loose rock.
48. **Never Never Land** (5.11b) 8 bolts plus anchors.
49. **Hooka** (5.11a) 7 bolts plus anchors.
50. **Unknown** (5.11c/d) 6 bolts plus anchors.
51. **Unknown** (5.11b/c) 4 bolts plus anchors.

SOCORRO BOX

OVERVIEW

The Socorro Box climbing area consists of five cliffs on the east and west sides of Box Canyon 6 miles west of Socorro on U.S. Highway 60. The area was developed by Bertrand Gramont, a visiting French geology graduate student at New Mexico Tech, and other locals in the late 1980s. The crags were the first sport climbing venues established in this part of the state. After the subsequent discovery of Enchanted Tower farther west, the crags saw little new activity and are seldom visited except by traveling climbers passing by. Many worthwhile routes, however, are found here, including New Mexico's second hardest route, *Keeping Up With the Joneses* (5.13d). A Palomas Peak route, *Snake Dance* (5.13d), climbed in 1995, also shares this distinction.

Moderate sport routes in the 5.10 to 5.11 range are plentiful here along with some excellent bouldering. Most of the routes are bolted, although some require the placement of gear for protection. The Box's rhyolite rock provides climbs that range from 20' to 100' long on a fine-grained, hard volcanic rock. Sharp edges and small positive holds on steep to overhanging face routes are characteristic of the area.

The Waterfall Wall, the canyon's first bolted cliff, is directly across from the parking area on the canyon floor. It's now a popular toprope crag. All the bolts on the wall were removed by first-ascensionist Gramont to equip his new routes at Enchanted Tower. The cliff features 18 toprope problems that range in difficulty from 5.5 to 5.12. The easier routes ascend the right or south side of the cliff, while the left or north side offers harder lines, including two 5.12s.

To the south and about 150 yards uphill from the Waterfall Wall is the Fillet a Papillon Wall, a sport climber's nirvana with many difficult and over-hanging bolt-protected routes. One of the best recommended routes on the crag is *Almost Blue* (5.12c) up the obvious black streak on the left side of the cave. Lots of glue has been used to reinforce loose holds on this cliff.

Red Wall, with the canyon's longest routes, lies down the Box from the parking area and Waterfall Wall on the canyon's east side. The climbs, up to 2 pitches long, are 5.6 to 5.11 and mostly bolt-protected with occasional required gear placements. *TNT* (5.11+) is the recommended route. At the north end of the Red Wall is the Corner Block. This large triangular boulder offers five routes that all share the same 2-bolt anchor on top. Routes range from 5.8 to 5.11R. All routes can be led (placing some protection required) or toproped. Access to the top anchors is by scrambling up the back of the block.

The North Wall is the northern-most cliff in the canyon and the closest crag to the highway. Many routes are established on this generally shady wall that range from 5.7 to 5.12. Some fine bouldering is found on large blocks in this area as well.

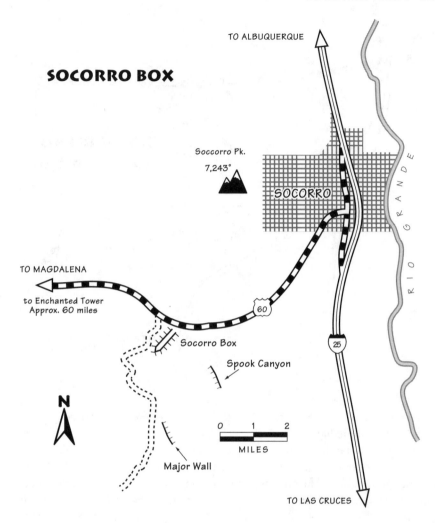

SOCORRO BOX

TO ALBUQUERQUE

Soccorro Pk.
7,243°

SOCORRO

RIO GRANDE

TO MAGDALENA

to Enchanted Tower
Approx. 60 miles

60

25

Socorro Box

Spook Canyon

N

0   1   2

MILES

Major Wall

TO LAS CRUCES

The so called "East Wall" lies directly north of the parking area on the west side of the canyon. A smattering of bolted routes, mostly 5.11s and 5.12s, work up overhanging choss on this loose, funky wall.

Less than 2 miles south from the main Box parking area are the Minor, Major, Pocket Change, and Alcohol walls. These areas are all worth a visit. Continue driving south from the parking area about 1 mile to Minor Wall and about 0.5 mile farther to Major Wall. A gate is across the road a short distance ahead. Both crags lie on dry slopes on the left or east side of the road. The Major Wall offers short routes ranging in difficulty from 5.7 to 5.13d. Uphill and to the north of Major Wall is Alcohol Wall. Many short, well-

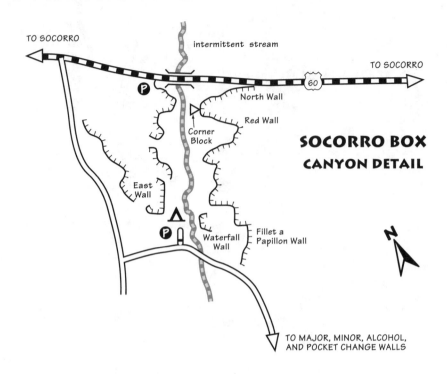

TO SOCORRO

intermittent stream

TO SOCORRO

60

North Wall

Red Wall

Corner Block

SOCORRO BOX

CANYON DETAIL

East Wall

Waterfall Wall

Fillet a Papillon Wall

N

TO MAJOR, MINOR, ALCOHOL, AND POCKET CHANGE WALLS

protected routes from 5.10 to 5.12 are found here. Good bouldering is also found in the immediate area.

Visitors may be disappointed at the initial impression of the rock here. It certainly is not one of New Mexico's most attractive crags, but the climbing is actually pretty good. The area does suffer from lots of glue reinforcement and some chipping. Check out the area as part of an Enchanted Tower trip. The bouldering alone is worth a stop. Try the overhanging wall, the "Streambed," on the north end of the canyon near the highway. The boulders near Waterfall Wall and Major Wall also offer good bouldering.

A rack of quickdraws augmented with wires, TCUs, and larger cam units up to 3.5" will suffice. A 150' rope is sufficient for most descents. Most routes are equipped with lowering anchors.

Trip Planning Information

Area description: The Socorro Box, a roadside crag, offers many short, difficult, bolt-protected sport routes. Many routes can be toproped.

Location: Central New Mexico, 6 miles west of Socorro.

Camping: Limited, undeveloped camping convenient to the crags can be found in the area. Fires are permitted but discouraged. There are no fees, wood, water, or sanitary facilities.

Climbing season: Early spring to early winter are best. High summer temperatures limit climbing time. The mild winter temperatures provide for many climbable days.

Restrictions and access issues: The area is administered by the Bureau of Land Management. No restrictions are currently in place.

Guidebook: *The Enchanted Tower, Sport Climbing Socorro and Datil, New Mexico* by Salomon Maestas and Matthew A. Jones, 1993. *A Climber's Guide to Box Canyon* by Erik Hufnagel and Bertrand Gramont is a well-done self-published effort that may be available from local climbers.

Nearby mountain shops, guide services, and gyms: None.

Services: Full tourist services in nearby Socorro.

Emergency services: Dial 911. The nearest phone to the crags is by the hospital. The hospital is near the western edge of town and visible when driving west on US 60 toward the Box.

Nearby climbing areas: The Enchanted Tower is 60 miles west. The Organ Mountains are 150 miles south. A small toprope area is located in San Jose Canyon about 65 miles south of Socorro. From Interstate 25, turn west at the Redrock exit and go about 1.5 miles to the Old Pankey Ranch House. Stop here and ask permission from Mr. Rex Klietz to climb.

Nearby attractions: The Bosque Del Apache Wildlife refuge is about 14 miles south of Socorro off I-25. Also see information in the Enchanted Tower section.

Finding the crags: The Socorro Box, a.k.a. Box Canyon, is about 7.2 miles west of Socorro off US 60 on the south side of the highway. Turn left on a dirt road just after crossing a bridge that spans the canyon. The crags are visible to your left when crossing the bridge. Drive about 0.5 mile on the dirt road, take the first left, and park at road's end as it circles left into the canyon. The popular toprope Waterfall Wall is across from the parking area to the east. Just to the south and uphill about 150 yards is the Fillet a Papillon Wall. The Red Wall and North Wall are farther down-canyon on the east side. Out of sight and about 1 mile farther south of the rough dirt road leaving the parking area are Minor Wall, Major Wall, Alcohol Wall, and Pocket Change Wall.

WATERFALL WALL

This is a popular toprope area. Runners are required for easily reached anchors. Routes generally get harder moving right to left on the cliff.

FILLET A PAPILLON WALL

Uphill and to the right of the Waterfall Wall. Many routes have glue-reinforced holds. Avoid climbing the fourth bolted line from the right (south) end. This route ends at a 2-bolt anchor and starts with an unsafe bolt placed in a hollow flake. Some of the routes here start with a variation out of the cave near the cliff's left (north) end.

1. **New Kids On the Block** (5.10+) 4 bolts and shared anchors. Ends on a ledge.
2. **Little Caterpillar** (5.12b) 4 bolts to anchors for *New Kids on the Block.*
3. **Bob Marley Meets Master Ganj** (5.11b) Glued flake near middle.
4. **Not recommended** (Unsafe bolt).
5. **If You Can't Do it, Glue It** (project).
6. **Dreadlock Holiday** (project).
7. **Red Tag Sale** (5.11b to middle anchors, 5.12b to top).
8. **Window Shopping** (5.12b/c) Starts inside the cave. Use bolts on the right. 9 bolts. Traverse right at top to anchors for *Red Tag Sale.*
9. **Fair Trade** (5.13c) Starts inside cave. Clip first 2 bolts on right then left across the lip to a bolt over the lip. 7 bolts and anchors.

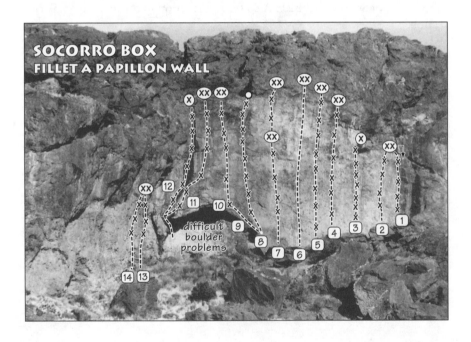

SOCORRO BOX
FILLET A PAPILLON WALL

10. **Insider Trader** (5.13c) Starts inside cave. Clip 2 bolts just left of right-most bolts, then bolt over lip (same as *Fair Trade*). Finish up *Fair Trade*. 3 difficult boulder problems can be protected by using the bolts inside the cave then lowering from bolts over the lip.

11. **Sinister Dane** (5.13c) Start on left side of cave. Climb up right past 3 bolts to a bolt over the lip. 5 more bolts lead to anchors.

12. **Almost Blue** (5.12c) Climb the black streak on the left end of the rock. 6 bolts to 1 cold shut.

13. **Uncle Fester Gets Sent to Europe** (5.12a/b) A long name for a short route. 3 bolts to cold shuts.

14. **Uncle Fester Gets Sent in Europe** (5.12c) Ditto above. Shares 3rd bolt and anchors.

RED WALL

This is the tallest crag in the canyon. Most routes terminate at about mid-height and require placing some protection.

15. **Lucid Fairyland** (5.10) A short route on the right end of the rock. Go right at second bolt. 4 bolts and shared anchors.

16. **Unnamed** (5.8) Same start as *Lucid Fairyland*, then left at 2nd bolt.

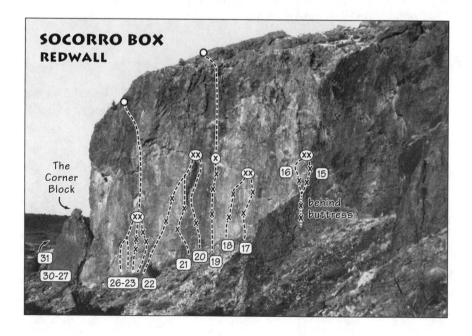

17. **Monkey Business** (5.11a) Clip 2 old fixed pins then over the roof. Gear protects the roof. Chained anchor.

18. **Unnamed** (5.10) 2 bolts on the face left of *Monkey Business*. Shares anchors.

19. **Spiderman** (5.7) Not recommended. Loose. 2 pitches. It is possible to escape to the left after the 3rd bolt. Clip 3 bolts and bring some gear if you must climb this one. 1 bolt anchor that can be backed up with gear at the top.

20. **Redwall** (5.7) Climb the dihedral with bolts and gear for protection. Best to lower from the spacious ledge or traverse right and finish up the 2nd pitch of *Spiderman*.

21. **Earwig** (5.9+) Start under the dihedral then past 2 bolts left then up to the anchors for *Redwall*. Gear placements necessary.

22. **The Diagonal** (5.9) Groundfall potential. 2 bolts only. Gear placements difficult. Shares anchors with *Redwall*.

23. **Molotov Cocktail** (5.11a) 2 bolts and anchors on a bulging face. 1st bolt is above crux.

24. **TNT** (5.11+) Climb over the bulge past 2 bolts to shared anchors with *Molotov Cocktail*.

25. **Gun Powder** (5.10c) Protect the seam with gear then right to *TNT* anchors.

26. **Hawk's Nest** (5.7) Climb the right-trending dihedral to anchors for *TNT*. Continue up left to a tree anchor.

CORNER BLOCK

Located between the Red Wall and the North Wall on the east side of the canyon. All routes can be led or toproped from a 2-bolt anchor shared by all routes. Access anchors by climbing the back of the block.

27. **Unnamed** (5.8) Toprope variation.

28. **Nowhere to Go** (5.10+) 2 bolts plus gear placements.

29. **No Bozos** (5.11) 3 bolts.

30. **Last Tango** (5.11R) Runout near the bottom.

31. **Pluto** (5.9) On the north side of the block. Gear placements, no bolts.

SOCORRO BOX
CORNER BLOCK

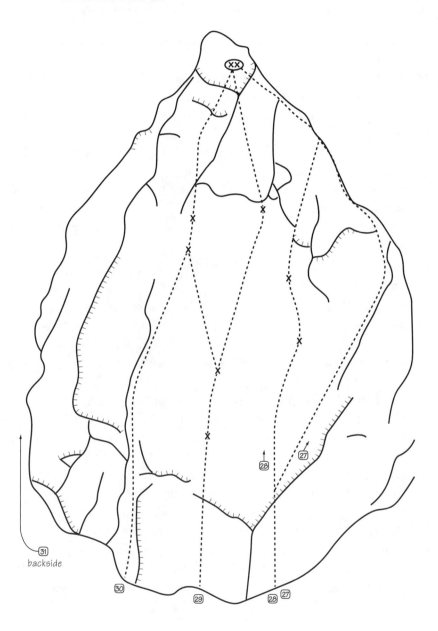

NORTH WALL

This cliff lies at the far north end of the Box just south of the highway. Access it by parking in the lot and working north down the streambed to the cliff. This site offers some good climbing and decent bouldering.

32. **Liposuction Massacre** (5.10+) Start behind the Corner Block. 4 bolts and chained anchor.

33. **The Truth** (5.7) Start on a slab then left past anchors to a crack. No bolts, gear placements required.

34. **Direct on The Truth** (5.9) A short difficult crack start to *The Truth*. Gear placements required.

35. **Alarm Arm** (5.11+) Steep climbing to a 2-bolt anchor. Gear placements required.

36. **Maria de la Sangria** (5.11+) Climb past fixed pins on a short overhanging face to an anchor.

37. **Unnamed** (5.11) Fixed pins plus bolts protect an overhanging seam to anchors.

38. **Boss Hog** (5.12a/b) 7 bolts plus anchors.

39. **Rock Trooper** (5.9) 1 bolt, no anchor. Loose.

40. **Black Crack** (5.10+) No bolts. Climb the right-leaning crack.

41. **Arch of Evil** (5.10+) Start up *Black Crack,* then left across a large black streak to a bolt. Continue past 1 more bolt to the top and anchors.

42. **Grease Mechanic** (5.12-) Start left of the black streak. Straight up past 5 bolts to shared anchors.

43. **Box Baby** (5.10b) Climb up right to the 3rd bolt of *Grease Mechanic*. Finish on *Grease Mechanic*.

44. **Modern Day Contrivances** (5.11+) Start same as *Box Baby*, then left at 3rd bolt of *Grease Mechanic* past 2 bolts to shared anchors.

45. **Box Frenzy** (5.10a) Same start as *Box Baby*. Climb straight up and move right near top past 2 bolts to shared anchors.

46. **Totem** (5.7) Same start as *Box Frenzy*. Climb straight up to the top following crack system. No bolts, no anchor, gear placements required.

47. **Tomahawk** (5.9) No bolts, no anchor, gear placements required. Climb a crack to a roof, finish on the left-hand crack.

48. **The "Z" Crack** (5.8) No bolts, no anchor, gear placements required.

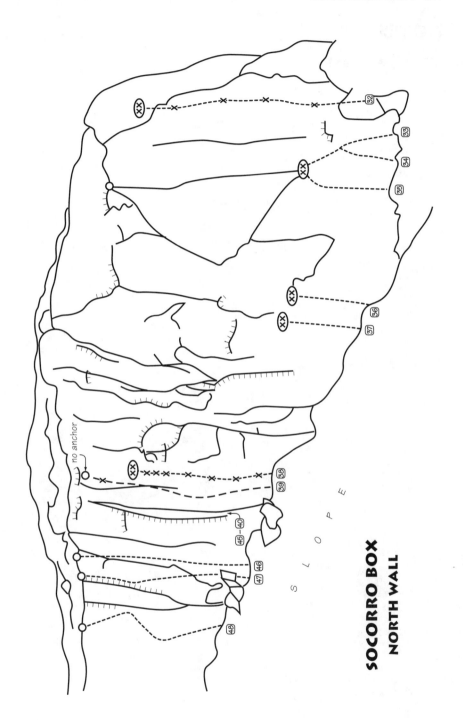

SOCORRO BOX
NORTH WALL

NOTES

Southern New Mexico

REGION

LAS CRUCES AREA

ORGAN MOUNTAINS

OVERVIEW

Adventure climbing in a pure traditional sense is what visiting rock climbers can expect to find in southern New Mexico's rugged Organ Mountains. A flashlight or headlamp is always carried by experienced Organ climbers in anticipation of the usual late return due to the rugged, forced-march approaches, long multi-pitch routes, and devious scrambling descents that are the hallmarks of climbing in this complex mountain range.

The Organ Mountains, a 20-mile ridge of spires and rough peaks, form an immense, ragged skyline above Las Cruces and the Rio Grande valley. Topped by 9,012' Organ Needle, the range stretches south from 5,719' San Augustine

WEST SIDE OF ORGAN MOUNTAINS

Paul Drakos on the airy third pitch of *Tooth or Consequences* (III 5.10) The Tooth, Organ Mountains, New Mexico. *Photo by Jim Graham.*

Pass to the Franklin Mountains on the Texas border. This massive uplifted fault block rears almost 5,000' above the surrounding lowland valleys. Granite composes most of the Organs, although snatches of sedimentary and volcanic rocks appear on its lower elevation fringes. A lot of mining took place in the northern part of the range in the latter half of the 19th century, yielding rich deposits of lead, silver, gold, zinc, and copper.

This wild, desolate range, once an enclave of the Apache Indians, was originally named *La Sierra de la Soledad* or Mountains of Solitude by the Spanish who trekked past the range along El Camino Royal en route to Santa Fe. The ruggedness of the Organ Mountains still preserves the area's solitude and wilderness character. Despite its proximity to Las Cruces, no roads (save U.S. Highway 70 over San Augustin Pass) and few trails cross the lofty range. The Wheeler Survey, which explored the sierra in the 1870s, described them as "lofty, rugged, and inaccessible." This description still rings true today.

Climbing history: The first recorded climb in the Organs was in 1904 when two college students from Las Cruces scaled Organ Needle, the range high point, and planted a flag on the summit. German rocket scientists, brought to nearby Fort Bliss after World War II, initiated the first mountaineering of the Organ Mountains over 50 years ago. These early pioneers were driven by the tradition of reaching the summits of the sierra's many granite spires. Later efforts concentrated on the more difficult faces found in canyons and on rugged slopes on the range's west side. Difficult routes were established on Southern Comfort Wall, The Citadel, and The Tooth.

Dick Ingraham, Jim Graham, Ed Ward, Mark Motes, and Karl Kaiser are long-time activists responsible for many routes. Jim Graham has been leading the effort to replace many of the 1/4" bolts found on the more popular climbs. These three excellent crags continue to attract the bulk of the area's climbing attention. Recent development has been concentrated on The Citadel, Wedge, and Lesser Spire.

Except for a small local climbing community, the Organs see very little climbing activity. Assistance from locals in locating trails and other route information is often sought by visitors. Trails to the cliffs are obscure and require careful hiking and navigating across the rugged desert landscape. Once on the rocks, climbers must utilize many of the traditional skills of rock climbing for a successful outing. On all but the shorter, modern climbs, creative gear placements and route-finding skills are necessary. Proper preparation and the ability to self-rescue is also required. Any emergency here that requires outside assistance is usually an involved and difficult affair. The routes in the Organ Mountains are not underrated.

Use caution when climbing here, and always err on the side of good judgment. The Organs are probably not a good beginner area. Even the moderate routes require good climbing skills and many are long multi-pitch lines that require expertise in placing protection and setting up belay and rappel stations.

Climbers should be prepared for a long day whenever venturing into the Organs, particularly if you're a first-time visitor. The crags, access trails, and descent routes all take time to locate. Lots of water is a must in this arid climate. A good starting point is two quarts per person per day. Hot weather may require more water. Don't plan on finding any water here. If any is located, purify it before drinking. Other Organ essentials include a headlamp for the often necessary night descent. A space blanket and some extra clothes and food will make any forced bivy more tolerable. You should be able to avoid any epics on the described routes if you start early, climb efficiently, and monitor the daylight.

Rack: Carry a wide variety of gear including sets of RPs, wired stoppers, and Friends. Extra sizes in the mid-ranges are good to bring. Bring lots of slings of various lengths and about twelve quickdraws. Bring some extra webbing to back up old rappel slings. Use caution whenever climbing or rappelling with existing fixed gear and bolts. Many old 1/4" bolts are found, although some rappel stations are retro-fitted with 3/8" bolts and chains. Climbing with two ropes on most multi-pitch routes is generally best in the Organs. Double-rope technique may alleviate rope drag on long, circuitous pitches. Double ropes are also needed on many rappels.

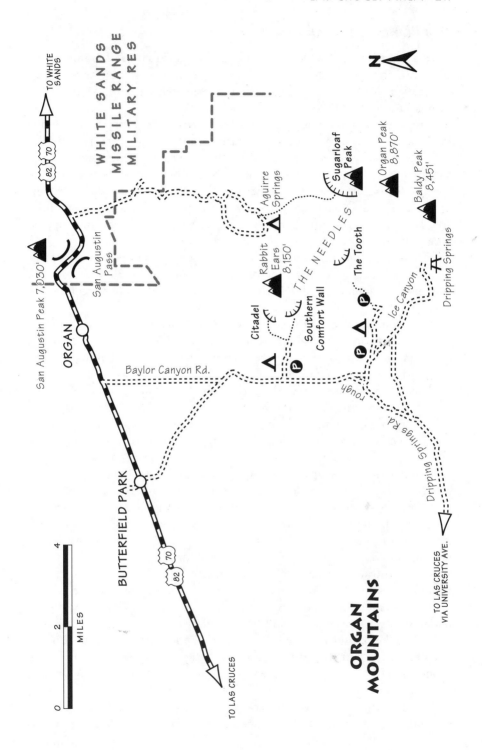

TO WHITE SANDS

WHITE SANDS MISSILE RANGE MILITARY RES

N

82 70

San Augustin Peak 7,030'

San Augustin Pass

ORGAN

Aguirre Springs

Sugarloaf Peak

Organ Peak 8,870'

Baldy Peak 8,451'

Rabbit Ears 8,150'

THE NEEDLES

The Tooth

Dripping Springs

Citadel

Southern Comfort Wall

Ice Canyon

Baylor Canyon Rd.

Fough

Dripping Springs Rd.

BUTTERFIELD PARK

82 70

TO LAS CRUCES

TO LAS CRUCES VIA UNIVERSITY AVE.

ORGAN MOUNTAINS

0   2   4

MILES

Trip Planning Information

Area description: The Organ Mountains, a rugged range of granite spires and faces, offers excellent traditional, multi-pitch routes in remote settings.

Location: South-central New Mexico. Immediately east of Las Cruces and 40 miles north of El Paso.

Camping: Any level spot along the access roads to the Topp Hut or Modoc Mine can serve as a camp site. The nearby Doña Ana Mountains also offer lots of free, undeveloped camping. Wherever you camp, bring your own water, do not build fires, do haul out all trash, and bury human waste. Aguirre Springs Recreation Area offers 56 developed campsites. No water. Restrooms on site. Fees and time restrictions apply. The only drinking water in the entire area is at the Cox Visitor Center on the west side at the end of Dripping Springs Road.

Climbing season: Year-round. The range rarely receives snow but routes with a southern exposure are the best choice during colder winter months. Summer days are hot and dry. Early morning starts and shady north faces are best bets.

Restrictions and access issues: The Organ Mountains are administered by the Bureau of Land Management. Most of the climbing areas are in a wilderness study area. The only present restriction is no motorized bolting.

Guidebook: Dick Ingraham, a local climbing pioneer, has been compiling information on the area since the early 1960s. His guide is available at the New Mexico State University Library or sometimes from Bikes Plus at the corner of Lohman and Solano in Las Cruces. Local climbers are a valuable resource willing to share copies and other information about the area. *Rock and Ice* issue 48 featured a guide to the Organ and Doña Ana Mountains.

Nearby mountain shops, guide services, and gyms: Las Cruces.

Services: Food, fuel, and lodging are available in Las Cruces.

Emergency services: Call 911. Memorial Medical Center in Las Cruces.

Nearby climbing areas: Hueco Tanks State Historical Park (70 miles southeast), City of Rocks State Park (80 miles west). The nearby Dona Ana Mountains offer excellent bouldering, cragging, and camping.

Nearby attractions: Las Cruces and nearby Mesilla historical sites, the Gadsden Museum, Fort Selden State Monument, White Sands National Monument, and Ciudad de Juarez in Mexico. Visitors should inquire about entry requirements before entering old Mexico, although generally a visit is simple.

Finding the crags: Climbing is found on both the east and west sides of the mountains. The best climbing on the east side is on Sugarloaf. Sugarloaf is the prominent 800' white granite spire visible looking south from the east side of San Augustin Pass.

The majority of climbing is found on the west side of the mountains and is visible from Las Cruces. Popular rocks include The Citadel, Southern Comfort Wall, The Tooth, and The Wedge.

Trailheads for The Citadel and Southern Comfort wall start from the Topp Hut Road, and the trailhead for The Tooth and The Wedge start from the Modoc Mine Road. Both roads, neither of which is signed, are accessed from the Baylor Canyon Road that parallels the Organs' west side. Baylor Canyon Road can be accessed from US 70 about 10 miles east of its junction with I-25. This is just west of the small village of Organ. Baylor Canyon Road is also accessed by University Avenue east out of Las Cruces. Drive about 7 miles east on University Ave. to the well-marked left turn for Baylor Canyon Road. Refer to each crag's description for trail directions.

THE CITADEL

The Citadel, a 400' crag perched on the west side of the Organ Mountains, offers a good selection of moderate climbs on its north face. Some routes go to the summit, but most parties choose to descend after 1 or 2 pitches. Many of the 1/4" bolts have been replaced with 3/8" bolts and descent anchors have been added. Caution is advised when relying on the occasional 1/4" variety. *Glad You Came*, (5.9) a 1-pitch bolt-protected face climb, and *Wish You Were Here* (5.8) are area classics. Equally recommendable are *Hercamur Snurd* (5.11) and *Finger Zinger* (5.10+), a bolt-protected, classic Organ face climb. Some climbers choose to tackle only the first 2 pitches of *Hercamur Snurd* at 5.9 and rappel from a 2-bolt anchor.

The approach is relatively easy for this fine crag. Follow the above directions to Baylor Canyon Road. If approaching from the east or west via US 70, turn south on Baylor Canyon Road a little west of the village of Organ and drive 3.7 miles to the left turn onto the Topp Hut Road. This is just past the sixth cattle guard. This very rough road eventually gets to the Topp Hut but few will choose to drive this far. Several pullouts are handy for parking when you call it quits, then continue walking to the Topp Hut, a rock structure. Continue walking the road past the Hut for nearly a mile to a fork in the road. Go left a short distance to an abandoned mine. The trail to The Citadel starts above the mine tailings above and left of the mine. This relatively easy trail goes into Rabbit Ears Canyon. Climbing *Glad You Came* and *Hercamur Snurd* requires bushwhacking up the canyon to the east end of the crag and backtracking to the routes. Allow about 1 hour for this approach.

1. **Glad We Came** (5.9) 1 pitch. The arete on the northeast corner of the rock. A #3 Friend protects the bottom moves up to 8 bolts to descent anchors. Excellent climb.

2. **Wish You Were Here** (5.9) **Pitch 1:** Start in the dihedral to the right of *Glad We Came*. Traverse left near the top to belay from *Glad We Came's*

anchors. Descend from here or traverse right to the roof to a 2-bolt anchor. **Pitch 2:** Face climb (5.11) to a right-facing corner and belay above a roof. 2 moderate pitches reach the top from here. Most parties descend after the 1st pitch, although a fine route can be pieced together to the summit for the accomplished climber.

3. **Hercamur Snurd** (5.10-) About 150 yards right of *Glad We Came*. **Pitch 1:** Traverse left on mossy rock left of a gully onto a face. Climb steeply up on poor looking rock past 3 bolts (5.10-) to a fixed anchor. **Pitch 2:** Face climb (5.9) past a bolt and a fixed pin, then angle left via an awkward crack (5.10) to a 2-rope rappel station.

4. **The Whole Banana** (5.10) Difficult face climbing leads to a crack. Belay on a good ledge.

5. **Murray's Crack** (5.8) Carry large SLCDs for this large crack.

6. **Tugboat** (5.10) Toprope.

7. **Finger Zinger** (5.10c/d) Near the west end of the crag. Excellent bolt-protected face and edge climbing to fixed rappel anchors. Rappel from here or continue to the top via the *West Ridge* (5.6). Classic Organ face climbing.

8. **Anticipation** (5.9R) Runout near the bottom.

9. **West Ridge** (5.6) Adventure climbing to the top.

10. **The Nose** (5.9) Rappel from *Finger Zinger* anchors or continue up the *West Ridge*.

ORGAN MTNS.
NORTH FACE
OF CITADEL

ORGAN MTNS.
SOUTHERN COMFORT WALL

SOUTHERN COMFORT WALL

Southern Comfort Wall, featuring a relatively easy approach and a smattering of good routes, is worth a visit. The crag is popular with locals, especially during the winter and late fall.

To reach the trail to Southern Comfort Wall, follow the directions in "Finding the crags" to the left turn to the abandoned mine above the Topp Hut. Stay on the main road to the right at this junction until you reach a large white road cut. Leave the road here and slog up the slope on a well-defined trail to the base of a cliff. Southern Comfort Wall finally becomes visible after a short traverse up and right to the crag's left-hand side. Allow about 1 hour for this approach.

11. **Irish Cream** (5.10+) Not pictured. About 80' left of *Black Velvet* near the left end of the crag. **Pitch 1:** Up a right-leaning discontinuous hand crack, (#3 and #4 Friends very helpful) to a belay stance in a crack. **Pitch 2:** Climb right past a fixed pin (5.10), then up past 1 bolt and some unprotected 5.9 face climbing to a 2-bolt rappel anchor. 2-rope, 165' rappel. Several 5.7 and 5.8 routes are to the left.

12. **Lowenbrau Light** (5.7) **Pitch 1:** Start at large tree at base of *Black Velvet*, then up a left-facing corner system. Belay below a left-slanting short crack. **Pitch 2:** Face climb left or up the crack to where the crack bends right. Move up and left from here to gain the top. Scramble to fixed rappel anchors on the central wall for a 2-rope (165') rappel to the base.

13. **Black Velvet** (5.9) The prominent left-facing corner. **Pitch 1:** Start at the large oak tree and do a short 5.6 section right to reach the corner. Belay at a stance in the corner after a short blocky vertical section. **Pitch 2:** Go up the corner to where it bends right (5.9). Three choices from here: 1. Face climb (5.9) straight up past 2 bolts to the top; 2. Go right to a crack that traverses left under a large roof (5.7) and belay or take the 5.7 roof to the top; and 3. Continue traversing right (5.2) to anchors. If a belay is installed, one more rope-length of moderate climbing to the right reaches rappel anchors for the central wall. **Descent** from all variations is by a 2-rope (165') rappel from fixed anchors on the central wall.

14. **Margaritaville** (5.10-) **Pitch 1:** Up a left-facing corner (5.10-) right of *Black Velvet* to a bolted belay. **Pitch 2:** Continue straight up (5.9) to a belay. Traverse right to rappel anchors for the central wall.

15. **Hangover** (5.11R) About 200' right of *Black Velvet*. **Pitch 1:** Climb a thin, short crack, then face climb up and left (5.10-R) to a belay below an overhanging finger crack. **Pitch 2:** Right and up (5.11) on thin crack and face climbing, then right to a fourth-class section leading to the top.

THE TOOTH

The Tooth offers long quality routes. The requisite long steep approach ends at the best granite in the area. Locals agree that this is the best climbing on the west side.

To reach The Tooth follow directions to Baylor Canyon Road by driving east on University Avenue on the south side of Las Cruces. After about 7 miles, turn left (north) on Baylor Canyon Road and go about 0.5 mile to the right to an east turn onto the Modoc Mine Road. Take this road past the mine, through a gate, and park above the mine. This is a hideous road and you may choose not to drive all of it. Find the trail above the mine by walking right (east by southeast) down the road and then up a steep hill. At the hilltop the trail begins, going east on a short section of tire tracks, and then continues around the hillside to a large gully. Follow the trail across the large gully and then up to the base of The Tooth. Continue up the large gully to the base of the crag. Allow at least 1 hour for the approach. Plan for a minimum of 10 hours car to car.

Rack: A rack for The Tooth is a single set of camming units up to a #3 Friend and a good selection of wired nuts. The 1/4" bolts found here are more than 15 years old, so use caution and back them up whenever possible. Retro-bolting efforts are underway. Check with locals for current status of climbs.

Descent: To descend, rappel from fixed anchors just below the summit.

16. **Tooth Fairy** (III 5.10) Super route. **Pitch 1:** Start on low-angle slabs near the left (northern) edge of the rock. Climb a crack up toward a large triangular roof. After clipping the 1st bolt, (ignore the bolts going left), traverse about 20' to the right and belay at the right end of the roof. 1 bolt and gear placements can be found here. **Pitch 2:** Turn the roof and crack climb (5.9) past a bush, past a tree with rap anchors, then up to another tree and belay. **Pitch 3:** Face climb left to a 1/4" bolt, then up left to a finger crack (5.10). Belay at a 4-bolt anchor left of the slot where the crack widens. This is the crux pitch. **Pitch 4:** Climb a short crack (5.7) up past a bush to a belay ledge. Alternately, face climb (5.9) left with 2 bolts for protection to same belay ledge. **Pitch 5:** Crack and face climbing lead up to anchors below summit. Rappel from here. **Descent:** Multiple double-rope (165') rappels down the route. Super route.

17. **Tooth or Consequences** (III 5.10) Maybe the best route in the Organs. **Pitches 1 and 2:** Same as first 2 pitches of Tooth Fairy. Some prefer to belay at the first tree. **Pitch 3:** Traverse left onto face, then up left (5.10a/b) with widely spaced bolt protection to a bolted belay station. An airy, exposed, and exciting pitch. **Pitch 4:** Step right to a crack, over blocks, then face climb left near the formation's north edge (5.9+). Move back right to a 2-bolt belay. **Pitch 5:** Face climb past 2 bolts and 1 fixed pin to a crack and belay on a ledge. **Pitch 6:** Climb either the 5.7 crack on the left or the 5.9 crack on the right to belay and rap anchors shared by all 3 routes below the summit. **Descent:** Rappel the route or *Tooth Fairy.* 2 165' ropes necessary.

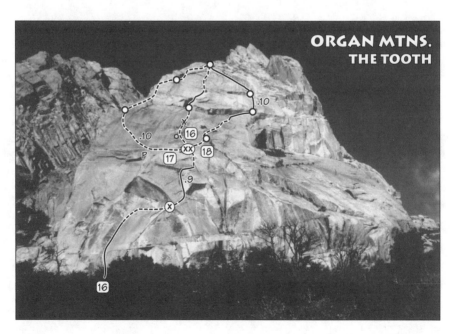

ORGAN MTNS.
THE TOOTH

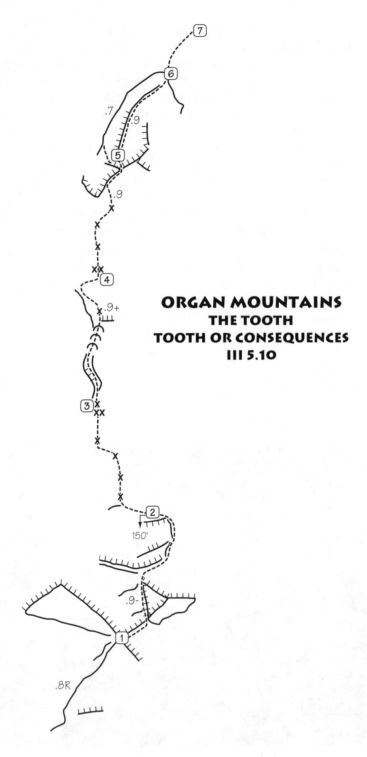

ORGAN MOUNTAINS
THE TOOTH
TOOTH OR CONSEQUENCES
III 5.10

18. Tooth Extraction (III 5.10) Highly recommended route. **Pitches 1 and 2:** Same as first 2 pitches of *Tooth Fairy*. Move right along ledge at end of 2nd pitch and establish a belay. **Pitch 3:** Climb up right-trending grass-filled crack, then face climb right (5.9-) underneath a small roof to the base of the large left-facing dihedral system that angles up left. **Pitch 4:** 5.10 climbing leads up the dihedral to a belay on a sloping ledge. **Pitch 5:** Continue up the dihedral (5.9) hand crack to a ledge. Go left about 15' to an off-width (look for the hand crack in the back) to the rap anchors shared by all 3 routes. **Descent:** Multiple double-rope (165') rappels down *Tooth Fairy.*

THE WEDGE

Up left (north) of the Tooth is The Wedge. At least 4 routes can be found here including one done by Royal Robbins while he was stationed at Fort Bliss in the early 1950s. The *West Ridge* (II 5.7) on the left-hand skyline is a local favorite. *Shillelagh* (II 5.9) starts near the center of the face and climbs 3 pitches before it connects with the *West Ridge* several pitches from the top.

These remote routes are seldom climbed and little is known about them. They are included here for the adventure seekers that may want to recapture the spirit of exploration and discovery that is so much a part of early Organs climbing history. Ask locals for more information or better yet, tag along. Remember your headlamp!

Follow all directions to The Tooth to find The Wedge. From the base of The Tooth stay north (left) of the next large gully. The Wedge is above to the left. Allow about 1.5 hours for the approach. Rappel the east face to descend.

Ask locals about the following routes: *West Ridge* (5.7), *Robbins Route* (5.9+), *Heads and Motes* (5.11+), and *Shillelagh* (III 5.9).

SUGARLOAF

Climbing Sugarloaf will round out the visitor's Organ Mountains experience. Located on the east side of the Organ Mountains, the sweeping lines of this 800' granite spire have lured climbers for more than 30 years. In keeping with the mountaineering tradition of those times, the original lines up the northern and southern slabs were ascended to reach the top. Today these lines provide climbs of moderate difficulty and continue to be enjoyed by locals and other visitors to the area. The steeper sections in the middle of the rock offered fewer opportunities for protection and waited until the 1970s for ascents. Recently some of the original 1/4" bolts have been augmented by 3/8" bolts. Climbers can still expect to encounter many of the old 1/4" bolts protecting long runouts on difficult face climbing. Exercise caution and discretion when relying on these bolts.

Allow 10 to 12 hours car to car for this remote spire. The approach is usually done in 2 to 3 hours with 1 to 2 hours to return to the car. Once on the top allow yourself at least 1 hour to get back to your packs at the cliff base.

The *Left Eyebrow* (10 pitches, 5.6) and *Right Eyebrow* (7 pitches, 5.7) are recommended moderate climbs to the summit. *Science Friction* (3 pitches, 5.11) can be combined with the *Left Eyebrow* for a great 9-pitch route to the summit. On all routes be prepared for a long day with widely spaced protection and many route-finding decisions.

Rack: A rack for Sugarloaf should include quickdraws, runners, small wired stoppers and RPs, and nuts and Friends up to fist-size. It's a good idea to bring two ropes.

Descent: Descent from the top requires rappelling from fixed anchors on the east face (go left at the top) to gain access to the descent gully. Two ropes are helpful here. Several rappel stations can be found in the gully itself, along with much down-climbing. Resist the temptation to exit the gully too early near the bottom.

Finding the crag: Access to Sugarloaf is via US 70, connecting Las Cruces and Alamogordo. From Las Cruces drive east on US 70 about 14 miles to the Aguirre Springs Recreation Area exit on the east side of San Augustin Pass. Drive about 6 miles to the campground. Once in the campground, continue on the one-way loop almost exactly 1 mile from the self-pay station and restrooms to a pullout on the right. This is about 0.5 mile before the road becomes two-way. Park here and then walk back up the road about 50 yards to the road sign that advises a sharp left turn ahead. The trail starts here and goes south across the acacia forest to a saddle, down and across a drainage, and then heads uphill all the way toward Sugarloaf.

Finding the start of the trail and making an effort to stay on it will greatly facilitate this long approach. Traveling up the main gully system is the next best alternative. The trail is almost always to the right (west) of the gully, often following an old fence line. A 30' waterfall (generally dry) in the gully is a good landmark. This marks the halfway point of the approach. Just below the waterfall, the trail crosses the gully for the final time and travels up a ridge. If you haven't been successful in finding the trail and have traveled up the drainage, you can cross over the top of the waterfall from right to left and find the trail here. Eventually the trail will cross a large drainage coming down from the southern part of Sugarloaf. Leave the trail here and go up the drainage. Turn out of it when you get close enough to traverse left to the base of the rock. Aim for the large roof system close to ground near the middle of the rock. *Science Friction* and the *Left Eyebrow* start left of this feature.

Routes are described left to right.

19. **North Face** (IV 5.6) This 14-pitch climb features 50' to 60' runouts on moderate climbing. Start near the lowest or north end of the formation, well below and left of the prominent roof system that is close to the ground. **Pitch 1:** Go up through a roof with trees at both ends. A fixed pin protects the easy roof. Continue up moderate climbing 5 pitches up right to a belay below a band of roofs. Trend up and right over the roofs onto the upper slabs for 7 or 8 pitches more to the summit.

20. **The Left Eyebrow** (IV 5.6) Start below and left the prominent roof system that is close to the ground. **Pitch 1:** Face climb up to a right-facing crack to a tree on its left end. Two more trees are on the right side. Climb a short right-facing corner up left to another tree and belay. **Pitch 2:** Face climb left, then up a crack past a bush to a belay (5.6). **Pitch 3:** Crack climb up right, then work up left to a belay. **Pitch 4:** Face climb past a bush and belay at the end of a roof system. **Pitch 5:** Face climb right to a tree and belay. **Pitch 6:** Angle right and up into a left-facing corner. 4 more pitches (with many choices and options for easy climbing and belay stances) lead up to the summit. Look for a 2-bolt belay at the end of Pitch 8.

21. **Science Friction** (II 5.11) Grade IV if combined with upper pitches of 'Left Eyebrow. **Pitch 1:** Start in short right-angling cracks below and left of the prominent roof system close to the ground. Face and crack climb (5.10) past 2 fixed pins. Face climb left past 2 bolts to a belay stance. **Pitch 2:** Move right, then face climb past 3 bolts and 1 fixed pin (5.10-). It is 130' to the ground from here. **Pitch 3:** Face climb straight up (5.11) past

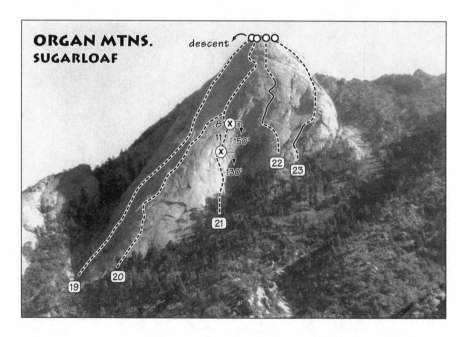

ORGAN MTNS. SUGARLOAF   descent

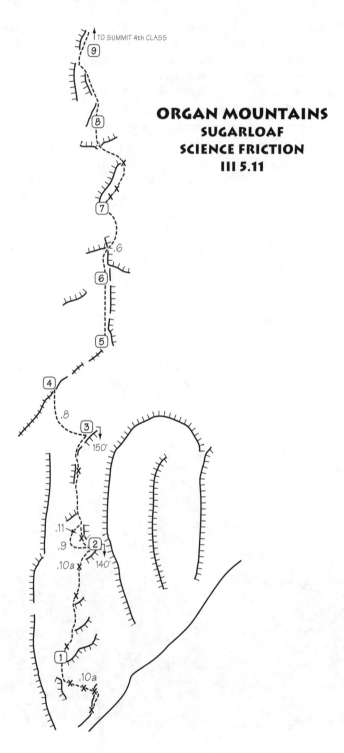

TO SUMMIT 4th CLASS

ORGAN MOUNTAINS
SUGARLOAF
SCIENCE FRICTION
III 5.11

9

8

7

.6

6

5

4

.8

3

150'

.11

.9   2

.10a   140'

1

.10a

a bolt (a 5.9- face climbing variation to the left can circumvent this hard short section) and into a crack system with a fixed piton. Move up and right to a belay stance. A 2-rope rappel reaches the ground from here. But after coming all this way you might as well keep going. The upper pitches are fun and the view from the summit is outstanding. **Pitch 4:** Face climb right, then up to the tree at the end of Pitch 5 of the *Left Eyebrow.* To continue to the top, follow the route description starting with Pitch 6 of the *Left Eyebrow.* An Organ classic. Highly recommended.

22. **The Right Eyebrow** (III 5.7) Start on the right side of the prominent roof system close to the ground. **Pitches 1 and 2:** 2 pitches of face climbing end at the top center of the prominent roof system. **Pitch 3:** Climb a left-facing corner. **Pitch 4:** (crux) Start in a right-facing corner, then up a left-facing corner to its end. **Pitch 5:** Face climb left up to a right-facing corner. **Pitches 6 and 7:** Face climb easy slabs to the summit.

23. **Flea Tree Dihedral** (III 5.8) Starts right of the *Right Eyebrow.* Climb a dihedral system for 4 or 5 pitches to the "lonesome pine" on the right skyline. 2 more pitches of moderate slab climbing lead to the top.

DOÑA ANA MOUNTAINS

OVERVIEW

Outcrops of coarse porphyritic desert granite scatter throughout the Doña Ana Mountains in southern New Mexico, providing pockets of excellent climbing. This small range, north of Las Cruces, is topped by 5,835' Doña Ana Peak. The range, the peak, and the nearby town of Doña Ana were named for Doña Ana (Lady Ann) Robledo, a 17th century resident. The Doña Ana Mountains, like the neighboring Organ Mountains, is a superb off-the-beaten track area that yields good climbing in a wild desert setting. Numerous 1- to 3-pitch traditional routes scale the range's rock cliffs, and seven lines ascend Checkerboard Wall, a 500' crag on the north flank of Doña Ana Peak. The face is grooved with slicing cracks that give it a huge checkerboard appearance. Besides its easily accessible routes, the range also offers some great bouldering along the area's dirt roads.

The crags here offer adventure climbing. There is one sport route in the entire area. Traditional skills of placing gear, route finding, and self rescue are necessary. Use caution on all routes and watch for sandbag ratings. Watch for loose rock on routes and on cliff tops. Rattlesnakes are common here. Keep an eye and ear out for them when crossing talus fields and hiking up rocky slopes. Remember if you are bitten by a snake to seek medical help immediately. Do not apply ice or a tourniquet, or cut the bitten area.

Climbers on *The Best* (5.10-) at The Columns in the Doña Ana Mountains, New Mexico. *Photo by Dennis Jackson.*

The Doña Ana Mountains have the same climate as the adjoining Organs as well as Hueco Tanks farther south. Autumn, winter, and spring are the best times to visit. Expect warm days and cool nights. Winter nights can drop as much as 50 degrees below the daytime high. Snowfall is usually light and rare. Expect windy afternoons in spring. Summers can be very hot, with daily highs in the 90s and low 100s. Get an early start and climb in the morning coolness. Carry plenty of water to the crags; at least two quarts a person daily is a good starting point. Don't expect to find any water here.

Climbing history: Little recorded history exists of early climbing in the Doña Ana Mountains, although R. Ingraham and Anuta made the first ascent of the Checkerboard Wall in 1964. Later local climbers established numerous routes on the range crags. Jim Graham has been active recently replacing some of the old 1/4" bolts.

Bolts, placed on the lead by first ascent parties, are found at some belay and rappel stations. Use all old 1/4" bolts cautiously. Always back them up with gear if possible, particularly at belays.

Rack: All routes require gear placements. A rack of camming units up to 4" along with a set of wired stoppers, and an assortment of quickdraws, runners, and a 150' rope is adequate for most routes.

Descent: Descent is usually by rappel from fixed anchors. Be prepared to fashion your own rappel anchors on some routes.

Trip Planning Information

Area description: The Doña Ana Mountains, rising above the desert north of Las Cruces, yield excellent bouldering and routes on rough granite outcrops in a wild setting.

Location: Southern New Mexico, north of Las Cruces.

Camping: Undeveloped free camping is available at the Bear Boulders and the Pizza Boulders just off the access road. Fires are discouraged. Bring water. Please practice minimum impact camping to protect this fragile area.

Climbing season: Climbing is possible year-round in the Doña Ana Mountains. Fall, winter, and spring are best. High summer temperatures and occasional cold winter days can limit climbing opportunities. Expect wind in the spring.

Restrictions and access issues: The area lies on BLM land. No climbing restrictions are currently in place. The area has a long traditional history and excessive bolting is frowned upon. Follow existing climber access trails whenever possible and pick up all your litter.

Nearby mountain shops, guide services, and gyms: Las Cruces. There are no guide services or gyms in the area.

Services: Food, fuel, and lodging are available in Las Cruces.

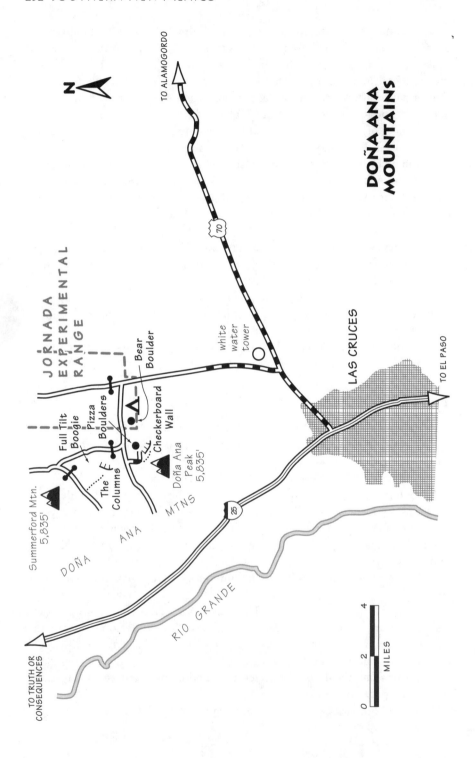

N

DOÑA ANA MOUNTAINS

TO ALAMOGORDO

70

JORNADA EXPERIMENTAL RANGE

Bear Boulder

white water tower

Full Tilt Boogie

Pizza Boulders

Checkerboard Wall

The F Columns

Doña Ana Peak 5,835'

Summerford Mtn. 5,835'

DOÑA   ANA   MTNS

LAS CRUCES

TO EL PASO

25

TO TRUTH OR CONSEQUENCES

RIO GRANDE

0   2   4

MILES

Emergency services: Call 911 for emergency assistance.

Nearby climbing areas: The Organ Mountains are a short drive south and east. Hueco Tanks State Historical Park is 75 miles southeast. City of Rocks State Park is 80 miles west.

Nearby attractions: The Gadsden Museum in Mesilla, Fort Selden State Monument (12 miles north on Interstate 25), and White Sands National Monument (45 miles northeast via U.S. Highway 70). Ciudad de Juarez is a short drive south on I-25. Visitors should inquire about entry requirements before entering old Mexico, although generally a visit is simple.

Finding the crags: The Doña Ana Mountains are east of Interstate 25 and north of Las Cruces. Exit I-25 onto US 70/82 and head east toward Alamogordo. Turn north (left) after about 3 miles on Jornada Road. Signs here say Jornada Experimental Station. Also look for a large white water tower on the northeast corner and a Shell gas station. Drive 6.4 miles north on the road to USDA signs by a rock pillar and turn left (west). After about 1.9 miles turn left to the Bear Boulders. Camping and bouldering opportunities are found here. The turn to the Pizza Boulders is 3.5 miles from the rock pillars. This area is about 1.2 miles south on a fairly rough dirt road. To the southeast of the boulders is the popular Checkerboard Wall, a 30-minute hike southeast.

To get to The Columns and Full Tilt Boogie, continue past the Bear Boulders about 0.6 mile to a right turn through a gate. Continue on the road 1.6 miles to a left turn that travels back under the power line, through a gate, and into another left turn to the parking area. This is about 1.2 miles from the left turn that goes under the power line. A short hike south reaches the base of The Columns.

BEAR BOULDERS

Because of their ease of access and good bouldering, this is where locals are generally introduced to the Doña Ana Mountains. One large boulder and several smaller ones are located here. A toprope can be installed on the largest boulder by slinging the top. A bolt on the top helps in directing the rope.

CHECKERBOARD WALL

The Checkerboard is a 500' east-facing cliff with routes that range in difficulty from 5.6 to 5.10+. This has traditionally been a popular beginner area and is very good in the winter. Bring a standard rack for these 3-pitch routes and a 165' rope. Expect long runouts on easy and moderate climbing, with crux moves on the summit overhangs. Approach by parking at the Pizza Boulders and walking southeast. Allow 30 minutes to reach the cliff base. Descend to the south or north, depending on which side you are climbing on.

DOÑA ANA MOUNTAINS
CHECKERBOARD WALL

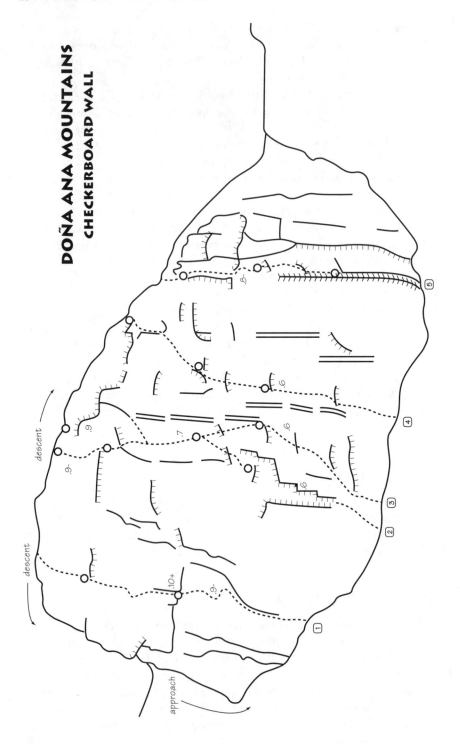

Routes are described left to right.

1. **Unnamed** (5.10+) 3 pitches up the left side of the wall. **Pitch 1:** Work up a right-leaning crack past some bushes. Face climb up left (5.9-) to an intermittent crack system and belay on a small ledge below an obvious roof. **Pitch 2:** Pull the roof and follow an off-width crack (5.10+) to runout face climbing. Belay on a ledge up right. **Pitch 3:** Climb easy rock to the summit.

2. **Unnamed** (5.9-) **Pitch 1:** Start well right and downhill from #1 in a right-facing crack just right of a left-facing crack. Easy climbing (5.6) ends on a ledge. **Pitch 2:** Start in a crack, then face climb above a ledge to another ledge and belay. **Pitch 3:** Face and crack climb (5.7) past a ledge, then face climb to a roof. Belay by bushes under the roof. **Pitch 4:** Crack and face climbing lead to the top. Crux pitch.

3. **Circus Finish** (5.9) **Pitch 1:** Start on a ledge right of #2 and face climb (5.6) to a belay on a ledge. **Pitch 2:** Face climb to the left of a large crack past a ledge to the top of the second pitch of #2. **Pitch 3:** Face and crack climb (5.7) to a ledge, then right and up to a ledge below a left-facing crack. **Pitch 4:** Climb the crack and roof system to the top. Crux pitch.

4. **Unnamed** (5.6) Start on a ledge right of the large cracks. **Pitch 1:** Face and crack climb (5.6) to a belay on a ledge. **Pitch 2:** Discontinuous cracks lead to a belay on a ledge. **Pitch 3:** Face climb right, then up a large crack to the top.

5. **Knight's Move** (5.8) Start in a right-facing corner left of trees. **Pitch 1:** Climb the corner to a ledge belay. **Pitch 2:** Continue up the corner, then right via a ledge to face climbing that ends on a sloping ledge. **Pitch 3:** Climb a short crack, then face climb (5.8-) to a right-facing corner. Belay at the top of the corner.

THE COLUMNS

The Columns has a moderate approach of about 10 to 20 minutes. From the parking area, hike south up a drainage then turn left up the hill through boulders to the base of the rock.

The described route is on the Southwest Face. Additional routes are on the North Face. Start these from a large "perched" ledge. *Crack 5* (5.9) is a hand and fist crack on the left. *Crack 4* (5.10-) goes up the roof in the center. *Baskin Robbins* (5.8) climbs the prominent dihedral to an off-width.

1. **The Best** (5.10-) **Pitch 1:** Climb the off-width to a good belay stance. Crux pitch. **Pitch 2:** Climb a short section of fourth class to the right, then jam the overhanging hand and fist crack to the top. Excellent route.

To the left of this route are several more good routes. Look for a chained anchor at the top of a short finger crack (5.10+). Left of the chains is a bolt ladder up a steep face that has not been free climbed to date.

OTHER DOÑA ANA AREAS

Local consensus says that the best route in the area is *Full Tilt Boogie* (5.10b/ c). The best approach is to hike west from where the main approach road to The Columns leaves the power line. This is about 0.5 mile before the left turn to The Columns. Look for a 50' vertical crack that leans left for another 50' near the top. The route is visible from the road. The area's only sport climb, *Anorexic* (5.11), climbs the face below and then through *Full Tilt Boogie*. Descend to the east.

DEMINGAREA

CITY OF ROCKS STATE PARK

OVERVIEW

City of Rocks State Park, a secluded jumble of boulders in arid southwestern New Mexico, is a virtually undiscovered bouldering paradise. The area has seen little serious activity and the potential for thousands of boulder problems awaits future boulderers. Hundreds of 10' to 30' welded volcanic tuff formations cover this 680-acre parkland. The strangely shaped rocks are the result of nearby volcanic activity some 30 million years ago. The erosive sculpting by wind and water produced edges, huecos, and cracks similar to the rock at Hueco Tanks and Enchanted Tower. Bouldering here is an end in itself or preparation for the more developed and famed Hueco Tanks boulders to the east. While City of Rocks doesn't offer the diversity and outstanding quality of Hueco Tanks, the lack of crowds, pleasant camping among the rocks, and the pure potential for personal statements on untried problems make it an attractive alternative.

Bob Murray is City of Rocks' most prolific boulderer. Murray, one of the West's best boulderers, left his mark here as well as at Hueco Tanks. He considers the City one of the best bouldering areas he explored and developed while living in Tucson in the 1980s. Murray often wrapped the boulder summits at the City with long lengths of webbing and worked out the hard moves protected by a Gibbs ascender. John Sherman, in his excellent book *Stone Crusade*, notes that "...there's always the feeling that when you're doing something hard, it probably isn't a first ascent. Still, 100 Thimbles wait to be done by someone with chrome-moly nerves and freon-filled veins."

Unlike Hueco Tanks, no guidebook or named and rated problems are found at City of Rocks. It's best for the adventurous boulderer to roam the area and search out what looks good. A network of roads and trails lace the park, allowing easy access to every area. A few suggestions include the boulders

Ian Spencer-Green bouldering at City of Rocks State Park, New Mexico.
Photo by Stewart M. Green.

above campsites on the east side of the one-way road and at The Suburb, a boulder grouping at the far northwest end of the park. Some excellent boulders and problems rise above the few campsites in this sector.

Most of the park's bouldering is on sharp edges and flakes, with occasional problems that jam or layback up cracks. Many problems are quite painful to the fingertips. Descent off many boulders is problematic. Sometimes it's easiest to downclimb some desperate problem to a point where it's possible to launch onto the crash-pad. Others require trailing a tied-off rope up and rapping down the backside. Remember to bring your bouldering ethics with you. Don't chip, alter, or file holds. Not only is this illegal, but it's cheating and destroys the area's future for hard bouldering. A crash pad and a spotter will help avoid injuries.

Trip Planning Information

Area description: City of Rocks offers hundreds of boulders scattered across a rolling plain in an arid desert environment.

Location: Southwestern New Mexico. 27 miles north of Deming and Interstate 10.

Camping: City of Rocks State Park features a tidy, well-maintained campground that is open year-round. Most of the sites sit among the boulders. Just camp and climb. An added plus are showers and drinking water. Fees and time limits apply. Campsites at The Suburb on the north end of the park are usually deserted.

Climbing season: Year-round. The best seasons are spring, fall, and winter. Summer temperatures typically exceed 90 degrees. At an elevation of 5,200', occasional cold winter days may restrict opportunities. Expect windy days, particularly in spring, at this exposed area.

Restrictions and access issues: Rock defacement and bolting are the primary concerns of park personnel. Both are illegal. Rescuing stranded visitors on the boulders is a park problem. Determine descent routes before starting out, and have a rope available to lower or rap off with the assistance of an anchored belayer. Park officials also ask climbers to use chalk sparingly to avoid unsightly marks on the rocks. If climber visitation and use increases, the possibility of additional restrictions is virtually guaranteed. The present park manager is willing to work with visitors to accommodate bouldering. Picking up your trash, walking on existing trails, and leaving no evidence of your visit are recommended.

Guidebook: None.

Nearby mountain shops, guide services, and gyms: Nothing close; try Las Cruces.

Services: All services are found in Deming, Silver City, and Las Cruces.

CITY OF ROCKS STATE PARK

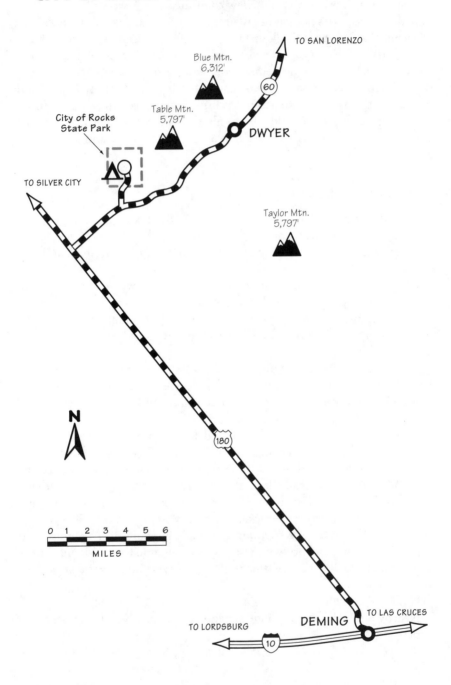

TO SAN LORENZO

Blue Mtn.
6,312'

60

Table Mtn.
5,797'

DWYER

City of Rocks
State Park

TO SILVER CITY

Taylor Mtn.
5,797'

N

180

0 1 2 3 4 5 6

MILES

TO LORDSBURG

DEMING

TO LAS CRUCES

10

Auto fuel and a convenience store are in Hurley, 18 miles north on U.S. Highway 180.

Emergency services: For all incidents in the park, contact the rangers at the visitor center. Emergency medical services are available in Deming, 28 miles south on US 180 and in Silver City 34 miles north on US 180.

Nearby climbing areas: Organ Mountains and Doña Ana Mountains, 60 miles southeast; Hueco Tanks, 130 miles southeast; and Enchanted Tower, 190 miles north. Areas in Arizona include Cochise Stronghold.

Nearby attractions: Gila Cliff Dwellings National Monument, Gila Wilderness Area (hiking, backpacking, fishing, hot springs, and whitewater boating), Gila National Forest, Pancho Villa State Park, Rock Hound State Park, Deming Luna Mimbres Museum, and Columbus Historical Museum. The Great American Duck Race with attendant festivities is held every year in Deming on the fourth weekend in August. A privately owned hot spring, about 2 miles south of the park on New Mexico Highway 61, is sometimes open.

Finding the boulders: From Las Cruces or Arizona take I-10 to Deming. Turn right and drive 23 miles north on US 180, then turn right on NM 61. Drive 3 miles and turn left at a sign to City of Rocks State Park. Continue 2 miles north to the visitor center. From Albuquerque and Santa Fe take I-25 south and exit west at the Hillsboro exit 12 miles south of Truth or Consequences. Drive 51 miles west on NM 152. This highway is steep, hilly, and winding; allow lots of time for driving. Turn south onto NM 61 at San Lorenzo and drive 23 miles southwest to the City of Rocks State Park sign. Turn right (north) here. A fee is charged to enter and use the park. A one-way loop drive circles the park. Find whatever boulders you like, park, and climb.

Jean DeLatallaide on the overhang *Custer's Last Stand* (5.13b) Sitting Bull Falls, New Mexico. *Photo by Dennis Jackson.*

CARLSBADAREA

SITTING BULL FALLS

OVERVIEW

Sitting Bull Falls, a small limestone cliff tucked in a canyon on the northeast flank of the Guadalupe Mountains, is New Mexico's newest sport climbing crag. The crag's fourteen established routes range in difficulty from 5.10 to 5.13b. The area's most difficult route, *Kootenai Cruiser* (5.13d), saw its first free ascent in 1996 by Chris Grijaiva. Most of the lines are 5.12+, with *Custer's Last Stand* (5.13b) the cliff's most difficult route. In addition to the difficult overhanging climbs on the Big Horn Wall on the cliff's left side, The Rosebud Wall on the right features shorter, more moderate routes in the 5.10 to 5.11 range. A bulging prow topped with a cave-like feature separates the two sectors. Sitting Bull Falls, one of New Mexico's best sport climbing venues, is worth many visits.

The area is named after an American Indian chief but not the more famous Sioux war chief, Sitting Bull. This Sitting Bull was chief of a small band that lived in the area in the 1880s. The falls were named for him after he led a group of ranchers on a merry chase after stealing some of their horses and cattle.

The 80' north-facing cliff is composed of tufa or travertine, a limestone formed in freshwater. The sponge-like rock is riddled with many pockets and holes that result from calcification around organic material like algae, small plants, and trees. The organic material was deposited, rotted, and weathered, leaving pockets from mono-doigts to potholes large enough to rest inside. The limestone's relative softness has eroded to a scooped-out, arching, cave-like cliff that overhangs as much as 40' in 80' of vertical.

Climbing history: The area has long been used by local cavers for rappelling and ascending practice. John Gogas, along with other climbers, visited Sitting Bull Falls in the early 1980s but rejected the area as a climbing locale because of the lack of protection possibilities. After gaining experience on many Texas crags, Gogas returned with his soon-to-be-wife Carol and Eric Isaacson on Memorial Day, 1992. Thinking they had proper permission, they began developing the cliff. The "permission" as it turned out was granted by unauthorized personnel. The painted hangers, glued-in Petzl anchors, and low-key approach, however, went unnoticed until the summer of 1995 when all development, although not climbing, was suspended pending a Forest Service Environmental Assessment of the area. Subsequent meetings between Gogas and Forest Service personnel have since paved the way for area management to include climbing as a legitimate recreational activity. Please read and adhere to all climbing rules and regulations to keep this excellent area open.

Rack: The rack for all routes is quickdraws and a 165' rope.

Descent: Descend from lowering anchors at each route's end.

Trip Planning Information

Area description: Sitting Bull Falls offers excellent sport climbing routes on a 50' to 80' tufa limestone cliff. Routes range in difficulty from 5.10 to 5.13+.

Location: Southeastern New Mexico between Artesia and Carlsbad.

Camping: The crag rises from the picnic area at Sitting Bull Falls. Camping is not allowed in the immediate area. Undeveloped sites, with no facilities or water, are located along the road several miles northeast of the picnic area. Practice clean, primitive camping and leave little evidence of your visit. Use existing fire-rings and campsites. Water and restrooms are available at the picnic area. Be self-sufficient—it is a long distance to any amenities.

Climbing season: Climbing is best in early spring and late fall. Summer temperatures in this desert climate can limit climbing, although the north-facing cliff may be bearable on hot days. Climbing is possible on all but the coldest winter days. Check the Carlsbad temperatures for an idea of daily highs and lows.

Restrictions and access issues: The area is in Lincoln National Forest. It is first and foremost a picnic area. After somewhat of a rough start, the area is open to climbing with the following stipulations and restrictions: climbing is limited to the one wall behind the restrooms; all other areas are off-limits. The area will not accommodate more routes so leave your drills at home. Citations and fines will be issued to violators. The extreme right end of the cliff is a bat nursing area and closed to climbing and other disturbing activities. Periodic closures of some of the routes just to the left of this area to protect bat habitat may be necessary in the future. The area's Environmental Assessment calls for closing the present trail and building a new one. Local climbers are committed to helping with trail maintenance and trash clean-up. All climbers are encouraged to aid this effort. The picnic facilities will soon be upgraded which will

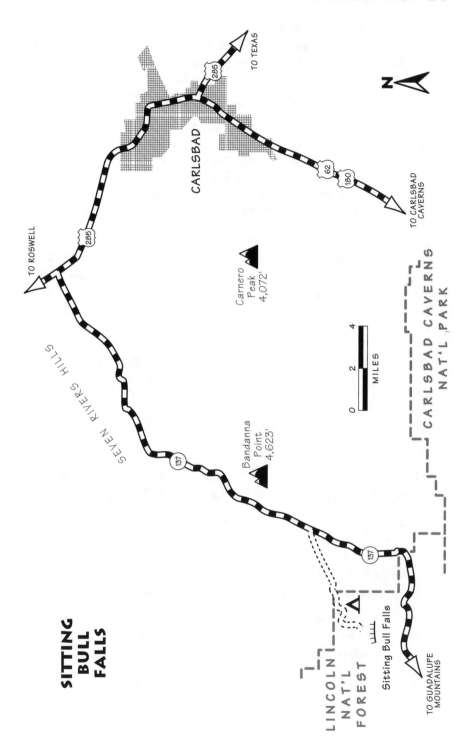

SITTING
BULL
FALLS

TO ROSWELL

SEVEN RIVERS HILLS

285

CARLSBAD

TO TEXAS

285

62
180

TO CARLSBAD
CAVERNS

N

Carnero
Peak
4,072'

Bandanna
Point
4,623'

137

137

0   2   4
MILES

CARLSBAD CAVERNS
NAT'L PARK

LINCOLN
NAT'L
FOREST

Sitting Bull Falls

TO GUADALUPE
MOUNTAINS

likely curtail climbing during the construction phase. Climbers can call Guadalupe Ranger District, (505) 885-4181, for conditions and closures before visiting.

Guidebook: None.

Nearby mountain shop, guide services, and gyms: None. The nearest mountain shops are in El Paso and Las Cruces to the south and in Albuquerque to the north.

Services: None. Carlsbad, a 1-hour drive east and south, offers all services. Artesia, about 1 hour northeast, offers full services.

Emergency services: None. Getting assistance here would be a time-consuming process. Either self-evacuate or drive back on New Mexico Highway 137 to U.S. Highway 285 and go south to Carlsbad and emergency facilities.

Nearby climbing areas: Hueco Tanks is about 190 miles south and west.

Nearby attractions: Carlsbad Caverns National Park (50 miles south), Guadalupe National Park (in Texas).

Finding the crag: From US 285 exit onto NM 137 (about 24 miles south of Artesia and 12 miles north of Carlsbad). Drive west and south on paved NM 137 (somewhat difficult to follow) for about 20 miles. The main highway trends to the left past several right turns to ranches and drill sites until it reaches a signed right turn to Sitting Bull Falls. Follow this dirt road about 8 more miles. The cliff band is in view from the end of the road at the Sitting Bull Falls Picnic Area behind the restrooms. A 5-minute hike leads directly to the cliff's left side. Future plans include closing this trail because of erosion problems and rerouting the trail farther south.

Routes described left to right.

THE ROSEBUD WALL
(A.K.A. "THE WARM-UP WALL")

1. **The Brit Route** (5.11b) The least popular climb on the crag. Start just right of the cave-like formation on the left end of the cliff.
2. **Firewalker** (5.10b) Excellent.
3. **Wounded Knee** (5.10a) A good introduction to Sitting Bull Falls.
4. **Six Little Indians** (5.10c) Quality. Difficult at top.
5. **Big Medicine** (5.11c) Difficult near the top. Quality.
6. **Sweat Lodge** (5.11b) Quality.

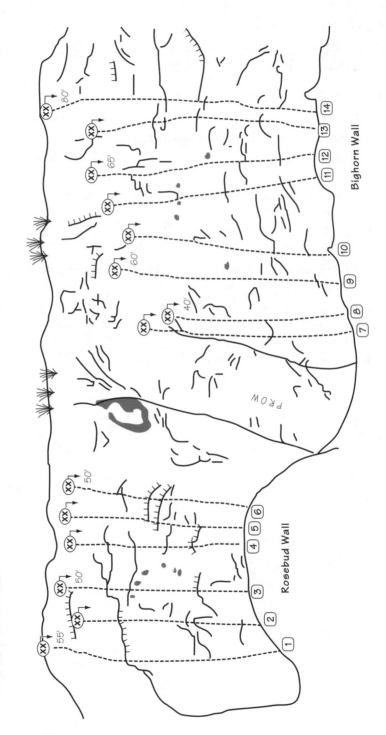

**CARLSBAD AREA
SITTING BULL FALLS**

Bighorn Wall

Rosebud Wall

PROW

THE BIG HORN WALL

The following routes are located on the Big Horn Wall on the same cliff band about 40' right of *Sweat Lodge*.

7. **Smoke Signals** (5.11b) Quality. Another good warm-up for harder things to come.

8. **Ghost Dancers** (5.12a) Short and fingery. Excellent.

9. **Counting Coup** (5.12b) A runner up for the best 5.12b route in New Mexico.

10. **Eagles aren't Crows** (5.12c/d) Not as steep as *Counting Coup* but thinner. Quality.

11. **Tribal War** (5.12c/d) Similar to *Broken Arrows* with easier crux and harder climbing to the anchors. An area favorite.

12. **Broken Arrows** (5.12d) Pumpy climbing leading to a powerful crux, then easy climbing to the anchors. Quality.

13. **Kootenai Cruiser** (5.13d/.14) 30' of 5.12d, then a V9 boulder problem followed by a burley dyno, then 5.12a/b to the anchors. Get ready for big air time if you miss the dyno.

14. **Custer's Last Stand** (5.13b) Quality moves.

Texas

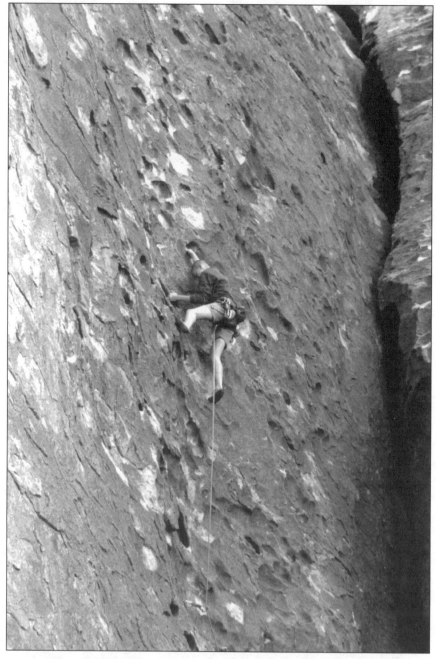

Brett Spencer-Green pulling huecos on the first pitch of *Sea of Holes* (5.10R) on The Front Side at Hueco Tanks, Texas. *Photo by Stewart M. Green.*

WEST TEXASAREA

HUECO TANKS STATE HISTORICAL PARK

OVERVIEW

Hueco Tanks State Historical Park in the desert east of El Paso, Texas, offers some of America's finest bouldering and climbing opportunities on its soaring rock walls and fabulous boulder gardens. The 860-acre park, with a warm, dry climate, is now regarded as the premier winter climbing area in the United States. A multitude of stunning 1- to 3-pitch routes scale the sculpted rock walls at Hueco Tanks, offering overhanging jug-hauls, technical faces, thin slabs, occasional crack lines, long chimney systems, and lots of exposure on the 250'-high Front Side. It's on the boulders, however, where most rock jocks come to sample and test their mettle. John Sherman, author of the area's complete guidebook and first ascensionist of many of the park's superlative problems, calls Hueco "simply the best bouldering in America."

Such high praise attracts many climbers to Hueco Tanks, particularly in the winter months when snow and frigid temperatures encase most of the United States. It's not that the weather is always so warm here—it's just warmer than the rest of the country! While Minnesota suffers under a minus-20 cold wave, it's usually a balmy 55 degrees here. Hueco Tanks, lying above 4,000 feet, is not immune to winter's storms, but they are usually short-lived. After a day or so of bleak skies and showers, the clouds part and the sun again shines down on the crags. January temperatures average 44.4 degrees, with daytime highs in the 50s and 60s and lows in the mid-30s. Snow flies only two or so days each winter and almost never accumulates. Besides the storm of sunlight, west Texas is also renowned for its occasional wind and accompanying dust storms. The typical climbing season at Hueco runs from November through March. April and October offer warmer weather, but the climber will seek shady problems during mid-day. The rest of the year is hot, with daily highs regularly climbing into the 100s. The park averages about 8" of rainfall every year.

Hueco Tanks is a Texas state historical park that preserves the area's unique natural and archeological resources. The park, lying in the Chihuahuan Desert ecosystem, has long sheltered humans, from the ancient Archaic hunters thousands of years ago up to the Mescalero Apache Indians. These Native Americans relied on the area's natural rock basins, or *huecos,* filled with water to slake their thirst in this arid climate. These peoples' presence remains with a remarkable legacy of rock art on cliff faces in the park. They also left deep grinding holes under shady overhangs, where they gathered to grind seeds into flour. Historic attractions here also include the stone remains of an old ranch house and the ruins of a relocated stage station from the old Butterfield Stage Line, which ran across the southern United States. Evidence of even earlier visitors are found on many of the park's boulders on The Front Side. Look at the Mushroom Boulder's north side and notice the rock's glassy, smooth finish. This "mammoth rub" was caused by mammoths rubbing against the boulders to dislodge lice during the moist Pleistocene Period some 10,000 years ago. The park's primary mission is to protect these and other natural features. Recreational activities like rock climbing are secondary and managed in a way not to conflict with the historic preservation.

The rock at Hueco Tanks is composed of syenite porphyry, a type of granitic rock. This rock began forming some 34 million years ago when a mass of molten rock from deep within the earth's crust was pushed upward and intruded into overlying layers of limestone. Before reaching the surface the rock cooled and solidified. Subsequent weathering slowly exposed the erosion-resistant igneous rock while the softer, surrounding layers were eroded away, leaving today's humped rock mountains towering over an outwash plain west of the Hueco Mountains. The weathered rock gives the immediate impression that it was made to climb on. Huecos, the spherical depressions etched and eroded into the rock, grace both the boulders and cliff faces in the park. These, combined with "ironrock," a local term for the hard surface coating, define the area's unique bouldering opportunities.

Climbing history: Hueco Tanks was unknown to climbers before 1975. Area locals usually traveled north to the Organ Mountains in New Mexico to tackle the seemingly unlimited supply of rock. Climbing activity was limited to rappelling until Mike Head, a talented young climber, stumbled on the area in the summer of 1975. Hampered by a lack of partners, Mike waited until 1978 to begin developing Hueco's walls. Head, along with John McCall and Mark Motes, had the area entirely to themselves. The park restricted climbing from the beginning, with no bolting or climbing on the west face of North Mountain, clearly the area's most attractive cliff. Bolting was officially viewed as "rock defacement" similar to the graffiti and trash problems found throughout the park. The trio, unwilling to be thwarted by park rangers, felt compelled to adopt guerrilla tactics when attempting new routes up the crackless

Sunset on The Front Side at Hueco Tanks, Texas. *Photo by Stewart M. Green.*

faces. Strategies using lookouts, decoy cars, and drilling at night were mostly successful but occasionally met with failure and a fine. A tenuous accommodation of climbing was finally accepted by park personnel when it became evident that the climbers were capable of not killing themselves. A growing reputation for long runouts with difficult climbing kept outside visitation to a minimum.

In 1985 Mike Head wrote the area's first guide book. That same year an article in *Climbing Magazine* boosted climber visitation dramatically. A few new visiting climbers demonstrated insensitivity to local issues by rap-bolting new routes and leaving siege ropes strung up cliffs. This raised the ire of park officials enough to prompt a climbing ban in March, 1988. This closure was intended to show climbers that they must cooperate with park officials or forfeit their privilege to climb at Hueco Tanks.

The park reopened to climbing in 1989 through the combined efforts of the American Alpine Club's Access Fund, Texas Parks and Wildlife Department, and the El Paso Climbing Club. A three-phase program was implemented to manage climbing. Phase I replaced all 1/4" bolts with 3/8" anchors; Phase II provided for the addition of bolts to existing lines; Phase III provided a petition system for new routes. In December 1989 the El Paso Climbing Club began Phase II. Most of the original lines, put up surreptitiously in the late 1970s and early 1980s, were bold, dangerous affairs that were infrequently

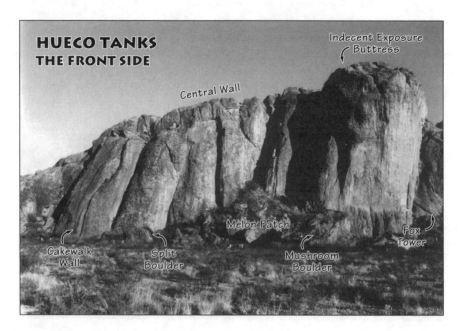

HUECO TANKS
THE FRONT SIDE

Indecent Exposure
Buttress

Central Wall

Melon Patch

Fox
Tower

Cakewalk
Wall

Split
Boulder

Mushroom
Boulder

attempted. Retro-bolting was considered important to render these bold creations safer. Some of the retro-bolted routes include *Flake Roof, Flake Roof Direct, Malice in Bucketland, Alice in Bananaland, Busted, Amplified Heat, Eternal Apples, Sea of Holes,* the 1st pitch of *Rainbow Bridge, Lunar Abstract, Deliverance, All the Nasties, Braindead, Perverts Delight, Head Fox, Fox Trot, Uriah's Heap, Divine Wind, Fast Foods, Window Pain, Catwalk, Catwalk Direct, Hueco Syndrome, Secret Sharer, Tarts of Horsham, Max Headroom,* and *Tanks for the Mammaries.* The area's popularity skyrocketed after these efforts. The tradition of run-out climbing continues at Hueco, although in a more limited and somewhat safer way. Visiting climbers will find most of the Front Side routes somewhat risky, with occasional hard moves a long way out from protection. Be advised—this isn't a sport climbing area.

Rack: Climbing here is a curious blend of traditional and sport approaches. Do not expect to clip bolts every 5'. Most routes have been retro-bolted taking into consideration gear placement possibilities, so a rack should include TCUs, wires, and occasionally, larger Friends. Some are just plain run-out. Proficiency at placing gear will lessen the stress level on many climbs. Have at least 12 quickdraws on hand for the longer routes. A 200' rope is useful on many lines, although a standard 165' rope is adequate.

Descent: Two-rope rappels are necessary for routes that do not go to the top of the Front Side, especially on the longer middle and right sections of the wall. A 200' rope is helpful but not necessary for many descents. When in doubt, use two ropes to rappel. Many climbers do only the 1st pitch of many of the routes and rap off to avoid the walk-off descent. All routes that reach the top of North Mountain require a long and somewhat confusing, but not difficult, descent off the northeast side of the mountain.

Bouldering: The term bouldering had not yet been invented but the first inhabitants of the area, the Native Americans who made the area their home, surely scrambled through the myriad of canyons looking for shade, water, and favorable sites to paint the haunting legacy of their presence. For centuries these obscure, basically unimpressive mounds of rock baked in the desert sun waiting to be given new meaning and importance. In the 1970s and 1980s a small intrepid group of adventurers from El Paso including Donny Hardin, Fred Nakovic, and John McCall, and Mark Motes from Las Cruces, started tapping the area's vast bouldering resources. Mike Head also took a break from his frenetic climbing activity and established many classic moderate problems as well as modern testpieces. *Mushroom Roof* is a good example of Mike's patience and skill in producing quality problems. The route now exemplifies how a classic problem can be destroyed by the unconscionable practice of enhancing holds.

The El Paso boys opened up the area and set the standards, but it was the awesome talents of Bob Murray that took bouldering to new dimensions in the 1980s. In his relentless search throughout the Southwest for quality bouldering, Murray discovered a bouldering bonanza at Hueco. Many of Hueco's classic bouldering problems are Murray creations, perhaps the most famous of which are *El Murrays Left, Center,* and *Right* on the mega-classic Mushroom Boulder. Although he rarely named problems, Murray originally called these *Stuck Inside of Baltimore, Texas Medicine,* and *Railroad Gin* after Bob Dylan songs. Future climbers changed the names to honor Murray. Another Murray problem, the *45 Degree Wall,* is thought by many to be one of the finest boulder problems in the world. A wrist ligament injury shortly after his peak year of 1984 cut short Murrays' career as America's premier boulderer, but his legacy is alive and well at Hueco along with hundreds of other areas in the Southwest.

John Sherman spent more than a year here in 1989-90 climbing every established route while writing the seminal guide to the area, *Hueco Tanks, A Climber's and Boulderer's Guide.* The exhaustive guide, along with Sherman's entertaining writing, is largely responsible for the area's immense popularity. Sherman's arcane open-ended V (V for "Vermin," John's nickname) rating scale originally went from V0 (about 5.9) to V10 (5.13/14). As word of the fantastic bouldering at Hueco spread to the general public, climbers from all over the world assembled to repeat the classic problems and to create new ones. As the area became well known as a winter climbing destination, European superstars Elie Chevieux, Jerry Moffat, and others graced Hueco's rigid syenite with quick repeats of established lines and added quite a few desperates of their own. In the spring of 1995, Frederic Nicole of Switzerland took the area by storm, by establishing the hardest boulder problems in the area, with standards comparable to the hardest problems in the country, with his two new problems, *Mer Diaphane* (V12/13) and *The Crown of Aragon* (V13).

Hueco continues to reveal hidden problems for both the expert and beginner. New problems are discovered each time you wander through this magical garden of rock. The Hueco bouldering experience is defined by everything from steep slabs to severely overhanging weaknesses that permit climbing on small edges and slopers. Shoulder your day pack, leave the crowd behind, and let the spirit lead. When a boulder beckons and you unlock its passage to the top you will be in harmony with yourself and the natural world in a way few are privileged to experience. This is the essence of bouldering.

Hueco Tanks park is divided geographically into four areas: North Mountain, East Mountain, West Mountain, and the East Spur. North Mountain offers most of the park's rock climbing with more than 70 1- to 3-pitch routes on the 250' Front Side. This tall, west-facing wall yields some brilliant lines up slabby and vertical walls studded with huecos or solution pockets. Climbing is generally on sharp edges and pockets. The rest of North Mountain offers several excellent bouldering areas, including the famed Mushroom Boulder below the Front Side by Outhouse 2 and The Gymnasium, a shallow canyon with a superb huecoed wall. East Mountain offers good climbing in Comanche Canyon and on Pigs in Space Buttress, as well as superb bouldering at the Dragon's Den area. The East Spur, a low rocky bluff on the park's southeast corner, boasts the classic *45 Degree Wall* boulder problem as well as the East Spur Maze. The less visited West Mountain offers the park's hardest crack climb (*The Gunfighter*), as well as it's boldest lead (*When Legends Die*). It also gives some excellent bouldering on some hard-to-find walls on its east flank and in the unique Round Room, a huge, circular, hueco-lined pothole tucked into the mountain's cliffs.

Most climbers come to Hueco to sample the excellent boulders. However, it's initially confusing to find many of the bouldering areas and problems. The best advice is to buy or borrow John Sherman's comprehensive guide and study it. Once the obvious areas are located using his maps and overview photos, then the more elusive ones can be found. Locals can also point you in the right direction if you get lost. A free bouldering guide is sometimes available when registering. This small guide has a map to the general areas and selected problems that new visitors will find most helpful. The problems here are rated using the "V" scale, which currently tops out at V15. The best way to understand and use the system is to attempt the standard problems for each grade that are listed in Sherman's guidebook.

In addition to the comprehensive guide, landing pads variously called "crash" or "sketch" pads, a spotter, a brush, and a first aid kit are useful items for

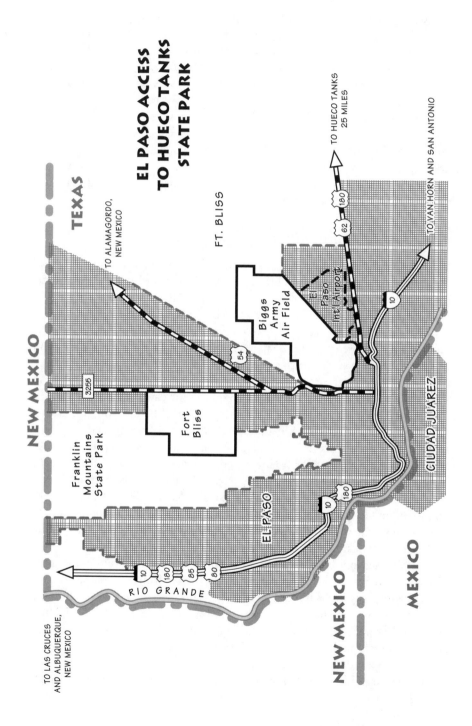

bouldering at Hueco. The pad, used along with a competent spotter, effectively cushions landings after falling off a problem. A simple pad can be constructed from an old sofa cushion. Toothbrushes or small stiff fiber paintbrushes work well to clean chalk and dust off holds. The sharpness of the holds here almost guarantees cuts to the fingertips. A basic first aid kit containing small scissors, hydrogen peroxide, tincture of benzoin (Tuff Skin), and tape will take care of most injuries. Early treatment will prevent further damage and reduce loss of climbing time. Benzoin is also helpful for getting the tape to stick. If you use glue to bond the tape to your fingers, use Krazy Glue, not Super Glue (which is toxic). Both can glue your fingers together so be careful. When done for the day, rewash any wounds and treat with an antibiotic ointment to avoid infection.

Trip Planning Information

Area description: Hueco Tanks State Historical Park offers excellent bouldering and climbing on cliffs up to 250' high and numerous boulders scattered throughout the park.

Location: West Texas. 30 miles east of El Paso.

Camping: Camping is available in the park or at Pete and Queta's Country Store, 1 mile before entering the park. Pete's is strictly a climber's destination resort with a large gravel tenting area in front of the quonset hut that serves as a small store and restaurant. Limited sleeping quarters upstairs in the hut are sometimes available. Reservations are required for camping in the park. Call Central Reservation Center at (512) 389-8900 well before your visit. There are 17 sites with electricity ($9) and 3 sites with no electricity ($6). One bathroom with showers services the sites. Water and tables are provided in all sites. Up to 8 people and 2 cars are covered by the fee. A fee of $2 is charged for additional cars. If you plan on entering the park for more than 7 days, consider purchasing an annual pass at the visitor center. This $13 pass entitles you to unlimited entrances for the year. The park diligently enforces camping rules. Complying with all rules is strongly recommended. Additional camping in the immediate area is virtually non-existent.

Climbing season: Hueco Tanks is one of the premier winter climbing area in the United States. The best climbing weather is from November through March, with daily highs in the 50s and 60s. This is also the time of the heaviest visitation. Occasional winter snow and low temperatures can limit climbing from December to February. Climbing is possible in the spring and early summer by seeking the cooler north faces and other shaded areas. Uncomfortably hot temperatures in the summer and fall severely limit climbing.

Restrictions and access issues: Hueco Tanks is a heavily restricted climbing area. The park's primary mandate to preserve the area's record of historic cultural habitation often conflicts with climbing activity. Since 1989, visiting climbers account for the majority of park usage. Developing a fair and equitable management plan to accommodate all visitation is a fluid, on-going process. Consequently, the management of climbing activities changes frequently. Checking with the park at (915) 857-1135 is recommended for first time visitors. The newest rules require reservations for camping and a $2 "activity fee" besides the $2 daily entrance fee. These fees are required each day you climb or boulder. Registering to climb or boulder plus payment of entry fees are required each day of visitation. Climbers are expected to comply with all other park rules during their visit.

White chalk only is acceptable but should be used sparingly or not at all. Colored chalk and rosin are not allowed. Using chalk as "tic marks" to chart out new problems looks disgustingly like graffiti spray painted liberally throughout the park. Please avoid this practice. Cleaning up the rock and surrounding area after each visit is strongly recommended. The use of chalk is a continuing issue with park personnel.

Chipping or altering handholds on any of the park rocks is illegal. This practice has altered many existing problems in the park and may well usher in further restrictions or closure of the area to climbing.

Applications to establish new climbing routes are available at the visitor center. This program has operated successfully since 1989.

Climbing in the park is considered by park personnel to be a privilege. Please obey all rules to help insure the future of climbing here.

The Small Potatoes, the Kiva Cave, Nuclear Arms/Blood and Gore area, Bucket Roof, Gold Star Roof, Artists, and Opposition are closed to bouldering.

Guidebook: *Hueco Tanks, a Climber's and Boulderer's Guide* by John Sherman, Mike Head, James Grump, and Dave Head is the definitive guide to Hueco Tanks. The guide is now in its second edition. Both climbing and bouldering are covered, with an emphasis on bouldering. *Great Rock Hits of Hueco Tanks* by Paul Piana details select climbing routes.

Nearby mountain shops, guide services, and gyms: El Paso.

Services: Full services are found in nearby El Paso. Pete and Queta's Country Store, just outside the park, has inexpensive meals and some groceries. The nearest fuel is 13 miles from the park, west on U.S. Highway 62/180 (Montana Boulevard). A 24-hour service station is located on the corner of Montana and Lee Trevino.

Emergency services: Contact the rangers at the visitor center for all emergencies. A public pay phone is also available here. After hours, try their two residences just east of the entrance. If unsuccessful with the rangers, contact the Montana Vista Volunteer Fire Department or El Paso County Sherrif.

Nearby climbing areas: Organ Mountains and Doña Ana Mountains are 50 miles northwest in New Mexico.

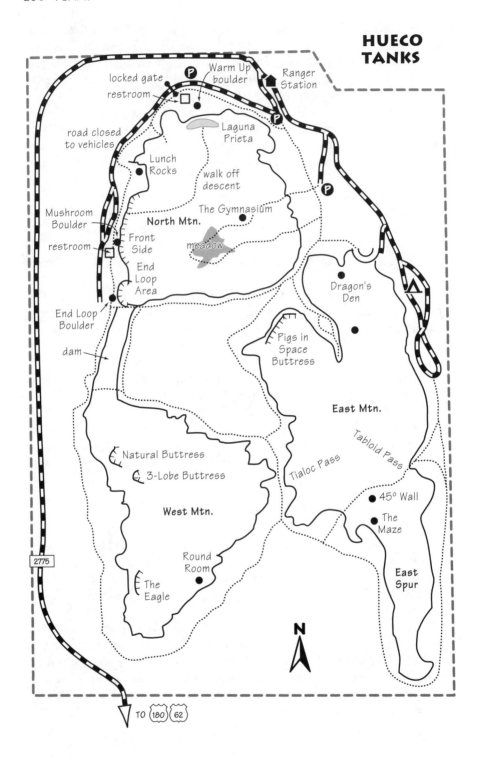

HUECO TANKS

locked gate
Warm Up boulder
Ranger Station
restroom
road closed to vehicles
Laguna Prieta
Lunch Rocks
walk off descent
The Gymnasium
Mushroom Boulder
North Mtn.
restroom
Front Side
meadow
End Loop Area
Dragon's Den
End Loop Boulder
Pigs in Space Buttress
dam
East Mtn.
Tabloid Pass
Natural Buttress
3-Lobe Buttress
Tialoc Pass
2775
West Mtn.
45° Wall
The Maze
Round Room
East Spur
The Eagle
N
TO 180 62

Nearby attractions: El Paso Centennial Museum on the campus of the University of Texas, El Paso Museum of History, Insights-El Paso Science Center, Tigua Indian Reservation (Ysleta del Sur Pueblo), Wilderness Park Museum.

An easy way to visit Juarez (in Mexico) is by using the El Paso/Juarez Trolleys. These air-conditioned rubber-tired vehicles depart from the Civic Center on the hour from 9 a.m. to 4:45 p.m., Wednesday through Sunday. Another easy option is to park your car near the border and walk across. Park in a patrolled lot or your vehicle might emigrate to Mexico without you. Visas or passports are not necessary for U.S. citizens. Foreign nationals should have a passport and appropriate visas both for entering Mexico and returning to the United States. Duty free purchases of up to $400 are allowed for U.S. citizens. You can return with a maximum of 1 liter of duty-free alcohol. Make sure you know and obey all regulations regarding entry and return from Mexico before visiting.

Finding the area: Hueco Tanks State Historical Park is 30 miles east of El Paso, Texas, on Ranch Road 2775 just north of US 62/180. El Paso is reached via I-10 from both the north and south. An alternate approach from the north is via US 54. From I-10 exit onto US 62/180 east toward Carlsbad, New Mexico. Be alert in this section when approaching from the west on I-10 to go past Chelsea then onto Paisano. In a short distance, bend right onto Montana Blvd. (US 62/180). Follow Montana Blvd. east through suburbia and out into the desert. An easier way to avoid the road congestion is to continue east on I-10 a few more miles to Lee Trevino. Exit onto Lee Trevino and drive a few miles north to Montana Blvd. Continue about 20 miles east on US 62/180 to Ranch Road 2775. This junction is signed for Hueco Tanks State Historical Park. Follow the paved road 8 miles north and into the park. The park gate is locked from 10 p.m. to sunrise. A combination is available for campers upon registration. Park Headquarters hours are 8 a.m. to 5 p.m.

NORTH MOUNTAIN

The greatest concentration of quality routes at Hueco is found on North Mountain. To get to North Mountain, also called the Front Side, take the first right turn after the visitor center to reach the parking area. From here continue walking on the road for about 400 yards to the base of the cliff. **Descent:** For routes that do not reach the summit, rappel, generally from fixed anchors, back to the base. 2 ropes are often needed; when in doubt use 2 ropes. For routes that go to the summit, hike east or straight ahead then north or left down ramp systems. Pick the easiest way, no roped climbing necessary, across various gullies and slabs. At night head for the lights at the ranger's houses. Follow the natural drainage down to Laguna Prieta, a marshy pond, near the bottom. Exit the pond area near the west end on its right by easy scrambling through a gap on the rock to rejoin the road. Turn right to the parking area or turn left to the base of the cliff.

1. **Hueco Walk** (5.6R) Start left of a 5' boulder at ground level. Great moderate hueco climb to a wide crack and up. Somewhat unprotected.

2. **Flake Roof** (5.11+) A classic Hueco Tanks roof problem. Boulder up to a sloping ledge at the base of a left-facing dihedral. Climb the dihedral to the right side of the roof, traverse left 10' then over the roof. Use the 2 bolts over the lip to belay or continue up *True Grip* for a great finish.

3. **Flake Roof Indirect** (5.11b) Begin as *Flake Roof,* then up the arete to a crack. Continue up the crack then right to the *True Grip* belay.

4. **True Grip** (5.10a) **Pitch 1:** Face and crack climb the dihedral on the far right side of *Flake Roof* to a small roof, then stem left and climb a low-angle face with many huecos, past a bush to a horizontal crack. Traverse left and up to a 2-bolt belay. **Pitch 2:** Move left to a bolt, then up left to a horizontal crack and up a steep face with large huecos (crux) over another horizontal crack, then up to the summit. A #2 and #3 Friend plus TCUs needed for the belay. **Rack:** Up to a #4 Friend to supplement fixed pro. **Descent:** Gain the summit and walk off north toward Laguna Prieta. Excellent route.

CAKEWALK WALL

5. **Son of Cakewalk** (5.6) **Pitch 1:** Start 10' right of the hourglass formation. Climb a short distance to a small roof by a left-facing dihedral. Pull the roof then straight up on excellent holds to a crack 150' off the ground and belay. **Pitch 2:** Continue up the crack to a short headwall. Gain the summit by first crossing the chockstone in the crevice at the top or rappel into the crevice. **Descent:** Walk off to Laguna Prieta.

6. **Return of Cakewalk** (5.7) **Pitch 1:** Start on the left side of the highest boulder at the base of the wall. Climb up to a large hueco, then up right through a steep section to easier climbing above. Belay 150' off the ground. **Pitch 2:** Climb left, turn the large white roof on the left. **Descent:** Same as *Son of Cakewalk.*

7. **Cakewalk** (5.6) **Pitch 1:** Start 15' right of the boulders at the base of the wall. Good holds lead up the black water trough. When the angle eases, traverse right and up to a hand crack and belay from bolts. **Pitch 2:** Jam the crack to the summit overhang. Traverse up right to belay. **Descent:** Walk off the summit toward Laguna Prieta. A local favorite.

8. **Cakewalk Direct** (5.10a) **Pitch 1:** Start behind trees located behind picnic table #37. Trend up right to a black water streak to a bulge. Climb the

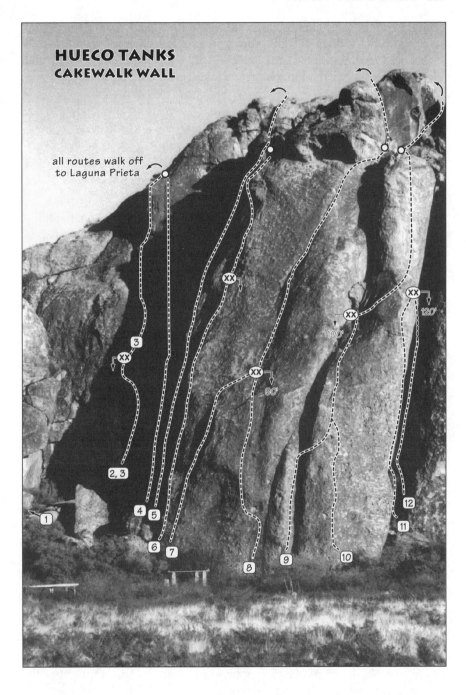

HUECO TANKS
CAKEWALK WALL

all routes walk off
to Laguna Prieta

right side of the bulge to easier terrain above. Belay from 2 bolts in a crack. 6 bolts. **Pitch 2:** Climb the upper pitch of *Cakewalk* to the top. A harder variation begins in the *Banana Patch* thin crack and climbs up and left past a bolt to the black water streak. **Rack:** Stoppers and TCUs protect this excellent start.

9. **Banana Patch** (5.10) **Pitch 1:** Start in the thin 20' crack 15' left of a chimney, or start 4' left of the chimney, both 5.10. Climb about 35' until it is possible to step across the chimney to gain a thin crack on its right side. Continue up the thin crack to a 2-bolt belay next to a tree. **Pitch 2:** Either continue up the chimney or finish on *Busted* to the top. **Rack:** Carry TCUs, small Friends, and wires for the crack variation.

10. **Alice in Bananaland/Busted** (5.10a/5.9) **Pitch 1:** Start 13' right of the chimney. Climb up huecos to a thin vertical crack (same as *Banana Patch*) about 60' up. Belay above at a 2-bolt anchor next to a tree on a sloping ledge. 6 bolts. **Pitch 2:** *Busted.* Climb right then face climb to the steep buttress to the top, (5.9). 3 bolts. **Descent:** Gain the summit and walk off toward Laguna Prieta. An excellent 2-pitch climb. **Rack:** Carry TCUs, wires, and small Friends.

11. **Malice in Bucketland** (5.10a) Start from the top of the 15' boulder at the base of the large chimney. Giant huecos lead to the first clip which is way up there. A 30' ground fall is the penalty for failure; be ready for this one. Climb past 6 bolts to a 2-bolt anchor on an airy stance above a horizontal crack. 2-rope rappel to the ground. Spectacular route. Not hard, but exposed.

12. **Cowboyography** (5.13c/d) Right of *Malice in Bucketland* and to the left of the large chimney. Steep and pumpy face climbing. 8 bolts and anchors.

THE CENTRAL WALL

13. **Divine Wind/Brain Dead** (5.8/5.10+) **Pitch 1:** Start just right of the large chimney. Trend right and up on small holds past 5 bolts to a good ledge 100' off the ground. Belay from 2 bolts. (5.9). **Pitch 2:** *Brain Dead.* Work right then up past 7 bolts on steep rock to the top. 165'. No anchors, gear required. **Rack:** TCUs, wires, and camming units up to 2". It is possible to get one more crack pitch in at the top or scramble to the summit and do the walk north to Laguna Prieta. Excellent link-up route to the summit. Most parties rap 100' to ground from *Divine Wind* anchors.

14. **All the Nasties** (5.9+) **Pitch 1:** Start in the center of the face right of the large chimney directly under the belay ledge for *Divine Wind*. Climb up past 1 bolt on good holds to a thin crack 35' off the ground. Climb the crack, move right on poor-quality rock past 2 bolts, and work up left to

all routes walk off
to Laguna Prieta

HUECO TANKS
CENTRAL WALL

the *Divine Wind* anchors. A scary lead with only 4 bolts. **Pitch 2:** Start on the left end of the ledge. Climb up to a steep headwall. Either go straight up (1 bolt), or traverse right then straight up on good rock (small wires) to the top. No anchors. **Rack:** Carry TCUs, wires, and camming units to 2". One more good crack pitch of your choice leads to the top or scramble left to the summit for the walk-off to Laguna Prieta.

15. **Purple Microdot** (5.11R) **Pitch 1:** Start on the second crack right of the large right-facing dihedral. Difficult climbing leads to a 2-bolt belay below the upper Y-cracks. **Pitch 2:** Climb right under the roof to a right-facing dihedral. Work up past a roof on the left to a good ledge. **Pitch 3:** Either traverse the ledge left or climb one of the cracks above the ledge. Gear and lots of skill in placing it required to do this line.

16. **Walking on the Moon** (5.10R) Start at a tree to the right of *Purple Microdot*. Climb a small overhang to a tiered ledge with 1 bolt. Climb up past 1 bolt then left and up to a crack 100' off the ground. Go right up to a left-facing dihedral. Climb the dihedral and angle right to the belay for *Final Stone*. **Descent:** 2-rope rappel from here or traverse left to the upper portion of *Purple Microdot*. 4 bolts and anchors. **Rack:** Carry TCUs and wires for the cracks.

17. **Final Stone** (5.11R) Start in a shallow dihedral that leans right. Climb past 6 bolts straight up to a flake system. The crux is pulling the horizontal rib. Continue on 5.10+ runout climbing for 35' to the last bolt. Belay from 2 bolts at the top of the crescent-shaped crack. 5 bolts. 2-rope rappel from here or continue unprotected 5.9 to the top.

18. **Window Pain** (5.10b/c) Start on a ramp left of an obvious left-facing dihedral. Face climb straight up past 11 bolts to a 2-bolt anchor on a small ledge. 165' pitch. 2-rope rappel from here. Superb and continuous.

19. **No Fear of Flying** a.k.a. **Dos Equis** (5.11c) Start 10' left of the left-facing dihedral. 8 bolts and anchors. **Rack:** RPs and camming units to 1.5" protect the cracks. **Descent:** 2-rope rappel.

20. **Lunacy** (5.10) **Pitch 1:** Start in the left-facing dihedral. Stem and jam 75' over a small roof to a finger crack. Belay higher on a good ledge from 2 bolts. **Pitch 2:** Continue up the dihedral to a large roof. Climb the wide crack to the chimney finish.

21. **Lunar Abstract** (5.12a) Start just right of the left-facing dihedral. Climb a thin discontinuous crack system to a 2-bolt anchor. RPs and TCUs protect the lower crack. 3 bolts. A short difficult pitch.

22. **Lunatic Friends** (5.10+R) **Pitch 1:** Start near a bush on the buttress right of the left-facing dihedral. Difficult climbing past a bulge emerges onto a steep headwall. Work left around a corner. Continue up steep rock with good protection to the *Lunacy* belay ledge. Belay on the right side. 165'. 6

bolts. **Pitch 2:** Climb right under a small roof, then continue above on easier terrain to the top. Take the left crack near the top. **Rack:** Wires, TCUs, and small camming units plus runners.

23. **Desperado** (5.10+) This excellent pitch is near the top of the wall. A good way to reach it is to climb *Lunatic Friends* and traverse right at the small roof on the 2nd pitch. Follow overhanging jugs past 3 bolts to a thin crack in a dihedral that leads up left to the top. **Rack:** TCUs and wires protect the top section.

24. **Hueco Syndrome** (5.10-) **Pitch 1:** Start 5' to 10' left of the pillars laying against *Uriah's Heap* left side. Moderate, 5.8+ hueco climbing works past 5 bolts to a 2-bolt belay. **Pitch 2:** 2 bolts plus optional gear protect the left-facing corner above, then 3 more bolts lead up the face above to a 2-bolt anchor. **Descent:** Descend by a 2-rope rappel from here or climb an easy pitch to the top. Excellent climb.

25. **Uriah's Heap** (5.7+) **Pitch 1:** Start either on the right side of the pillars (longer, harder) or on the left side. Climb moderate cracks to a good belay stance a little below the top of the highest pillar. **Pitch 2:** Traverse right to a brown water streak and climb to the end of a crack. Climb right and up to a 2-bolt anchor. **Pitch 3:** Climb easy rock passing a roof and loose rock on the right. A good 5.8 variation traverses right at the base of the left facing corner on the 2nd pitch to the anchors for *Sea of Holes*. An excellent moderate climb.

26. **Sea of Holes** (5.10R) **Pitch 1:** Start 10' left of the large left-facing dihedral. The first bolt is 45' away: be focused. 2 more bolts lead straight up through large huecos to a 2-bolt belay 130' off the ground (5.9). **Pitch 2:** Climb straight up to a bolt, then trend right and up to a steep face 15' left of a tree in a dihedral. Climb the face above (crux) to the summit. Gear required for the belay and to supplement bolts (5.10). 4 bolts. One of the most popular climbs at Hueco.

INDECENT EXPOSURE BUTTRESS

27. **Tree Route** (5.9) Start in the large dihedral with a brushy tree near the top. 2 pitches up the dihedral end at the summit. **Rack:** Bring lots of camming units, TCUs, wires, and runners. Not often climbed although highly recommended.

28. **Eternal Apples** (5.11c/d) **Pitch 1:** Start 10' right of the huge dihedral. Climb huecos past 2 bolts to a right-leaning arch, then step left to surmount the arch at the 3rd bolt. Climb up to and over the roof above then easier rock right to a 2-bolt anchor on a good ledge. **Pitch 2:** Climb excellent huecos

HUECO TANKS
RIGHT FRONT SIDE &
INDECENT EXPOSURE BUTTRESS

200'

Mushroom Boulder

to a small roof, clip a hidden bolt, then traverse right on the crack to a 2-bolt anchor. Quality rock, quality route.

29. **Amplified Apples** (5.10d) **Pitch 1:** Climb the 1st pitch of *Eternal Apples* or *Amplified Heat,* or do a 5.7R traverse from the anchors on the 1st pitch of *Sea of Holes.* **Pitch 2:** Climb up left from *Eternal Apples/Amplified Heat* anchors on huge huecos 10' to 15' right of the *Tree Route* and left of *Eternal Apples.* 3 bolts. One of the best pitches at Hueco.

30. **Amplified Heat** (5.11b) **Pitch 1:** Start at the bottom of the huge dihedral. Climb up a green streak then the crack and the face above to a 2-bolt belay. **Pitch 2:** Climb the 2nd pitch of *Eternal Apples* or *Amplified Apples.* 7 bolts on 1st pitch. Excellent.

31. **Indecent Exposure** (5.9+) **Pitch 1:** Start on top of boulders 30' right of the tree at the base of the large dihedral. Climb right to the 1st bolt 20' off the ground then straight up past 1 more bolt and a traverse right to a 2-bolt belay. **Pitch 2:** From the right end of the belay ledge, climb to a right-facing dihedral then to a flake. Climb 10' up the flake, then traverse right on great holds with lots of exposure to easier terrain. 3 bolts. Continue right to the top of a small crack then straight up to a belay stance. The 2nd pitch is rated 5.10 by some climbers. One of the must-do climbs at Hueco. Seconds should be competent and carry prussiks for 2nd pitch.

32. **Rainbow Bridge** (5.11bR) **Pitch 1:** Start on top of large boulders downhill and right of *Indecent Exposure.* Difficult 5.10+ face climbing up and right leads to the bottom of a flake system. Climb the flake then step right into the dihedral (*Deliverance*) and climb up to a 2-bolt belay. 6 bolts and gear. **Pitch 2:** Climb right to a black rib of rock, then straight up for 50' to a good belay ledge. 5.8. **Pitch 3:** This wild pitch climbs the overhanging buttress above. Step right from the belay, work up to a bolt, then right and up to a good rest and a bolt. Continue up left under a bulge and up its left side to easier terrain above. **Rack:** Carry wires, TCUs, and small camming units. Difficult, sustained, and classic.

33. **Deliverance** (5.12a) **Pitch 1:** Start up easy hueco climbing to thin face climbing past 3 bolts to the bottom of the dihedral. Lower from a 2-bolt anchor to do only the 5.12 section or continue up the dihedral (5.9) to a 2-bolt anchor. **Pitch 2:** Continue up a dihedral to the anchors for the 1st pitch of *Indecent Exposure.* **Pitch 3:** Climb left off the belay to a seam angling left about 15' right of a white-water streak (5.10+) 5 bolts. Belay on a good ledge just below the top.

34. **Optical Promise** (5.11d) This exposed pumpy, pitch begins at the top of the 2nd pitch of *Rainbow Bridge.* **Pitch 1:** From the belay, traverse right to a belay on a sloping ledge below the 150' of overhanging rock above. It is 200' to the ground from here. **Pitch 2:** 3 bolts protect the face up to a crack. Gear required for the crack plus the anchors. Exciting and airy.

HUECO TANKS
FOX TOWER

FOX TOWER

35. **Head Fox** (5.10b/c) Climb the face next to a left-angling crack to its end then straight up to a 2-bolt anchor. 10 bolts. **Rack:** Wires, TCUs useful. Excellent.

36. **Fox Trot** (5.10a) Start 6' right of *Head Fox*. Climb huecos to 2 cracks. **Rack:** Wires and TCUs and camming units to 1.5" protect the cracks. 160'. 7 bolts. **Descent:** 2-rope rappel from a 2-bolt anchor. One of the best routes at Hueco.

37. **Fox Tower Indirect** (5.9) To the right of *Fox Trot*. Jam left of 2 cracks for 75', then step into the right crack.

38. **Fox Tower** (5.8) To the right of *Fox Trot*. The right of 2 cracks. Chimney problem after 100'.

END LOOP WALL

End Loop Wall is the last cliff located on the south end of the Front Side.

39. **Cave Exit** (5.7) Start on the south side of the deep chimney just east of table #55. Climb the right side of the right wall up large huecos to a sloping ledge then left to a black water streak. 60'.

40. **Short Hands** (5.7) Climb a right-facing dihedral offering good hand and fist jams to a 2-bolt anchor. 40'. Popular toprope.

HUECO TANKS
END LOOP WALL

End Loop
Boulder

41. **Fast Foods** (5.8) Start 10' right of *Short Hands*. Face climb to shared anchors with *Short Hands*. Usually toproped.

42. **Eclipse** (5.9) Climb up 15' to an overhanging fist crack. Continue above the overhang on easier terrain to the top. 110'.

43. **Show Me** (5.9) Start 15' right of *Eclipse*. Climb the right-leaning crack system to the top. Recommended.

END LOOP BOULDER

This large boulder sits on the far south end of The Front Side.

44. **Wyoming Cowgirls TR** (5.11+) Start 11' left of the crack on the northwest face. This short 35' pitch has also been led although is a popular TR. Previously rated 5.12-.

45. **The End TR** (5.10+) The crack on the northwest face. Unique rest opportunity inside a hueco.

WEST MOUNTAIN

West Mountain is the large formation on the south end of the park. A large earthen dam is between North Mountain and West Mountain. Walk on a good trail from the south end of North Mountain, past the dam to reach West Mountain and the following crags.

NATURAL BUTTRESS

Located about 350 yards south of the earthen dam. **Descent:** Walk east at the top then south down the first canyon south of the buttress.

46. **All Natural** (5.8) This is an old hangerless bolt ladder to the large sloping ledge that is the start for #'s 47 and 48.

47. **Supernatural Anesthetist** (5.12a) **Pitch 1:** Start on the sloping ledge. Climb a crack through the roof above and onto the headwall (5.12). Belay 20' up. **Pitch 2:** Continue up the thin crack in a shallow corner (5.10).

48. **Mr. Natural** (5.11) Climb to the sloping ledge and start 20' right of *Supernatural Anesthetist*. Climb the overhang, then follow bolts to the top. The hangers on bolts and anchors have historically fallen prey to souvenir hunters so check before you climb. 75'.

49. **Sunny Side Up** (5.12b) Start on the south face of the buttress. Large huecos and steep crimps up 5 bolts to a 2-bolt lowering station. 60'.

50. **Max Headroom** (5.10d/.11a) Start in a left-facing corner/ramp system. Climb 40' to a large block. Move left up huecos past 6 bolts to a 2-bolt anchor. 110'. **Rack:** Camming units to 3.5" supplement bolts. Excellent.

THREE LOBE BUTTRESS

The Three Lobe Buttress (not pictured) is 100 yards south of the Natural Buttress at the top of a wide gully on the crest of West Mountain.

51. **Natural Mystic** (5.11) Climb 40' of jugs on an overhanging wall to the base of a right-leaning crack. Go left up a short steep section then onto easy low-angle rock. 85'. **Descent:** Rappel to base of rock.

52. **Huecool** (5.11d R) Start 15' right of *Natural Mystic*. The 1st bolt is mispositioned, requiring the crux moves to be done before the clip. A stick clip from 40' up is the other option. Excellent climbing above on big holds up a very steep wall makes it worth the effort. A former toprope problem that still needs some attention.

THE EAGLE

The Eagle is visible on the south end of the west side of West Mountain on the drive into the park. It is easily reached by walking south on the trail that starts on the south end of North Mountain. Resist any temptation to bypass paying entrance fees by jumping the fence and climbing in this area. It just doesn't work.

53. **The Gunfighter** (5.13b) Thrash up to the north face of the rock to a bolt belay on a boulder below the north face. Jam up an overhanging thin crack in a tight corner that trends right to a bulge. Climb the bulge and go right for an easier finish or left up a good looking thin crack (5.11d). Sustained and difficult. Lots of fixed wires.

54. **When Legends Die** (5.13a) Start 10' right of *The Gunfighter.* Climb right on large huecos. Move up the overhanging face past 7 bolts to a 2-bolt anchor. Runout near the top. Exposed and wild climbing.

55. **Road to Nowhere** (5.11+) Start on the "breast" of The Eagle. Climb a radically overhanging dihedral to an anchor at its end. Strange yet odd.

56. **Through The Looking Glass** (5.11a) **Pitch 1:** Start in the main left-trending crack on the west face. Climb this to an alcove under a roof. Follow the crack left under the roof, then climb the wide crack and jugs to a small ledge. Move up right to the next ledge and belay. **Pitch 2:** Difficult climbing (5.10) off the right end of the ledge leads to easier terrain. Continue

up then left to a dark water streak, then left through poor rock and up to the top. A variation (*Electric Hueco Land*) to the 2nd pitch is to climb left from the belay up overhanging rock past a pin and a bolt to an optional 1-bolt belay (which can be backed up).

EAST MOUNTAIN: PIGS IN SPACE BUTTRESS

The 150' Pigs in Space Buttress lies on the northwest side of East Mountain. From the headquaters continue toward the campgrounds and take the first right turn into a large parking area. Hike an easy trail south between North Mountain and East Mountain. The crag is just past Comanche Canyon, the first large canyon on the left or east. Reach the cliff base by scrambling. **Descent:** Descend all routes that reach the top by walking north then left to a ledge with a tree. Downclimb many huecos, then walk around the east end of the formation.

57. **Plastic Fantastic** (5.11cTR) 60 yards east or left of Pigs in Space Buttress. Access the toprope anchors by scrambling in from the left. Climb huecos up a steep wall left of a black streak.

58. **Death Dihedral** (5.8) Start in the main crack system in a large dihedral near the center of the buttress. From the alcove 35' up, climb left then back right into the dihedral to a tree about 75' above the ground. Complete the dihedral to the top. 120'.

59. **Pigs to Pork** (5.10+/.11a) Start at the bottom of the dihedral, then go straight up the face on the right to a large ledge. Above climb past the Great White Hueco to the top. Difficult gear placements and sustained difficult climbing. Use runners to reduce rope drag. 140'. Recommended.

60. **Pigs in Space** (5.10c) **Pitch 1:** Start same as *Pigs to Pork* and belay on the ledge below the Great White Hueco. **Pitch 2:** Straight up to the top. 140'. This climb passes close to a bee nest.

61. **Kings Highway** (5.9) Start on the north face of the buttress. Climb moderate rock up a corner to a bulge. Above the bulge, move left into a crack. Jam or face climb past the crack, move up right on easier rock to summit.

THE GREAT WALL

Located above and south or right of Pigs in Space Buttress.

62. **Star Dust** (5.12b) Start near the left side of the wall 35' right of a large right-facing corner. Boulder up to a good ledge with tree. Belay here and

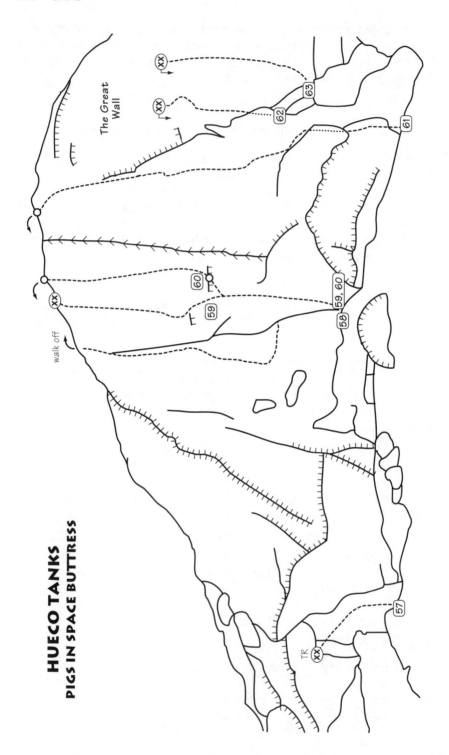

**HUECO TANKS
PIGS IN SPACE BUTTRESS**

climb the overhanging face above past 4 bolts to a 2-bolt anchor. 70'. Wires supplement bolts. Classic, steep, and pumpy.

63. **Tarts of Horsham** (5.12d) Start by bouldering up to the ledge with a tree. Belay from the right end of the ledge. Crimp up right past 2 bolts then straight up at the 3rd. 75'. 7 bolts to a 2-bolt anchor.

POINT OF ROCKS

OVERVIEW

Point of Rocks is an old-time Texas climbing area near Davis Mountains State Park in west Texas. The crag is one of many in an ocean of outcrops that make up the Davis Mountains. Presently, Point of Rocks is the only crag with climbing access, although it is on private land. The remaining cliffs outside the park are on the large ranches prominent in this area of Texas.

At least 20 routes are established on the 150', moderately angled, west-facing slab, the only such slab in a area of vertical pinnacles and cliffs. The slab is composed of good quality syenite rock. The syenite is a Tertiary intrusive igneous rock. The slab rises above a pleasant picnic area on the southeastern edge of the park. Access to the base of the slab is an easy, 10-minute hike from the picnic area. Most of the routes are moderately difficult and range from one to three pitches in length. The climbs become more difficult on the west side of the slab, with the hardest lines being on the far western end.

Climbing history: Around 1975, climbers from Midland, Texas, began visiting Point of Rocks. Rappelling and aid climbing were the main attractions. Chuck Lohn became interested in free climbing in 1978 and opened up new territory by freeing some old aid lines. Experience gained at other climbing areas, principally Tuolumne Meadows, enabled John and other climbers to test the crackless faces in the late 1970s. The arrival of Bill Davey from Big Springs in 1980 resulted in most of the present development and a rise in the standards. John Gogas became interested in the area at this time and brought his talents to further exploration. Development has slowed since then, with most of the quality lines already done. Today few climbers visit this relatively remote area. A solitary and enjoyable experience is virtually guaranteed for the occasional climbing visitor.

Rack: A rack of ten quickdraws, camming units up to 4", and a 165' rope is sufficient for most routes. Gear supplements bolts on most routes.

Descent: Lower from anchors, rappel, or walk off either side from the top. A large ramp on the left end of the crag is a good descent for most routes.

More routes have been developed on the north side of the Point of Rocks outcrop. Routes from 5.5 to 5.10 are found here with many in the easy to moderate range. On the east end of the outcrop is the Oriental Wall with harder routes in the 5.9 and 5.10 range. This crag is on private property. Access is via a dirt road just east of the picnic area and permission is required from the Largents, who live in the first house on the left. Please be courteous and obey all of their wishes. The abundant spires and faces in the area hold promise for future development. Consultation with park rangers should precede any new climbing development in the park. Rocks outside the park boundaries are all on private land. Permission to climb on any of these areas is required before crossing any fence line.

Trip Planning Information

Area description: Point of Rocks, a roadside crag in Davis Mountains State Park, features numerous bolt-protected, 1- to 3-pitch routes on a wide syenite slab.

Location: West Texas.

Camping: Good camping is available in Davis Mountains State Park. Reservations are advisable on holidays and weekends. Sites have tables, grills, and bathrooms with showers. Also in the park is the Indian Lodge, a hotel and restaurant.

Climbing season: Climbing is possible year-round in this area. Elevations between 4,900' and 5,500' provide for cool summers and mild winters. Occasional winter cold spells can limit climbing.

Restrictions and access issues: Register to climb at Point of Rocks even though it is on private land. Climbing is permitted and even encouraged at other areas in the park. Please cooperate with the rangers to help maintain this unique situation. Climbers are asked to register, pay entry fees, and observe other park rules.

Guidebook: *Point of Rocks and Environs* by C. Eggleston has circulated informally for a number of years. Ask locals for a copy of this hard-to-find guide if considering other climbing opportunities in the area.

Nearby mountain shops, guide services, and gyms: None.

Services: Food, fuel, and lodging are found in nearby Fort Davis or Alpine, 26 miles to the southeast. Alpine, the largest city in this area of Texas, offers full services.

Emergency services: Contact the rangers at Davis Mountains State Park for all emergencies in the park. The Big Bend Regional Medical Center in Alpine (turn east off Texas Highway 118 North as you enter Alpine), is the only hospital in the area.

Nearby climbing areas: Big Bend National Park is 100 miles southeast. Hueco Tanks State Historic Park is 200 miles northwest.

Nearby attractions: Fort Davis National Historic Site, open daily 8 a.m. to 5 p.m. Admission fees are required. McDonald Observatory on Mount Locke

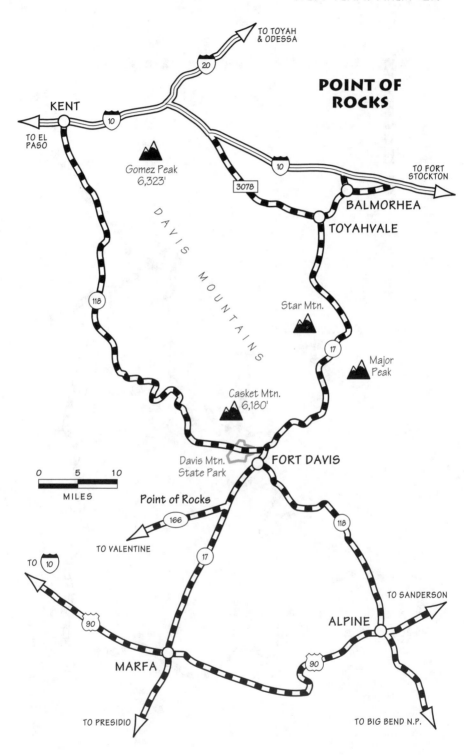

POINT OF
ROCKS

TO TOYAH
& ODESSA

20

KENT

10

TO EL
PASO

Gomez Peak
6,323'

10

3078

TO FORT
STOCKTON

BALMORHEA

TOYAHVALE

D A V I S

118

Star Mtn.

17

M O U N T A I N S

Major
Peak

Casket Mtn.
6,180'

Davis Mtn.
State Park

FORT DAVIS

0   5   10

MILES

Point of Rocks

166

118

TO VALENTINE

TO 10

17

TO SANDERSON

90

ALPINE

90

MARFA

TO PRESIDIO

TO BIG BEND N.P.

POINT OF ROCKS

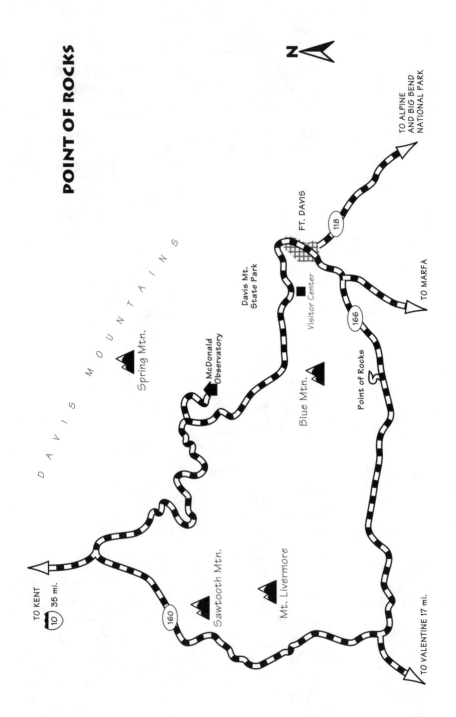

N

DAVIS MOUNTAINS

Spring Mtn.

McDonald Observatory

Davis Mt. State Park

Visitor Center

Blue Mtn.

Point of Rocks

FT. DAVIS

118

TO ALPINE AND BIG BEND NATIONAL PARK

166

TO MARFA

TO KENT

10 35 mi.

160

Sawtooth Mtn.

Mt. Livermore

TO VALENTINE 17 mi.

(visitor center and celestial viewing), Scenic Drive (74-mile loop through the Davis Mountains), town of Fort Davis, restored historic Limpia Hotel, Neill Museum, and the Overland Trail Museum. In nearby Alpine visit the Sul Ross State University Museum of the Big Bend.

Finding the area: Point of Rocks lie near the southern boundary of Davis Mountain State Park, just southwest of Fort Davis. From Interstate 10 eastbound, exit onto TX 118 and drive 51 miles south to Fort Davis. Westbound on I-10, exit onto TX 17 at Balmorhea and drive 34 miles south. Look for signs to Davis Mountain State Park on the north end of Fort Davis. Drive a short distance to the visitor center to register and pay entrance fees. Paying fees and registering will facilitate cooperation between climbers, the park, and the private owner. Check with locals for more information. The visitor center is on the north end of town, off route to the rocks, but folks should go there to register before climbing. To reach the crag from Fort Davis drive south on Texas 17 for 2 miles then west on 166 for 10 miles. Maps to the climbing area and other visitor information are available when you register.

Routes are described from right to left when viewed from the bottom of the crag.

1. **Solo Slabs** (5.0-5.7) Climb the low-angled slabs on the right side of the large slab. Good practice friction routes for beginners.

2. **Frog Fright** (5.10) Smear up *Solo Slabs* to a belay spot under the obvious large roof. Jam a short strenuous crack up the overhang's middle.

3. **Scarcity** (5.7) Begin left of *Solo Slabs*. Work up right to the edge of the low angle and high angle slabs. Climb straight up past 2 bolts and angle up left to a belay ledge. Do a short pitch to the summit.

4. **Density** (5.9) Begin just left of *Scarcity*. **Pitch 1:** Edge up past 2 bolts on the steep slab (crux at bolt 2) and belay at the 3rd bolt. **Pitch 2:** Move up right to a bolt and climb up the slab (5.6) to a spacious ledge.

5. **Lucky Ledges Direct** (5.9) Start left of *Density*. **Pitch 1:** Thin climbing leads to 1st bolt. Work up right to a flake and another bolt. Go up left to a belay ledge with 2 bolts. 60'. **Pitch 2:** Climb to a bolt above and go up right on easy climbing past a flake to a large ledge, or work up left to a large flake (5.6), climb the flake, and head for the ledge. 110'.

6. **Lucky Ledges** (5.6) Begin by a large boulder. **Pitch 1:** Smear up right 30' to a bolt. Climb up on good holds to a down-sloping ledge system and move right to a 2-bolt belay stance. **Pitch 2:** Go up right to a bolt and continue up right past a hollow flake (5.4) to easy climbing and a belay ledge.

POINT OF ROCKS

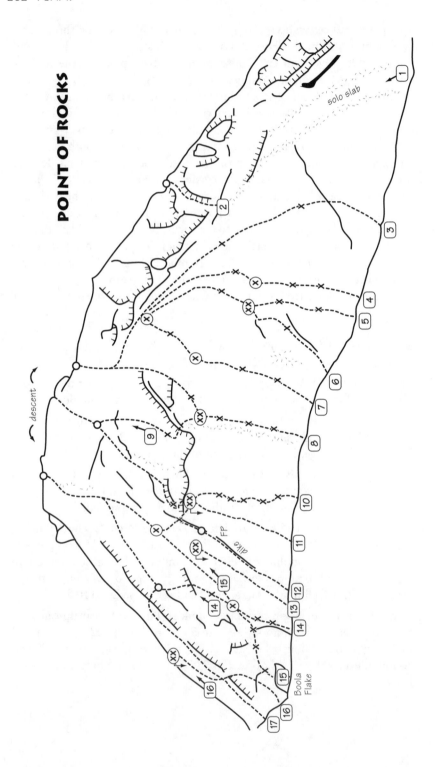

7. **Tuolumne** (5.9) **Pitch 1:** Delicate moves past 2 bolts (5.9-) lead to a flake. Climb up to a ledge with a fixed piton/1- bolt belay. 60'. **Pitch 2:** Edge up right to a shelf, a bolt, and an overlap. Belay high above on the large ledge. 140'.

8. **Breach of Faith** (5.8) Start below a hollowed scoop beneath the right side of the arch above. **Pitch 1:** Work up and over the scoop to a bolt. Climb left (5.8) and up to another bolt. Move straight up to a 2-bolt belay stance. 65'. **Pitch 2:** Edge up right past a bolt to a flake. Climb up good holds to a right-facing corner. Continue up to the summit. 150'.

9. **Travesty** (5.9) Climb the first pitch of *Breach of Faith*. From the belay work into a corner by a prickly pear cactus. Step left around the edge of the arch to a bolt and climb fun, easy rock above to a ledge. 150'.

10. **Double Determination** (5.9) **Pitch 1:** Thin, sustained edging and friction leads past 5 bolts to a thin flake topped with 2 bolts. Friction climbing heads up left to the arch and a bolted belay stance. 100'. **Pitch 2:** Pull over the arch to a bolt (5.8) and sling a spike above. Work up right on easier climbing to the summit. 140'.

11. **Bad Air** (5.10a) Begin near a boulder. Climb straight up past several bolts to the bolted belay stance on *Double Determination*. Continue to the summit on its 2nd pitch or rap with 2 ropes.

12. **The Dike** (5.8) Find the obvious right-angling dike of white rock. **Pitch 1:** Move up the dike and past the route crux (5.8+) after 15'. (Find a pothole

thread for pro.) Pass a fixed pin and belay in a stance in a hollow. 60'. **Pitch 2:** Continue up right to a bolt and climb up and then left (5.7) to a sloping shelf with a fixed pin. 50'. **Pitch 3:** Climb a long right-leaning ramp (one 5.7 move) to a left-facing corner and the summit.

13. **Cowboy Logic** (5.11a) Begin just left of *The Dike*. Great thin face climbing moves up right past several bolts to a double-bolt anchor. 70'. Rap or lower.

14. **The Chute** (5.9) Begin left of *Cowboy Logic*. **Pitch 1:** Thin face climbing (5.9) works up an incipient crack with 2 bolts to a single belay bolt. 40'. **Pitch 2:** Move up right to a bolt and work back left past a thin crack. Climb over a 5.9 bulge to a short crack and the right-angling ramp/crack. 60'. **Pitch 3:** Continue up right on easier climbing to the top. 150'.

15. **Crossfire** (5.9) Start on the left side of a large flake-boulder (The Boola Flake). **Pitch 1:** Climb to a bolt and traverse up right to another bolt (5.9 crux). Move past another bolt and climb up right (stoppers for pro). Continue up right to *The Dike's* second belay stance. 150'. **Pitch 2:** Friction straight up (5.7) to easier climbing and the summit. 70'.

16. **Palomino Gals** (5.10c/d) Begin up the slope from Boola Flake. Face climb up across *Cross Country Crack's* ramp to a 2-bolt belay/rap station.

17. **Cross Country Crack** (5.6) Start by a tree below an obvious right-angling ramp. **Pitch 1:** Follow the ramp for a long way to a spot where you can drop down right to a ledge. Climb up to a better ledge and belay. 140'. **Pitch 2:** Move up the ledge to a hand traverse (5.6) and a left-facing corner. 145'.

PECOS RIVER GORGE

OVERVIEW

More than 1,000 miles from its headwaters high in the Sangre de Cristo Range in the southern Rockies of New Mexico, the Pecos River finally joins with its sister river, the Rio Grande, for its final journey to the Gulf of Mexico. At the confluence, the river has cut down through the Permian limestone bed that pervades much of western Texas.

Long a barrier to travel for western pioneers, the gorge is now easily crossed by a bridge connecting the vast reaches of "Texas west of the Pecos" with the equally vaster reaches of eastern Texas. The Amistad (Spanish for "friendship") Reservoir, a joint American and Mexican venture dedicated in 1969, now partially fills the gorge, offering ample recreational opportunities for boating and angling enthusiasts.

Natalie Merrill Leading *Spike Shabook* (5.10b) on the Pecos River Cliffs, Texas.
Photo by Ian Riddington.

PECOS RIVER GORGE

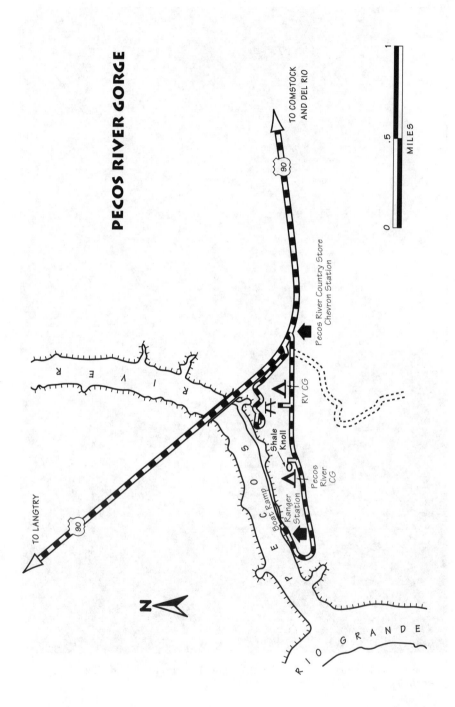

PECOS RIVER GORGE

Gecko Wall

Random Wall

Slain Buffalo Wall

Shaman Wall

Metalogic Wall

Lawless Wall & Cove

Whiskey Wall

Dock Wall

Recently, Texas climbers have begun to tap the gorge's vast climbing resource as well. Limestone cliffs from 50' to 150' high stretch for miles on both sides of the rivers—enough climbing for a lifetime. That's the good news. The bad news is that most of the cliffs are on private property, a common occurrence in Texas ranch country. The vast potential here is yet to be tapped, but right now climbers can enjoy a good selection of bolted lines, all with easy access, a friendly scene, cheap camping, and a truly remarkable setting.

Climbing history: The very first area to be developed here is now closed to climbing due to its location in a highly sensitive archaeological area. Some 4,000 years ago, a sophisticated culture of Native Americans lived and prospered in this area. They left a legacy of art in the form of pictographs, paintings or "rock art," on many of the canyon walls. One of the most spectacular sites was visited by Texas climbers in the late 1980s. Mike Lewis and Jacob Valdez led these efforts. More than 40 routes were developed before the person who leased the land proposed charging $150 per day to climb there, the same fee he charged to hunters. Negotiations with this individual proved to be futile, so when his lease expired the Rock Art Foundation was formed and the group was able to purchase the strip of land and an access right of way from the owner to preserve this extraordinary glimpse of a lost culture. Cooperative efforts between the Foundation and the Access Club began at this time with a preliminary agreement to allow climbing for those who became members of the Foundation ($50 a year). The area however, is presently completely closed to climbing. Up-to-date information can be obtained from the Rock Art Foundation at (210) 525-9907, or the Access Fund.

Forced to look elsewhere, locals found equally good cliffs a short distance south. More than 40 well-bolted routes can be enjoyed here, all on private land but with the owner's permission. Early developers included Carol Sproul and John Gogas. This duo put up over half of the routes on the crags. Dave McArthur and Andy Ruude; two Air Force instructor pilots from Del Rio, were also active during this time, establishing good moderate routes. Jeff Jackson and Alex Catlin are responsible for many of the most difficult climbs on the cliff's middle and southern sectors.

Climbing in the Pecos River Gorge is on high-quality, pocketed, vertical to overhanging limestone cliffs overlooking the Pecos River. Using small flutes and scoops for holds is characteristic of the area. Many of the routes are in the 5.10 to 5.11 range, making it a popular intermediate area. The Lawless Wall and Whiskey Wall crags, with easy access and a plethora of 5.10 and 5.11 routes as well as a smattering of 5.7 to 5.9 routes, are the most popular venues. The longer 150'-high Random Wall also offers easy access and the longest routes in the gorge. Most of the routes here also run between 5.10 to 5.11. There is something for everyone at the Gorge however, with several 5.12s, 5.13s, and an unconfirmed 5.14. Most parties choose to rappel down the Lawless and Random walls, although it is possible to walk to the base from the gorge bottom. Climbers of all abilities will enjoy the area.

Rack: Bring a large rack of quickdraws, up to 20 for the Random Wall, a 150' rope for the sport routes, and camming units for the occasional crack. A 165' rope is recommended for the Random Wall.

Descent: Descend by lowering or rappelling from fixed anchors.

Trip Planning Information

Area description: Pecos River Gorge offers excellent intermediate to expert sport climbing on 80' to 150' limestone cliffs.

Location: Southwestern Texas at the confluence of the Pecos River and Rio Grande about 40 miles east of Del Rio, Texas.

Camping: A private campground operated by the owner of the crag is located on the rim above the climbing area. Day-use and camping fees are $3 per person per day/night. Picnic tables, shelters, restrooms, and showers available. Register at the Chevron station on the south side of U.S. Highway 90 on the way to the area. Additional camping, more deluxe and more expensive, is available about 1 mile east of US 90 at Seminole Canyon State Historical Park. Entrance fees of $3 and $6 to $9 camping fees are strictly enforced. Picnic tables, shelter, restroom, and showers available. Mid-December to mid-January camping can be problematic here on weekdays due to a closure for "permit hunting."

PECOS RIVER GORGE

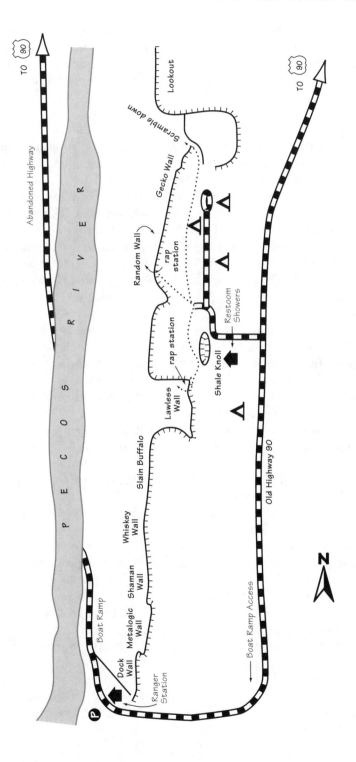

Climbing season: Pecos River Gorge is primarily a winter climbing area. Moderate temperatures in the late fall and early spring are also conducive to climbing. Temperatures in excess of 100 degrees are characteristic of the summer months. The west-facing cliffs are shaded throughout the day in the winter.

Restrictions and access issues: All of the crags are on private land with climbing allowed at the discretion of the owner. One serious accident prompted a temporary closure in the past. Currently, the area is open to climbing with the only restrictions being a $3 fee for use. Farther up-river is the original developed area in a sensitive archeological area. This land, with help from the Access Fund, is now owned by the Rock Art Foundation and is closed to climbing to protect and preserve an amazing array of pictographs along this section of the Pecos River. Please honor this closure until a management plan can be developed that may include climbing activities. Contact Jim Zintgraff in San Antonio, (210) 525-9907, for information on how you can help.

Guidebook: The area is included in *Texas Limestone II*, by Jeff Jackson and Kevin Gallagher. *Climbing Magazine,* May-June 1995, featured a mini-guide to the area also by Jeff Jackson.

Nearby mountain shop, guide services, and gyms: None.

Services: It is best to arrive self-sufficient when climbing at Pecos River Gorge. Two restaurants, a post office, and a gas station are found in Comstock about 10 miles east on US 90. About 1 mile before Comstock is the Owl's Nest, a small grocery store with domestic brews and auto fuel.

Emergency services: Dial 911.

Nearby climbing areas: None. Pecos River Gorge is an isolated crag. The limestone crags around San Antonio and Austin are 270 miles and 200 miles east. Enchanted Rocks State Natural Area is 230 miles east and Hueco Tanks State Historical Park is 350 miles west. Big Bend National Park and Point of Rocks are 250 miles west.

Nearby attractions: Seminole Canyon State Historical Park (pictographs), Judge Roy Bean Visitor Center in Langtry.

Finding the crag: The Pecos River Gorge is on the east side of the Pecos River just south of the high bridge on US 90. If approaching from the west, cross the bridge, drive a short distance past the Overlook entrance to the Chevron station on the south side of the highway. Pay fees and register for camping here. Continue driving west on a paved road for a little less than 1 mile to the well-marked right (north) turn into the campground operated by the owners. Ignore the RV campground passed on the way. If approaching from the east, look for the Chevron station about 1 mile west of Seminole Canyon State Historical Park.

Once in the campground, turn right and then left around the small shale knoll located near the center of the campground. Head toward the river straight ahead beyond campsite electrical boxes 19/20 for about 100 yards to a parking area with a picnic table and fire ring. Access the Gecko Wall by walking about 250 yards to the right to the second gully and then down to the base of the cliff. Alternately rappel from anchors bracketing the left and right margins of the wall. Long slings are useful here.

To get to the Random Wall, walk straight ahead from the picnic table towards the river for about 75 yards and locate anchors that are north (up-river) of a steep gully. The first anchors (welded cold shuts) are for *Humping the Camel* and the second (preferable to access all climbs) are for *She Rode Horses*. The descent is a 150' rappel, 2 ropes required. You can also walk to the base of the cliff from both the Lawless and Gecko walls. Go up-river from the Lawless and down-river from the Gecko.

To get to the Lawless and all other walls, go left from the picnic table on a good trail for about 100 yards to a gully. Walk a short distance down the gully and then do a short rappel from anchors (welded cold shuts for *The Way Out*). Turn left (facing the wall) for routes on the Lawless or turn right for all other routes on Lawless Cove to Dock Wall.

It is also possible to walk in from the bottom to access all walls. To use this approach, continue driving past the campground less than 1 mile to the Amistad Recreation Area. Park in the lower lot by the information shelter. An easy-to-follow trail starts by the porta potties opposite the Information Shelter and leads uphill to the concrete abutments that define the right margin of the Dock Wall. Go left at the abutments to access all walls.

THE GECKO WALL

This small cliff is the most recently developed crag at Pecos River Gorge. 4 moderate routes are currently established. Little information is available. The main attractions appear to be easy access and moderate routes. Routes described from left to right when viewed from the base of the cliff.

1. **Prosimian** (5.8)
2. **Lizard's Lust** (5.9) 7 bolts and anchors.
3. **Butterfly Gecko** (5.10d) 7 bolts and anchors
4. **Renegade** (5.10a) 7 bolts and anchors.

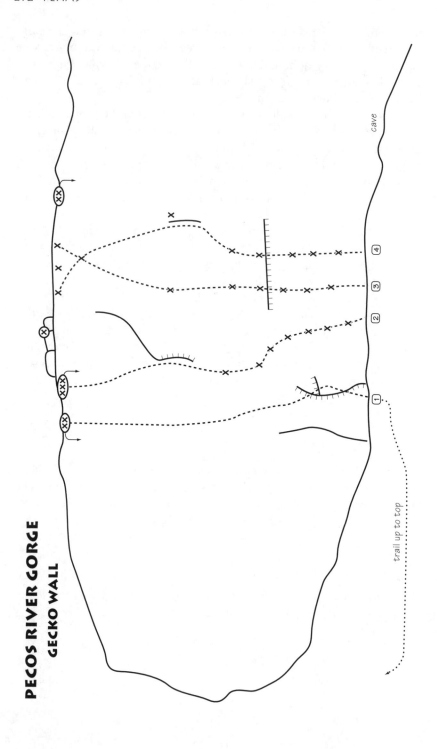

PECOS RIVER GORGE

GECKO WALL

cave

① ② ③ ④

trail up to top

THE RANDOM WALL

The longest routes (up to 150') in the climbing area are found here. Either walk up river from the Lawless Wall or rappel in from anchors for *She Rode Horses*. Routes are described left to right when viewed from the base of the cliff. Ignore the project anchors to the south or down river of the gully for any access.

5. **All This Way for the Short Ride** (5.11d) 13 bolts and shared anchors. Start on *Well Tuned Evinrude* to the large vegetated ledge. Move left past a tree to a shallow vertical crack. Easier climbing above. Shares anchors with *Well Tuned Evinrude*.

6. **Well Tuned Evinrude** (5.11d) 11 bolts and anchors. Steep climbing protected by 4 bolts leads to the large vegetated ledge/cave. Move a little left and climb a steep face to a blunt arete. Recommended.

7. **Bucket Rider** (5.11c) 11 bolts and anchors. Climb past 1 bolt to the large ledge/cave with a left-facing crack ascending to a good ledge with yellow streaks. Climb face left of crack, turn ledge with yellow streaks on left. Recommended.

8. **Smoking Guns** (5.12a) 12 bolts and anchors. Start on right side of yellow chossy rock near the center of the cliff. Difficult climbing up suspect rock at start to easier climbing above. One of the best routes on the cliff. Loose flakes near the bottom.

9. **He Drove Porsches** (5.11b) 16 bolts and anchors. Climb low-angle face past 2 bolts to the left end of a long ledge. Continue slightly left and up to the left of a round hole, then up and left of another smaller hole. Continue straight up, passing good rest ledges and small roofs to a 2-bolt anchor. Loose flakes near the bottom. Excellent route.

10. **She Rode Horses** (5.11b) 18 bolts and anchors. Same start as *He Drove Porches*. Trend right above the 2nd bolt to a left-facing crack, then up good pockets and edges to a 2-bolt anchor. Loose flakes near the bottom. Excellent.

11. **Humping the Camel** (5.10) 9 bolts and welded cold shut anchors. Start at bottom of *He Drove Porches*. Climb easy low-angle ledge to right to set up a belay at the base of the climb. Face climb to left of crack system. Recommended.

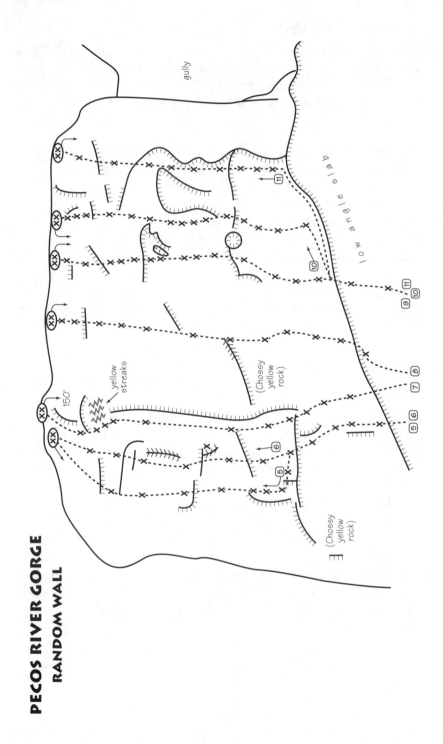

PECOS RIVER GORGE
RANDOM WALL

THE LAWLESS WALL AND LAWLESS COVE

Routes are described left to right when viewed from the base of the cliff.

12. **Crescent Conundrum** (5.11a) No topo. Walk about 50' left or up-river from *Texas 2-Step*. Start in a left facing crack and meander up and left past 11 bolts to anchors. Strange, but worth the effort.

13. **Texas 2-Step** (5.9) Good hand jams to a 2-bolt anchor. Lower from here or ignore the anchors and veer left lower in the crack to climb the arete on the left. Traverse right near the top to belay from anchors for *Dancing With Too Many Girls*. Difficult clips and slightly contrived. Friends up to #3.5 protect the hand crack.

14. **Dancing With Too Many Girls** (5.12b) Start in the 5.9 handcrack and continue up the attractive steep pocketed face to lowering anchors. Quality route.

15. **Chimney Sweep** (5.10a) Take the crack all the way to the rim. No anchors, gear placements required.

16. **The Real U.T. is in Tennessee** (5.10a) 9 bolts and anchors. Excellent face climbing just to the right of the dihedral.

17. **Wetback Expressway** (5.9) 8 bolts and anchors. Start at ground level (recommended) or from the belay ledge above. Excellent moderate climbing.

18. **Scott Free** (5.10a) 9 bolts, shares last bolt and anchors with *Wetback Expressway*. Start at ground level or from the belay ledge above. Quality.

19. **Hanging Judge** (5.10a) 8 bolts and anchors. Start on the belay ledge 10' right of *Scott Free*. Recommended.

20. **Andy's Encore** (5.11d/.12a) 4 bolts and anchors. Difficult climbing up a steep face to easier climbing above.

21. **Running From the Law** (5.12a) 4 bolts, shares anchors with *Andy's Encore*. Difficult climbing up an arete.

22. **Fool's Way Out** (5.11a) 4 bolts, shares anchors with *The Way Out*. Start left of a thin crack. Steep face climbing.

23. **The Way Out** (5.9+) Also the usual way in. 2 bolts protect a crack to welded cold shut anchors. Harder than it looks.

24. **Basta** (5.13) 60' feet left of *The Way Out* past the overhanging "Lawless Cove." Bouldering possibilities are found in the cave. 8 bolts and anchors. The first bolt protects the crux overhang start. Angle right near the top to anchors.

25. **Wrangler Savvy** (5.11b) 8 bolts, shares anchors with *Basta*. Joins *Basta* left of the tree. Excellent.

26. **Cow Smarts** (5.10) 7 bolts and anchors. Start right of *Wrangler Savvy*.

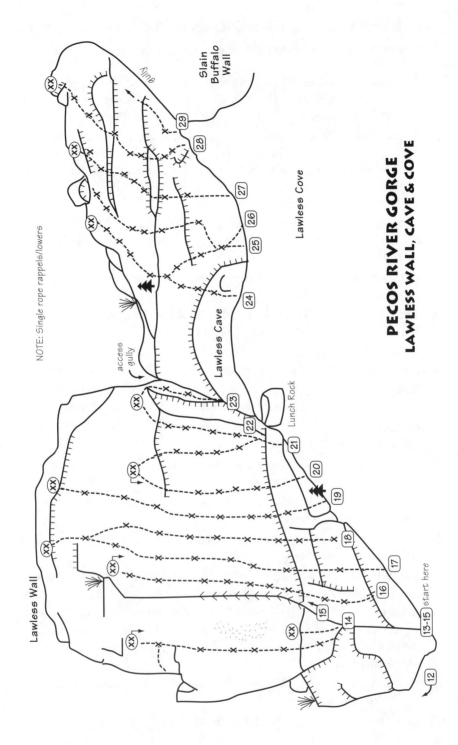

NOTE: Single rope rappels/lowers

PECOS RIVER GORGE
LAWLESS WALL, CAVE & COVE

Slain Buffalo Wall

Lawless Cove

Lawless Cave

gully

access gully

Lunch Rock

Lawless Wall

start here

29

28

27

26

25

24

23

22

21

20

19

18

17

16

15

14

13-15

12

Clip 1st bolt of *Wrangler Savvy,* then right for one more clip, then up past 5 bolts to anchors right of the hole near the top.

27. **Giddy-Up** (5.10b) 7 bolts, shares anchors with *Cow Smarts.*

28. **War Path** (5.11b) 7 bolts and anchors.

29. **Jurisdiction** (5.11+) Located up the gully on loose rock. Not recommended.

SLAIN BUFFALO WALL

This wall is named after a likeness of a buffalo discernible on the cliff face. *Medicine Wheel* climbs past the alledged beast's head.

30. **Monopoly** (5.10) No topo. On the left side of Slain Buffalo Wall, 50' right of *Jurisdiction.* A white face protected by bolts.

31. **Shape Shifter** (5.11b) 8 bolts up an attractive arete. Shares anchors with *Highland Fling.* Recommended.

32. **Highland Fling** (5.7) 9 bolts protect a flake system. Recommended. A good place to practice gear placements.

33. **Unknown** (5.8) 25' feet right of *Highland Fling.* Either lead the crack or toprope the face from anchors located above the large belay ledge near a large hole.

34. **Coup Stick** (5.13-) **Pitch 1:** (5.13-) Starts at ground level. Climb the black face past 3 bolts to anchors on the large belay ledge. **Pitch 2:** (5.12c). Climb the overhang just left of the yellow and black streaks past 5 bolts to lowering anchors.

35. **Cat on a Hot Tin Roof** (5.12b) Start on the large belay ledge below a wildly overhanging black and yellow streaked wall right of a small cave. Climb the arching crack and face above to lowering anchors. 5 bolts. Excellent.

36. **Medicine Wheel** (5.13+) Uncompleted project as of 1995.

37. **Flaming Arrow** (5.12a) Start 100' right of *Medicine Wheel.* Steep face climbing past 5 bolts to lowering anchors.

38. **Unknown** (5.7) Starts at ground level. Crack climb. Gear placements required.

WHISKEY WALL

Rappel in from anchors for #40 or walk right from the Lawless Wall. Routes described left to right when viewed from the base of the cliff.

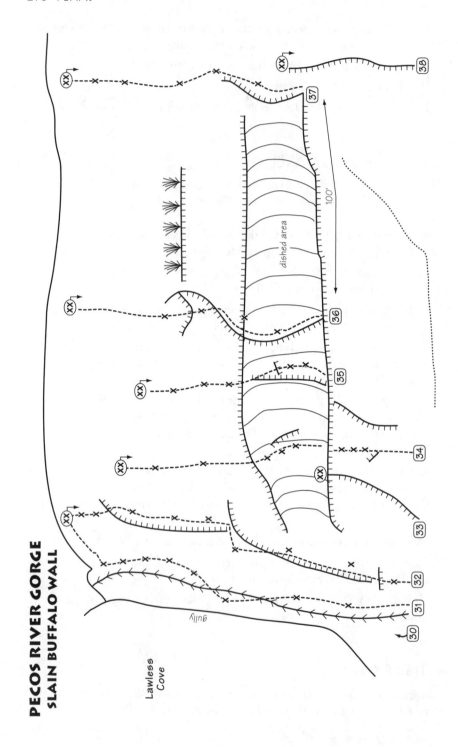

PECOS RIVER GORGE
SLAIN BUFFALO WALL

Lawless
Cove

gully

100'

dished area

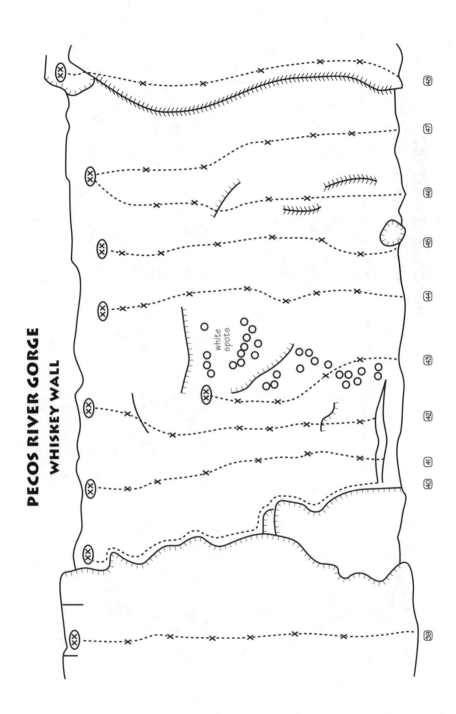

PECOS RIVER GORGE

WHISKEY WALL

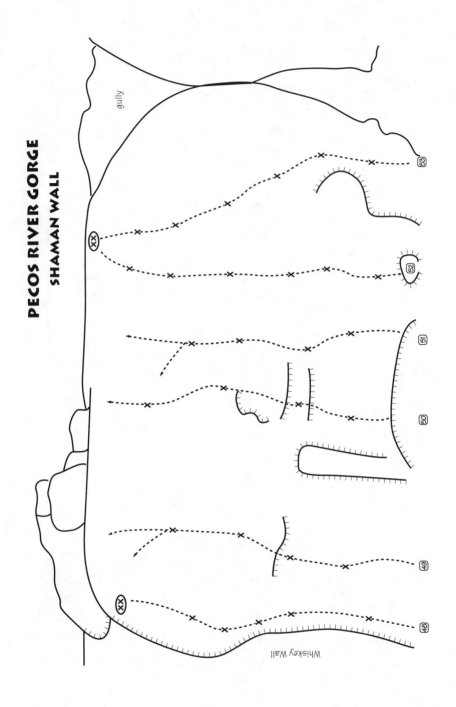

PECOS RIVER GORGE
SHAMAN WALL

39. **Anomaly** (5.11d) 6 bolts and anchors.

40. **Unknown** (5.7.) No bolts, gear placements required. Anchors at top. Good moderate lead.

41. **Stab it and Steer** (5.11a) 6 bolts and anchors.

42. **Unknown** (5.10d) 6 bolts and anchors.

43. **Frosted Flake** (5.10d) 4 bolts and anchors.

44. **Tugboat Granny** (5.10a) 7 bolts and anchors.

45. **Spike Shabook** (5.10b) 6 bolts and anchors.

46. **Unknown** (5.11) 4 bolts and shared anchors.

47. **The Bear Paw** (5.11) 5 bolts and shared anchors.

SHAMAN WALL

The Shaman Wall is a continuation of the Whiskey Wall. It starts right of Bear Paw. Routes are described left to right when viewed from the base of the cliff. Anchors not obvious. Plan accordingly.

48. **Shaman in a Bottle** (5.12b) 5 bolts and anchors. Arete right of *The Bear Paw.*

49. **Dwarf Shaman** (5.13) 4 bolts.

50. **Uber Shaman** (5.12c) 4 bolts.

51. **Shamaroid** (5.13) 4 bolts.

52. **Sky Shaman** (5.13a) 6 bolts to shared anchors.

53. **Geisha Man** (5.12) 6 bolts to shared anchors.

METALOGIC WALL AND DOCK WALL

Located right of the Shaman Wall after a short walk past undeveloped cliffs. These walls, featuring upper grade climbs, can also be reached easily by a good trail starting by the porta potties in the lower parking area for the boat ramp serving the Amistad Reservoir. Routes are described left to right when viewed from the base of the cliff.

54. **Aporia** (5.12b) 4 bolts and shared anchors. This and the following 2 routes likely have anchors or shared anchors. Locate before you climb.

55. **Terry's** (5.12) 4 bolts and shared anchors.

56. **Metalogic** (5.14-) 4 bolts, shares anchors with *Reading Iculus.*

57. **Reading Iculus** (5.13) 4 bolts and anchors.

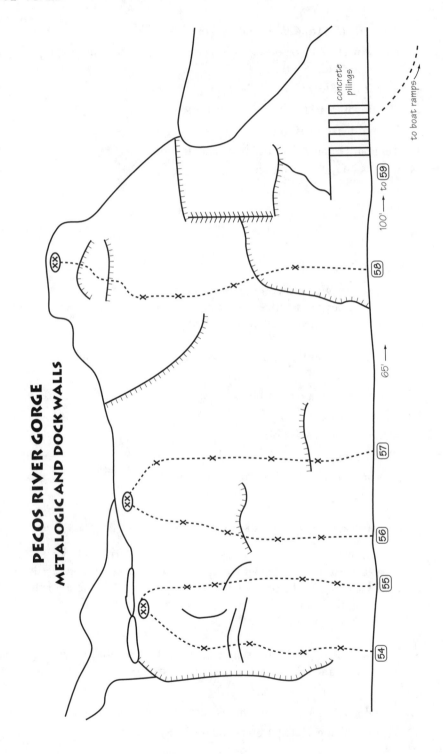

PECOS RIVER GORGE
METALOGIC AND DOCK WALLS

concrete
pilings

to boat ramps

100' → to 59

65'

THE DOCK WALL

Located 65' right of Metalogic Wall.

58. **Coyote Trickster** (5.11a) 65' right of *Reading Iculus*. 4 bolts and anchors.

59. **Conjure it Up** (5.12b) No topo. 100' right of *Coyote Trickster* past the concrete pilings. 4 bolts and anchors.

BIG BEND NATIONAL PARK

OVERVIEW

Big Bend National Park, named for the great sweeping northern curve of the Rio Grande along the United States/Mexican border in west Texas, offers climbing adventures on vertical limestone cliffs up to 1,000' high and on smaller volcanic outcrops. The towering mountains and arid deserts of Big Bend country are not often regarded as a climbing destination. Climbers, however, will find an amazing array of rock scattered across the park's 801,163 acres. Although much of the area's rock is suspect, small pockets of good climbing can be found.

Limestone cliffs rise from the river's banks to the cool mesa tops high above the desert floor. Steep side canyons hide sheer 1,000' walls. Most of these cliffs are sharp fluted faces sliced by few cracks. Syenite, a volcanic rock similar to granite, is found both on the desert floor and in the Chisos Mountains. Most of the park's established climbing is on the good quality volcanic crags found at Indian Head Hills and Grapevine Hills on the desert floor. The volcanic rock found in the Chisos appears to be of a poorer quality, although little climbing activity has tested this hypothesis.

No guides exist to Big Bend's crags and little recorded information is found— and most Big Bend climbers prefer it that way. This guide only points the intrepid climber in the direction of some of the park's rocks and routes. The rest is up to you. Decide what looks good; decide what gear you need; and go for it.

A small group of local rock climbers boasts the luxury of climbing in both the national park and on adjoining private lands. Visitors can climb legally only on park crags. The park areas offer good potential for further exploration and new routes. Most of the developed climbing areas are found on private lands; visitors, however, need permission from area landowners to visit these cliffs.

Climbing history: The Big Bend region is relatively unknown to anyone outside of a small group of locals. Consequently, little climbing activity has occurred. A small transient local group led by Mark Mills, Billy Blackstock,

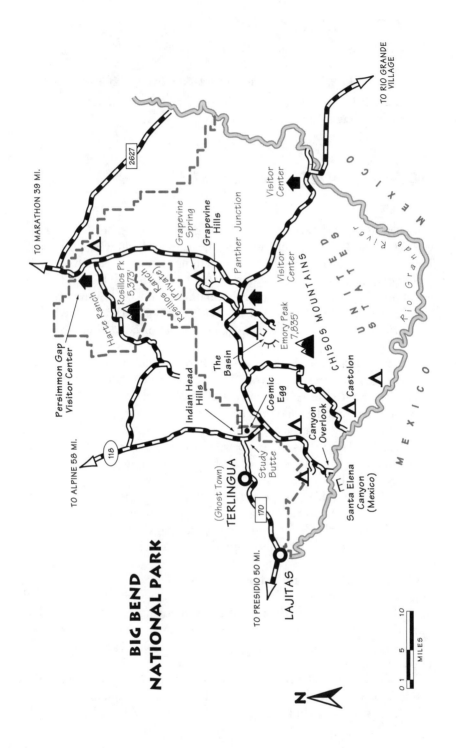

BIG BEND
NATIONAL PARK

Martin Ziebell, and Bill Davey has been active since the 1980s in developing some areas. Most of these efforts are on the smaller volcanic cliffs in the Indian Head Hills. Many of these areas are located on private land. The eastern portion of the crag extends into the park. This area is legal to explore and offers some climbing potential. The routes on the Mexican side of the river established by Davey are not currently subject to any restrictions. Fording the river is problematic but many opportunities exist here for the adventure seeker.

Directions, permits, and climbing regulations for park climbing areas are available at the visitor center in Panther Junction. Rangers recommend areas in The Basin, a popular visitor attraction in the Chisos Mountains. The best area is Pulliam Ridge (Alsate's Nose), a low fifth class affair with a tricky descent. Boot Rock and Appetite Peak, the other suggested areas, offer little or no climbing. Mesa de Anguilla, another suggestion, is a remote area in the park's western corner that has few climbing opportunities. Other areas, including Grapevine Hills and Santa Elena Canyon, offer better climbing potential. Bill Davey, using a canoe to access the cliffs, established two Grade IV climbs on the Mexican side here in the 1980s. *Border Incident* and *Coming of Age in Chihuahua* represent the first ascents of these imposing walls. Both climbs are 5.11 with some aid. Neither has had a second ascent. Vast potential for short and long climbs exists in this canyon for new routes, but only for those willing to accept the harsh conditions imposed by the tall, foreboding walls and the remote surrounding desert.

Trip Planning Information

Area description: Big Bend National Park offers a selection of adventure routes on remote limestone cliffs and volcanic crags.

Location: West Texas.

Camping: Park campgrounds are found in The Basin, Rio Grande Village, and Castolon. All are fee areas. Camping regulations are rigorously enforced. Use is heavy during spring and fall. Christmas and Thanksgiving holidays are very popular. Some primitive roadside campsites are available in the park. Many of these can be reached only by high-clearance or four-wheel-drive vehicles. Permits and other information are available at the visitor center. Camping outside the park is difficult because most of the surrounding area is privately owned. Big Bend Ranch State Natural Area near Lajitas is the one exception; check on availability beforehand. Terlingua Oasis RV Park has tent sites and small cabins.

Climbing season: Winter, early spring, and late fall offer the best opportunities to climb. Expect warm days and low precipitation. Uncomfortably high summer temperatures restrict climbing except in the Chisos Mountains.

Restrictions and access issues: Technical climbing, although discouraged, is allowed in Big Bend National Park. A day-use permit and park entry fee are

climb
ascends
dihedral

BIG BEND
BORDER INCIDENT

required. Climbers can most easily register at the visitor center in Panther Junction. Visitor centers are also located in the Basin, Persimmon Gap, and Rio Grande Village. Area maps, trails, and other useful information are available in all locations. Regulations prohibit the use of portable electric drills and climbing on or around cultural resources. Closure of some areas from February 1 to July 15 protect peregrine falcon nesting sites, including Santa Elena Canyon. Climbing activity is given only tacit approval by park personnel. The park does not feel it has rescue capabilities and that most of the rock is unsuitable for climbing. Be careful and respectful when climbing here to avoid focusing negative attention on climbing activities. Climbing areas outside park boundaries are all on private land. These areas include most of Indian Head, Willow Mountain, and Wild Horse Mountain. Climbers are advised to seek permission from landowners to climb in these areas. This can be difficult or impossible. The friendly local climbing community may be helpful here. For information on Big Bend National Park write Superintendent, Big Bend National Park, TX 79834.

Guidebook: None.

Nearby mountain shops, guide services, and gyms: None.

Services: Gas stations, restaurants, and grocery stores are located within the park at Basin, Castolon, Panther Junction, and Rio Grande Village. Minor auto repairs are available at Panther Junction or outside the park between Study Butte and Terlingua. Lodging, food, and fuel can be found at Study Butte, Lajitas, and the restored mining town of Terlingua. The Chevron Food Mart at the junction of Texas Highway 118 and County Road 170 offers inexpensive meals, fuel, and groceries.

Emergency services: Contact the visitor center for all emergencies within the park boundaries. The nearest hospital is in Alpine, 108 miles north on TX 118. Terlingua Medics and Big Bend Family Health Center are 26 miles west of the park visitor center.

Nearby climbing areas: Point of Rocks is 130 miles north. Pecos River Gorge is about 250 miles east.

Nearby attractions: River running on the Rio Grande (commercial and private trips from 1 day to 10 days). Also, Chisos Mountains trails (including 7,835' Emory Peak), free public hot springs, and, in Mexico, the village of Boquillas.

Finding the crags: Big Bend National Park is 103 miles south of Alpine, Texas, on TX 118 or 68 miles south of Marathon, Texas, on U.S. Highway 385. TX 118 enters the western portion of the park 26 miles from the visitor center. US 385 goes directly to the visitor center.

Indian Head Hills: Many park visitors drive the dirt road along the base of Indian Head Hills to reach the park's western portion. The dirt road, beginning on the north side of Big Bend Motor Inn off TX 118 just before Study

Butte, heads east and ends on the park's western boundary. The road starts by following a telephone line. At 0.7 mile the road bends north around an old land fill. At 1.2 miles the road reaches a Y junction. Take the right fork heading east. Willow Mountain is visible to the north. At 1.8 miles the road crosses an arroyo. Traversing this obstacle is sometimes problematic; in early 1995 a metal culvert was placed to facilitate the production of the movie *Gambler IV.* Summer flash floods occasionally wash out this culvert. A short distance ahead is the easily recognizable Cosmic Egg, a 30' round boulder sitting on the desert floor. There are established routes on the Egg and on the cliffs to the road's end at the park boundary. A trail enters the park at road's end. Many of the boulders along this park trail are graced with Indian rock art. The cliffs passed along the way and rocks beyond a small spring offer climbing possibilities.

Santa Elena Canyon is reached by driving the Maverick Road, located about 1 mile from the western entrance of the Park. It is 12 miles south to the Rio Grande. This dirt road is rough and sometimes closed during and after severe thunderstorms. Check with rangers for conditions. Border Incident is about 1 mile up-river from the take-out for boaters on the south or Mexican side of the river. A canoe or similar craft is needed to reach the base of the climb. Check with locals (Far Flung Adventures) for help in logistics and locating the climb.

Grapevine Hills is easy to reach and offers bouldering and climbs on short volcanic crags. The road to the trailhead starts about 3 miles west of the Panther Junction visitor center. Go north on a dirt road just west of the Chisos Basin exit. A pleasant 2-mile hike through the desert reveals many boulder problems as well as some short fifth-class opportunities. Almost no recorded climbing has been done in this area.

Chisos Basin climbs and Emory Peak are accessed by driving 3 miles west of the Panther Junction visitor center to a well-signed exit. Turn left and drive 6 miles south on a paved road to The Basin.

AUSTINAREA

ENCHANTED ROCKS STATE NATURAL AREA

OVERVIEW

A pleasant surprise awaits first-time visitors to Enchanted Rocks in central Texas. This delightful area, a 1,643-acre preserve operated as a Texas State Natural Area, is home to a wide diversity of plant and animal species. Its unique ecological features alone would make a visit here worthwhile, but Texas rock climbers are attracted by the immense, pink granite domes that rise above the surrounding mesquite grasslands and oak forest. Good weather, easy access, pleasant camping, and great routes and rock combine to make Enchanted Rocks one of the best climbing venues in all of Texas.

Climbers from all over the state travel vast distances to climb the park's granite slabs and to hone their strength and gymnastic skills bouldering on the hundreds of smaller rocks liberally sprinkled throughout the area. Every crag, cliff, and boulder more than a body length in height has been climbed, named, and rated. The climbing is excellent, with more than 250 established routes that range in difficulty from 5.0 to 5.13. This guide highlights some of the most popular, recommendable routes. Consult with locals for advice on other routes and boulder problems.

Friction and face climbing enthusiasts will find ample opportunities throughout the park, but the best and longest are on the Backside Area on the north side of the Main Dome. Crack climbers will like Buzzards Roost, the Triple Cracks area on the west face of the Main Dome, and the Orange Peel area on the northwest end of the Main Dome. Climbers of all abilities will enjoy a cragging visit to Enchanted Rocks.

The pink granite domes are part of a huge, ancient Precambrian batholithic structure about 1.2 billion years old. Uplift and erosion exposed the domes. They represent some of the oldest exposed rocks in Texas. The porphyritic texture of the rock is rich in feldspar crystals that provide delightful and plentiful hand and foot holds. The domes are characteristically rounded and smooth in appearance due to the weathering process of exfoliation. Although not as

Natalie Merrill top-roping the first pitch of *Texas Radio* (5.11c) at Enchanted Rocks, Texas. *Photo by Tom Struzik*.

ENCHANTED ROCK STATE NATURAL AREA

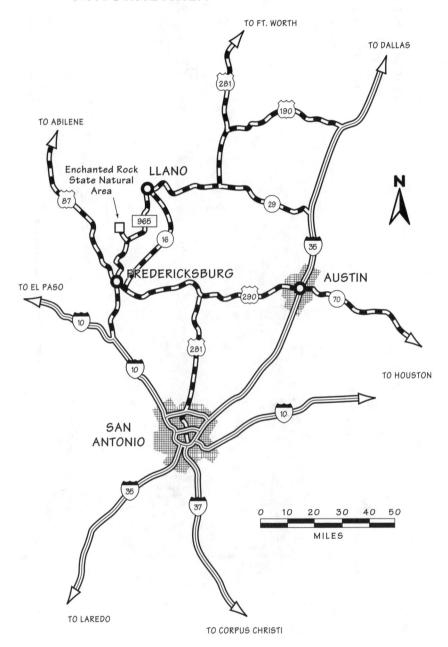

TO FT. WORTH

TO DALLAS

TO ABILENE

Enchanted Rock State Natural Area

LLANO

87

965

16

29

281

190

35

N

TO EL PASO

FREDERICKSBURG

AUSTIN

290

70

10

TO HOUSTON

10

281

10

SAN ANTONIO

10

35

37

TO LAREDO

TO CORPUS CHRISTI

0 10 20 30 40 50

MILES

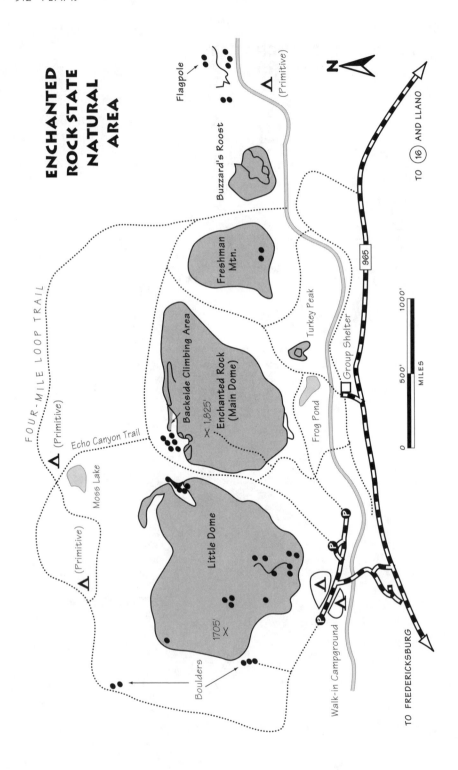

ENCHANTED ROCK STATE NATURAL AREA

N

Flagpole

Buzzard's Roost

Freshman Mtn.

FOUR-MILE LOOP TRAIL

(Primitive)

Echo Canyon Trail

Moss Lake

(Primitive)

Little Dome

Backside Climbing Area

×1,825'
Enchanted Rock
(Main Dome)

Turkey Peak

Frog Pond

Group Shelter

965

(Primitive)

TO 16 AND LLANO

1705'
×

Boulders

Walk-in Campground

P

P

P

TO FREDERICKSBURG

1000'

500'

MILES

0

Natalie Merrill on the superb *Fear of Flying* at Enchanted Rocks, Texas.
Photo by Ian Riddington.

Jack Petree topropes *Fly on a Windshield* (5.10a) at Enchanted Rocks, Texas.
Photo by Tom Struzik.

large or extensive, they resemble Tuolumne Meadows formations. Climbs up to 200' ascend the Main Dome, the park's largest formation.

Climbing is possible all year long at Enchanted Rocks. Summer temperatures can reach 100 degrees, which limits activity to early mornings and evenings. Occasional winter storms and low temperatures also limit climbing. The prime time to visit is late January to mid-May.

Many routes are commonly toproped. All can be led on thoughtfully placed bolts, mostly drilled on the lead. Some retro-bolting has occurred, making routes safer and accessible to more climbers. Serious runouts on easier climbing, however, are found on many of the Backside slab routes. A single 165' rope is necessary for most routes. Carry at least a dozen quickdraws on the longer bolted lines. Most routes terminate below the cliff top. Rappels with two ropes from established bolt-anchors are the descent of choice. Many routes in the park appear to be over-rated by Colorado and New Mexico standards.

If possible, plan to visit Enchanted Rocks on weekdays. The area is extremely popular and receives heavy visitation on the weekends and holidays. The friendly local climbing scene, however, will make you feel at home any day you visit.

Trip Planning Information

Area description: Enchanted Rocks State Natural Area, offering good beginner through expert routes, features excellent granite climbing on domes, slabs, and steep faces that range in height from 20' to 200' high.

Location: Central Texas west of Austin.

Camping: Reservations are recommended to ensure a campsite at Enchanted Rocks. This is particularly important on weekends and holidays. For $9 per night, the 46-site campground offers a tent pad, picnic table, fire pit, water, bathroom, and shower. Primitive sites are $7 per night. These feature new self-composting toilets. No water at primitive sites. Moss Lake or Walnut Springs primitive sites are nearest to the popular Backside climbing area. For Buzzard's Roost routes camp at Buzzard's Roost Primitive area. These require a 1- to 2-mile hike. There is a $5 per vehicle daily entrance fee. Robinson City Park in Llano allows tent camping by the river.

Climbing season: The long spring and fall seasons are the most pleasant times to climb. Spring starts here in late January and lasts to mid-May. Fall is from late September to as late as December. From June through August summer temperatures of 90 to 100 degrees limit climbing activity to the early morning and late evening.

Restrictions and access issues: Climbers are required to sign a waiver at park headquarters prior to climbing. The park is subject to a multitude of rules about climbing and camping that visitors should become familiar with. A visit to headquarters will ensure a hassle-free visit.

Guidebook: The first guidebook to the area, *Stranger Than Friction* by Dale Bergeron and James Crump, 1984, has served as the basis for at least two later publications, including *The Dome Drivers Manual* by James Crump, Robert Price, and Scott Harris, Best Printing Company, 1993. The guide is available at park headquarters, but is somewhat flawed in places by incorrect route numbers on topos and photos. A free 1-page map and list of climbs is supplied when you sign in.

Nearby mountain shops, guide services, and gyms: Guide service in Austin. There are no shops or gyms in the area.

Services: There is a small country store at Crabapple Crossing, about 5 miles east of the park. Fredericksburg, 15 miles south, offers full services.

Emergency services: Report any climbing or hiking accident occurring in the park to park headquarters. Hospitals and ambulance services are available in Fredericksburg and Llano.

Nearby climbing areas: There are short limestone sport areas in both the Austin and San Antonio areas. *Central Texas Limestone, A Climber's Guide* by Jeff Jackson and Kevin Gallagher, 1992, details these areas. A second edition was printed in 1995. Mineral Wells State Park is about 175 miles north.

Nearby attractions: The Nimitz Museum State Historical Park in Fredericksburg, LBJ National Historic Park, Pedernales Falls State Park.

Finding the area: Enchanted Rocks is in the Texas Hill Country of central Texas about 15 miles north of Fredericksburg and 20 miles south of Llano. From the Austin area, go 80 miles west on U.S. Highway 290 to Fredericksburg. Then go north 18 miles on FM 965 and look for signs on the left (west) to Enchanted Rocks State Natural Area. From the west, take Interstate 10 to the US 290 exit to Fredericksburg. From the San Antonio area, take I-10 north to the US 87 exit to Fredericksburg.

THE BACKSIDE AREA

The Backside Area of the Main Dome holds the greatest concentration of quality routes. The majority of fifth class routes are here with more than 60 established lines and variations. Climbs range in difficulty from 5.4 to 5.12b. Most of the climbing is in the easy to moderate range, with the harder problems being variations of the more popular lines. The described routes represent the most popular lines. Most of the other routes are recommended. Ask a friendly local for advice. Access is via the Loop Trail starting at the southwest end of the campground parking lot. The well-marked, easy-to-follow trail goes north between Little Dome on the left (west) and the Main Dome on the right (east). Continue around the Main Dome on the trail to the east end of the formation for beginning of route descriptions.

Descent: Descent from the Backside is best accomplished by rappelling from the *Ripple* rap station (single rope, 80') in the cliff mid-section, or from the *Baba Wawa* rap station (single rope, 80'). Do not belay off these anchors. Use them only for rappelling to avoid crowding the stations, especially on busy days. Walk-off the dome by following the summit trail.

Routes are described from left to right (east to west) when viewed from the bottom of the Dome. Routes 1 through 6 are the longest in the park at 250'.

1. **Rites of Spring/Increasingly Vague** (5.8-R) *Rites of Spring* is a long girdle traverse of the face. This route climbs its 1st pitch. Begin atop some broken boulders below the right side of a prominent arch. **Pitch 1:** Angle up left on easy rock (5.4) to a grassy ledge 100' up. Traverse right on grassy ledge below right side of overlap and set up a belay. **Pitch 2:** Climb the headwall above to a crescent-shaped ledge. Continue on easy slab climbing to summit belay. Runout.

2. **Easier Than It Looks** (5.5) Begin atop boulders. **Pitch 1:** Climb on good holds up corners to a right-angling ramp. Belay at the "Fatman Flake" below a steeper headwall. **Pitch 2:** Scale the flake and angle up left to a ledge. Continue straight up on easy rock (no pro) or traverse up left to a summit belay. Bring a small rack of wires and Friends.

3. **Harder Than It Looks** (5.6) An area favorite. Begin on boulders at the lowest point of the Backside wall. **Pitch 1:** Face climb up left past 3 bolts to a belay stance at "Fatman Flake." (Same belay as *Easier Than It Looks*.) **Pitch 2:** Work up the flake and face climb to a ledge and gear placements. Continue to a summit belay by climbing straight up (no pro) or angling up left.

4. **Christene Variation** (5.6R) Begin just right of *Harder Than It Looks*. Angle up left along a rock rib on a broad ramp. Work up right to the left side of *Boston* ledge. Belay here. Go right on the ledge and finish up *Dome Driver*. 1 pitch. Sparse pro.

5. **Boston** (5.7R) Begin right of ramp below a notch on the left side of an obvious arch. **Pitch 1:** Face climb up to the notch. Pull over, step left, and angle up and right past 2 bolts to a good ledge with trees. **Pitch 2:** Work up right on a large flake. Cross top of flake to a small tree and climb straight up a black streak to summit. Excellent.

6. **Dome Driver** (5.7) Start atop a boulder right of *Boston* under the the highest part of the overlap. **Pitch 1:** Work up left to a tree in the overlap. Pull over and pass 2 bolts en route to *Beer Can Alley* (5.7), a long right-angling crack/ledge system. Belay near a tree below the *Boston* flake. **Pitch 2:** Scale the flake and step left onto a black streak. Waltz up the unprotected streak to a 2-bolt belay. Exposed, somewhat runout, and excellent—an area classic.

7. **M.D. 20/20** (5.9R) Climb *Dome Driver* but angle right over the overlap. Continue straight up to a belay on *Beer Can Alley* ledge. Rap 80' from 2 bolts.

ENCHANTED ROCKS
BACKSIDE OF MAIN DOME (LEFT SIDE)

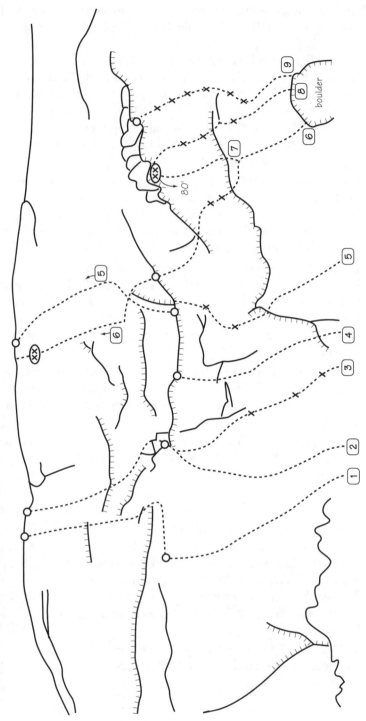

boulder

80'

8. **TJ Swan** (5.8) Begin on the boulder right of *M.D. 20/20*. Slab climb up to a bolt below the right side of the arch. Pull over to another bolt and continue upward past a bolt to the large ledge (*Beer Can Alley*). Rap 80' from a 2-bolt station.

9. **Ripple** (5.9) Popular and classic 110' pitch. Begin atop a slab boulder just right of *TJ Swan*. Climb a water groove up right to a bolt. Edge through the crux and continue upward past more bolts to the long ledge. Belay from hand-size pro or by the rap anchors. 6 bolts.

10. **Carpet Crawl** (5.9+) Begin on the ground right of the slabby boulder. Climb up to a bolt, step left to a mantle and a ledge above. Continue up past 2 more bolts and angle up right along a runout rib. Climb up to a sickle-shaped flake (protect with small TCUs) and finish up and right on Beer Can Alley. 3 bolts. 160'.

11. **Intensive Care** (5.10bR) Begin where the overlap/arch nears the ground right of *Carpet Crawl*. Work over a small bulge to a dish and a bolt. Continue up right 40' to another bolt. Run it out to a 3rd bolt and angle up right to a 2-bolt belay ledge. Do a short easy pitch to the ledge above and walk left to the *Ripple* rap station.

12. **La Dolce Vita** (5.11a) Hard climbing leads over an obvious overlap to a bolt. Work up left to a bolt. Above climb to a sloping stance and straight up to a 3rd bolt. Above join *Carpet Crawl* at a 4th bolt and climb up right to a 2-bolt ledge. 4 bolts.

13. **Bold Talk for a One-eyed Fat Man** (5.10d) This fine line begins by a large tree. Climb straight up past 2 bolts. Above, edge up on sustained face climbing for 25' to a slight bulge (crux) and a 3rd bolt. Work up left to bolt 4. Above lies 45' of runout, sustained face climbing (5.9+). Continue to a 2-bolt belay ledge. **Descent:** Descend by walking off above or traversing left on Beer Can Alley to the *Ripple* rap station.

14. **Gravitron** (5.11c) Begin atop boulders. Climb the left side of a wide black streak past 4 bolts to a 2-bolt belay shared with *Bold Talk for a One-eyed Fat Man*.

15. **Real Gravy** (5.11a) This line ascends the black streak right of *Gravitron*. Climb directly over the overlap to a bolt. Hard face climbing (5.11) leads to another bolt. Mantle on a knob to a 3rd bolt. After 30' more of hard climbing (5.10+) the angle eases. Belay at a 2-bolt stance. 3 bolts.

16. **Texas Radio** (5.11c) One of the better routes on the cliff with excellent, sustained face climbing and decent protection. Climb over the obvious arch/overlap to a bolt. Work up and right on stiff face climbing (5.10 and 5.11) past 3 more bolts (5.11 mantle at bolt 4). 25' of runout 5.10 climbing on crystals leads to bolt 5. Continue up for 60' on runout 5.7 friction to a 2-bolt belay. A short pitch leads to the cliff summit. 5 bolts.

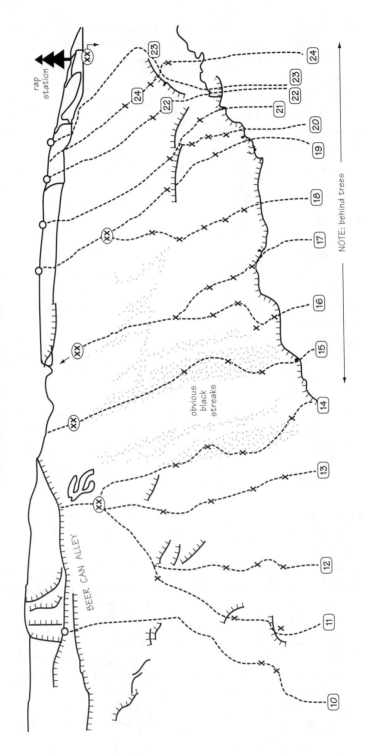

ENCHANTED ROCKS
RIGHT SIDE OF MAIN DOME

rap station

NOTE: behind trees

BEER CAN ALLEY

obvious black streaks

10 11 12 13 14 15 16 17 18 19 20 21 22 23 24

17. **Sixth Happiness** (5.12a) A tough lead put up by Hueco pioneer Mike Head. Work up and over the arch to a bolt. Continue straight up on thin climbing past 2 bolts. Higher work left across a hard, scary traverse to *Texas Radio's* 5th bolt. Continue straight up on easier climbing (5.7) 60' to a 2-bolt belay. 3 bolts.

18. **Stranger Than Friction** (5.10a) Classic, popular, and well-protected. From the top of a flake move up left to a concave dish and a bolt. Work left to a tough mantle. Climb up and right past more bolts to a final easy 35' runout to a 2-bolt belay. A short easy slab pitch leads to the rock summit. 5 bolts. Scramble right along ledges to the descent rappel.

19. **Terminal Orogeny** (5.10cR) Climb up a flake (TCUs or stoppers) to crystal face and a bolt. Continue over the arch above to a bolt and angle up left to *Stranger Than Friction's* belay.

20. **French Route** (5.11a) Good thin slab line. A full-rope pitch. Easy climbing leads up left to a small ledge. Continue straight up past 3 bolts to a break in the leaning arch. Clip a bolt above and run it out on good holds up a rib to a flake that offers pro. Continue to the upper ledges and belay. Rap from anchors farther right.

21. **Fly on a Windshield** (5.10a) Begin just left of an hourglass-shaped flake. Climb up to a flake and continue on fun climbing to a bolt. Friction up left (5.10-) to the overlap, pull over to a bolt above (same bolt as *French Route*), and continue up rock rib to cliff summit.

22. **Edge of Night** (5.8R) Work up the middle of the hourglass flake to the shallow arch. Edge up run-out 5.8 climbing above to a bolt. Head straight up to a belay ledge. Bring small gear for the arch crack.

23. **Runamuck** (5.7) Same start as *Edge of Night*. Friction up to thin, right-angling arch. Follow the arch (bring small pro) to its end. Climb straight up a shallow, committing corner to the top. Numerous other *Prok* variations exist on this wall. A couple follow here, but it's possible to climb most anywhere.

24. **Deep Prok** (5.8) Begin 10' right of *Runamuck*. Climb straight up to a bolt below the arch. Step left into the arch itself and pull over the bulge with a crack. Continue up past 2 bolts to summit. Rap from anchors to right.

Many more good but shorter routes lie right of here. Classics include *Baba Wawa*, a good 5.6 face climb to the rap station, and *Sweat*, a fun 5.7 layback/finger crack to a tree.

BUZZARD'S ROOST

Buzzard's Roost, on the eastern side of the park, offers the park's best opportunities for crack climbing. Some fine face climbs can be found here as well. The relative seclusion of this area, the availability of primitive camping sites, and good climbing make this dome an attractive alternative to the often crowded Backside area. Access is by walking northeast or downstream in Sandy Creek located to the right or east of park headquarters. Hike past Turkey Peak and join the eastern portion of the Loop Trail where it travels northwest between Freshman Mountain on the left and Buzzard's Roost on the right or north. Leave the trail near the southern end of Buzzard's Roost and traverse right to the east face. These climbs are located on the bouldery southeast face. More routes are in the immediate area; these represent the most recommendable lines.

25. **P.G. 13** (5.10c) Start off a flake boulder on the far left side of the Southeast Face. Face climb up crystals to a shallow right-facing corner/crack. Continue above on harder climbing to the clifftop. 4 bolts to a 2-bolt belay. Often toproped. Newly added bolts add security for the leader. 40'.

26. **Eat** (5.10a) One of the most popular crack climbs in the park—continuous, steep, and excellent. 30' right of *P.G. 13*. Step off a boulder and jam up right in a double crack system. The final crux pumps out many leaders. Belay on a ledge with a tree. 40'. *Fun and Grins* (5.9-) is just right. Layback out a left-leaning corner to a dihedral.

27. **The Wick** (5.10d) Start in a corner. Climb left to a concave dish with a bolt. Step around the corner then up the crystal face above past 2 pins in a seam to the headwall finish. More routes are to the right.

The following climbs are on the East Face, the park's steepest wall. Approach by scrambling up and right from the southeast face. These routes lie to the left and right of a large, obvious dihedral (*Fear of Flying*).

28. **Texas Crude** (5.10b) This excellent 40' handcrack is the left-most of 3 cracks on the wall right of the obvious dihedral. Follow the overhanging handcrack to a ledge. Medium gear required for protection and the belay.

29. **Shrike** (5.12bR) An area testpiece. Start just right of *Texas Crude*. Jam and lieback up the 40' crack protected by small TCUs and wires. Sustained.

30. **Aquatic Anxiety** (5.11a) Start in a curving dihedral right of *Shrike*. Finger and hand crack climbing lead to a good belay.

31. **Fear of Flying** (5.10R) The obvious open dihedral located right of *Aquatic*

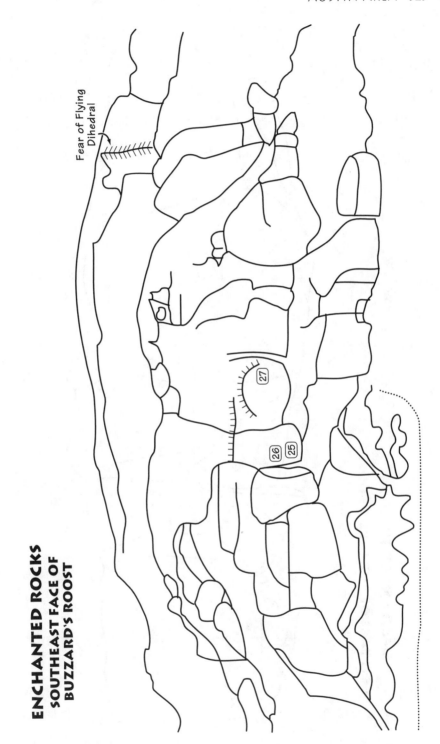

ENCHANTED ROCKS
SOUTHEAST FACE OF
BUZZARD'S ROOST

Fear of Flying
Dihedral

27

26 25

ENCHANTED ROCKS
EAST FACE OF BUZZARD'S ROOST

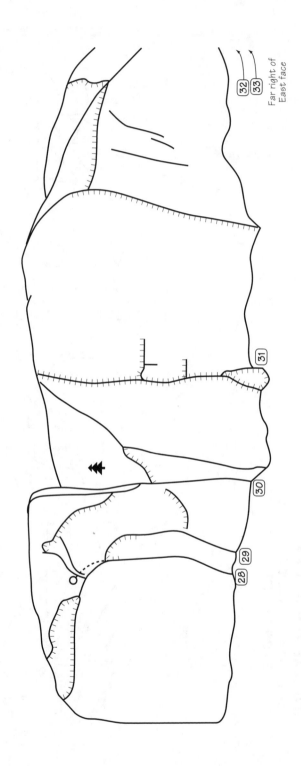

Far right of
East face

Anxiety. This area favorite is usually toproped. Carry #4 Friends and Big Bros to lead it. Lieback up the dihedral. Tie off blocks back from the cliff rim for toprope anchors and pad the rope where it runs over the sharp lip.

32. **Little Feat** (5.9) On the far right end of the East Face. Good hand jams lead to low-angle rock. Belay off gear. Save some 3" to 3.5" Friends for the belay. Quality.

33. **Unknown** (5.10+) Right of *Little Feat.* Bolts lead to a 2-bolt anchor. Difficult at top. Excellent.

OTHER PARK CRAGS

Short but worthwhile routes are found in the Echo Canyon area between Little and Main Dome. Near here is the Triple Cracks Sanctuary. A good selection of moderate cracks makes this a popular intruction area, which often means waiting your turn for a route. Lunch Rock is a pleasant bouldering spot and a good place to meet other climbers. The Orange Peel area has some quality short climbs including *Orange Peel,* probably the first 5.10 lead done at Enchanted Rocks. The Frog, a large boulder, offers a good concentration of rap-bolted face routes ranging from 5.10 to 5.12. These routes can also be toproped. Turkey Peak, just southwest of Buzzard's Roost, offers several routes worth climbing if not occupied by one of the many groups that provide instruction in the park. Toproping is very popular here although you may want to lead one of the area's classic overhanging problems, *Mighty Dog* (5.11c/d). The free guide provided when registering gives directions and route descriptions to all of these areas.

DALLASAREA

LAKE MINERAL WELLS STATE PARK

OVERVIEW

Lake Mineral Wells State Park, a 1- to 2-hour drive from the Dallas-Fort Worth metroplex, is one of the most popular climbing areas in Texas. Park officials and climbers are working together to preserve this valuable resource, the only available climbing area in the Dallas metroplex. The 3,000-acre park offers bouldering, rappelling, and toproping on vertical 40' to 65' metamorphosed sandstone-conglomerate cliffs. Lead climbing is prohibited. The area, with more than 80 established toprope routes, is excellent for beginner and intermediate climbers. All climbing activity is conducted at the Penitentiary Hollow Climbing Area.

The area receives heavy use on the weekends from youth groups and climbers from the Dallas/Fort Worth area. Weekdays are usually less crowded. A map with trail information and route topos is supplied upon registering at park headquarters. Future plans may include the development of additional climbing areas on recently purchased land.

Rack: A 165' rope, a selection of carabiners, and slings are required to set up topropes off trees and boulders. Future plans call for installing fixed anchors atop the cliffs. The park's face and crack routes range in difficulty from 5.5 to 5.11.

Trip Planning Information

Area description: Lake Mineral Wells State Park is a toprope climbing and rappelling area.

Location: Northern Texas. 50 miles west of Fort Worth.

Camping: Campsites are available in the park. Tent sites with water, picnic tables, grills, and shared restrooms with showers cost $8 per day. Sites with

LAKE MINERAL WELLS STATE PARK

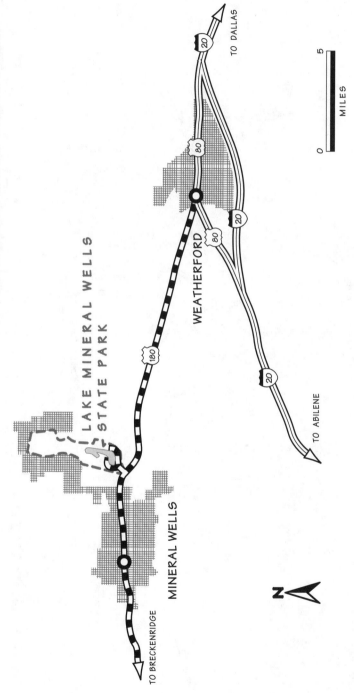

TO DALLAS

20

80

WEATHERFORD

20

80

20

TO ABILENE

180

LAKE MINERAL WELLS
STATE PARK

MINERAL WELLS

TO BRECKENRIDGE

N

MILES

0   5

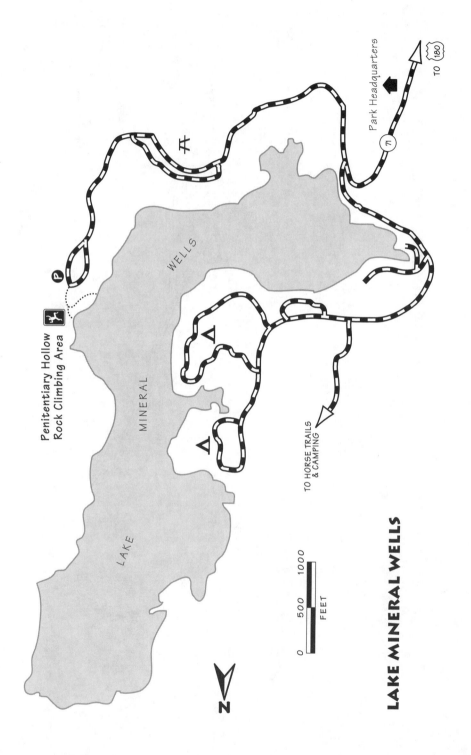

Penitentiary Hollow
Rock Climbing Area

P

Park Headquarters

TO 180

71

MINERAL

WELLS

LAKE

TO HORSE TRAILS
& CAMPING

0   500   1000
FEET

N

LAKE MINERAL WELLS

electricity range from $11 to $15 a day. Weekly rates are available. Backpacking campsites ($6) require a 2.5-mile hike and have no water or sanitary facilities.

Climbing season: Year-round. Occasional cold winter days limit climbing. Expect hot temperatures during summer months. April and May are the wettest months.

Restrictions and access issues: In addition to normal entrance fees, climbers and rappellers must pay a $2 "activity fee." Climbing is regarded as a privilege and is monitored by the Texas Parks and Wildlife Department with help from the Texas Climbing Coalition. All climbers and rappellers must register and sign a release. Participants must be 17 years of age or have parental permission. Youth group leaders must sign a Youth Group Compliance form. All rappels require a belay. Lead climbing is prohibited. Climbers are asked to refrain from climbing when the rock is visibly wet to minimize rock deterioration. Call (817) 328-1171 to check on conditions. Climbing is limited to the Penitentiary Hollow Area.

Guidebook: A map to the climbing area and topos of the climbs are available at park headquarters.

Nearby mountain shops, guide services, and gyms: Dallas/Fort Worth.

Services: Full tourist services are available in the town of Mineral Wells.

Emergency services: Report all emergencies to Park Headquarters 24 hours a day.

Nearby climbing areas: There are no climbing sites in the immediate area.

Nearby attractions: Excellent fishing for bass, crappie, and catfish in Lake Mineral Wells. Information and licenses are available at park headquarters. Horseback riding, hiking, and mountain biking are allowed on designated park trails. Possum Kingdom State Park, 1 hour west on US 180, features good fishing, water skiing, and scuba diving.

Finding the area: From the town of Mineral Wells, drive 3 miles east on US 180 and turn north on State Park Road 71. From Weatherford in the east, drive 14 miles west on US 180 west and turn north (right) on State Park Road 71. Continue 0.5 mile to park headquarters. Trail maps and route topos are provided when registering at park headquarters. From the parking lot at the end of the road an easy 100-yard trail leads to the climbing area.

APPENDIX A
Further Reading

Central Texas Limestone. Jeff Jackson, Kevin Gallagher. Homo Aggro Press, 1992.

A Climber's Guide to Box Canyon. Erik Hufnagel and Bertrand Gramont. Self-published.

The Dome Drivers Manual. James Crump, Robert Price, and Scott Harris. Best Printing Company, 1993.

The Enchanted Tower, Sport Climbing Socorro and Datil, New Mexico. Edited by Salomon Maestas, Matthew A. Jones. New Mexico Tech Student Association, 1993.

Great Rock Hits of Hueco Tanks. Paul Piana. Mountain N'Air, 1992.

Hiker's and Climber's Guide to the Sandias, third edition. Mike Hill. University of New Mexico Press, 1993.

Hueco Tanks, a Climber's and Boulderer's Guide. John Sherman, Mike Head, James Grump, Dave Head. Chockstone Press, 1991.

Hueco Tanks: Climbing and Bouldering Guide, second edition. John Sherman. Chockstone Press, 1996.

Rock 'n Road. Tim Toula. Chockstone Press, 1995.

Sport Climbing in New Mexico. Randal Jett and Matt Samet. 1991.

Stranger Than Friction. Dale Bergeron and James Crump. 1984.

Texas Limestone II. Jeff Jackson, Kevin Gallagher. Homo Aggro Press. 1995.

APPENDIX B
RATING SYSTEM COMPARISON CHART

YDS	British	French	Australian
5.3	VD 3b	2	11
5.4	HVD 3c	3	12
5.5	MS/S/HS	4a, 4a	12/13
5.6	HS/S 4a	4b	13/14
5.7	HS/VS 4b	4c	15-17
5.8	VS 4c/5a	5a	18
5.9	HVS 5a/5b	5b	19
5.10a	E1 5a/5b	5c	20
5.10b	E1 5b/5c	6a	20
5.10c	E2 5b/5c	6a+	21
5.10d	E2/E3 5b/5c	6b	21
5.11a	E3 5c/6a	6b+	22
5.11b	E3/E4 5c/6a	6c	22
5.11c	E4 5c/6a	6c+	23
5.11d	E4 6a/6b	7a	24
5.12a	E5 6a/6b	7a+	25
5.12b	E5/E6 6a/6b	7b	26
5.12c	E6 6b/6c	7b+	27
5.12d	E6 6b/6c	7c	27
5.13a	E6/E7 6b/6c	7c+	28
5.13b	E7 6c/7a	8a	29
5.13c	E7 6c/7a	8a+	30
5.13d	E8 6c/7a	8b	31
5.14a	E8 6c/7a	8b+	32
5.14b	E9 6c/7a	8c	??
5.14c	E9 7b	8c+	??

Sources: *Mountaineering: The Freedom of the Hills*, 5th Edition; *Climbing Magazine*, No. 150, February/March 1995.

APPENDIX C
MOUNTAIN SHOPS, GUIDE SERVICES, & CLIMBING GYMS

NEW MEXICO

ALBUQUERQUE

The Albuquerque Rock Gym
3300 Princeton NE
(505) 881-3073

Mountains and Rivers
2320 Central Ave SE
(505) 268-4876

REI
1905 Mountain Road NW
(505) 247-1191

The Sandia Climbing Guides,
(505) 891-3366

Sandia Mountain Outfitters
1700 Juan Tabo Blvd. NE
(505) 293-9725

LAS CRUCES

Bikes Plus
Corner of Lohman and Solano
(505) 523-7982

LOS ALAMOS

Trailbound Sports
771 Central Ave
(505) 662-3000

SANTA FE

Ace Mountain Wear
825 Early St. Suite A
(505) 982-8079

Active Endeavors
301 N. Guadalupe
(505) 984-8221

Base Camp
121 W. San Francisco
(505) 982-9707

Challenge Designs, Inc
Rt. 19, Box 115-J
Santa Fe, NM 87505
(505) 988-5207

The Santa Fe Climbing Gym
825 Early St. Suite A
(505) 989-7114

Wild Mountain Sports
541 West Cordova
(505) 986-1152

TAOS

Mountain Skills-Taos
P.O. Box 490
(505) 758-9589
or 1-800-584-6863

Mudd N-Flood Review
134 Bent St.
(505) 758-1059

PEA (Phil's Excellent Adventure)
105 B Camino de la Placita
(505) 751-1212

Taos Mountain Outfitters
114 South Plaza
(505) 758-9292

TEXAS

Austin

Mountain Madness (guide service)
(512) 443-5854

Whole Earth Provision Co.
2410 San Antonio St.
(512) 478-1577

Whole Earth Provision Co.
4006 S. Lamar Blvd.
(512) 444- 9974

Dallas/Fort Worth

Backwoods
Old Town Shopping Ctr.
5500 Greenville, Ste 308
Dallas, (214) 363-0372

Backwoods,
3212 Camp Bowie
Fort Worth
(817) 332-2423

Exposure Indoor Rock Gym
2389 Midway Road
Carrollton
(214) 732-0307

Mountain Hideout
5643 Lovers Lane
Dallas, (214) 350-8181

Mountain Hideout
14010 Coit Rd
Dallas, (214) 234-8651

REI
4515 LBJ Freeway
Farmers Branch (a suburb of Dallas),
(214) 490-5989

Stoneworks Rock Gym
1003 Forest Ave.
Carrollton
(214) 323-1047

Whole Earth Provision Co.
5400 Mockingbird Ln.
Dallas, (214) 824-8611

Houston

Whole Earth Provision Co.
6560 Woodway Dr.
(713) 467-0234

Whole Earth Provision Co.
2934 S. Shepard
(713) 526-5226

334 APPENDIX & INDEX

APPENDIX D
SERVICES

NEW MEXICO
ALBUQUERQUE
CAMPING

Central KOA
    (505) 296-2729

North KOA
    (505) 867-5227

Mountainair Ranger District
    USDA Forest Service
    P.O. Box 69

Mountainair, NM, 87036
    (505) 847-2990

FOOD

Pinky's Gourmet Pizza & Calzone
    5200 Eubank NE

Amadeo's Pizza & Subs, 417 Tramway

Ron's Camino Real
    416 Yale Blvd. SE
    (505) 255-0973

Scalo Northern Italian Grill
    3500 Central Ave SE

The Bangkok Cafe
    5901 Central Ave NE

Monroe's Restaurant
    1520 Lomas Blvd. NW &
    6021 Osuna Road NE

Tio Tito's Original Mexican Grill
    12999 Central Ave NE

El Patio
    142 Harvard Drive SE
    (505) 268-4245

LAS CRUCES
FOOD

Mesilla Valley Kitchen
    Arroyo Plaza
    2001 East Lohman

Napalitos, 310 S. Mesquite

My Brothers Place, 334 S. Main

Old West Brewery on Avenida De Mesilla
    in Mesilla (just south of Las Cruces)
    for speciality beers

LOS ALAMOS
CAMPING

Cochiti Dam
    U.S. Army Corps of Engineers
    (505) 242-8302

Bandelier National Monument
    HCR 1, Box 1, Suite 15
    Los Alamos, NM 87544-9701
    (505) 672-3861

SANTA FE
CAMPING

Santa Fe National Forest
    Pinon Building
    1220 St. Francis Drive
    Santa Fe, NM 87504
    (505) 988-6940

SOCORRO
FOOD

Capitol Bar, on the town plaza

La Pasadita, on Garfield Street

Coyote Moon, 5 miles north in Lemitar

The Owl Bar and Cafe, 10 miles south in
    San Antonio on US 380

SUGARITE STATE PARK

CAMPING

Sugarite State Park
HCR 63, Box 386
Raton, New Mexico 87740
(505) 445-5607

TAOS

CAMPING

Carson National Forest
224 Cruz Alta Road, Box 558
(505) 763-6200

BLM headquarters
224 Cruz Alta Road
(505) 758-8851

Orilla Verde Recreation Area
(505) 758-8851

FOOD

Mainstreet Bakery and Cafe
on Guadalupe Plaza
(505) 758-9610

Wild and Natural
1005 Paseo del Pueblo Norte
(505) 751-0480

Trading Post Cafe, at the corner of NM
68 and NM 518 in Rancho de Taos
(505) 758-5089

Eske's Brew Pub, one and half blocks east
of the Plaza

TEXAS
AUSTIN

CAMPING

Enchanted Rock State Natural Area
Rt. 4, Box 170
Fredericksburg, TX 78624 (915)
247-3903, (central reservation center
at (512) 389-8900)

Crabapple Crossing Campground
(915) 247-4260

KOA campground, near Fredericksburg
(210) 997-4796

BIG BEND
NATIONAL PARK

CAMPING

Big Bend National Park visitor center
(915) 477-2251
camping reservations
(915) 477-2291

Big Bend Ranch State Natural Area,
(915) 424-3327

Terlingua Oasis RV Park
(915) 371-2218 or
800-848-BEND

COMSTOCK

CAMPING

Seminole Canyon State
Historical Park
P.O. Box 125
Comstock , Texas 78837
(915) 292-4464.

DALLAS/FORT WORTH

CAMPING

Lake Mineral Wells State Park
    camping reservations
    (512) 389-8900

FORT DAVIS

CAMPING

Davis Mountains State Park
    Box 786 Fort Davis, TX
    (915) 426-3337
    Camping reservations
    (512) 389-8900

Indian Lodge
    P.O. Box 1458
    Ft. Davis, TX 79734 or
    (915) 426-3254

TERLINGUA

FOOD

The Starlight Cafe, downtown Terlingua.

RIVER GUIDES

Far Flung Adventures, 1-800-359-4138.

APPENDIX E
Emergency Services

NEW MEXICO
New Mexico Medical Crisis Center, 1-800-432-6866, is available 24 hours a day throughout New Mexico

ALBUQUERQUE
Kaseman Presbyterian Hospital
8300 Constitution Ave NE
(505) 291- 2000

Lovelace Medical Center
5400 Gibson Blvd. SE
(505) 262-7000

Presbyterian Hospital
1100 Central Ave SE
(505) 841-1234

St. Joseph Northeast Heights Hospital
4701 Montgomery Blvd. NE
(505) 888-7800

University of New Mexico Hospital
2211 Lomas Blvd. NE
(505) 843-2111

LAS CRUCES
Memorial Medical Center
2450 South Telshor
(505) 521-8641 or 521-2286
(24-hour emergency number)

LOS ALAMOS
Los Alamos Medical Center
(505) 662-4201

St. John's Search and Rescue and
State Police, (505) 827-9300

SANTA FE
St. Vincent Hospital, (505) 983-3361

TAOS
Holy Cross Hospital, (505) 758-8883

New Mexico State Police
(505) 758-8878

Taos County Sheriff, (505) 758-3361

Taos City Police, (505) 758-2216

TEXAS
ALPINE
Big Bend Regional Medical Center
801 E. Brown, Alpine
(915) 837-3447.

BIG BEND NATIONAL PARK
Terlingua Medics, (915) 371-2536

Big Bend Family Health Center
(915) 371-2661 or 371-2207

COMSTOCK
Comstock Volunteer Fire Department
emergency calls only at 292-4533

Texas Rangers in Del Rio, 775-3569

EL PASO
Montana Vista Fire Station, 857-0999

El Paso County Sheriff Eastside Substation, 546-2280

FORT DAVIS
Sheriff's department, (915) 426-3913

Ambulance service, (915) 426-3900

FREDERICKSBURG
Ambulance, rescue, and sheriff
assistance, (512) 997-7585

Llano ambulance, (512) 247-4221

APPENDIX F
GLOSSARY OF TERMS/CLIMBER JARGON

aid/artificial climbing—Type of climbing where equipment is used for upward progress (supporting body weight, used for hand and foot holds, etc.)

anchor—Secure attachment to the rock. Many different combinations exist:

    artificial/gear anchors—may consist of climbing hardware placed in cracks, etc.;

    fixed anchors—may be bolts or pitons permanently attached to the rock;

    natural anchors—may consist of a block, keyhole in the rock, or a tree, etc.

angle piton/angle—Specific type of piton with a "V" shape cross section (see piton); removable, yet invasive—damaging the rock and possibly the piton.

arete—Sharp, narrow ridge or spur; outside corner.

bashy—Malleable hardware for extreme aid climbing (see copperheads); otherwise known as a "mashy" or a "trashy" when the cable blows out; removable, yet invasive—damaging the rock and the equipment.

beak/bird beak—Specific type of piton for extreme aid climbing; very thin and in the shape of a bird's beak (see piton).

belay—Rope handling technique to hold a climber in the event of a fall; **belayer**—person securing the rope for a lead climber; **belay anchor**—the secure attachment of the rope to the rock.

beta—Detailed description of all information about a climb.

bolt—Permanent/fixed protection device (typically commercial grade concrete expansion bolt) that is driven into a hole drilled in the rock; invasive equipment that is removable but generally left on the cliff for other climbers to use. A specially designed metal alloy "hanger" is attached so carabiners can be attached easily.

bouldering—Type of free climbing on small cliffs and boulders; generally done without protective equipment such as a rope.

buttress—Formation of rock connected to a large wall or cliff, resembling a support or reinforcement.

cam—Variety of protection devices that when placed will rotate to take a load; removable and non-invasive.

Camalot—Specific type of spring-loaded 4-cam unit; removable and non-invasive; typically heavy and expensive.

carabiner/'biner—Metal alloy snap link used in many ways for connecting points of protection, rope, and person to a belay and anchor system.

chicken head—Bump or protrusion on the rock surface about the size of a chicken's head.

chimney—Narrow cleft in a cliff generally 8 inches or wider.

chock—Removable, non-invasive wedge, nut, or cam made of metal alloy used for points of protection and anchors typically placed in cracks.

copperheads/c-heads—Malleable wedges attached to a short cable; driven into seams and shallow cracks for extreme aid climbing (see bashy).

crack—Split, break, or fissure of various width and depth in rock.

dihedral—Rock formation resembling a two-sided open book or inside corner.

edge—Small indentations or steps in the rock used for hand and foot holds.

face—Feature of a cliff or mountain; also a type of climbing technique where the texture of the rock is used for holds.

fixed hardware—Permanent protection equipment placed in the rock (i.e. bolts, fixed pitons, nut or cam that is too stuck to remove without damage; see anchors).

flash—To free climb a route/pitch without falls, hangs/rests, or prior knowledge of the climb.

free climbing—Type of climbing where equipment is used only for protection, not for upward progress or to support body weight; may be done without a safety rope and belay (see free solo climbing).

free soloing—To climb alone without a rope or any protective hardware (see solo climbing).

Friend—Specific type of spring-loaded 4-cam device; removable and non-invasive.

gear—Equipment used for protection (invasive and non-invasive apparatuses; see anchors).

hangdogging—Type of climbing where leader free climbs from one point of protection to another, resting or supporting body weight on the equipment.

HB (Hugh Banner)—Specific type of protection wedge/nut made of metal alloy and equipped with a short loop of cable; removable, non-invasive.

hook—Specific type of metal hooks of various shapes and designs for extreme aid climbing on the texture of a cliff face; removable and non-invasive.

jam—Technique involves wedging parts of the body—fingers, hands, feet, etc.—for ascending cracks. The size/width of the crack dictates type of technique required.

jug—Large "thank God" hold.

knifeblade—Specific type of thin piton (see piton).

layback/lieback—Technique using counterforce; pulling with the hands while pushing with the feet.

lead—Situation where a climber goes first up a pitch, attached to a rope and belayer and placing protection along the way.

lost arrow—Specific type of piton named after the Lost Arrow Spire in Yosemite (see piton).

mono-doigt—One finger hold.

natural gear—Removable, non-invasive protection equipment (in addition to sharing the broad definition of "gear," natural gear also can mean placement of a sling around a tree or horn of rock or use of a rock as a chockstone, etc.).

nuts—Removable, non-invasive protection equipment (a.k.a. wedges, stoppers, chocks, etc.)

off-hands—Cracks typically 2 to 3.5 inches wide.

on-sight—Style of climbing where leader attempts to climb route from the bottom up without prior knowledge (see flash).

off-width (OW)—Cracks typically 3.5 to 8 inches wide.

pitch—Rope-length of climbing.

piton—Specially designed metal spike made to drive into cracks as a point of protection or an anchor; removable and invasive.

prow—Projection or portion of a cliff or mountain face that protrudes.

quick draw—Short loop of nylon webbing (see runner) with two carabiners attached for quick attachment to protection equipment.

rack—Assortment of protective hardware (see gear) needed for a climb.

rappel anchor—Secure attachment to the rock for rappelling (bolts and slings, bolts and chains, slings around rock horns or trees, welded cold shuts, pitons, nuts, etc.).

rappel/rap—Method of descending from a mountainside or cliff by means of a rope.

redpoint—To free climb a route/pitch without falls, hangs, or rests on equipment, but with prior knowledge or rehearsal of route.

roof—Severely overhanging rock formation.

RP (Roland Pauligk)—Specific type of protection wedge/nut originally designed in Australia and made of brass, equipped with a short loop of cable; removable, non-invasive.

runner—Tubular webbing tied or sewn into loops of various lengths and used as protection and anchor attachments.

runout—Section of climbing where protection is far apart.

RURP (Realized Ultimate Reality Piton)—Specific type of small, thin piton for extreme aid climbing (about the size of a postage stamp and about as useful for holding a lead fall; see piton).

sandbag—Underrated difficulty (most locals are "sandbaggers").

sling—See runners.

solo climbing—Climbing alone with or without a rope or protective hardware.

smear—Climbing technique using friction to stick to the rock surface (shoe rubber works better than skin).

thin crack—Crack up to 1.25 inches wide; typically small enough to accommodate portions of the fingers.

thin face—Holds that typically are narrow and small (see face).

thin hands/rattly fingers—Cracks (0.75 to 1.5 inches wide) typically too small to insert the entire hand but too large to get a good grip/jam with finger knuckles.

toprope—Technique of practice climbing where rope is anchored above the climber.

Tri-Cam—Specific type of passive cam device that has sewn slings attached to the cam; removable and non-invasive.

TCU (Three Cam Unit)—Specific type of small spring-loaded cam device; removable and non-invasive.

webbing—Nylon strapping made in a tube shape ("tubular" webbing) and specially designed for climbing applications.

wired stopper/wires—Wedge made of metal alloy and equipped with a short loop of cable; removable, non-invasive.

yo-yo—Type of free climbing style where the lead climber lowers to the ground if a fall occurs or for a rest and then ascends back to the previous high point and beyond without weighting the rope or any of the protection equipment.

Index

Symbols

45 Degree Wall   255, 256
5.8 Crack   85
5.9 Crack   86

A

A Climber's Guide to Box Canyon   205
A Date With Death   160
Abiquiu   58
Accrojovia   114
Acid Rain   122
Across the View   150
Adam Ant   89, 90
Adolescent Fantasy   132
Advanced Start   94
Aero Questa   29
After the Pillar Came Down   49
Alamogordo   226
Alarm Arm   210
Albuquerque   108, 109, 110, 144, 145, 157,
        161, 163, 164, 178, 241
Alcohol Wall   203, 205
Alice in Bananaland   254
Alice in Bananaland/Busted   264
Alien, The   68
All Natural   272
All the Nasties   254, 264
All This Way for the Short Ride   293
Almost Blue   202, 207
Alpine   278, 307
Alsate's Nose   305
Amazon   42
American Alpine Club   253
American Mountain Foundation   13
Amistad Recreation Area   291
Amplified Apples   269
Amplified Heat   254, 269
Anazazi Momma   138
Andy's Encore   295
Animal Magnetism   150
Anomaly   301
Anorexia   139
Anorexic   236
Another Lichen Nightmare   119
Another Pretty Face   30
Anticipation   220
Anuta   231
Aporia   301
Appetite Peak   305
Apprentice   103
Apprentice, The   132
Aquatic Anxiety   322
Arch of Evil   210
Are You Lichen It   114
Arroyo Hondo   41

Arroyo Seco Creek   31
Art Gecko   132
Artesia   246
Artists   259
Ash, Jeff   160
Aspen Alley   68
Austin   315, 316
Autobahn   132
Aviary Ort Overhangs   161
Awkward Chimney   41

B

Baba Wawa   316, 321
Babalouie   182
Baby Cakes   64
Back of Jack   70
Back to Montana   125
Backside   315
Backside Area   309
Backside Area, The   316
    Bold Talk For A One-Eyed Fat Man   319
    Boston   317
    Carpet Crawl   319
    Christene Variation   317
    Deep Prok   321
    Dome Driver   317
    Easier Than It Looks   317
    Edge Of Night   321
    Fly On A Windshield   321
    French Route   321
    Gravitron   319
    Harder Than It Looks   317
    Intensive Care   319
    La Dolce Vita   319
    M.D. 20/20   317
    Real Gravity   319
    Ripple   319
    Rite of Spring/Increasingly Vague   317
    Runamuck   321
    Sixth Happiness   321
    Stranger Than Friction   321
    Terminal Orogeny   321
    Texas Radio   319
    TJ Swan   319
Bad Air   283
Baker, Mike   141
Baker, Robbie   160
Balance of Terror   138
Baltzenator, The   183
Bambi   197
Banana Patch   264
Banana Rama   114
Bandelier National Monument   80, 82, 97, 98
Bandelier Tuff   6
Barlow's Buttress   94
Basin   307
Basin, The   305, 308
Baskin Robbins   235
Basta   295
Bats in the Belfry   65

Batshit Roof 98
Battle of the Bulge 94
Bear 185
Bear Boulders 231, 233
Bear Paw, The 301
Beastie Alley 59
Beastie Crack 97, 99
Beauchamp, Ron 160
Bede, Hans 160
Beginner's Crack 93
Beginners Hand Jam 94
Bell, George 79
Below the Old New Place 77, 80, 82, 89
    Adam Ant 90
    Color of My Potion 92
    Got a Nightstick, Got a Gun, Got Time on My
        Hands 92
    Fat Boys Don't Fly 92
    Flesh Eating Gnats 90
    I Dogged Your Wife and She is a Doofus 92
    Inflight Movie 90
    Instant Dogma 92
    L Dopa 90
    Little Shop of Horrors 90
    Lost Nerve 90
    Manic Crack 90
    Manic Nirvana 90
    Monsterpiece Theater 90
    P.M.S. 90
    Polyester Terror 90
    Putterman Cracks 90
    Ralph's Dilemma 90
    Ralph's Leisure Suit 90
    Ralph's Revenge 90
    Sardonic Smile 92
    Scandinavian Airlines 90
    Strong Urge to Fly 92
    Wailing Banshees 90
Benyak, David 160
Bergeron, Dale 315
Bernalillo 178
Best, The 236
Better Red than Dead 54, 63
Bevis 181
Bienvenidos 63
Big Bend National Park 2, 303, 305, 307
Big Horn Wall 243, 248
    Broken Arrows 248
    Counting Coup 248
    Custer's Last Stand 248
    Eagles Aren't Crows 248
    Ghost Dancers 248
    Kootenai Cruiser 248
    Smoke Signals 248
    Tribal War 248
Big Medicine 246
Black Crack 210
Black Mantel 100
Black Panther 182
Black Streak 63

Black Velvet 221, 222
Black Wall 94
Blade, The 114
Blessed and Blissed 201
Blind Faith 47
Blind Man's Bluff 191
Blind Prince, The 192
Blowhole, The 93, 94
Bob Marley Meets Master Ganj 206
Bold Talk for a One-eyed Fat Man 319
Bolts to Nowhere 63
Bookworm 103, 132
Boot Rock 305
Border Incident 305, 308
Bosker Boozeroo 83, 85
Bosque Del Apache Wildlife 205
Boss Hog 210
Boston 317
Bovine Inspiration 146
Box Baby 210
Box Canyon 205
Box Frenzy 210
Box Overhang Left 86
Box Overhang Right 86
Boy Scout 96
Boy What Assholes (You Guys Turned Out To Be)
        83, 85
Boya From La Jolla Who Stepped On A Cholla,
        The 130
Boyce, Cayce 43
Braindead 254
Brazos Cliffs 3
Breach of Faith 283
Bridgers, Doug 160
Brit Route, The 246
Broadway 98
Broken Arrows 248
Bucket Rider 293
Bucket Roof 259
Buhler, Carlos 160
Bulges, The 42
Bulimia 139, 140
Bunga Bunga 116
Burns, Cam 141
Bush Shark Tower 161
Busted 254
Butterfly Gecko 293
Buzzard's Roost 309, 322, 325
    Aquatic Anxiety 322
    Eat 322
    Fear Of Flying 322
    Little Feat 325
    P.G. 13 322
    Shrike 322
    Texas Crude 322
    The Wick 322

C

Cacti Cliff 103, 110, 134, 135, 139
    Anazazi Momma 135

Balance of Terror 135
Cheese Grater 135
Clandestine Desire 135
Cross-eyed and Painless 135
Crank Addiction 135
Direct Terror 135
Flameout 135
Full Cortex Meltdown 135
Funktuation 135
Gravity's Angel 135
Hump Me Dump Me 135
Izimbra 135
Pendejo Park 135
Premature Infatuation 135
Reach Or Bleach 135
Slums of Bora Bora 135
Technobiscuit 135
The Sample 135
Vibrator Dependent 135
Cactus Climb 94
Cactus War 133
Cakewalk 262
Cakewalk Direct 262
Cakewalk Wall 262
    Alice in Bananaland/Busted 264
    Banana Patch 264
    Cakewalk 262
    Cakewalk Direct 262
    Cowboyography 264
    Malice in Bucketland 264
    Return of Cakewalk 262
    Son of Cakewalk 262
Campbell, Larry 80
Captain Hook Area 198
    Captain Hook 198
    Peter Pan Flies Again 198
Captain Smarmbag 86
Capulin Mountain 74
Cardinal Sin 122
Carlsbad 244, 246, 261
Carlsbad Caverns. 6
Carpet Crawl 319
Carson National Forest 27, 33, 38, 45
Castolon 305, 307
Cat on a Hot Tin Roof 297
Catlin, Alex 288
Cattle Call Wall 141, 145
    Bovine Inspiration 146
    Cow Flop Crack 145
    Cud for Lulu 145
    Cowpies for Breakfast 145
    Moon over Belen 145
    Ow Now 146
    Pie In Your Eye 145
Catwalk 254
Catwalk Direct 254
Cave Exit 271
Cavemantle 97
Central Texas Limestone, A Climbers Guide 316
Central Wall 264
    All The Nasties 264

Desperado 267
Divine Wind/Brain Dead 264
Final Stone 266
Hueco Syndrome 267
Lunacy 266
Lunar Abstract 266
Lunatic Friends 266
No Fear Of Flying 266
Purple Microdot 266
Sea Of Holes 267
Uriah's Heap 267
Walking On The Moon 266
Window Pain 266
Chama 58
Checkerboard Wall 229, 233
    Circus Finish 235
    Knight's Move 235
Checkers 183
Cheeks, The 95
Cheese Grater 135
Cheshire Cat 197
Chess 183
Chevieux, Elie 255
Chicken Chop Suey 166, 167
Chicken Pox 139
Chickenheads 61
Child of Light 189
Chilly Willy Wall 141, 148
    Donkey Show 148
    Tasty Freeze 148
    Turkey Sandwich 148
    Wet Willies 148
Chimney, The 169
Chimney Canyon 169
Chimney Sweep 295
Chisos Basin 308
Chisos Mountains 303, 305
Chocolate Thunder 87
Cholla Backstep 49
Cholla Crack 85
Cholla Wall 83, 85
Christene Variation 317
Chute, The 284
Cibola National Forest 163, 178, 190, 191
Cinderella's Nightmare 199
Circle K 183
Circus Finish 235
Citadel, The 216, 218, 219
    Anticipation 220
    Finger Zinger 220
    Glad We Came 219
    Hercamur Snurd 220
    Murray's Crack 220
    The Nose 220
    The Whole Banana 220
    Tugboart 220
    West Ridge 220
    Wish You Were Here 219
Citizen Of Time 87
City of Rocks 239

City of Rocks State Park   237
Clandestine Desire   138
Classic Jam Crack   182
Clean Green Dream   63
Climbing Magazine   27, 108, 178, 253, 290
Cochiti Canyon   103
Cochiti Classic   129
Cochiti Lake   77, 108, 110
Cochiti Mesa   1, 2, 3, 6, 103, 104, 108, 110, 118, 135
Cochiti Mesa Crags   103
Coleur, Doug   24
Color of My Potion   89, 92
Columns, The   233, 235, 236
    The Best   236
Comanche Canyon   256, 275
Coming of Age   132
Coming of Age in Chihuahua   305
Common Cold   139
Comstock   290
Confusion Say   119
Conjure it Up   303
Corner Block   208
    Last Tango   208
    No Bozos   208
    Nowhere to Go   208
    Pluto   208
Coronado State Park   161
Corrido Del Norte   50
Cosmic Egg   308
Couleur, Doug   104
Counting Coup   248
Coup Stick   297
Cow Flop Crack   145
Cow Smarts   297
Cowboy Bob's Chicken Head Delight   64
Cowboy Logic   284
Cowgirl Pump   65
Cowpies for Breakfast   145
Coyote Trickster   303
Crabapple Crossing   316
Crack   235
Crack A Smile   119
Crackerjack   119
Crank Addiction   134, 138
Crash Test Dummy   181
Crescent Conundrum   295
Crisis In Utopia   88
Cross Country Crack   284
Cross-eyed and Painless   135
Crossfire   284
Crown of Aragon, The   256
Crump, James   315
Cryin' in the Rain   63
Crystal Suppository   122
Cud for Lulu   145
Cundiff, Reed   160
Curious George   182
Custer's Last Stand   243, 248

D

Dallas-Fort Worth   326, 329
Dancing With Too Many Girls   295
Danger Mouse   59
D'Antonio, Bob   80, 141
D'Antonio Approach, The   86
Dark Dreams   181
Darriau, Joe   160
Datil   185, 190, 191
Datil Mountains   185, 189
Davey, Bill   277, 305
Davis Mountain State Park   281
Davis Mountains State Park   277, 278
Dead Cholla Wall   22, 41, 43, 45
    After the Pillar Came Down   49
    Blind Faith   47
    Cholla Backstep   49
    Corrido Del Norte   50
    Doc's Dangle   50
    Either Or   50
    Esmerelda   50
    Fun   49
    Games   50
    Gorge Yourself   49
    Jam Time   47
    Just Arose   49
    Lava Flows   47
    Merge Left   49
    No Waiting   50
    Open Season   49
    Queso's Delight   47
    Somebody Loaned Me a Bosch   50
    Special Ed   49
    Toxic Socks   49
    Twisted Feet   50
Death Dihedral   275
Deception   41
Deep Prok   321
Del Rio   288
DeLataillade, Jean   104, 139
Deliverance   254, 269
Deming   239, 241
Density   281
Desert Shield   119
Desert Storm   119
Desperado   267
Diagonal, The   208
Didgemaster   116
Digital Pleasures   125
Dihedral Area, The   182
    Babalouie   182
    Black Panther   182
    Classic Jam Crack   182
    Floating World   182
    Green Eggs and Ham   182
    Lucky Boy   182
    Quickdraw McGraw   182
    Smoked Salmon   182
    Tim's Rig   182

Dihedrals, The   103, 118
   Art Gecko   132
   Autobahn   132
   Bookworm   132
   Cactus War   133
   Discipline   133
   Eternal Spring   133
   Inchworm   132
   Indiscipline   133
   Marlboro Country   133
   The Apprentice   132
   Wyoming Saw   133
Dike, The   283
Dinabolic   119
Direct on The Truth   210
Direct Start   63
Direct Terror   138
Dirty Black Nightmare   63
Dirty Diagonal   61
Discipline   133
Disease Wall   103, 110, 139
   Anorexia   139
   Bulimia   140
   Chicketn Pox   139
   Common Cold   139
   Endorphin   140
   Opiate of the Masses   140
   Small Pox   139
Divine Wind   254
Divine Wind/Brain Dead   264
Dock Wall   291, 301
Doc's Dangle   50
Doeren, Bruce   160
Dome Driver   317
Dome Drivers Manual, The   315
Dome Wilderness   111
Dome Wilderness Area   108
Doña Ana   2
Doña Ana Mountains   218, 229, 231, 233
Donkey Show   148
Double D   179
Double Determination   283
Double Jeopardy   119
Double Vision/Ream Dream   85
Doughnut Shop, The   82
Dragon's Den   256
Dragon's Lair   65
Dreadlock Holiday   206
Dream Tower   141, 150
   Animal Magnetism   150
   East Coast Dreams   150
   Hail Dancer   150
   Sanctuarium   150
Dreamscape   119
Drop in the Ocean   179
Drumheller, Doug   160
Dunlap, Dave   160
Duran, John   104, 110, 160
Dwarf Shaman   301

E

E Pluribis Cruxi Unum Puripus   114
Eagle, The   274
   Road To Nowhere   274
   The Gunfighter   274
   Through The Looking Glass   274
   When Legends Die   274
Eagle Canyon   103, 108, 110
   Accrojovia   114
   Are You Lichen It   114
   Banana Rama   114
   Bunga Bunga   116
   Didgemaster   116
   Earth Monster   114
   Ego Maniac   114
   E Pluribis Cruxi Unum Puripus   114
   Handsome Parish Lady   114
   Indecent Insertion   111
   Jug Abuse   111
   Killer Bee   111
   Kona   111
   New Wave   111
   Old Wave   111
   Omdulation Fever   114
   Pepto-Dismal   111
   Maalox Moment   111
   Manhattan   114
   Mr. Wong's Zipper   114
   Psycho Thriller   114
   Racist Fantasy   114
   The Blade   1114
   The Wrong Mr. Wrong   114
   Turkey Baster   113
   Tutti Frutti   111
   Wannabee   111
Eagle Nest   40
Eagles aren't Crows   248
Earth Monster   114
Earwig   208
Easier Than It Looks   317
East Coast Dreams   150
East Face   322
East Mountain   256, 275
   Death Dihedral   275
   Kings Highway   275
   Pigs to Pork   275
   Pigs in Space Buttress   275
   Plastic Fantastic   275
East Saddle of the Needle   159
East Spur   256
East Spur Maze   256
East Wall   203
Eat   322
Echo Canyon   325
Eclipse   272
Edge of Night   321
Edwin Terrell Memorial Route, The   34, 36
Eggleston, C.   278
Ego Maniac   114
Either Or   50

El Camino Royal 215
El Murrays Left, Center, and Right 255
El Paso 218, 246, 251, 258, 259, 261
El Queso Grande 99
El Salto 31, 34
Emory Peak 308
Empty and Meaningless 125
Enchanted Rocks 314
Enchanted Rocks State Natural Area 2, 4, 309,
    315, 316
Enchanted Tower, The 185, 189, 190, 191, 194,
    202, 204, 205, 237
    Golden Stairs 194
    Goliath 194
    Jabberwocky 194
    Medusa 194
    Once Upon a Time 194
    Ripped Van Winkle 194
    Rubber Mission 194
    Rumplestiltskin 194
    Shipwrecked 194
    Technowitch 194
    The Mad Hatter 194
    Tinkerbells' Nightmare 194
    Zee Wicked Witch 194
End TR, The 272
End Loop Boulder 272
    The End TR 272
    Wyoming Cowgirls TR 272
End Loop Wall 271
    Cave Exit 271
    Eclipse 272
    Fast Foods 272
    Short Hands 271
    Show Me 271
End of the French Revolution 119
Endorphin 139, 140
Ennslin, Norbert 80
Entertaining Mike Tyson 181
Entrada 6
Entrance Exam 179
Entrance Area 179
    Double D 179
    Drop in the Ocean 179
    Entrance Exam 179
    Fall From Grace 179
    Nature of the Beast 179
Esmerelda 50
Espanola 56
Eternal Apples 254, 267
Eternal Spring 133
Eyes That Lie 70

F

Face, The 42
Face Off 85
Factory Direct 181
Fainting Imam 122
Fair Trade 206
Fairfield, Tim/Timmy 176, 189

Fall From Grace 179
Far Side, The 182
    Chess 183
    Checkers 183
    Curious George 182
    Lonesome Dove 183
    Midnight Rider 182
    Patchwork 183
    Pussy Whipped 183
    Ramblin' Man 182
    R.I.P. 182
    Tiger By The Tail 183
Fast Foods 254, 272
Fat Boy's Don't Cry 89
Fat Boys Don't Fly 92
Fear of Flying 322
Fee Fi Fo Fum 192
Fillet a Papillon Wall 202, 205
    Almost Blue 207
    Bob Marley Meets Master Ganj 206
    Dreadlock Holiday 206
    Fair Trade 206
    If You Can't Do It, Glue It 206
    Insider Trader 207
    Little Caterpillar 206
    New Kids On The Block 206
    Red Tag Sale 206
    Sinister Dane 207
    Uncle Fester Gets Sent To Europe 207
    Window Shopping 206
Final Stone 266
Finger in the Socket 122
Finger Zinger 219, 220
Fingerfest 65
Fingertip Layback 94
Firewalker 246
First Strike 93, 96
Five Years After 61
Flake Roof 254, 262
Flake Roof Direct 254
Flake Roof Indirect 262
Flameout 138
Flaming Arrow 297
Flea Tree Dihedral 229
Flesh Eating Gnats 89, 90
Floating World 182
Fly on a Windshield 321
Flying A, The 93, 95
Fool's Way Out 295
Fort Davis 278, 281
Fort Worth 326
Fortuitous Circumstance 132
Foster, Gus 56
Fox Tower 271
    Fox Tower 271
    Fox Tower Indirect 271
    Fox Trot 271
    Head Fox 271
Fox Tower Indirect 271
Fox Trot 254, 271

Franks, The
  Bevis   181
  Crash Test Dummy   181
  Dark Dreams   181
  Entertaining Mike Tyson   181
  Funky Junkie   181
  Junkhead   181
  Monkey Man   181
Franklin Mountains   215
Fredericksburg   316
French Route   321
Freshman Mountain   322
Fried Chickens   61
Frijoles Canyon   80
Frog Fright   281
Frog, The   325
Frog Prince, The   189, 191
Frog Prince Wall   191
  Blind Man's Bluff   191
  Frog Prince   191
  Gollum   191
  Red Queen   191
  Through The Looking Glass   191
  White Knight   191
  White Queen   191
Front Side   256, 261
Frosted Flake   301
Full Cortex Meltdown   138
Full Tilt Boogie   233, 236
Fun   49
Funktuation   138
Funky Junkie   181

G

Gallagher, Kevin   3, 290, 316
Gallery Wall   141, 150
  Accross the View   150
  Presume to be Modern   150
Gallinas   185
Games   50
Gateway Rock   141, 146
  Woof Toof Noof Roof   146
Gecko Wall   291
  Butterfly Gecko   291
  Lizard's Lust   291
  Prosimian   291
  Renegade   291
Geez Louise   68
Gemstone Slabs   161
Gemstone West Slabs and East Slabs   161
Ghost Dancers   248
Giddy-Up   297
Glad You Came   219
Glass Coffin   197
Glass Slipper   199
Gogas, John   243, 277, 288
Gold Star Roof   259
Golden Stairs   194
Goliath   194
Gollum   191

Gompper, Eric   176
Gorge Yourself   49
Got a Nightstick, Got a Gun, Got Time on my
  Hands   92
Graham, Jim   216, 231
Gram, Peter   80
Gramont, Bertrand   185, 202, 205
Grandma's Cancer   65
Grapevine Hills   303, 305, 308
Gravitron   319
Gravity's Angel   135, 138
Gray, Clark   160
Grease Mechanic   210
Great Rock Hits of Hueco Tanks   259
Great Wall   275
  Star Dust   275
  Tarts of Horsham   277
Green Eggs and Ham , The   182
Groth, John   176
Grump, James   259
Grunge up the Munge   125
Guadalupe Mountains   6, 243
Gun Powder   208
Gunning for The Buddha   125
Gunslinger   181

H

Hadfield, Lance   176
Hail Dancer   150
Hammack, David   160
Handsome Parish Lady   114
Hanging Judge   295
Hangover   222
Happy Entrails   148
Hard Start   98
Harder Than It Looks   317
Hardin, Donny   255
Harris, Scott   315
Have Slab Will Travel   181
Hawk's Nest   208
He Drove Porsches   293
Head, Dave   259
Head Fox   254, 271
Head, Mike   252, 253, 255, 259
Heads and Motes   225
Headwall Crack Left   85
Headwall Crack Right   85
Heart of Stone   33, 34, 38, 51
  Heart of Stone   34
  Laid Back Limey   36
  The Edwin Terrell Memorial Route   34
Heart of Stone Rock   22, 31, 41
Heaven Above   41
Hendry, Bill   80
Herb's Roof   99
Hercamur Snurd   219, 220
Hesse, Mark   103
Hessing Route   100
Hicks, Gary   160
Highland Fling   297

Hiker's and Climber's Guide to the Sandias 161, 163
Hill, Mike 163
Hollywood Tim 151
Holthouse, Bruce 53
Holthouse to Hell 63
Holthouse's Haulsack 63
Holy Crack 85
Holy Wall 83, 85
Holy Wars 125
Hondo Cliffs 38
Hooka 201
Hopewell Lake 54
Horak, Carl and Lou 79
Horak, Paul 24, 160, 176
How Ed's Mind Was Lost 68
Hueco Mountains 252
Hueco Syndrome 254, 267
Hueco Tanks 4, 237, 251, 252, 253, 255, 256, 259
Hueco Tanks, A Climber's and Boulderer's Guide 255, 259
Hueco Tanks State Historical Park 2, 251, 258, 261
Hueco Walk 262
Huecool 273
Huecos Rancheros 86
Hufnagel, Erik 205
Hump Me Dump Me 135
Humping the Camel 291, 293
Humpty Dumpty 197
Humpty Dumpty Wall 197
  Bambi 197
  Humpty Dumpty 197
Hurley 241

I

I Dogged Your Wife and She is a Doofus 92
IDBI Wall 100
If You Can't Do it, Glue It 206
Illusion Dissolution 122
Immaculate Deception 122
In the Lime-Lite 182
Inchworm 132
Indecent Exposure 269
Indecent Exposure Buttress 267
  Amplified Apples 269
  Amplified Heat 269
  Deliverance 269
  Eternal Apples 267
  Indecent Exposure 269
  Optical Promise 269
  Rainbow Bridge 269
  Tree Route 267
Indecent Insertion 111
Indian Head 307
Indian Head Hill 307
Indian Head Hills 303, 305
Indiscipline 133
Inflight Movie 90
Ingraham, Dick 159, 216, 218

Ingraham, R. 231
Inside Dihedral 99
Insider Trader 207
Instant Dogma 92
Intensive Care 319
Irish Cream 221
Isaacson, Eric 244
Izimbra 138

J

Jabberwocky 194
Jackson, Jeff 3, 288, 290, 316
Jam Time 47
Jaramillo, Ed 40, 43, 45, 53, 56
Jemez Caldera 103, 141
Jemez Mountains 1, 96, 108, 141, 157
Jemez River 141
Jemez Springs 144
Jemez Volcanic Field 6
Jemez Volcano 103
Jett, Randal 82, 108, 144
John Dunn Bridge 38
John's Wall
  Amazon 42
  Awkward Chimney 41
  Deception 41
  Heaven Above 41
  Memory Lane 42
  Rope-a-Dope 41
  Route 66 42
  The Bulges 42
  The Face 42
  The Nose 42
  The Trapeze 41
John's Wall 22, 38
Jones, Matthew 190
Jones, Matthew A. 205
Jug Abuse 111
Juniper Campground 80
Junkhead 181
Jurisdiction 297
Just Arose 49
Just Say No To Crack 119
Just Say No To Jugs 86

K

Kacon, Kathy 160
Kaiser, Karl 216
Kalakay, Tom 104
Keeping Up With the Joneses 202
Keller, Carl 80
Kids in Toyland 122
Killer Bee 111
King Crack 69
Kings Highway 275
Kiva Cave 259
Kline, Larry 159
Knight's Move 235
Kona 111
Kootenai Cruiser 243, 248
Kor, Layton 79

Kutz, Jack and LaDonna 159
Kyle's Crack 182
Kyrlack, Bob 159

L

L Dopa 90
La Dolce Vita 319
La Espina 129
La Sierra de la Soledad 215
Laeser, Luke 141
Laid Back Limey 31, 33, 36
Lainbo 125
Lake Maloya 75
Lake Mineral Wells State Park 2, 326
Land Beyond 189
Las Conchas 141, 144
Las Cruces 214, 215, 226, 231, 233, 239, 241,
    255
Last Tango 208
Latir Peak Wilderness 24
Latir Wilderness 27
Lava Flows 47
Lawless 291
Lawless Cove 291, 295
Lawless Wall 288, 295
    Andy's Encore 295
    Basta 295
    Chimney Sweep 295
    Cow Smarts 295
    Crescent Conundrum 295
    Dancing With Too Many Girls 295
    Fool's Way Out 295
    Giddy-Up 297
    Hanging Judge 295
    Jurisdiction 297
    Running From the Law 295
    Scott Free 295
    Texas 2-Step 295
    The Real U.T. is in Tennessee 295
    The Way Out 295
    War Path 295
    Wetback Express 295
    Wrangler Savvy 295
Leaning Tower, The 141, 153
    Lichen Attack Crack 153
    Mainliner 153
    The Mean Leaner 153
Left Eyebrow 226, 227
Left Mother 99
Len's Roof 86
Leonard, Mark 160
Leonardo da Smeari 161
Leslie's Little Fingers 118
Less Hard Start 99
Lesser Spire 216
Lewis, Mike 287
Lichen Attack Crack 153
Lincoln National Forest 244
Liposuction Massacre 210
Liska, Don 79
Little Caterpillar 206

Little Dome 316, 325
Little Feat 325
Little Horse Mesa 71, 75
Little Roof 97, 100
Little Shop of Horrors 90
Lizard Man 100
Lizard's Lust 293
Llano 315, 316
Llano Uplift 4
Lohn, Chuck 277
Lonesome Dove 183
Lookout Shelf 58
Lopez, Juan 141
Los Alamos 74, 82, 96, 98, 108, 111, 144
Los Alamos Mountaineers 3, 79
Los Alamos Mountaineers Club 82
Los Alamos. 80
Lost Nerve 90
Lounge, The 82
Love Shack Area 141, 148
    Happy Entrails 148
Lowenbrau Light 221
Lower La Cueva Canyon area 161
Lower La Cueva Domes 161
Lubme 88
Lucid Fairyland 207
Lucky Boy 182
Lucky Ledges 281
Lucky Ledges Direct 281
Lumpy Gravy 122
Lunacy 266
Lunar Abstract 254, 266
Lunatic Friends 266

M

M.C. Epic 86
M.D. 20/20 317
Maalox Moment 111
MacFarlane, Tom 80
Mad Bolter 68
Mad Dogs and Englishmen 151
Mad Hatter 194
Magdelena 185
Main Dome 309, 314, 316, 325
Mainliner 153
Major Wall 203, 204, 205
Malice in Bucketland 254, 264
Mama Jugs 61
Mamby Hot Spring 41
Manhattan 114
Manic Crack 89, 90
Manic Nirvana 90
Marathon 307
Margaritaville 222
Margolin, Len 79, 80, 96
Maria de la Sangria 210
Marlboro Country 133
Mauldin, John 160
Max Headroom 254, 273
McArthur, Dave 288
McCall, John 252, 255

McGill, Mike 141
McKernan, Jenny 160
Mean Leaner, The 141, 153
Medicine Wheel 297
Medusa 194
Memory Lane 42
Mer Diaphane 256
Merge Left 49
Merlin's Mantra 201
Merrill, Steve 160
Mesa de Anguilla 305
Metalogic 301, 303
Metalogic Wall 301
    Aporia 301
    Conjure It Up 303
    Coyote Trickster 303
    Metalogic 301, 303
    Reading Iculus 301
    Terry's 301
Mexican Breakfast 160, 161, 172
    Mexican Breakfast Crack 174
    Tarantula 174
Mexican Breakfast Crack 172, 174
Meyerriecks, Thad 160
Middle Mother 99
Middle Rock 58, 64
    Bats in the Belfry 64
    Cowboy Bob's Chicken Head Delight 64
    Cowgirl Pump 64
    Dragon's Lair 64
    Fingerfest 64
    Grandma's Cancer 64
    Raging Chicken 64
Midnight Pumpkin Wall 199
    Cinderella's Nightmare 199
    Glass Slipper 199
    Midnight Pumpkin 199
Midnight Rider 182
Mighty Dog 325
Mills, Mark 305
Mineral Wells 329
Minor 203
Minor Wall 205
Modern Day Contrivances 210
Moffat, Jerry 255
Molotov Cocktail 208
Mona Feetsa 161
Monk, Don 79
Monkey Business 208
Monkey Do 182
Monkey Lust 125
Monkey Man 181
Monkey See 182
Mononucleosis 118
Monopoly 297
Monster 100
Monsterpiece Theater 89, 90
Montana Deviate 125
Moon over Belen 145
Mosaic Rock 53, 58, 59, 61
    Baby Cakes 64

Better Red Than Dead 63
Bienvenidos 63
Black Streak 63
Bolts to Nowhere 63
Chickenheads 61
Clean Green Dream 63
Cryin' in the Rain 63
Danger Mouse 59
Direct Start 63
Dirty Black Nightmare 63
Dirty Diagonal 61
Five Years After 61
Fried Chickens 61
Holthouse Haulsack 63
Holthouse to Hell 63
Learn to Forget 63
Mama Jugs 61
Pony Express 59
Raise the Titanic 64
Seaman Girl 61
Serpentine Crack 63
Serpentine Face 63
Summer Dreams 64
T.B.O.L. 61
Techtonic 61
Tech-no-star 61
Thunder Toad 59
Walking Dread 63
Mosaic Wall 58
Moss Lake 315
Motes, Mark 216, 252, 255
Mother Goose 189
Mount Taylor 157
Mountain Momma 171, 172
Mountaineers 3
Mountains of Solitude 215
Mr. Foster's Lead 94
Mr. Natural 272
Mr. Toad's Wild Ride 125
Mr. Wong's Zipper 114
Muralla Grande 160, 161, 169
    The Second Coming 171
    Warpy Moople 169
Murray, Bob 237, 255
Murray's Crack 220
Mushroom Boulder 252, 256
Mushroom Roof 255

N

Nakovic, Fred 255
Napoleon Blown-Apart 125
Narcissistic Dream 85
Natural Buttress 272
    All Natural 272
    Max Headroom 273
    Mr. Natural 272
    Sunnyside Up 273
    Supernatural Anesthetist 272
Natural Mystic 273
Nature of the Beast 179
Navajo Reservation 3

Needle, The 160, 161, 163, 167
The Southwest Ridge 167
Never Never Land 201
New Age Nightmare 130
New Kids On the Block 206
New New Place, The 82
New Rage 68
New Wave 111
Nicole, Frederic 256
No Bozos 208
No Exit 83, 85
No Fear of Flying 266
No Lines 50
No Waiting 50
North Cliff 125
Back to Montana 125
Conchiti Classic 129
Digital Pleasures 125
Empty and Meaningless 125
Grunge up the Munge 125
Gunning for the Buddha 125
Holy Wars 125
La Espina 129
Lainbo 125
Montana Deviate 125
Monkey Lust 125
Mr. Toad's Wild Ride 125
Napoleon Blown-Apart 125
New Age Nightmare 130
Open Mouth Syndrome 130
Path of the Doughnut Man 130
Pickpocket 130
Praise the Lunge 125
Proctologist's Fantasy 125
Shunning Teocracy 130
The Boya From La Jolla Who Stepped On A
Cholla 130
Thief in Time 129
To Catch A Thief 129
Touch Monkey 125
North Face 227
North Mountain 256, 261, 272, 274, 275
Flake Roof 262
Flake Roof Indirect 262
Hueco Walk 262
True Grip 262
North Rock 58, 69
Back of Jack 70
Eyes That Lie 70
King Crack 69
Queen Crack 69
North Summit Direct 161
North Wall 96, 202, 205, 208
Alarm Arm 210
Arch of Evil 210
Black Crack 210
Boss Hog 210
Box Baby 210
Box Frenzy 210
Direct on The Truth 210
Grease Mechanic 210

Maria de la Sangria 210
Modern Day Contrivances 210
Liposuction Massacre 210
Rock Trooper 210
The Truth 210
The "Z" Crack 210
Tomahawk 210
Totem 210
Northwest Ridge 161
Nose, The 42, 79, 97, 99, 220
Notch, The 99
Nowhere to Go 208
Nutcracker Rocks 27, 28

O

Ojo Caliente 58
Ojo Caliente Mineral Springs 56
Old New Place, The
Got a Nightstick, Got a Gun, Got Time on my
Hands 92
Old New Place, The 77, 82, 88
Old Wave 111
Olympian Crack 122
Omdulation Fever 114
On Beyond Zebra 83, 86
Once Upon a Time 197
One Hundred Thimbles 237
Ooey Gooey 201
Open Book 97, 98
Open Mouth Syndrome 130
Open Season 49
Opiate of the Masses 139, 140
Opposition 259
Optical Promise 269
Orange Peel 309, 325
Organ Mountains 2, 159, 214, 216, 218, 219, 225
Organ Needle 214, 215
Oriental Wall 278
Original Horak Route 93, 95
Original Open Book 99
Orilla Verde Recreation Area 33, 45, 47
Outhouse 2 256
Overkill 88
Overlard 86
Overlichen 87
Overlook, The 80, 82, 83, 93
5.8 Crack 85
5.9 Crack 86
Bosker Boozeroo 85
Box Overhang Left 86
Box Overhang Right 86
Boy, What Assholes (You Guys Turned Out To
Be) 85
Captain Smarmbag 86
Chocolate Thunder 87
Cholla Crack 85
Cholla Wall 85
Citizen Of Time 87
Crisis In Utopia 88
Double Vision/Ream Dream 85
Face Off 85

Headwall Crack Left 85
Headwall Crack Right 85
Holy Crack 85
Holy Wall 85
Huecos Rancheros 86
Just Say No To Jugs 86
Len's Roof 86
Lubme 88
M.C. Epic 86
Narcissistic Dream 85
No Exit 85
On Beyond Zebra 86
Overkill 88
Overlard 86
Overlichen 87
Overlord 86
Overripe Fresh-squeezed California Females 86
Overture 86
Paul's Boutique 85
Polly's Crack 85
Primal Scream 88
Putterman Gully Jump 88
Sale at Mervyn's 85
Squeeze Chimney 85
The D'Antonio Approach 86
Thief in Time 85
Thorazine Dream 86
View With a Room 86
Way Beyond Zebra 85
Overlook Park 80
Overlord 86
Overripe Fresh-squeezed California Females 86
Overture 83, 86
Ow Now 146

P

P.G. 13 322
P.M.S 89
P.M.S. 90
Pajarito 82
Pajarito Plateau 96
Palomas Peak 2, 202
Palomino Gals 284
Pandorf, Doug 104
Panorama Wall 43
Panther Junction 307
Parks, Dan 24
Party Pogues 201
Patchwork 183
Path of the Doughnut Man 130
Paul's Boutique 83, 85
Pecos River 284, 288, 290
Pecos River Gorge 2, 3, 6, 288, 290
Pegg, Dave 176
Pendejo Park 135
Penitentiary Hollow Climbing Area 326
People Mover 183
Pepto-Dismal 111
Perverts Delight 254
Peter Pan Flies Again 198
Piana, Paul 259

Pickpocket 130
Pie In Your Eye 145
Pigs in Space 275
Pigs in Space Buttress 256
Pigs to Pork 275
Pilar 43, 45, 47
Pizza Boulders 231, 233
Placitas 178
Plastic Fantastic 275
Playground, The 77, 82, 93
    Advanced Start 94
    Barlow's Buttress 94
    Battle of the Bulge 94
    Beginners Hand Jam 94
    Black Wall 94
    Cactus Climb 94
    First Strike 96
    Fingertip Layback 94
    Mr. Foster's Lead 94
    Original Horak Route 95
    Texas 95
    The Blowhole 94
    The Cheeks 95
    The Flying A 95
    Unrelenting Nines 96
    Upper Left Roof 94
    Vulture Roof 95
    Zander Zig Zag 95
Pletta, Brian 176
Pluto 208
Pocket Change 203
Pocket Change Wall 205
Pogue's Arete 201
Pogue's Cave 189
Pogue's Cave Wall 201
    Blessed and Blissed 201
    Hooka 201
    Merlin's Mantra 201
    Never Never Land 201
    Ooey Gooey 201
    Party Pogues 201
    Pogue's Arete 201
Point of Rocks 2, 11, 277, 278, 281
    Bad Air 283
    Breach of Faith 281
    Cowboy Logic 284
    Crossfire 284
    Cross Country Crack 284
    Density 281
    Double Determination 283
    Frog Fright 281
    Lucky Ledges 281
    Lucky Ledges Direct 281
    Palomino Gals 284
    Scarcity 281
    Solo Slabs 281
    The Chute 284
    The Dike 283
    Travesty 283
    Tuolumne 283
Point of Rocks and Environs 278

Poison Apple 197
Pojoaque 98
Polly's Crack 85
Polyester Terror 90
Pony Express 59
Porter, Jim 79, 80, 96
Porter Route 100
Porter Route, The 97
Praise the Lunge 125
Prandoni, Peter 24, 103, 160, 171
Precious 181
Premature Infatuation 135
Presumed to be Modern 150
Pretzel Logic 182
Price, Robert 315
Primal Scream 88
Procrastination 166, 167
Proctologist's Fantasy 125
Project (Butthead) 181
Project (Kick Stand) 182
Project (Love Hate Love) 181
Project (Radio Flyer) 183
Project (Sick Man) 179
Project (Wooden Jesus) 179
Prosimian 291
Prow 163
Prow, The 119
Psycho Thriller 114
Pulliam Ridge 305
Pumpin' Huecos 151
Purple Microdot 266
Pussy Whipped 183
Put Up Wet 181
Putterman Cracks 90
Putterman Gully Jump 88

Q

Que Wasted 28
Queen Crack 69
Queso's Delight 47
Questa 24
Questa Dome 22, 24, 27, 28, 38, 41, 51
    Aero Questa 29
    Another Pretty Face 30
    Que Wasted 28
    Question Of Balance 29
    Tostados Comquesta 31
Questa, Heart of Stone 11
Question Of Balance 29
Question of Balance 22
Quickdraw McGraw 182
Quintana 33

R

R.I.P. 182
Racist Fantasy 114
Raging Chicken 65
Railroad Gin 255
Rainbow Bridge 254, 269
Rainbow Dancer 164
Rainbow Route 164, 166

Raise the Titanic 64
Ralph's Dilemma 90
Ralph's Leisure Suit 89
Ralph's Revenge 90
Ramblin' Man 182
Ramp, The 96, 100
Random Wall 288, 291, 293
    All This Way for the Short Ride 293
    Bucket Rider 293
    He Drove Porsches 293
    Humping the Camel 293
    She Rode Horses 293
    Smoking Gun 293
    Well Tuned Evinrude 293
Randy's Wall 182
    In the Lime-Lite 182
    Kyles Crack 182
    Monkey Do 182
    Monkey See 182
    Pretzel Logic 182
    Stremulation 182
Raney, Lorne 176
Rapunzel's Revenge 192
Rapunzel's Wall 189, 192
    Fee Fi Fo Fum 192
    Rapuzel's Revenge 192
    The Blind Prince 192
    The Thorn Bush 192
Raton 71, 74, 75
Ratshit Cave 96, 98
Reach Or Bleach 135
Read, Adam 104, 139, 160
Reading Iculus 303
Real Gravy 319
Real U.T. is in Tennessee, The 295
Red Light District 183
    Circle K 183
    People Mover 183
    Pony Ride 183
    The Baltzenator 183
    X-File 183
Red Queen 191
Red River 28
Red Tag Sale 206
Red Wall, The 202, 205, 207, 208
    Earwig 208
    Gun Powder 208
    Hawk's Nest 208
    Lucid Fairyland 207
    Molotov Cocktail 208
    Monkey Business 208
    Redwall 208
    Spiderman 208
    The Diagonal 208
    TNT 208
Redwall 208
Reimer's Fishing Ranch 3
Renegade 255
Return of Cakewalk 262
Riepe, Brian 80
Right Eyebrow 226

Right Eyebrow, The 229
Right Mother 100
Ringjam 96, 98
Rio Grande 288
Rio Grande Gorge 22, 27, 38, 43
Rio Grande Gorge Bridge 45
Rio Grande Rift 4
Rio Grande Village 305, 307
Rio Hondo 22, 38
Ripple 316, 319
Rites of Spring/Increasingly Vague 317
Road to Nowhere 274
Roadside Attraction 145
Roadside Attraction Rock 141
Robbins Route 225
Rock and Ice 108, 218
Rock and Ice Magazine 82
Rock Art Foundation 287, 288, 290
Rock Trooper 210
Rocket In My Pocket 122
Rode Hard 181
Rombach, Ed 110
Romback, Ed 104
Rope-a-Dope 41
Rosebud Wall 243, 246
    Big Medicine 246
    Firewalker 246
    Six Little Indians 246
    Sweat Lodge 246
    The Brit Route 246
    Wounded Knee 246
Ross, Kermith 79
Round Room 256
Route 66 42
Roybal, Mike 79, 97, 103, 160, 171
Rubber Mission 194
Rumplestiltskin 197
Runamuck 321
Running From the Law 295
Rutherford, Lewis 176
Ruude, Andy 288

S

Sale at Mervyn's 83, 85
Salomon Maestas 205
Sal's Neuroses 151
Samet, Matt 82, 108, 144, 160
Sample, The 138
San Antonio 164
San Augustine Pass 214
San Lorenzo 241
San Mateo 185
Sanadine Dream 122
Sanctuarium 150
Sandia Crest 164, 169
Sandia Mountain 2, 3, 4, 6, 11, 157, 159
Sandia Mountain Wilderness 157
Sandia Wilderness Area 161, 163
Sangre de Cristo 1, 2
Sangre de Cristo Mountains 10, 43
Sangre de Cristo Range 3, 4, 24, 83, 157, 284

Santa Elena Canyon 305, 307, 308
Santa Fe 80, 82, 98, 108, 109, 144, 157, 241
Santa Fe National Forest 80, 108
Sardonic Smile 89, 92
Scandinavian Airlines 90
Scarcity 281
Schillaci, Mike 80, 141
Schum, Steve 160
Science Friction 226, 227
Scott Free 295
Sea Hag 198
Sea of Holes 254, 267
Seaman Girl 54, 61
Second Coming 169, 171
Secret Sharer 254
Seminole Canyon State Historical Park 288
Sequestered 28
Serpentine Crack 63
Serpentine Face 63
Shadowdancer 119
Shaman in a Bottle 301
Shaman Wall 301
    Dwarf Shaman 301
    Geisha Man 301
    Shaman in a Bottle 301
    Shamaroid 301
    Sky Shaman 301
    Uber Shaman 301
Shamaroid 301
Shape Shifter 297
She Rode Horses 291, 293
Sheftel, Lee 80, 104
Sherman, John 237, 251, 255, 259
Shield, The 159, 160, 163, 164
    Chicken Chop Suey 167
    Procrastination 167
    Rainbow Dancer 164
    Rainbow Route 166
    Slipping Into Darkness 167
Shillelagh 225
Shiprock 3
Shipwrecked 194
Showdown Wall 181
    Gunslinger 181
    Precious 181
    Sidekick 181
    Sweet Jane 181
    Velcro Booties 181
Show Me 272
Shrike 322
Shunning Theocracy 130
Sidekick 181
Sidewinder 179
Silver City 239
Sims, Ken 31, 103
Sinister Dane 207
Sitting Bull Falls 2, 243, 246
Six Little Indians 246
Six Pack Crack 96, 98
Sixth Happiness 321
Skinner, Todd 104

Sky Shaman   301
Slab City   179
Slain Buffalo Wall   297
   Cat On A Hot Tin Roof   297
   Coup Stick   297
   Flaming Arrow   297
   Highland Fling   297
   Medicine Wheel   297
   Monopoly   297
   Shape Shifter   297
Sleeping Beauty   197
Sleeping Beauty Wall   189
   Cheshire Cat   197
   Glass Coffin   197
   Poison Aplle   197
   Sea Hag   198
   Sleeping Beauty   197
   Tarred and Feathered   197
Slipping Into Darkness   167
Slums of Bora Bora   135
Small Potatoes   259
Small Pox   139
Smith, Rick   80
Smoke Signals   248
Smoked Salmon   182
Smoking Guns   293
Snake Dance   176, 179, 202
Socorro   189, 190, 204, 205
Socorro Box   190, 204, 205
Socorro Box, The   202
Solo Slabs   281
Solomon Maestas   190
Somebody Loaned Me a Bosch   50
Son of Cakewalk   262
South Cliff   118
   Acid Rain   122
   Another Lichen Nightmare   119
   Cardinal Sin   122
   Confusion Say   119
   Crack A Smile   119
   Crackerjack   119
   Crystal Suppository   122
   Desert Shield   119
   Desert Storm   119
   Dinabolic   119
   Double Jeopardy   119
   Dreamscape   119
   End of the French Revolution   119
   Fainting Iman   122
   Finger In The Socket   122
   Illusion Dissolution   122
   Immaculate Deception   122
   Kids In Toyland   122
   Leslie's Little Fingers   118
   Lumpy Gravy   122
   Just Say No To Crack   119
   Mononucleosis   118
   Rocket In My Pocket   122
   Olympian Crack   122
   Sanadine Dream   122
   Strange Attractor   122

Shadowdancer   119
Terminal Ferocity   119
The Prow   119
Tolerated and Excused   122
Velocity Unto Ferocity   119
South Rock   56, 58
South Wall   96
Southern Comfort Wall   218, 221
   Black Velvet   222
   Hangover   222
   Irish Cream   221
   Lowenbrau Light   221
   Margaritaville   222
Southwest Ridge   167
Southwest Ridge, The   167
Special Ed   49
Spiderman   208
Spike Shabook   301
Spiral Staircase   96, 98
Sponge, The   141, 151
   Hollywood Tim   151
   Mad Dogs and Englishmen   151
   Pumpin' Huecos   151
   Sal's Neuroses   151
Sport Climbing in New Mexico   82, 108, 144
Sport Climbing Socorro and Datil   190, 205
Sproul, Carol   288
Squeeze Chimney   85
Stab it and Steer   301
Star Dust   275
Stemulation   182
Stone Crusade   237
Strange Attractor   122
Stranger Than Friction   315, 321
Streambed   204
Stridex   132
Strong Urge to Fly   92
Stuck Inside of Baltimore   255
Suburb, The   239
Sugarite   3
Sugarite Canyon State Park   71
Sugarite State Park   74
Sugarloaf   218, 225, 226
   Flea Tree Dihedral   229
   North Face   227
   Science Friction   227
   The Left Eyebrow   227
   The Right Eyebrow   229
Summer Dreams   64
Sundeck Wall   68
   Digital Dilemma   68'
   Gila Monster   68
   Zorro   68
Sunny Side Up   273
Sununu Place, The   82
Supernatural Anesthetist   272
Support Your Local Bolter   181
Sweat   321
Sweat Lodge   246
Sweet Jane   181

T

T.B.O.L 61
Tanks for the Mammaries 254
Taos 28, 31, 33, 34, 38, 43, 45, 56
Taos Box 22
Taos Junction Bridge 47
Taos Rock 27, 45
Taos Rock III 40
Tarantula 172, 174
Tarred and Feathered 197
Tarts of Horsham 254, 277
Tasty Freeze 148
Taylor, Bob 79
Taylor, Wayne 160
Tech-no-star 61
Technobiscuit 135
Technowitch 197
Techtonic 61
Techweenie 61
Techweeny Buttress 160, 161
Tefertiller, Joey 176
Tejano Canyon 157
Terminal Ferocity 119
Terminal Orogeny 321
Terrell, Edwin 31
Terry's 301
Texas 95
Texas 2-Step 295
Texas Climbering Coalition 2
Texas Climbing Coalition 329
Texas Crude 322
Texas Limestone II 290
Texas Medicine 255
Texas Parks and Wildlife Department 2, 253
Texas Radio 31
The Y 77, 82, 96, 98
    Batshit Roof 98
    Beastie Crack 99
    Black Mantel 100
    Broadway 98
    El Queso Grande 99
    Hard Start 98
    Herb's Roof 99
    Hessing Route 100
    IDBI Wall 100
    Inside Dihedral 99
    Left Mother 99
    Less Hard Start 99
    Little Roof 100
    Lizard Man 100
    Middle Mother 99
    Monster 100
    Open Book 98
    Original Open Book 99
    Porter Route 100
    Ratshit Cave 98
    Right Mother 100
    Ringjam 96, 98
    Six Pack Crack 98
    Spiral Staircase 98
    The Nose 99
    The Notch 99
    The Ramp 100
    Triple Overhang 98
    Twin Cracks 100
    Wisconsin 99
Thief in Time 85, 129
Thomas, Mark 176
Thompson Canyon 185, 190, 191
Thorazine Dream 83, 86
Thorn Bus, The 192
Three Guns Springs 163
Three Lobe Buttress 273
    Huecool 273
    Natural Mystic 273
Three Mother Cracks, The 97
Through The Looking Glass 191, 274
Thumb, The 161
Thunder Toad 59
Tierra Amarilla 58
Tiger By The Tail 183
Tina's Rig 182
Tinkerbell's Nightmare 197
TJ Swan 319
TNT 208
To Catch A Thief 129
Tolerated and Excused 122
Tomahawk 210
Tooth Extraction 225
Tooth Fairy 223
Tooth or Consequences 223
Tooth, The 219, 222
    Tooth Fairy 223
    Tooth or Consequences 223
Torreon 160, 161
    Mountain Momma 172
    Voodoo Child 172
Totem 210
Touch Monkey 104, 125, 132
Toxic Socks 49
Training Wall 189
Transition Zone 181
    Factory Direct 181
    Have Slad WIll Travel 181
    Put Up Wet 181
    Rode Hard 181
    Support Your Local Bolter 181
    Trigger Happy 181
    Wavy Gravy 181
Trapeze, The 41
Travesty 283
Tree Route 267
Tres Piedras 2, 15, 38, 41, 51, 54, 56, 58, 61
Tres Piedras Rocks 22, 69
Tribal Council of Cochiti Pueblo 103
Tribal War 248
Trigger Happy 181
Triple Cracks 309
Triple Cracks Sanctuary 325
Triple Overhang 97, 98
Trout, Ken 24

True Grip 262
Truth, The 210
Tsankawi 98
Tugboat 220
Tugboat Granny 301
Tuolumne 283
Tuolumne Meadows 314
Turbo Trad 176, 179
Turbo Trad is Slab City 176
Turkey Baster 114
Turkey Peak 322, 325
Turkey Sandwich 148
Tusas Mountains 2
Tutti Frutti 111
Twin Cracks 97, 100
Twisted Feet 50

U

Uber Shaman 301
Udall, Dennis 160
Ugly Duckling, The 189
Uncle Fester Gets Sent in Europe 207
Underlook, The 82
UNM Spire 163
Unrelenting Nines 93, 96
Upper Left Roof 94
Uriah's Heap 254, 267

V

Valdez, Jacob 287
Valle Grande Caldera 145
Vandiver, Chris 80, 141
VanWinkle, Dirk 160
Velcro Booties 181
Velocity Unto Ferocity 119
Verchinski, Steve 160
Vibrator Dependent 138
View With a Room 86
Vista Point 132
Vista Point Overlook 110
Voodoo Child 171, 172
Vulture Roof 95

W

Wailing Banshees 80, 89, 90
Walking Dread 63
Walking on the Moon 266
Wannabee 111
War Path 297
Ward, Ed 216
Ware, Charlie 160
Warm-up Wall, The 246
Warpy Moople 169, 171
Wasted Youth 132
Water Canyon 190
Waterfall Wall 202, 204, 205
Wavy Gravy 181
Way Beyond Zebra 85
Way Out, The 291, 295
Weatherford 329
Weber, Cayce 40, 45, 53, 56, 160

Wedge, The 216, 219, 225
Well Tuned Evinrude 293
West Mountain 256, 272, 274
West Ridge 220, 225
West Rock 1 68
    Geez Louise 68
    How Ed's Mind Was Lost 68
    New Rage 68
    The Alien 68
    The Mad Bolter 68
West Rock 2 68
West Rocks 58
Wet Willies 148
Wetback Expressway 295
Wezwick, Tom 104, 110, 160
Wheeler Peak 10
When Legends Die 256, 274
Whiskey Wall 297, 301
    Anomaly 301
    Frosted Flake 301
    Spike Shabook 301
    Stab It and Steer 301
    The Bear Paw 301
    Tugboat Granny 301
White Knight 191
White Queen 191
White Rock 1, 3, 80, 82, 110
White Rock Canyon 77, 83
Whitelaw, Dave 176
Whole Banana, The 220
Wick, The 322
Wild Horse Mountain 307
Williams, Mike 79
Willow Mountain 307, 308
Window Pain 254, 266
Window Shopping 206
Wisconsin 96, 97, 99
Wish You Were Here 219
Woof Toof Noof Roof 146
Wounded Knee 246
Wrangler Savvy 295
Wrong Mr. Wong, The 114
Wyoming Cowgirls TR 272
Wyoming Saw 133

X

X-File 183

Y

Yosemite Decimal System 17
Yucca Flower Tower 161

Z

Z Crack, The 210
Zander Zig Zag 95
Zee Wicked Witch 194
Ziebell, Martin 305
Zintgraff, Jim 290
Zuni 6

Dennis Jackson taking notes at The Overlook. *Photo by Stewart M. Green.*

ABOUT THE AUTHOR

The four corners region of the Southwest has been the venue for Dennis Jackson's work as a professional guide and outdoor educator for the last twenty-five years. His travels have taken him to many great climbing areas including Yosemite, Alaska, Canada, Mexico, Europe, and South America. In this, his first guidebook, he describes many of the classic climbs in New Mexico—the Land of Enchantment—and the delightful climbing areas of the Lone Star State of Texas.

Dennis is the founder and president of Challenge Designs, Inc., providing adventure-based services throughout the United States. He lives in Santa Fe, New Mexico, with his wife Carol.